ECONOMIC DEVELOPMENT IN COMMUNIST RUMANIA

CENTER FOR INTERNATIONAL STUDIES
MASSACHUSETTS INSTITUTE OF TECHNOLOGY

Studies in International Communism

ECONOMIC DEVELOPMENT IN COMMUNIST RUMANIA

John Michael Montias

THE M.I.T. PRESS

Massachusetts Institute of Technology
Cambridge, Massachusetts, and London, England

FOREWORD

Professor Montias' book on the economic development of Rumania complements Professor Fischer-Galati's on the contemporary history and politics of the country. Together, I think it fair to say, they represent the first major scholarly treatment of the new Rumania and the process by which Bucharest achieved major autonomy from Soviet control.

As a result of his exploitation of the economic literature of other Communist countries relevant to Rumanian economic matters, Professor Montias' book also, in my view, represents a major methodological contribution to the study of East European economics. Professor Montias is too modest to point out that only his mastery of all the languages concerned made this possible; he has set a standard that all will wish but few will be able to meet.

I should also like to record my gratitude, and that of the Center, to the Ford Foundation, which through a generous grant to the Institute for research and teaching in international affairs made the publication of this book possible.

Munich, Germany
January 1967

WILLIAM E. GRIFFITH
Director, Project on
International Communism

PREFACE

This study was begun in early 1962 after I was asked to write a paper on the postwar economic development of an East European country. I chose to work on Rumania, chiefly because it attracted my curiosity as one of the least studied countries of the area. I came to the subject with little knowledge but with some scepticism about the ostensible accomplishments of the Rumanian economy as they were propagated in official publications. My paper, based on preliminary findings, was delivered in December 1962 and published in May 1963.[1] Its generally positive appraisal of Rumania's progress toward industrialization did not differ in any essential way from the conclusions of the present study, based on more systematic and thorough research.

While I was aware of a change in the orientation in Rumania's foreign trade when I wrote this initial paper, I had no inkling of the issues dividing Rumania from the Soviet Union and from her fellow members of Comecon.[2] In 1962, signs of intra-CMEA friction could already have been perceived by an alert observer — especially one who already knew what to look for — but because I concentrated my research almost exclusively on domestic development, I did not detect the incipient dispute.

The "generally positive appraisal" of my paper on Rumanian development was not based on any measure of consumers' satisfaction but on the ability of the planners to carry out the industrialization policy ordered by the Rumanian Communist Party. This was also my approach in the present study. To argue that individual consumption has failed to keep pace with production or that bathroom plugs are now just as hard to find in retail shops as they were eight years ago is beside the point. The question I pose is whether development has proceeded along the general lines charted by the Party and at more or less the pace anticipated in the long-term plans. For the period 1958 to 1965, I think it is hard to deny that this criterion of success was

[1] "Unbalanced Growth in Rumania," Proceedings of the American Economic Association, *American Economic Review*, May 1963.

[2] Throughout this book I use the terms Comecon and CMEA interchangeably to denote the Council for Mutual Economic Assistance.

met by the industrial sector, whose expansion was at the core of the
development program. It was not, however, met by agriculture, although even here the situation might have been worse considering
the cataclysmic experience of the Soviet Union with compulsory collectivization in the early 1930's.

The present survey of the Rumanian economy under Communist
aegis, while it is probably the first of its kind published in English[3]
is still perhaps premature in the sense that the information at hand
may be too fragmentary and incomplete to form a balanced and
intelligent perception of what has happened in the last twenty years.
While lengthy tomes could now be written about the economic development of Poland, Hungary, or Czechoslovakia, the lack of statistics
about crucial aspects of the Rumanian economy — such as the value
of national income produced and distributed, the wage bill, the components of net investment, imports and exports in domestic prices
and in constant foreign trade prices, agricultural procurements, retail
and wholesale price indices, costs and profits in industry — make it
hazardous to draw any firm conclusions about these subjects. In writing this book, I have incurred the risk that the publication of new
data by the Central Direction of Statistics in Bucharest may invalidate
some of my findings or open up new problems that I did not even
suspect existed.

My ignorance stems not only from the absence of data but from
the systematic concealment in almost all Rumanian publications of
the difficulties the economy has been encountering in its development.
In the other Communist countries of Eastern Europe public discussions over the last few years have called attention to the obstacles lying
in the path of development; in Rumania most economic writings are
still intended to point up achievements rather than to analyze existing
problems (although Party Secretary Nicolae Ceauşescu has been
franker in his recent criticism of shortcomings than his predecessor
Gheorghiu-Dej).

It is partly for lack of information about inefficiencies at the micro-
economic level that I have glossed over the subject but also because
I have chosen to describe the growth of the economy at an aggregated
level. I have no doubt that inefficiencies occurred and that they were
important enough to reduce growth below its potential, but I doubt
very much whether the cumulative evocation of specific cases and
examples will go far toward explaining why the Rumanian economy
expanded faster in one period than another or why it should perform

---

[3] See, however, the excellent article on Rumania in the United Nations, Economic Commission for Europe, *Economic Bulletin for Europe*, Vol. 13, No. 2 (1961).

better or worse than other centrally planned economies similarly afflicted with these deficiencies.

The crucial question that any analyst of the Rumanian economy must consider is whether official statistics — published or reconstructed from fragmentary data — are reliable enough to support generalizations about the state of the economy. I can only say that in all my work with Rumanian statistics in the last five years, I have not been able to find an example of a serious and demonstrable inconsistency between any two sets of figures.[4] Even the trends in real wages and consumption of workers and peasants, which are probably the weakest of all the Rumanian data I have worked with, appear roughly consistent with independently derived data on total individual consumption. It is also significant, I believe, that when consumption trends became less auspicious, as in the period 1963–1965, statistical information of this sort was no longer commonly divulged in economic publications. If the information had been systematically falsified, there would have been no obvious reason for imposing this secrecy. However that may be, one must at all times be mindful of possible biases in the data, especially of the type that would give an unrealistically favorable impression of developments. If I have not given sufficient warning in the text of my lack of confidence in the precision of some of my data — especially those relating to national income and individual consumption — let me enter my caveat at this point.

Still on the subject of data gathering, I should like to draw the reader's attention to one essential point: no analysis of an economy described in such a one-sided fashion by its own nationals can be complete if it does not avail itself of materials published about it in other Communist countries, where a good deal of the pertinent information is known to qualified specialists and, on occasion, gets to be released by inadvertence or by design. Many examples could be cited, but the one that affected me most was the discovery, after two years of intermittent research on Rumanian foreign trade, of a Hungarian source that disclosed the value of Rumania's imports and exports in foreign-exchange prices from 1950 to 1957. This information, as far as I know, had never been made public before, nor has it appeared anywhere else since that time. One may also mention statistics of Rumania's consumption per capita of food staples and of textiles, which are to be found nowhere except in a Czechoslovak publication on CMEA problems. One of the best sources on the Rumanian petroleum

---

[4] A partial exception is mentioned in Appendix B, p. 273; but I suspect this inconsistency is the result of an error made in the Central Statistical Office rather than of any desire to mislead the public.

industry until the late 1950's was a Soviet book on the subject. The Soviets have also released unique data on Rumania's foreign trade by commodity groups and by region for 1950 and 1960 that were essential to my study of the reorientation of Rumania's exchanges. The basis for my calculations of "rates of accumulation" out of national income is a figure for 1963 from a Polish source, reprinted in a Slovak daily paper. All these materials were available in publications that were, or should have been, easily accessible in the United States.

While Rumanian statistics published in Rumanian sources provided the basic material for my study, sources from other countries helped me to fill important gaps in this original store of information. I found some of my documentation in the West, some in Bucharest at the library of the Economic Institute, whose materials were kindly made accessible to me during my stays in Rumania in 1962 and 1965, and some in the public libraries of Budapest — while I was participating in the exchange program sponsored by the Inter-University Committee on Travel Grants and by the Hungarian government. I concentrated my efforts during my study trip in Hungary on the analysis of the economic relations between the more and the less developed countries of CMEA, which required a detailed examination of Rumania's foreign trade. This investigation happened to dovetail with the present project. I am grateful to the Inter-University Committee for this opportunity and to the Hungarian government for providing me with library and other facilities to carry out my research.

I should like to thank the editors of *Soviet Studies*, its publishers, Basil Blackwell, Ltd., and the editors of *The Slavic Review* for their permission to reproduce parts of articles that I wrote in these publications, which cover, in revised form, sections of Chapters 3 and 4, respectively.

This study was partly carried out with the financial aid of the Economic Growth Center of Yale University, whose assistance is gratefully acknowledged.

I am indebted to Mr. Jozef van Brabant for his painstaking calculations and checks on my estimates throughout the five chapters of the text and the appendices. Professor Pong S. Lee is responsible for most of the work on the index of industrial production of Appendix A, although Professor George Staller's assistance in preparing this index was also invaluable to me. In addition, I am grateful to Professor Staller for his perceptive comments on the text. My thanks are also due to Professors Jerzy Karcz, Frederic L. Pryor, Charles S. Rockwell, Harry Trend, and to Mr. George Brown for their valuable suggestions on various portions of the manuscript. I benefited greatly from the advice of Professor Raymond P. Powell on the measurement of changes in factor productivity. Professor Stephen Fischer-Galati was kind enough to check and correct Rumanian citations. I am beholden to Professor William E. Griffith for his initiative, prodding, and encouragement without which this study might never have been written. Finally, I owe Mrs. Martha Sheckleton a special debt for her careful typing and retyping of the text and footnotes in a variety of unfamiliar languages.

New Haven, Connecticut   JOHN MICHAEL MONTIAS
February 1967

CONTENTS

ECONOMIC DEVELOPMENT IN COMMUNIST RUMANIA

CHAPTER ONE

THE INDUSTRIALIZATION OF RUMANIA

Then and Now

Official Rumanian propaganda is so strident and repetitious in proclaiming the economic accomplishments of the Communist regime that a Westerner accustomed to more subtle means of persuasion may become quite obdurate to its claims. Nonetheless, much of what it blares is true. Industrial output has indeed grown very fast; health conditions have vastly improved; education has spread; new technical skills have been developed; and consumption levels have risen since the late 1930's not only because the majority of peasants and industrial workers live somewhat better but also because so many peasant families have moved to town and acceded to the higher standards of urban living.

In this chapter I shall try to assess some of these accomplishments, beginning with industrial output and ending with education. But my main concern will be with the economic policies pursued by the Communist authorities after the war, with what may be called their strategy of industrialization. What resources did they mobilize to move toward their goals? How did other sectors fare when heavy industry was expanded at forced draft? How did Rumania's economic relations with the Soviet Union help or hinder her industrialization drive? What was the effect of political events in the Soviet bloc, such as the death of Stalin and the Hungarian revolution of October–November 1956, on the Rumanian economic course? How did realizations compare with long-term plans, and what were the causes of such deviations as could be observed?

My preoccupation will be with allocative decisions, not with the methods by which decisions were reached. I may say at once that planning in Rumania has remained tightly centralized. It differs at present in no essential way from the system that prevailed in Poland, Hungary, and Czechoslovakia in the early 1950's, with which many readers will already be acquainted. Rumania and Albania are the only Communist countries of Europe that have not experimented with

1

any significant measures of decentralization in recent years.[1] Rumania's successful progress toward industrialization, the fact that the internal links binding her economy together are still relatively simple and clear cut and that, thanks to her natural wealth, she has been able to use foreign trade to loosen constraints imposed by a limited range of resources and production capacities may explain why Rumanian leaders have found no compelling reason to devolve decision-making powers on lower government organs.

To moor the general coordinates of the economy in time and space, I shall introduce this survey of Rumania's development with a few basic statistics.

At the time of the last prewar census in 1930 Rumania had a population of slightly over 18 million inhabitants. Of this number, 2.5 million lived in Bessarabia and nearly half a million in northern Bukovina, both of which were annexed by the U.S.S.R. in June 1940.[2] Southern Dobrogea, which was ceded to Bulgaria in 1940, had about 340 thousand inhabitants. The total population of the present-day

---

[1] On what appear to be rather formal and diffident moves toward a reduction of the Planning Commission's responsibilities after 1956, see R. Moldovan, "Conducerea planificată a economiei naționale a Republicii Populare Romîne," in *Economia Romîniei între anii 1944–1959* (Bucharest, 1959), pp. 50–52. In May 1965, a decision of the Council of Ministers called for the participation of large enterprises working for the export market in drawing up contracts with foreign clients, along with the representatives of the Ministry of Foreign Trade and of foreign trade enterprises (see *Probleme economice*, No. 12 [1965], p. 77). In his speech at the Ninth Party Congress of July 19–24, 1965, Alexandru Bîrlădeanu, a top-level economic planner, criticized excessive centralization in the administration of the economy, but up to the time of writing only minor measures had been taken to widen the powers of nationalized enterprises. See *Congresul al IX-lea al Partidului Comunist Român* (Bucharest, 1965), pp. 579–581.

[2] The territories given up to the U.S.S.R. are again a fit subject for discussion in Rumania after many years of total silence in the Rumanian press. (There was no entry under Bessarabia in the *Dicționar enciclopedic Romîn*, Vol. I, 1962. This "un-region" was only represented by its adjective "bessarabian," a stage in the geological evolution of that part of Europe.) It is noteworthy that 56.2 percent of the inhabitants of Bessarabia spoke Rumanian as their mother tongue in 1930 (30 percent of the urban, 60 percent of the rural population). The next largest group was Ukranian or "Ruthenian" speaking and made up 11.6 percent of the population. Bessarabia in 1930 was 87 percent rural. Its largest city, Chișinău (in Russian, Kishiniev), had 117,000 inhabitants. Northern Bukovina, due mainly to the city of Cernauți (Chernovtsy), with 111,147 inhabitants, was somewhat more urbanized than Bessarabia. The illiteracy rate in Bessarabia for the ages 8 to 19 was the highest in Rumania. In 1935, Bessarabia accounted for 15 percent of the wheat, 25 percent of the rye and barley, and 17 percent of the corn harvests of Rumania. Per acre yields were significantly lower than in the Old Kingdom and Transylvania. The total personnel of industrial establishments in Bessarabia numbered 35,707 in 1935, or less than 6 percent of Rumania's total. (All data are from the Institutul central de statistică, *Anuarul statistic al Romăniei 1935–1936* [Bucharest], pp. 33–35, 43, and 182–183.)

territory of Rumania was officially estimated at 14.3 million. At the time of the 1956 census it had risen to 17.5 million; it equaled 19.1 million on March 15, 1966, when the last census was taken.[3]

The basic demographic statistics of Table 1.1 summarize the main trends in occupational distribution, literacy, birth and death rates in these twenty-six years.

TABLE 1.1. Rumania's Basic Demographic Data for 1930 and 1956 (*Postwar Territory*)

	1930	1956
Total population (millions)	14.3	17.5
urban population (millions)	3.1	5.5
urban population (percent)	21.4	31.3
Total active population (millions)	8.4[a]	10.4
in agriculture and forestry (percent)	76.7	69.4
in industry (percent)	7.9	13.3
in construction (percent)	0.6	2.5
Illiterates in population[b]		
males (percent)	26.9	5.5
females (percent)	50.4	14.4
Live births (per 1,000 inhabitants)	34.1	24.2
Deaths (per 1,000 inhabitants)	19.3	9.9
Infant mortality (per 1,000 live births)	175.6	81.5
Life expectation (years of age)	42.0[c]	63.2

[a] Based on estimates for Bukovina and Dobrogea.
[b] Over seven years of age in 1930 and over eight years of age in 1956.
[c] 1932.

Sources: Direcția centrală de statistică, *Recensămîntul populației din 21 Februarie 1956: Rezultate generale* (Bucharest, 1959), pp. XV–XXIX; *Anuarul statistic al Romăniei 1935 și 1936*, pp. 46–47; *Anuarul statistic al R.P.R. 1965*, pp. 76, 94, and 112.

Since the mid-1950's further progress has been made toward a demographic pattern typical of more developed countries. By March 1966 over 38 percent of the population had become urban.[4] The death rate in 1965 was down to 8.6 and infant mortality to 44.1 per thousand (lower than in Poland and Portugal, slightly higher than in Italy and Spain); the life expectancy of Rumanian citizens in 1963 was over 68

[3] Direcția centrală de statistică, *Anuarul statistic al R.P.R. 1965* (Bucharest, 1965), p. 65 (hereafter referred to as *Anuarul statistic al R.P.R. 1965*) and "Communiqué on the Preliminary Results of the Population and Housing Census of March 15, 1966," *Agerpres*, Supplement.
[4] "Communiqué on the Preliminary Results of the Population and Housing Census of March 15, 1966," *op. cit.*

years; the proportion of the active population working in industry in 1965 had risen to 19 percent, while the proportion in agriculture and forestry had dropped to 56.5 percent (from 7.3 million persons in 1955 to 5.5 million persons in 1965).[5]

The last percentage cited shows how far Rumania still has to go to attain the typical pattern of developed countries. In 1963 only 26.5 percent of Italy's active population was agricultural; even in Spain and Portugal this proportion was down to about 40 percent. With the exception of Albania, for which no data are available, the only European countries that may be compared with Rumania in this respect are Greece, where 53.9 percent of the active population was in agriculture in 1961, and Yugoslavia (57.3 percent in 1962). Within CMEA, Rumania had, by an appreciable margin, the highest proportion of her labor force in agriculture. In the Soviet Union 36 percent of the labor force was engaged in agriculture, in Czechoslovakia 23 percent, in East Germany 18 percent, in Hungary 35 percent, in Poland 48 percent, and in Bulgaria 47 percent, according to the censuses taken in these countries in the early 1960's.[6]

Despite, or perhaps because of, the preponderance of peasants in the labor force, agricultural production per head is still very low, much lower in fact than in many countries where the farm sector constitutes a smaller share of employment. It was recently estimated by American statisticians that Rumania's agricultural production per capita in 1955 was 53 percent of that of the United States, about 95 percent of that of East Germany and Czechoslovakia, and 85 percent of that of Hungary.[7] Rumania's inferiority is even more manifest when these output data are expressed per person employed in agriculture.

The rise in the proportion of the labor force working in industry is one measure of industrialization, but a very imperfect one if we consider that industrial employment has been held down in recent years, and capital investment has been the prime mover of output. Per capita production statistics for some of the most important manufactures,

[5] Direcţia centrală de statistică, *Anuarul statistic al Republicii Socialiste România 1966* (Bucharest, 1966), pp. 77, 96, 115; and data on the number of persons active in agriculture per 100 hectares of agricultural land in 1955 and 1965 in *Probleme economice*, No. 10 (1966), p. 45.

[6] Główny Urząd Statystyczny Polskiej Rzeczypospolitej Ludowej, *Rocznik statystyczny 1965* (Warsaw, 1965), pp. 559–560; and official statistical yearbooks for Italy, Portugal, and Spain.

[7] Rumania's agricultural production per capita, however, was still 18 percent higher than in the Soviet Union. For details, see Frederic L. Pryor and George J. Staller, "The Dollar Values of the Gross National Products in Eastern Europe, 1955," *Economics of Planning*, Vol. 5, No. 1 (1966), p. 79.

shown in Table 1.2, give a better idea of the industrial progress realized in the 1930's and over the entire span of the postwar period.

Production of electric power per capita in Rumania in 1938 was of the same order of magnitude as in Syria or India and much lower than

TABLE 1.2. PER CAPITA PRODUCTION OF SELECTED INDUSTRIAL COMMODITIES, 1929, 1938, AND 1965 (*In Kilograms*)

	1929 Prewar Territory	1938 Prewar Territory[a]	1938 Postwar Territory[b]	1950	1965
Electric power (kilowatt hours)	30.9	57.8	72.4	130	905
Iron ore	5.1	7.1	8.9	24	130
Pig iron	4.1	6.8	8.5	20	106
Steel (crude)	9.3	14.1	18.2	34	180
Coal (brown and bituminous)	173	151.7	181.1	238	637
Cement	18.1	23.6	32.7	63	285
Petroleum	275	336.0	422.7	310	662
Sulfuric acid	1.5	2.3	2.8	3.2	28
Sugar	6.1	7.0	6.1	5.3	21
Cotton cloth (millions of m²)	n.a.	n.a.	6.7	9.1	16
Woolen cloth (millions of m²)	n.a.	n.a.	.8	1.3	2.2

[a] Prewar population estimate on December 31, 1937.

[b] Postwar population estimate on July 1, 1938.

Sources: Institutul de statistică generală a statului, *Anuarul statistic al României 1933,* pp. 175–190; League of Nations, *Statistical Yearbook of the League of Nations, 1938–1939,* p. 166; and *1939–1940,* pp. 105–145; *Anuarul statistic al R.P.R. 1965,* pp. 168–172; *Statistical Pocket Book of the Socialist Republic of Romania, 1966,* p. 91.

in Brazil or Turkey in the early 1960's. By 1965 it was two and a half times as great as Brazil's, twice as great as Portugal's, on a par with Spain's and Bulgaria's, but still only about half of that of France or the Soviet Union. Pig iron production per head in 1938 was less than one half of India's at the present time; in 1965 it was seven times as great.[8] In general, Spain, Bulgaria, and Rumania have now reached approximately the same stage of development, but the divergent economic policies these countries have pursued have brought about substantial differences in the structure of their output. Thus, Spain, which produces 30–40 percent more iron ore per capita than Rumania, turns out only about one third as much crude steel as Rumania. (Bulgaria's ratio of iron ore to steel output, incidentally, is about half way between

[8] All comparisons in this paragraph are based on data for individual countries in 1962 and 1963 in *Statistisches Jahrbuch der Deutschen Demokratischen Republik 1965* (East Berlin: Staatsverlag, 1965), pp. 28*–40*.

Spain's and Rumania's.) On the other hand, the production of sulfuric acid, a basic ingredient for the chemical fertilizer industries, is more developed in Spain, with 47 kilograms per capita in 1963, than in either Bulgaria (33 kilograms in 1963) or Rumania (28 kilograms in 1965). The production of phosphate fertilizers per hectare of agricultural land in Rumania amounts to only about half of what it is in Spain, while that of nitrogen fertilizers is substantially the same in both countries. On the other hand, cement, which is needed to generate high rates of capital investment in all three countries, is at present produced at about the same level per head (250 to 280 kilograms). This is on a par with the U.S.S.R. and Poland but much below Switzerland (615 kilograms in 1963), West Germany (552 kilograms), Belgium (506 kilograms), or Austria (462 kilograms).

Rumania has improved her relative position as a producer of basic industrial staples vis-à-vis countries that were already industrialized before World War II, including Czechoslovakia and East Germany. But she has lost ground with respect to the one resource with which she was most generously endowed by nature and which she produced on an international scale before the war, namely petroleum. In 1937 Rumania produced 2.5 percent of the world output. Her production of about 7 million tons came to one fourth of the Soviet Union's and Venezuela's production and to 64 percent of Iran's. In 1963 Rumania was down to a little less than 1 percent of world output, 6 percent of the Soviet Union's, 7 percent of Venezuela's, and 17 percent of Iran's. She was the fifth largest producer in the world in 1937 but only the twelfth largest in 1963, below such countries as Mexico and Argentina, which she greatly surpassed before the war.[9]

Before reverting to our discussion of the main trends in Rumania's development, we may dwell for a moment on her relative importance as an industrial producer among the countries of the Council for Mutual Economic Assistance (CMEA or Comecon).[10] Table 1.3 assembles some data on Rumania's share in the total output of CMEA, both including and excluding the Soviet Union, before and after World War II. For all products except petroleum, these data show an increase in Rumania's share in the output of CMEA countries, excluding the Soviet Union, in the postwar period. This relative improvement in Rumania's standing has been most conspicuous for cement, electric power, metallurgical products, and heavy chemicals.

[9] *Ibid.*, p. 30.
[10] Up to the early 1960's the members were Albania, Bulgaria, Czechoslovakia, East Germany, Poland, Rumania, and the U.S.S.R. Since then Mongolia has become a member, and Albania, for all practical purposes, has left the organization.

TABLE 1.3. Percentage Share of Rumania in the Aggregate Output of CMEA Countries for Selected Industrial Products, 1937, 1950, 1963

	1937		1950		1963	
	CMEA Countries[a]	CMEA Excluding U.S.S.R.[a]	CMEA Countries	CMEA Excluding U.S.S.R.	CMEA Countries	CMEA Excluding U.S.S.R.
Petroleum	18.5[b]	92.1[b]	11.6	87.3	5.6[b]	86.1[b]
Gas (all sources)	28.3[c]	44.0[c]	19.9	32.0	11.9	46.5
Timber	4.9[d]	21.0[d]	5.4	21.4	3.7	24.4
Electric power	1.9	4.6	1.6	4.8	2.1	8.2
Pig iron	0.8[b]	4.2[b]	1.3	6.9	0.72	17.0
Steel	1.2[e]	4.8[e]	1.5	6.5	2.6	10.9
Coal	1.3[f]	3.5[f]	0.7	1.3	0.9	1.9
Cement	4.7	9.6	5.5	12.3	5.0	16.4
Sulfuric acid	2.1	6.0	1.7	5.8	3.4	10.6

[a] Figures for East Germany refer to 1936, for Rumania to 1938.

[b] Excluding Bulgaria, whose production was negligible.

[c] Excludes Czechoslovakia and Hungary, minor producers, for which no data are available.

[d] Data for East Germany and Bulgaria are not available; output statistics refer to 1938 for Hungary and to 1940 for the U.S.S.R.

[e] 1939 for Bulgaria.

[f] Net output of coal for Czechoslovakia, gross output elsewhere.

Note: CMEA countries are exclusive of both Albania and Mongolia.

Source: Statistisches Jahrbuch der Deutschen Demokratischen Republik 1965 (East Berlin: Staatsverlag, 1965), pp. 27*–36* and official statistics of individual countries.

Table 1.4 reproduces recent estimates of per capita industrial production in Eastern Europe, which give a more comprehensive measure than the selected statistics I have presented so far of Rumania's relative standing in the Soviet bloc.[11]

Industrial expansion in Rumania in the 1930's was, of course, slowed down by the world-wide depression but, in contrast with the situation in more developed countries — for example, in Czechoslovakia — its adverse effects were of short duration. Several branches of industry, including metallurgy, chemicals, paper, and textiles, made appreciable headway in the 1930's.[12] The situation in industry, however, was more

[11] For approximate data on the level of Rumanian national income relative to other CMEA members, see Chapter 4, p. 190, note 13.

[12] In 1937 the output of industries producing chiefly producer goods was about 44 percent greater than in 1928; the output of consumer goods industries, on the other hand, was only some 23 percent greater than in 1928. Among those that stagnated or retrogressed may be mentioned the building-materials, glass, ceramics,

TABLE 1.4. RELATIVE INDUSTRIAL PRODUCTION ($U.S.S.R. = 100$)

	Pryor-Staller Estimates		Other Per Capita Estimates			
	Total Production 1955	Per Capita Production 1955	Soviet 1957	Polish 1963	Czechoslovak 1961	Hungarian 1958
Rumania	4.3	49	50	89	52	59
Bulgaria	1.4	37	40	61	30	39
East Germany	13.0	142	129	167	133	130
Hungary	4.6	91	62	89	60	59
Poland	10.3	74	76	83	75	75
Yugoslavia	3.4	38	n.a.	n.a.	n.a.	n.a.

Sources: Frederic L. Pryor and George J. Staller, "The Dollar Values of the Gross National Products in Eastern Europe, 1955," *Economics of Planning*, Vol. 6, No. 1 (1966), p. 76.

favorable than in agriculture, the sector where a majority of the population gained its livelihood. Agricultural prices were still 30 to 35 percent below 1929 levels in 1937–1938, while the prices of industrial commodities bought by farmers had already recovered the ground lost during the recession.[13] Postwar calculations indicate consumption per capita of the peasant population in the mid-1930's was still below the level of 1929.[14] One may go so far as to argue that the industrial recovery was purchased — via protectionist import policies and direct government support — at the expense of the majority of consumers. Significant in this respect are the data on imports expressed in constant prices. According to quantum indices, based on 1929 prices, imports of manufactures in 1937 were still 30 percent below 1929 levels, whereas imports of raw materials and semifabricates had risen 45 percent above this base.[15] The displacement of iron and steel imports by domestic output is a case in point: while production of pig iron and crude steel

and electrotechnical industries. In a recent article, a Rumanian economist argued that government demand — for armaments, for army uniforms, etc. — was the chief driving force of industry in the 1930's. According to this source, 70 percent of the output of the metallurgical industry and 80 percent of the coal produced were purchased by the state or by state enterprises including the railroads (V. Axenciuc, "Contribuţii la studierea ciclului de producţie industrială 1929–1937 în Romînia burghezo-moşierescă," *Probleme economice*, No. 7 [1963], pp. 65–67).

[13] Data derived from the prewar economist V. Madgearu, quoted in *Probleme economice*, No. 11 (1961), p. 78.

[14] *Probleme economice*, No. 11 (1961), pp. 73 and 82.

[15] M. Constantinescu *et al.*, *Comerţul exterior al României 1928–1937*, Bibliotecă monetară economică şi financiară (Bucharest, 1939), Vol. I, p. 490.

rose from 72,000 tons and 163,000 tons, respectively, in 1929 to 127,000 and 235,000 tons in 1937, imports of iron and steel, including rolled steel products, dropped from 87,000 tons to less than 17,000 tons between these two dates.[16] Imports of machinery and equipment, the indispensable wherewithal of industrialization in this early period, fared better than imports of most manufactures. Their value in terms of current prices was already as high in 1937 as in 1929.[17] (The physical volume of these imports probably exceeded 1929 levels.)

The structure and evolution of foreign trade, both in the prewar and the postwar period, reflect the general nature of the economy and its broad tendencies as in a magnifying mirror. Take for example the cultivation and marketing of cereals. Back in 1913, when Rumania was still confined to the borders of the Old Kingdom, cereals made up two thirds of total Rumanian exports. The extensive land reform of 1917–1921 expropriated 6 million hectares from large landowners and foreign nationals; most of these farms were distributed in small parcels to the peasantry.[18] As a result, the share of the agricultural area belonging to farms in excess of 50 hectares fell from 44.7 percent in 1918 to 18.8 percent in 1930.[19] Since the large farms accounted for the bulk of cereals marketed, much of which was exported, their breakup led to a decline in the exports of cereals in the 1920's, especially of wheat, which typically was cultivated on the large estates. (Urbanization and Rumania's incorporation of Transylvania, several regions of which specialized in animal breeding and tended to import cereals, also contributed to the decline in the export of cereals.) In 1925–1929 wheat exports were one fifth of what they had been in 1910–1915 and corn exports slightly over four fifths, even though the production of both these cereals within the new Rumanian borders exceeded the prewar harvest in the Old Kingdom. Wheat exports did not recover pre-World War I levels until the late 1930's.[20] Even in the

[16] *Ibid.*, Vol. II, pp. 638–639. Note that in the prewar foreign trade nomenclature, iron and steel — including pig iron, forgings, and rolled items — were classified as processed products.

[17] *Ibid.*, Vol. II, pp. 248–249.

[18] Aurelian Z. Strat, *Des possibilités de developpement industriel de la Roumanie* (Paris, 1931), pp. 10–11.

[19] S. Fischer-Galati, ed., *Romania* (New York: Praeger, 1957), p. 203.

[20] *Probleme economice*, No. 11 (1961), pp. 72–73. In the Old Kingdom, alone, the wheat harvest in 1928 and 1929 came to slightly more than half of the average harvest for the years 1909–1912; the corn harvest was about the same in the two periods; an increase in the harvest (and exports) of barley — a cheaper but less risky crop typically cultivated on small farms — partially compensated the fall in wheat output in the old provinces (Direcţiunea generală a statisticei, *Anuarul statistic al României 1915–1916* [Bucharest, 1919], pp. 28–29; Institutul de statistică generală a statului, *Anuarul statistic al României 1929* [Bucharest, 1931], p. 72).

period 1935–1939 only 14.9 percent of the total production of cereals was exported, compared to 48.2 percent in 1909–1913.[21]

The importance of petroleum products in Rumanian foreign trade in the interwar period grew as that of cereals declined. In 1913, when cereals, as we have just seen, made up two thirds of the value of exports, the share of petroleum products (chiefly kerosene and gasoline) in total exports was slightly less than 20 percent.[22] At that time the output of crude oil was 1.8 million tons. It had risen to 4.3 million tons in 1928, at which time petroleum products represented about 30 percent of a larger volume of exports than in 1913. In 1937 production was up to about 7 million tons (slightly below the prewar record reached in 1936), and the industry now contributed nearly 40 percent of total exports. By this time the share of cereals in total exports had fallen to less than a third.[23]

Industrial progress in the interwar period was mainly of the import-substituting kind, typical of developing countries in the world today. As late as 1938 finished industrial products still represented only 2 percent of total exports,[24] while exports of machinery and equipment were negligible up to World War II.

Under Communist leadership, however, industrialization has not been limited to import substitution; the transformation of the economy has also had a remarkable impact on exports. In 1948 finished industrial products made up 7.2 percent of exports, in 1956, 19.6 percent.[25] In 1965 machinery and equipment alone contributed 18.5 percent and manufactured consumer goods 11 percent of exports. Petroleum exports were down to 12.6 percent and unprocessed goods to 7.3 percent of total exports. On the import side, the role of manufactured consumer goods has undergone an extraordinary regression, from over 50 percent of total imports in 1938 to not quite 7 percent in 1965.[26] This structural metamorphosis will be described in greater detail in Chapter 3, which is devoted to foreign trade.

After this brief survey of Rumania's past and present, we are ready to analyze the industrial expansion that took place in the last two

[21] O. Parpală, "Exportul de produse agricole şi dezvoltarea unilaterală a agriculturii Romîniei burghezo-moşiereşti," *Probleme economice*, No. 11 (1960). This article is one of the best documented postwar publications on the problem of agricultural exports in pre-Communist Rumania.

[22] Strat, *op. cit.*, p. 11.

[23] Constantinescu *et al.*, *op. cit.*, pp. 10–11, 294–295, and 324–345.

[24] *Probleme economice*, No. 12 (1957), p. 32.

[25] *Ibid.*

[26] Central statistical office of Rumania, *Statistical Pocket Book of the Socialist Republic of Romania, 1966*, pp. 250–252. For further details on the structure of postwar trade, see Chapter 3, Table 3.9.

decades. We shall first present alternative measures of the expansion of industry as a whole between "benchmark years," then discuss changes in the structure of industry, and finally make a few observations on diversification and specialization in the production of the sector.

Industrial Output and Structure

Rumanian statistics of gross industrial output, as in all other Communist countries, are based on the "enterprise method." The gross output of an industry is essentially the summation of the total value of output at fixed prices (net of turnover taxes) of all enterprises in that industry. The value of the output of an enterprise may include, in addition to its main production program, various ancillary activities, including construction and repairs. It differs from its marketed output, net of taxes, mainly by the extent of its accumulation of inventories of raw materials, goods in process, and finished production. The gross value of output of branches of industry and of manufacturing industry as a whole does not provide a firm foundation for an index of production. The official indices built up from gross output are affected by extraneous factors, such as vertical integration — the merging of enterprises at successive stages of production — and vertical disintegration — the breaking up of such enterprises — which are not directly related to the growth of the sector as economists would understand the concept.

The gross output index suffers also from the defect that it lies, or lay for many years, at the core of the incentive system for the managers of enterprises, who were induced to manipulate it for their own ends. In particular, the introduction of new products, which presents a delicate problem in the construction of any index, has often been a pretext for enterprises to tamper with "constant prices," with the aim of raising artificially the value of their output.[27]

An alternative index of industrial output, of a type mainly used in Western countries but which has no counterpart in official Rumanian statistics, measures the average growth of a sample of industrial products whose physical outputs are known. Such an index has been constructed by Professor Pong Lee and myself on the basis of production data for 215 products, of which, after the elimination of a number of intermediate products within subsectors, 183 products were retained.[28]

[27] On this and similar biases in the Polish gross output index, see Maurice Ernst, "Overstatement of Industrial Growth in Poland," *Quarterly Journal of Economics*, Vol. LXXIX, No. 4 (November 1965).

[28] The construction of the index is described in Appendix A.

Wherever possible we weighted our physical series with Rumanian prices of 1948–1950, which, with minor adjustments, remained in use until 1955. For 80 out of our 183 series, however, we had to resort to Soviet wholesale prices, which we related to Rumanian prices for comparable items. In order to limit possible errors due to the poor representation of our sample, we used our physical series only to construct indices of output for subgroups of industry (for example, for electrotechnical equipment, for meat and meat products). The subgroups were aggregated into branches (machine building, food processing, and so on) by the use of employment weights, except for lumber and woodworking and machine building where weights were derived from available breakdowns of official gross output. The branches of industry were aggregated into the index for industry as a whole by value added (wages and salaries plus amortization charges).

We confined ourselves to "benchmark years" — 1938, 1948, 1950, 1953, 1955, 1958, 1960, and 1963 — which, in our opinion, represent critical years in Rumanian development.

Our index is compared in Table 1.5 with the official index for industry as a whole and for its most important branches for 1948, 1953, 1958, and 1963.

The rates of growth for industry as a whole averaged 18.2 percent according to our index (24.0 percent according to the official index) from 1948 to 1953, 8.2 percent (9.7 percent officially) from 1953 to 1958, and 13.4 percent (13.5 percent officially) from 1958 to 1963. The striking differences between the rates for the three periods will be analyzed in separate sections in the remaining part of this chapter.

The large disparity between our index and the official index for the period 1948 to 1953, which is discussed in greater detail in Appendix A, presumably reflects differences in coverage of the two indices and in the treatment of new products as well as the organizational changes that influenced the official index.[29] The much closer correspondence between the two indices since 1955 does not necessarily validate either measure of output for this later period. For it is still possible that an upward bias in our index, due to the overrepresentation of fast-growing items in the published statistics, may be of the same magnitude as the official index's own bias, due to the defects already mentioned in the text. The yearly growth rates for later years may still be overstated by a percentage point or two.

In general, as we should expect from its priority standing in the Communist scheme of things, "heavy industry" grew much faster than "light industry." According to our index, the machine-building indus-

[29] See Appendix A, pp. 248–249.

TABLE 1.5. OFFICIAL AND INDEPENDENTLY COMPUTED INDICES OF
INDUSTRIAL OUTPUT, 1938, 1948, 1953, 1958, AND 1963
(*1938 = 100*)

Industry	1948		1953		1958		1963	
	(1)	(2)	(1)	(2)	(1)	(2)	(1)	(2)
Electric power	156	133	450	302	846	547	1,700	1,034
Fuel	76	78	159	156	224	199	351	245
Ferrous metallurgy	121	107	284	206	399	293	1,000	876
Machine building and metal-working	87	87[a]	393	225	751	536	1,700	1,063
Chemical	101	117	376	329	787	633	2,300	2,060
Building materials	117	119	583	313	989	484	1,800	825
Lumber and woodworking	99	84	215	183	319	205	526	374
Cellulose and paper	120	118	208	195	287	273	658	486
Glass and ceramics	133	141	382	271	693	413	1,200	705
Textiles	91	86	246	217	339	249	553	393
Leather and hides	102	128	217	330	351	476	555	848
Food	62	82	149	166	219	236	319	434
Soap and cosmetics	84	89	223	333	345	355	440	422
Nonferrous metallurgy	68	68	306	306	403	403	809	809
Clothing	123	123	419	419	566	566	1,000	1,000
Printing and bookbinding	131	131	261	261	444	444	822	822
All industries	85	90[a]	247	207	393	306	741	575

[a] The official index for machinery output was used for the period 1937 to 1948
because of the small number of machinery products for which output data were
available between these dates.

Note: Columns (1) give the official index, based on 1955 constant prices.
Columns (2) give the Lee-Montias index, based on 1948–1950 prices and 1958
value-added weights, except for nonferrous metallurgy, clothing, and printing for
which the official indexes were used; these indices were weighted by value-added
weights and included in our computed index for all industries.

Sources: Appendix A, Table A.2, and *Anuarul statistic al R.P.R. 1965*, pp. 150–151.

try averaged a growth of 18.2 percent per year from 1948 to 1963,
ferrous metallurgy 15.1 percent, chemicals 21 percent, fuels 7.9 percent, and building materials 13.7 percent; on the other hand, textiles
averaged 10.6 percent, leather and hides 13.5 percent, and food processing 11.7 percent.

As a consequence of the disparate rates of growth of its various
branches, the structure of industry underwent a profound transformation. We need look only at the composition of gross output in the official
statistics to be persuaded of this: the producer-goods industries included in group A made up 45.5 percent of output at 1955 prices in
1938; their share in 1964, at the same prices, had risen to 65.9 percent,
while the share of the consumer goods' industries (group B) had fallen

from 54.5 percent to 34.1 percent.[30] Among those industries whose relative weight increased may be listed machinery and metalworking (from 10.2 percent in 1938 to 28.0 percent in 1964), chemicals (2.7 percent in 1938 to 9.3 percent in 1964), building materials (from 1.2 to 3.6 percent, respectively), electric power (from 1.1 to 2.9 percent), and ferrous metallurgy (from 4.1 to 5.8 percent). These industries made relative gains mainly at the expense of consumer-goods industries, such as textiles (9.4 percent in 1938, 6.9 percent in 1964), food processing (32.4 and 15.3 percent, respectively), and leather and hides (3.3 and 2.3 percent). What makes the relative decline of the textile, leather, and food-processing industries all the more remarkable is that a part of the output of these industries before the war was not included in "industry" as defined in the census of manufactures, which supplied the basis of prewar statistics, but was produced in small shops and by handicraft methods. These activities have now either been absorbed by modern industry or have disappeared, with the consequence that the importance of these industries may be understated in 1938 and their growth overstated since that time.

Two producer-goods industries based on abundant domestic raw materials — and which at one time were mainstays of the Rumanian economy — have also receded in importance: these are petroleum (down from 13.1 percent of total industrial output in 1938 to 5.0 percent in 1964) and lumber and woodworking (from 9.5 percent to 7.1 percent). In recent years, the output of crude oil and raw timber, the unprocessed products of these sectors, has increased by less than 2 percent per year,[31] so that the gains in the value of output these sectors have registered are due, for the most part, to a greater degree of processing (for example, petrochemicals and higher-octane gasolines from petroleum, plywood and furniture from lumber).

Pong S. Lee has compared the structure of Rumanian industry with the structure of a "typical economy" outside the Communist bloc at the same stage of economic development. This "typical" or "composite" economy is based on Hollis Chenery's regressions of industrial output by branch on national income per head and population for a

[30] *Anuarul statistic 1965*, pp. 158–159. In these percentage shares, each industry is assigned to group A or group B according to the "preponderant destination of its products." In recent years all output has been divided into group A and group B according to the destination of each individual product. This principle of classification raised the share of group A in 1964 from 65.9 percent to 68.9 percent.

[31] *Anuarul statistic al R.P.R. 1965*, p. 169; and Direcția centrală de statistică, *Dezvoltarea industriei Republicii Populare Romîne: Culegere de date statistice* (Bucharest, 1964), p. 307 (hereafter referred to as *Dezvoltarea industriei R.P.R. 1964*).

sample of fifty-one countries outside the Communist area.[32] Lee found that Rumania's industrial structure in 1963 differed from that of a "composite" Western economy with a comparable level of national income per head and size of population mainly in that the share in total industrial output of the industries producing petroleum, lumber and wood products, and leather goods were significantly greater than those one would expect to find at that level of development. These disparities presumably reflected Rumania's specific resource endowment. In heavy industry, chemicals occupied about the same relative importance in Rumanian industry as in the composite economy, while the share of machinery was somewhat greater than expected, but this difference may not have been statistically significant. There is no evidence, in any case, that the concentration of investments in heavy industry significantly biased the structure of Rumanian industry away from the typical pattern prevailing in countries at a similar stage of development. As we shall see, the branches of industry that received a relatively small share of total investment — such as textiles, food, and leather — absorbed a good deal more manpower than average. This is one of the principal reasons why the preponderance of investments in heavy industry did not bring about a more profound transformation of the structure of output.

Has the rapid development of heavy industry been concentrated on the relatively few products that Rumania could specialize in on an international scale or has it been "extensive," based, that is, on the systematic enlargement of the nomenclature of products manufactured? While there are many products — including various types of equipment, tractors and engines and electric motors — for which domestic and/or foreign demand has been sufficient to permit production on a large scale, my impression is that expansion has been, on the whole, of the extensive type. This is reflected, on the one hand, in the constant preoccupation of the planners to raise the number of "new products mastered" in each plan period[33] — these products usually representing a net addition to the old nomenclature — and, on the other, in the small export-to-output ratios in the modern, technically advanced branches of the machine-building and chemical industries,

[32] Hollis B. Chenery, "Pattern of Industrial Growth," *American Economic Review*, Vol. 50 (September 1960), pp. 624–654. Professor Lee's unpublished study is titled "Growth and Structural Change of Rumanian Industry, 1958–1963" (1967).

[33] For a detailed description of the new products introduced in the machine-building industry between 1959 and 1963, see *Industria Romîniei 1944–1964* (Bucharest, 1964), p. 490.

where many new products have been introduced whose domestic market must be quite limited.[34] It is also instructive that the efforts of the more developed members of the Council for Mutual Economic Assistance to convince the Rumanians that they should eschew the production of standardized manufactures (produced more efficiently elsewhere) and specialize in the products for which they have a sound material base have been largely frustrated. According to a Czech economist, for instance, CMEA had recommended in 1955 that Rumania specialize in fifty-five types of machines and equipment. "Because, however, the majority of these items were already specialized in by a number of other countries of CMEA (four to six), this recommendation had relatively little effect on increasing the scale of production of these items." [35] It is very doubtful that the situation has been improved in more recent years in view of the deterioration of Rumania's relations with her CMEA partners.

To recapitulate, we found in this section that industrialization proceeded at a rapid but uneven pace throughout the postwar era. In spite of year-to-year fluctuations in the growth rates of industry, we may break down the span of years from the end of World War II to the present into four periods: (1) 1944 to 1948, a period of relatively slow recovery to prewar levels; (2) 1948 to 1953, marked by extremely rapid growth; (3) 1953 to 1957, characterized by significantly lower average rates than in the preceding period and ample fluctuations from year to year; (4) 1958 to 1965, when high, relatively constant growth rates were resumed after an initial acceleration. In each period industrial expansion was influenced by special exogenous circumstances and governed by distinct policies established by the central Party authorities. We shall study each of these periods in turn.

The Reconstruction Period: 1944 to 1948

Statistics of war damage are both methodologically suspect and factually tenuous; they can at best afford a general notion of the extent of a country's losses. We hear, for example, that Rumania's total wartime losses in fixed capital represented some 29 percent of the national income of 1938.[36] But we have no idea how this figure was arrived at.

---

[34] See Chapter 3, pp. 155–156.

[35] J. Novozámský, *Otázky vyrovnávání ekonomické úrovně evropských socialistických zemí*, candidate dissertation (Prague, July 1962), p. 154. There is conscious or unconscious irony in "specialization" by four to six members out of eight. For further details on the discussion in CMEA on specialization, see Chapter 4, pp. 209–214.

[36] This was said to be a smaller proportion than in any other East European nation. Poland, whose cumulative fixed-capital losses are said to have amounted

According to another source, apparently based on material submitted to the Paris Peace Conference of 1946, from August 23 — the date of the *coup d'état* as a result of which Rumania severed her ties with the Axis and joined the Allies — to October 25, 1944, when German troops were finally expelled from Rumanian territory, the destruction of property was evaluated at 30 billion lei of 1938 value or 11 percent of national income in 1938.[37] If we assume that the two sources were at least roughly comparable, we may infer that something like a third of the total war damage was incurred in the last months of the war. Another figure of doubtful precision that may be set against these data evaluates the economic contribution of Rumania to the war against Germany after August 23, 1944, at 106.4 billion lei of 1938 value (767.2 million dollars of 1938 parity), or 40 percent of 1938 national income.[38] Rumania's war effort, according to these calculations, was a good deal more costly than all losses suffered at the hands of the Germans. Almost the entire railway network and rolling stock of Rumania existing at the beginning of September 1944 was utilized "for the needs of the anti-Hitler front"; 80 percent of the output of coal was delivered to the railroads and thus indirectly served war needs, and a large part of Rumanian light industry was mobilized to supply uniforms and shoes for the Rumanian and Soviet armies. And, as we should expect, agriculture contributed significant quantities of foodstuffs for the military, out of crop harvests that were much smaller than before the war.[39] It is not explicitly stated whether these "contributions" include confiscations and spoliations by the Soviet army, though I think this is likely to be the case.[40]

---

to three and a half times 1938 national income, recovered prewar industrial output before Rumania. This testifies to the special difficulties under which Rumania was laboring after the war (for example, heavy reparations and the control of Rumania's primary resources by the joint Soviet-Rumanian companies).

[37] V. Anescu, "Efortul economic al poporului Romîn în Războiul antihitlerist," *Probleme economice*, No. 6 (1964), p. 31. This interesting article, based on original research in the archives, helped to bolster Rumania's claims about her substantial contribution to the allied (particularly Soviet) war effort after August 1944. It may be contrasted with the equivocal treatment by a Soviet author of Rumania's contribution to the allied effort in V. A. Karra's *Stroitel'stvo sotsialisticheskoi ekonomiki v Rumynskoi Narodnoi Respubliki* (Moscow, 1953), pp. 49–57. National income in 1938 was evaluated at 262.8 billion lei in *Enciclopedia României*, Vol. IV (Bucharest, 1938–1939), p. 964.

[38] Anescu, *op. cit.*, p. 31.

[39] *Ibid.*, pp. 28–30.

[40] R. L. Wolff estimates that the total loot taken between August 23 and September 12 may have reached 2 billion dollars (cited in Ghita Ionescu's *Communism in Rumania, 1944–1962* [London, New York, and Toronto: Oxford University Press, 1964], p. 88). This figure, given the depreciation of the U.S. dollar between 1938 and 1945, is not greatly superior to the one given in the Rumanian source

Despite her exertions on behalf of the Allies, Rumania was treated essentially as an enemy country by the Russians. The Soviet-Rumanian armistice convention of September 12, 1944, stipulated that Rumania would have to pay Soviet Russia an idemnity of 300 million dollars in goods over six years for "Soviet losses caused by military operations and occupation" and "restitute all goods taken from Soviet territory during the war." [41] One half of the reparations proper were to consist of petroleum and petroleum products and the other half of machinery, ships, timber, and grain. In addition, the Rumanians were to pay in grain (one million tons), livestock (300,000 head), other foodstuffs (60,000 tons), and rolling stock for goods evacuated or taken away from the Ukraine, Bessarabia, and Bukovina whose value was set at 950 billion lei, or 508.5 million U.S. dollars at the 1945 exchange rate.[42] The commodities delivered by Rumania were to be evaluated at 1938 prices, which were substantially below those prevailing in 1945–1946.[43] Later on the Soviets, mindful of the adverse effects of the reparations on the recovery of the Rumanian economy, trimmed their demands. They extended the period of delivery from 6 to 8 years and adjusted prices to Rumania's advantage. Finally, in mid-1948, they cut the balance of undelivered reparations in half.[44]

No accounting of Rumanian reparations to the Soviet Union has ever been released. Professor Spulber, who has explored the subject of reparations more thoroughly than any other Western economist, esti-

---

already quoted. According to Ionescu, Rumania's entire fleet, the major part of its merchant marine, large quantities of oil industry equipment, half of the available rolling stock, and all motor cars were seized by the Soviet army.

[41] Ionescu, op. cit., p. 91. One Western author estimates the total cost of reparations from September 1944 to June 1948 at $1.8 billion. This sum includes, in addition to petroleum, the value of 100,000 carloads of wheat, 55,000 carloads of sugar, 5,000 railroad cars, 2,600 tractors, and 260,000 head of cattle (Karel Holbik, "Economic Miracle Through Investment Priorities? The Case of Rumania," Weltwirtschaftliches Archiv, Vol. 94, No. 2 [1965], p. 310). The Rumanian official who drew my attention to this source said he could neither confirm nor impugn Holbik's estimates at this time. My own impression is that this estimate is on the high side. The Paris Peace Treaty of February 1947 essentially confirmed the provisions of the armistice, even though it recognized that Rumania had taken "an active part in the war against Germany" (Ionescu, op. cit., p. 128).

[42] Nicholas Spulber, The Economics of Communist Eastern Europe (New York and London: Technology Press and Wiley, 1957), pp. 172 and 175.

[43] For example, U.S. prices of crude oil (Pennsylvania) were 64 percent higher in 1945 than in 1938 (J. Mervart, Význam a vývoj cen v mezinárodním obchodě [Prague, 1960], p. 227). The price increases for refined products, however, which made up the bulk of deliveries to the Soviet Union, were much smaller than for crude oil. For gasoline, U.S. prices in 1945 were 12 percent higher than in 1938 and in 1946 28 percent higher (Spulber, op. cit., p. 175).

[44] Spulber, op. cit., p. 176.

mates that some 9 million tons of oil and oil products were supplied to the Soviet Union on reparations account between 1944 and 1948, or nine tenths of the total provided for in the armistice convention.[45] In July 1948 the Soviets stated that Rumanian reparations amounted so far to 153 million dollars (at 1938 parity), but gave no details as to the contents of these deliveries.[46] It is suspected, in view of the difficulties the Rumanians had in resuming grain exports — in 1945 and in 1946 the Russians exported grain to Rumania — that oil products made up the bulk of reparations.

The burden of reparations and restitutions would not have been so heavy if the Rumanians had been able to avail themselves of all their resources to meet their obligations. But in point of fact the Soviet Union had managed to get hold of a substantial part of Rumania's natural wealth through the instrumentality of the Soviet-Rumanian companies, the first of which were founded in July 1945. The Soviet contribution to the fifteen joint companies[47] was made up chiefly of German shares in Rumanian oil companies, banks, mines, and metalworking factories, together with Rumanian boats, seized from the Germans by the Soviet armed forces, and Soviet aircraft.

The share of total assets or of productive capacities in each of the sectors controlled by the Soviet-Rumanian companies could only be estimated for a few of these companies. In 1947 Sovrompetrol, probably the most important of these enterprises, is said to have been responsible for 29.8 percent of Rumanian crude oil extraction and for 36.5 percent of the output of refined petroleum products.[48] In 1950, "Muntenia" and "Petrolifera Moldova," the two strictly Rumanian companies, merged with Sovrompetrol, which as a result became responsible for the entire petroleum production of the country.[49] The metallurgical complex at Reşiţa, which was under the control of Sovrommetal from July 1949, produced 46.7 percent of Rumania's total output of pig iron, 52.3 percent of the output of steel, and 30.8

[45] *Ibid.*, p. 172.

[46] *Ibid.*, p. 173.

[47] Sovrompetrol (founded in 1945), Sovromtransport (1945), Tars (air transport, 1945), Sovrombanc (banking, 1945), Sovromlemn (lumber, 1946), Sovromchim (chemical industry, 1948), Sovromtractor (1948), Sovromgaz (1949), Sovromcărbune (coal, 1949), Sovrommetal (metallurgy, 1949), Sovromconstrucţii (1949), Sovromasigurărí (insurance, 1949), Sovromutilaj (oil equipment, 1952), Sovromnaval (ship building, 1952), Sovromcvarţ (uranium mining, 1952). Source: Spulber, *op. cit.*, p. 190.

[48] *Probleme economice*, No. 8 (1959), p. 70. The share of Sovrompetrol in exploratory drilling was close to 50 percent.

[49] I. Oleinik, *Dezvoltarea industriei Romîniei în anii Regimului Democrat Popular* (Bucharest, 1960), p. 209.

percent of the output of rolled steel in 1949.[50] Most of the oil-drilling equipment and tractors produced in Rumania were manufactured in plants belonging to the joint companies.[51]

Of course, not all the production of these joint companies was lost to Rumania. The agreements typically provided that each party would contribute 50 percent of current outlays and would obtain "50 percent of the product of the companies' activities." [52] For the petroleum industry this "parity principle" implied that the Soviets could claim 15 to 20 percent of the country's *total* petroleum output in 1946 and 1947. If we now consider that deliveries on reparation account came to 44 percent of total petroleum output in 1946 and that additional oil products had to be supplied for the Soviet occupation forces,[53] we may conclude that less than 40 percent of the output remained at the disposal of the Rumanian authorities.[54]

Up to 1964, when the Rumanians vigorously rejected the notion of multinational enterprises limiting domestic sovereignty,[55] it was frequently claimed in official Rumanian propaganda that the joint companies had helped to expand output at a time when private firms were sabotaging their own production.[56] One should keep in mind that until the nationalization law of June 1948 the major part of Rumania's industry was still in private hands; the joint companies were the core of the "state sector." That the joint companies might have been more

[50] *Economia Romîniei între anii 1944–1959, op. cit.*, p. 175. It is not known whether Sovrommetal produced metallurgical products in any other plants (cf. *Dezvoltarea industriei socialiste în R.P.R.* [Bucharest, 1959], p. 153).

[51] Č. Konečný, *Socialistický mezinárodní úvěr* (Prague, 1964), p. 130.

[52] *Ibid.*, p. 131.

[53] Spulber, *op. cit.*, p. 174. In 1945, total production was 4.68 million tons and total exports were 3.17 million tons. Of the latter, 2.54 million tons were delivered to the Soviet Union on reparations account and 418,254 tons as provisions for Soviet occupation forces (*ibid.*).

[54] The comparison is between deliveries of refined products and crude oil output. In 1948, the combined tonnage of refined products came to 94 percent of crude oil output.

[55] "During the development of the relations of cooperation between the socialist countries which are members of CMEA, forms and measures have been projected, such as . . . enterprises jointly owned by several countries. . . . Our party has very clearly expressed its point of view, declaring that, since the essence of the projected measures lies in shifting some functions of economic management from the competence of the respective state to that of superstate bodies or organisms, these measures are not in keeping with the principles that underlie the relations among the socialist countries." ("Statement on the Stand of the Rumanian Workers' Party Concerning the Problems of the International Communist and Working-Class Movement" [Bucharest: Meridiane Publishing House, 1964], reprinted in full in William E. Griffith, *Sino-Soviet Relations, 1964–1965* [Cambridge, Mass.: The M.I.T. Press, 1967], pp. 269–296.)

[56] Among other sources, see *Dezvoltarea industriei socialiste în R.P.R.* (Bucharest, 1959), pp. 96–98.

dynamic than private firms between 1945 and 1947 would not be surprising; the former could get equipment from the Soviet Union and foreign exchange to buy parts and essential materials,[57] while the latter were forced to work with antiquated equipment and were afflicted with crippling shortages of materials.

The dearth of foreign exchange, which underlay the lack of materials, spare parts, and replacements for worn-out equipment in industry, cannot be attributed entirely to the Soviet lien on Rumanian resources. It also resulted from the catastrophically low level of agricultural output.[58] Marketings were barely enough to prevent starvation in the towns, let alone to produce an exportable surplus. Commercial exports in 1947 — that is, exports exclusive of reparations — were evaluated at $34 million, compared to $143 million in 1938. Soviet credits helped Rumania to import nearly twice as much (61.3 million dollars) as it exported, although this level of imports was less than a quarter of the prewar level, if we make allowance for the depreciation of the dollar.[59]

The foreign exchange crisis can largely be blamed for the stagnation — and in some sectors the retrogression — of industrial output in 1946 and 1947 (shown in Table 1.6), although it must be recognized that the shortage of food to supply industrial workers, the disruption caused by the inflation (which was only temporarily arrested by the currency reform of August 1947), the obstructionist tactics of trade unions in the private sector, and the paralyzing effects on entrepreneurs of impending nationalization measures also shared responsibility for the slowdown. (This halting performance, incidentally, contrasted with the situation in such countries as Poland and Czechoslovakia where industrial production at the time was rapidly — and uninterruptedly — progressing toward the recovery of prewar levels.)

Of the essential products listed in Table 1.6, only cement, which was of course manufactured from domestic materials, had recovered prewar

[57] Cf. Article V of the official text of the convention for the creation of the Soviet-Rumanian oil company (Spulber, *op. cit.*, pp. 217–223), in which it is stated that the Soviet-Rumanian company "shall be granted by the Romanian authorities, without any difficulty, the foreign currency it requires for purchasing from abroad the materials and equipment necessary for its operations from the foreign currency that results from the company's own exports payable in such currency."

[58] In 1946, the wheat harvest amounted to 50 percent of the 1935–1939 average, the corn harvest to 19 percent and the potato harvest to 35 percent (Ministerul agriculturii şi silviculturii, *Dezvoltarea agriculturii în Republica Populară Romînă* [Bucharest, 1958], p. 54). On the land reform of 1945, see Chapter 2, p. 89.

[59] V. A. Karra, *Stroitel'stvo sotsialisticheskoi ekonomiki v Rumynskoi narodnoi Respublike* (Moscow, 1953), p. 88. According to Karra, 1938 exports should be reduced to $115 million and imports to $100 million to adjust for changes in territory and population.

TABLE 1.6. OUTPUT OF KEY INDUSTRIAL PRODUCTS IN 1938 AND 1944-1947

Units	1938	1944	1945	1946	1947
Crude oil (millions of tons)	6.6	3.5	4.6	4.1	3.9
Pig iron (thousands of tons)	133	142	56	68	93
Crude steel (thousands of tons)	284	245	134	165	203
Rolled steel products (thousands of tons)	289	202	114	126	137
Sulfuric acid (100 percent) (thousands of tons)	44	n.a.	21	25	25
Cement (thousands of tons)	510	n.a.	214	373	523
Cotton yarn (thousands of tons)	16.5	4.3	9.0	16.1	13.0
Cotton cloth (millions of square meters)	104	34.6	38.3	35.4	48.4
Woolen fabrics (millions of square meters)	12	8.8	8.1	8.0	8.9
Leather shoes (millions of pairs)	2.7	3.0	3.0	2.3	2.2

Note: 1938 data correspond to postwar territory.
Sources: Dezvoltarea industriei socialiste în R.P.R. (Bucharest, 1959), pp. 96, 148, 152, 231, and 384; *Anuarul statistic al R.P.R. 1965* (Bucharest, 1965), p. 168; S. Fischer-Galati, ed., *Romania* (New York and London: Praeger, 1957), p. 302.

output by 1947. The metallurgical industry performed much better than most branches of light industry in 1946 and 1947 by reason of the preference it received in the allocation of foreign currency for the importation of iron ore; light industry languished for lack of materials,[60] to the point where many private enterprises in the textile and food-processing industries discontinued all activity.[61]

I have expatiated on this early period because, in addition to its intrinsic interest, it illustrates a pattern of interdependence among

[60] In 1947, imports of iron ore came to 83.1 percent of the 1938 level, while domestic output, greatly expanded during the war, was already 50 percent above prewar levels in 1948 (no statistics are at hand for 1947, but it appears that 1938 output had already been recovered). Imports of cotton fiber, estimated at 20,000 tons in 1947, were about on a par with 1938. But imports of cotton yarn, which amounted to 27,000 tons in 1937, were negligible in the first postwar years. Imports of wool were running at an annual ratio of 1,700 tons from August 1945 to February 1948, compared to 3,281 tons in 1937, not counting the import of 2,616 tons of woolen yarns, which were certainly not matched in 1946 or 1947. (Prewar imports are taken from M. Constantinescu *et al., Comerțul exterior . . . , op. cit.,* Part I, Vol. 2, pp. 545, 551, 589, 593; postwar exports are taken from *Economia Rominiei între anii 1944-1959, op. cit.,* p. 572; I. P. Oleinik, *Dezvoltarea industriei Rominiei în anii Regimului Democrat-Popular* [Rumanian translation from the Russian original, Bucharest, 1960], pp. 154-155.)

[61] In 1947, 6,153 private firms in processing industries were inactive out of a total of 34,448. In mining, however, only 69 out of 1,095 were inactive (*Industria Rominiei 1944-1964* [Bucharest, 1964], p. 34). It may also be noted that the equipment of cotton-spinning works was utilized to the extent of 50.6 percent of capacity in 1947, compared to 79.5 percent in 1938. For cotton cloth, the corresponding proportions were 25.3 in 1947 and 62.8 in 1938, for woolen cloth 20.4 in 1947 and 31.7 in 1938 (*Dezvoltarea industriei socialiste în R.P.R., op. cit.,* p. 383).

sectors that will be observed again at several points in this survey of the Rumanian economy. Owing to the reliance of major sectors of industry on imported materials, industrial output hinges generally on the availability of foreign exchange, which in turn is bound up with the level of exports, of credits received and of external obligations incurred. In this first period, exports were depressed by the failure of the farm sector to generate surpluses above the minimal food requirements of the population and by the necessity of sharing the benefits of Rumania's natural resources with the Soviet Union, at a time when the country's meager foreign-exchange earnings were already depleted by onerous reparations payments. The rapid recovery and expansion of industry in the next few years were largely made possible by the spectacular amelioration of the foreign-trade situation.

The First Industrialization Drive: 1948 to 1953

The turning point, when economic recovery was resumed and then rapidly accelerated, may be set in the second half of 1947 or in early 1948. It may be true, as Rumanian economists now assert, that the monetary reform of August 1947, which slowed down the inflation, had something to do with the improvement.[62] I rather think, however, that the harvest of 1947 was the decisive factor in the upturn. From less than 50 percent of prewar, the aggregate value of all crops rose to roughly 75 percent.[63] The cereals crop was much better than in 1945 or 1946. The wheat crop remained substantially below prewar levels, but more corn was harvested than in 1938.[64] With more corn and other fodder on hand, peasants were at last able to reverse the downward trend in the size of their herds and make real headway toward the recovery of prewar levels.[65] When the Soviet Union cut the balance of undelivered reparations in half in 1948, foodstuffs and other primary products that would otherwise have been delivered as reparations were released for commercial exports. In 1948 the latter were composed

[62] *Dezvoltarea economică a Rominiei* (Bucharest, 1964), p. 47.

[63] Karra, *op. cit.*, pp. 85–86.

[64] The wheat and corn harvests may be calculated from estimated yields per hectare and from the acreage cultivated (*Dezvoltarea economiei R.P.R. pe drumul socialismului 1948–1957* [Bucharest, 1958], pp. 256, 262).

[65] Between January 1946 and January 1947, all major categories of farm animals had declined in numbers (Ministerul agriculturii și silviculturii, *Dezvoltarea agriculturii în Republica Populară Romînă* [Bucharest, 1958], p. 62). In January 1948 the size of herds of large-horned cattle and sheep surpassed 1938 levels, while the number of hogs was still less than prewar. The 1948 output of meat, measured in liveweight and slaughterings, was still less than two thirds of what it had been in 1938 (*ibid.*, p. 63).

in approximately equal halves of foodstuffs and raw materials, including mainly petroleum and lumber. In both of these two broad groups, 1948 exports amounted to 80 percent more than *total* exports in 1947 (for which no breakdown by commodity groups is available). As export earnings rose and purchases of foodstuffs abroad went down, it became possible to more than double imports of raw materials and semifabricates in 1948.[66] Thanks to these imports, manufactures could now operate closer to capacity. From May 1947 to April 1948, for instance, the textile industry is said to have operated at 85 percent of capacity, compared to an average of 64 percent in the period August 1945–April 1947.[67] The metallurgical industry, on the basis mainly of imported coke, two thirds of which came from the Soviet Union, raised the utilization of its capacity to 70–80 percent.[68]

From an estimated 75 percent of 1938 output at the end of 1947, Rumanian industrial production moved to 85 percent at the end of the following year and drew abreast with the prewar level sometime in 1949.[69] The peak wartime level, however, was probably not reached until at least 1950.

In 1949 and 1950 the Rumanian economy was governed by one-year plans, preparatory to the launching of the Five-Year Plan for 1951–1955. These annual plans already carried forward the government's development strategy, which found its clearest expression in the level and pattern of state investments. As can be seen in Table 1.7, the share of state investments devoted to industry, and, within this sector, the share allotted to producer goods, were not far below those envisaged in the First Five-Year Plan.[70]

After heavy industry, the largest claim on the state investment fund was made by the transportation sector (19 percent in 1949, 12 to 17 percent from 1950 to 1953). This was used mainly to bring the heavily damaged railroad system back into operation; but no major new railroad lines were undertaken, and the surface-road network was left in its underdeveloped state. Between 1950 and 1952 less than 1 percent of the goods transported — measured in ton-kilometers — was moved by truck. The only outstanding effort made to improve the country's infrastructure was the work done on the Danube–Black Sea Canal;

[66] Oleinik, *op. cit.*, p. 161. "Commercial exports" exclude deliveries on reparations account. All the export data cited in the text correspond to commercial exports.

[67] *Ibid.*, p. 154.

[68] *Ibid.*, p. 153.

[69] *Dezvoltarea economică a Rominiei 1944–1964, op. cit.*, p. 48. *Dezvoltarea economiei R.P.R. pe drumul socialismului 1948–1957* (Bucharest, 1958); *Anuarul statistic 1965*, p. 146.

[70] As it turned out both these shares were greatly surpassed.

TABLE 1.7. PATTERNS OF INVESTMENT IN THE STATE SECTOR (*Percentages*)

	1949 (*plan*)	1950 (*actual*)	1951–1955 (*plan*)	1951–1955 (*actual*)
Industry	47.2	48.3	51.4	57.5
producer goods	36.8	41.9	42.1	50.2
consumer goods	10.4	6.4	9.3	7.3
Transportation and communications	21.2	17.3	16.2	11.1
Agriculture and forestry	9.4	11.3	10.0	10.4
Housing, education, culture, science, and public health	11.0	14.2		11.0
			22.4	
Other branches	11.2	8.9		10.0
Total	100.0	100.0	100.0	100.0

Sources: 1949: I. P. Oleinik, *Dezvoltarea industriei Romîniei în anii Regimului Democrat-Popular* (Bucharest, 1960), p. 71; 1950–1955: *Anuarul statistic al R.P.R. 1958*, p. 168; United Nations, Economic Commission for Europe, "Economic Development in Rumania," *Economic Bulletin for Europe*, Vol. 13, No. 2 (January 1961), p. 73.

but this ill-conceived project, which had proved exorbitantly expensive in human lives and material resources, was finally abandoned in 1953, when only 7 kilometers of canal out of a total planned length of 75 kilometers had been excavated.[71]

Once the priority needs of industry and transportation for investment funds had been met there was little left to develop agriculture and other low-priority sectors. Only about 10 percent of state investments in fixed capital went to agriculture, which were, of course, concentrated on state farms. Housing was also neglected. In the cities, where practically all new housing was built directly by the state or with state credits, the expanding population had, for the most part, to be crowded into lodgings built before or during the war. In Bucharest, for example, a total of 872 new apartments were added to the housing stock from 1949 to 1952, nearly half of which were one-room dwellings; meanwhile the population increased by over 100 thousand inhabitants. By way of contrast, it may be mentioned that from 1919 to 1928, over 3,300 apartments were built each year, at a time when the rate of expansion of the city's population was somewhat slower than from 1949 to 1952.[72] In other cities, where industrial employment rose faster

[71] Fischer-Galati, ed., *op. cit.*, p. 340.
[72] Direcția Orășenească de Statistică București, *Anuarul statistic al orașului București 1959*, p. 70; E. C. Decusară, *O anchetă asupra construcțiunilor de clădiri noui în orașele municipi dela 1919–1928* (Bucharest, 1930), pp. 5–6.

after the war, the gap between prewar and postwar performance was narrower, but in most cases it was still significant. Housing built from private funds, most of which was located in the countryside, also fared poorly. The occupiable surface built under these auspices fell from 1.3 million square meters in 1951 to 1.18 million in 1952 and 1.04 million in 1953.[73] Retail sales of construction materials, an approximate indicator of private investments in houses and productive structures, also declined. A percentage index of these sales based on 1950 stood at 86 in 1951, 72 in 1952, and 64 in 1953. Sales of pine lumber, for instance, were down to 37 percent of their 1950 level in 1953[74] — clear evidence that state investments and the export program were cutting deep into domestic consumption.

Rumania's strategy of development, which paralleled in most respects that of the other people's democracies, was not limited of course to the concentration of investment resources on heavy industry; it also called for the mobilization of *additional* resources for "accumulation." [75] Gross fixed investment in the socialist sector went up from 1.4 billion lei in 1949 to 5.5 billion lei in 1949 and 7.5 billion lei in 1950, ostensibly in comparable prices.[76] Some of this increase undoubtedly reflected the encroachment of the state on private investment activities, an encroachment that also played a part in the government's strategy, since resources deflected from private investments could be applied to projects that were higher on the planners' scale of priorities.

Among the Communist countries Rumania is one of the last to hold back precise data on the absolute level of national income, as calculated by the Central Statistical Office, and on the ratios of net investment to national income ("rates of accumulation"), which have varied appreciably through the years. The scattered accumulation rates that are to be found in the economic literature usually refer to four- or five-year periods and are lacking in precise explanations as to the methodology employed and the prices underlying the calculations. The fact that taxes were levied on both producer and consumer goods

[73] *Anuarul statistic al R.P.R. 1965*, p. 370.

[74] *Ibid.*, pp. 412 and 428.

[75] Accumulation is defined as fixed investment, plus increases in inventories, in reserves, and in the value of cattle herds, minus depreciation. The rate of accumulation is obtained by taking the percentage ratio of this algebraic sum to national income measured at market prices, exclusive of "nonproductive services." Note that the surplus on current account in the balance of payments is included in national income produced but, as far as I can make out, not in accumulation (see, for instance, the discussion of accumulation in *Revista de statistică*, No. 2 [1963], p. 72, and the synthetic balances in *Revista de statistică*, No. 7 [1965], pp. 18–20).

[76] Karra, *op. cit.*, p. 134. Old lei have been converted into new lei at the rate of 5 new lei to 100 old lei.

up to 1954 and only on the latter thereafter renders tenuous, or at least imprecise, the long-term comparisons that can be made out.[77] Yet a measure of the country's aggregate saving is so essential for any analysis of development that we cannot avoid some reference to these ratios.

In Table 1.8 I have assembled a few statistics that are meant to give

TABLE 1.8. ESTIMATES OF NATIONAL INCOME, INVESTMENTS IN FIXED CAPITAL AND ACCUMULATION (1950–1953) AT 1950 PRICES (*Billions of Post-1952 Lei and Percentages*)

	National Income Produced (billions of lei)	National Income Distributed (billions of lei)	Gross State Investments in Fixed Capital (billions of lei)	Ratio of Investments to National Income Distributed (percent)	Rate of Accumulation (percent)
1950	33	39	7.5	19.2	11
1951	44	46	10.6	23	n.a.
1952	46	n.a.	14.3	31.1[a]	n.a.
1953	53	n.a.	18.0	34.0[a]	29

[a] Ratio of investments to national income produced.

Note: For definitions of national income produced and distributed, see Appendix B, pp. 267–268.

Sources and methods: National income produced: Estimates at current prices given in Table B.10 deflated by the price index of Table B.7. National income distributed in 1950 is from Table B.8; the estimate for 1951 is from Table B.10, deflated by the index in Table B.7. Gross state investments in fixed capital: for 1950, from V. A. Karra, *Stroitel'stvo sotsialisticheskoi ekonomiki. . . .* (Moscow, 1953), p. 134; for other years, investments were derived from data in 1955 prices on the assumption that the ratio between the estimates of investments in 1953 and in 1950 prices also applied in other years. Rates of accumulation: for 1950: Table B.8; for 1953: an official statement cited in United Nations, Economic Commission for Europe, *Economic Bulletin for Europe*, Vol. 13, No. 2 (Geneva, 1961), p. 63.

at least a general notion of the extraordinary increase in investments and "accumulation" that took place during the crucial period 1950 to 1953.

[77] According to calculations made for the years 1957 and 1958, the "rate of accumulation [was] reduced by two to three percent as a result of the fact that producer goods [were] relieved of paying turnover taxes [in 1955]." (I. Răvar, C. Ciotanu, P. Scarlat, and D. Şandru, "Unele probleme ale calcului venitului național după locul de creare," *Studii de statistică: Lucrările consfătuiri științifice de statistică 27–29 Noiembrie 1961* [Bucharest, 1962], p. 27.) Note that the rates of growth of national income are also affected by the inclusion of indirect taxes on consumer goods. Since most of these taxes are levied on industry, they artificially magnify the relative importance of this sector and, to the extent that industry rises faster than agriculture, impart an upward bias to national income as a whole.

While the rate of accumulation appears quite low in the year preceding the launching of the First Five-Year Plan,[78] the fact that the rate of accumulation rose more steeply than the ratio of fixed investments to national income from 1950 to 1952 is not necessarily the result of errors in the estimation of either set of figures. We should have in mind that increases in enterprise inventories and state reserves made up a large part of total accumulation during this period — perhaps as much as half — and that these inventories are likely to have risen faster than investments in fixed capital.[79]

How did the Rumanian authorities succeed in raising the nation's rate of aggregate saving so much and so quickly? One factor made a major contribution to this accomplishment: the recovery of agricultural output from its postwar low in 1946 to approximately prewar levels by 1953[80] made it possible to raise consumption per capita from the extremely depressed standards prevailing in 1948[81] and simultane-

[78] Note that the ratio of "productive accumulation" to national income, where productive accumulation is defined in the source as total accumulation minus investments in fixed assets in nonproductive sectors (for example, in housing, hospitals), was equal to 9.7 percent in 1950. This estimate seems to correspond precisely to the rate for total accumulation in Table B.8, if one adjusts the latter to exclude nonproductive investments in fixed assets, which were equal to 86.8 percent of total investments in that year (see *Voprosy ekonomiki*, No. 7 [1966], p. 72).

[79] An article in *Viaţa economică*, No. 36 (1965), p. 4, put accumulation in the form of additions to fixed capital at about 50 percent of total accumulation, excluding increments in state reserves from 1951 to 1955. Another source estimated that 60 percent of accumulation went to fixed funds (*Probleme economice*, No. 1 [1964], p. 30). According to this latter source, about 60 percent of accumulation as a whole was directed to the "sphere of material production" in 1951, although 87.7 percent of investments in fixed capital was assigned to this sphere in 1951 (*Anuarul statistic al R.P.R. 1965*, p. 337). These two figures imply that the greater part of inventory accumulation was in the "nonproductive sphere" (retail trade, state reserves).

[80] The official index of gross output on a 1938 base stood at 62 in 1948, 74 in 1950, and 100 in 1953. (*Dezvoltarea agriculturii 1965*, p. 563.)

[81] In 1952 after gross crop output had risen 48 percent over 1948, per capita human consumption of corn, the mainstay of the peasants' diet, was only 70 percent of the 1935–1939 average. Wheat consumption per capita was 10 percent higher than in 1935–1939, an increase that can satisfactorily be explained by migration from the country to the city where relatively more bread than corn meal is normally eaten. Per capita meat consumption in 1956 was estimated to be 12 percent above 1938 (*Dezvoltarea industriei socialiste, op. cit.*, p. 475). In that same year workers' consumption of meat per family was said to be 48 percent higher than in 1950, and peasants' consumption 45 percent higher than in 1953. According to interview information, real wages in the cities in 1948 were between one fourth and one half their prewar levels. They were stated to have risen by 59 percent from 1948 to 1951; they then stagnated until 1953 and resumed their increase thereafter (Karra, *op. cit.*, p. 208; and *Dezvoltarea agriculturii R.P.R.* [Bucharest, 1961], p. 370). No statistics of peasant families' consumption were apparently gathered before 1953, when the consumption of meat, fats, bread, and eggs was still at least 20 percent below prewar levels. Sugar consumption, however, may have been close to the prewar mark. (Cf. the consumption indices in M. Levente, E. Barat, and M. Bulgaru, *Analiza statistico-economică a agriculturii* [Bucharest, 1961], p. 220;

ously to raise the rate of accumulation. No doubt also the reduction of the reparations burden facilitated this two-pronged progress.[82]

Consumption in Rumania was never allowed to get out of hand; rationing of consumer goods for town dwellers was maintained throughout the reconstruction period and nearly until the end of the Five-Year Plan, in contrast to the situation in Poland where by 1949 (consumption having recovered prewar levels) rationing was abolished — only to be reinstated two years later when the rearmament effort, occasioned by the Korean War, and the mounting burden of an extraordinarily ambitious investment program forced the government to take direct measures to block consumption.

During the first industrialization drive, urbanization proceeded at a rapid pace in conjunction with the rise in employment in industry and in other socialized sectors: the urban population increased from 3,747,000 in 1948 (23.5 percent of the population) to an estimated 4,424,000 in 1953 (26.3 percent). This migration, by increasing the pressure on marketed food supplies, would in all likelihood have turned the terms of trade between industrial and agricultural prices in favor of the farm sector, if the state had not taken stringent measures to check any such tendency. The obvious "bolshevik" solution would have been to collectivize the land and squeeze out the farm surplus by outright confiscation; but the government was not yet well enough entrenched to force through such a policy on a massive scale, especially so soon after the peasants had begun to enjoy the fruits of the postwar land reform. In 1953, when the first peak of collectivization was attained, over three fourths of the country's arable land was still in private hands; only about 7 percent of the arable land had been incorporated into collectives of the Soviet type; the rest was divided between state farms (15 percent) and loose "associations" akin to the early Soviet T.O.Z. (which held 2.3 percent of the arable land).[83] The

---

Dezvoltarea economiei R.P.R. pe drumul socialismului 1948–1957 [Bucharest, 1958], p. 422; and *Economia Rominiei între anii 1944–1959* [Bucharest, 1959], p. 622.) If we consider also that peasants' real incomes in 1953 were supposed to be 43.2 percent above 1950 levels (*Dezvoltarea agriculturii R.P.R.* [Bucharest, 1961], p. 370), we can get some notion of the depressed levels of living in the countryside that must have prevailed before the inception of the First Five-Year Plan.

[82] International obligations, which represent the bulk of outlays on reparations, amounted to 46.6 percent of total planned expenditures in the 1947–1948 budget, 7.4 percent of actual expenditures in 1949, 4.6 percent of actual expenditures in 1950, and 3.8 percent of planned expenditures in 1951 (N. Spulber, "National Income and Product," in S. Fischer-Galati, ed., *op. cit.*, p. 192). The deficit in foreign merchandise trade, which excludes reparations, came to $43 million in 1953. This almost certainly exceeded the value of reparations Rumania may still have been paying in that year.

[83] See Chapter 2, p. 90.

state, during the period 1949–1953, was successful in raising the marketability of farm produce — which at first had been depressed by the land reform — by exacting quotas, in the form of compulsory deliveries, amounting in the case of cereals to about a quarter of total output.[84] It paid for these deliveries at exceedingly low prices and skimmed off most of the remaining surpluses by purchases at higher prices ("acquisitions" and "contracts"), which gave the peasants, at least on the margin, some incentive to market their produce. Peasants were also allowed to sell part of their surpluses on the free market once they had met their obligations to the state; in 1950 these free sales, for which much higher prices were usually obtained than in transactions with the state, contributed close to two thirds of the peasants' cash incomes from the sale of farm products.[85] For these crucial years, no indices of the relative prices of agricultural produce and of industrial goods purchased by farmers have been published, but we can still derive some measure of the deterioration in the parity index — that is, of the shift of relative prices against farmers — from scattered price quotations. It turns out that after the monetary reform of January 1952, which in effect confiscated most of the peasants' cash holdings, the weighted average of prices that the peasants received per kilogram of grain, meat, and milk from all sources, including compulsory deliveries and free market sales, bought only some 20 to 50 percent of the sugar, shoes, and cloth that might have been bought with a unit of each of these farm products in 1938.[86]

These exactions from the peasants were especially heavy on the "kulaks," who owned only 8 percent of the arable surface in 1952 but still contributed, from compulsory deliveries alone, about 12–13 percent of the fund of wheat, rye, corn, sunflower seeds, and meat collected

[84] *Rezoluții și hotărîri ale Comitetului Central al R.P.R.* (Bucharest, 1954), p. 500.

[85] *Economia României între anii 1944–1959* (Bucharest, 1959), p. 516; and *Probleme economice*, No. 12 (1959), p. 64.

[86] The estimated averages of farm prices have, if anything, an upward bias. They have been compared with the "commercial" (higher) prices of industrial products, since peasants were not issued ration cards and had only very limited opportunities of buying at the lower prices. Commercial prices of textile fabrics and shoes were about twice as high as rationed prices; the ratio for sugar was a little over 3 to 1 (*Hotărîrea consiliului de ministri cu privire la întocmirea și publicare cataloagelor de prețuri* [Bucharest, 1952]). Price quotations are taken from *Probleme economice*, No. 9 (1954), p. 93; No. 5 (1955), pp. 81–83; No. 9 (1955), p. 73; and No. 3 (1957), p. 89; and S. Țaigar, *Veniturile populației și nivelul de trai în R.P.R.* (Bucharest, 1964), p. 133. Interestingly enough, the parity index for prewar years, which *has* been published, shows that farmers were already much worse off in terms of purchasing power parity in 1938 than they had been in 1913 or in 1929: the parity index (based on 1929), which had stood as high as 119 in 1913, was down to 68 in 1938 (*Revista de statistică*, No. 5–6 [1960], p. 23).

or purchased by the state.[87] This policy was not without adverse consequences on agricultural output in the long run, but it did help to fulfill immediate aims: the swelling urban population was fed, and enough rations and commercial sales at higher prices were supplied to improve the diet; moreover, by 1952–1953, a fairly large surplus of cereals was left over for exports and reserves, amounting to 9.5 percent of the total cereals harvests of 1952 and 1953.[88]

A rising volume of exports during this period was essential to finance not only the rapidly growing imports of raw materials (cotton, iron ores, rubber) and semifabricates (rolled steel products and nonferrous metals) but also machinery and equipment at a time when 40 to 50 percent of the capital goods installed were purchased abroad.[89] Some of these imports of equipment (for example, from Czechoslovakia) were bought on credit, while the rest represented an immediate drain on Rumania's limited foreign exchange resources. Besides cereals and other food products, which made up less than a quarter of the value of exports from 1950 to 1953 (compared to 48.7 percent in 1948),[90] the principal sources of foreign exchange consisted of raw materials and semifabricates (71 percent of total in 1953). Petroleum products were, of course, the most important of these staples, at a time when 60 to 63 percent of the value of domestic production was exported; but other exports, such as lumber and cement, were also pushed as hard as possible to gain scarce currency.[91] The possibility of developing exports of mineral and forest products after 1948 relieved the pressure on food supplies and facilitated the recovery of living standards, despite the high rate of forced saving extracted from the population.

[87] *Probleme economice*, No. 7 (1961), p. 10.

[88] *Ibid.*, No. 7 (1958), p. 84. If exports of cereals consisted solely of wheat, the exports and additions to reserves came to 20 percent of the wheat harvest (averaged for 1952 and 1953), or about the same proportion as in 1938 (for exports alone).

[89] *Anuarul statistic al R.P.R. 1965*, p. 344.

[90] See Chapter 3, Table 3.8. The share of exports made up by food products varied widely depending on the state of the harvest. It was about 25 percent in 1950, nearly 30 percent in 1951 when gross crop output rose by 37 percent over 1950, 13 percent in 1952 when crop output declined by 10 percent from the preceding year, and 17 percent in 1953 when the crop output rose by 26 percent over 1952. The percentage for 1951 is based on the numbers linked to 1955 in the *Information Bulletin of the Rumanian Chamber of Commerce*, No. 3 (1956), p. 8. The percentage for 1952 was computed as a residual, the other components of exports being calculated from data in *Economia Romîniei între anii 1944–1959, op. cit.*, p. 577; other data are from Chapter 3, Table 3.8.

[91] See Appendix C, p. 286. The output of softwood timber, which made up the bulk of these exports, reached an all-time high in the years 1950 to 1953, then declined sharply in 1954; after staging a partial recovery, it has, more recently, been maintained at about 15 percent below the peak years of the early 1950's.

My schematic description of the main trends in the period preceding Stalin's death may have led the reader to the erroneous conclusion that the industrialization of Rumania developed smoothly under the guidance of a master plan. This was by no means the case. We have already mentioned *en passant* the monetary reform of 1952, which would not have been necessary if severe inflationary pressures had not developed, which in turn reflected hitches in fulfilling the plan.[92] Food prices on the free peasant market, one of the few reliable indicators of inflationary pressures, increased "over threefold" between 1947, the year of the previous reform, and 1951.[93] Compulsory deliveries of farm products, levels of which were pegged on optimistic estimates of year-to-year increases in agricultural output,[94] were so high that thousands of peasants fell into arrears and were obliged to abandon their land. In December 1961 Gheorghiu-Dej reported that "in the name of the struggle against the kulaks more than 80,000 peasants, most of them working peasants, were sent to trial; more than 30,000 of these peasants were tried in public which provoked great concern among the peasant masses brought to attend these infamous frameups."[95] We have no statistics of arrears on deliveries, but some financial data have been divulged that shed light on the peasants' inability to meet the government's heavy demands. In 1951 agricultural taxes actually collected came to 76.7 percent of the amounts budgeted; this proportion went up to 87.6 percent in 1952 and fell again to 81.1 percent in 1953. It was not until 1954 that the budget estimates for this category of revenue were regularly fulfilled.[96]

Stringent controls over urban and rural food consumption, paltry allocations of foreign exchange for importing consumer goods, and a vigorous export drive help to explain how the state managed to press forward its investment program. Something remains to be said about the distribution of labor and investment resources among the various branches of industry. This allocation was calculated to support a rapid expansion of the entire industrial sector and simultaneously to bring about a structural transformation in harmony with the planners' development strategy. For, as we shall have occasion to observe in the

[92] The second monetary reform converted all prices and wages at the rate of five new lei for 100 old lei, while currency in the hands of the population was refunded at the rate of only one new leu per 100 old lei for small balances and 0.25 new lei per 100 old lei for all sums exceeding a certain amount (see N. Spulber, *The Economics of Communist Eastern Europe, op. cit.*, p. 128).

[93] *Dezvoltarea economică a Romîniei 1944–1964* (Bucharest, 1964), p. 82.

[94] See Chapter 2, pp. 89–90 and p. 94.

[95] Cited in Ghita Ionescu, *op. cit.*, p. 201.

[96] Al. Şesan, *Aspecte din istoria aparatului financiar din R.P.R.* (Bucharest, 1958), p. 189. See also Chapter 2, note 44.

last chapter of this study on Rumania's relations with CMEA, none of the Communist leaders wished any part of a "calico industrialization," their term of opprobrium for an industrial development centered on light industry.[97] Development, in their view, must be spearheaded by electric power, engineering, and other branches of heavy industry.

Although for lack of data, especially on the earlier years of the period, we cannot assign a precise role to the various factors that made the expansion possible, we can segregate three inputs — labor, fixed capital, and raw materials — whose increased supplies had a preponderant influence on the growth of industrial production (Table 1.9).

TABLE 1.9. INDICES OF GROSS OUTPUT, EMPLOYMENT, AND FIXED ASSETS IN INDUSTRY, AND SELECTED INDICATORS OF RAW MATERIALS, FUELS, AND SEMIFABRICATES SUPPLIED TO INDUSTRY, 1948, 1950, AND 1953 (*1950 = 100*)

	1948	*1950*	*1953*
Gross output of industry (official index)	58	100	168
Industrial employment	71	100	131
Fixed assets in industry (official index)	n.a.	100[a]	132[a]
Imports of raw materials, fuels, and semifabricates	62	100	161
Deliveries of wool to industry from farm sector	n.a.	100[b]	176
Farm output of sugar beets	94	100	205
Farm output of cotton	15	100	328

[a] Evaluated at December 31 of year indicated. Socialized industry only.
[b] 1951.
Sources: Anuarul statistic al R.P.R. 1959, p. 83; *Anuarul statistic al R.P.R. 1965*, pp. 114 and 148; *Dezvoltarea agriculturii Republicii Populare Romîne* (Bucharest, 1961), pp. 182–185 and 368. Imports of raw materials, fuels, and semifabricates are computed from data in Chapter 3, Table 3.9. Industrial employment in 1948 is based on an estimate in S. Fischer-Galati, ed., *Romania* (New York and London: Praeger, 1957), p. 278.

Although from 1948 to 1953 industrial employment increased a good deal less than output, the intake of labor into industry was still considerable. The labor force rose from 550–600 thousand persons to over one million in five years. It was largely around the core of new employment in industry and construction, in which sector the labor force doubled between 1950 and 1953, that urbanization made its most rapid progress in postwar years.

When we examine the development of individual branches of industry, we are struck by remarkable differences in the relative importance of increments in labor and in capital assets assigned to various

[97] See Chapter 4, p. 203.

groups of industries. These disparities in incremental factor proportions emerge from the data in Table 1.10, which, for lack of more

TABLE 1.10. PERCENTAGE SHARES OF PRINCIPAL BRANCHES OF INDUSTRY IN
EMPLOYMENT, INVESTMENTS, AND FIXED ASSETS, 1950, 1953,
AND 1955

	Share in Total Employment[a]		Share in Total Increase in Employment	Share in Total Investments		Share in Total Fixed Assets of Industry[b]
	1950	1953	1950–1953	1950	1953	End of 1955
Electric power	1.3	1.2	1.1	9.7	13.9	9.9
Fuels	7.5	7.5	7.2	48.8	39.8	26.5
petroleum	3.7	3.1	1.0	38.6	29.3	n.a.
Ferrous metallurgy	4.2	3.9	2.5	6.7	6.9	8.4
Nonferrous metallurgy	2.0	1.9	1.5	2.4	6.4	2.6
Machine building and metal processing	21.3	22.4	26.7	7.4	8.0	16.3
Chemicals	2.6	3.2	5.4	3.3	7.8	4.8
Building materials	5.8	6.3	8.1	3.8	4.7	4.6
Lumber and wood-working	17.2	18.6	23.9	4.0	4.1	5.1
Cellulose and paper	1.1	0.9	—	1.3	1.5	1.9
Glass and porcelain	1.3	1.1	0.6	0.3	0.2	0.5
Textiles	12.7	12.0	9.4	3.9	1.3	8.0
Garment making	4.2	4.2	3.9	—	—	0.2
Hides, leather, and footwear	5.4	4.4	0.6	0.6	0.2	1.2
Food processing	11.0	10.2	7.2	5.2	3.6	7.8
Soap and cosmetics	0.2	0.1	—	0.1	0.1	0.2
Printing	1.3	1.4	1.6	1.6	0.8	1.3
Other branches	0.9	0.7	0.3	0.9	0.7	0.7

[a] Excluding private workshops and handicrafts, which made up 7.6 percent of
total output in 1950 and 3 percent in 1955.
[b] Republican industry only (accounting for 83 percent of industrial output from
all enterprises, including private workshops and handicrafts, in 1955).
Sources: Directia centrală de statistică, *Dezvoltarea industriei Republicii Populare
Romîne: Culegere de date statistice* (Bucharest, 1964), p. 117; *Anuarul statistic al R.P.R.
1965*, pp. 186 and 350.

pertinent evidence, are limited to employment and investments by
industry group in 1950 and 1953 and to the structure of fixed assets
in 1955.

While it is unfortunate that our earliest available data on fixed assets
refer to the end of 1955, we can still get an approximate idea of the
relative intensity of current investments in each branch of industry by

comparing the structure of investments with the structure of assets.[98] Certain branches of industry, including electric power, fuels, nonferrous metallurgy, and chemicals were getting a greater proportion of total investment funds in 1950 and 1953 than they had in the past — mainly before and during the war — insofar as this past can be gauged from the structure of assets in 1955. It is interesting that three out of four of these industries, which apparently enjoyed a priority status in the state's development program, received less than their share of the additional employment from 1950 to 1953 (the exception being the chemical industry). The petroleum industry offers a most striking example of this disparity in the allocation of investment funds and of employment: it was allotted an average of one third of all investments to industry between 1950 and 1953, but only one percent of the additional manpower employed in the entire sector between these dates. On the other hand, consumer-goods industries such as textiles, food processing, leather, and glass were awarded only a fraction of their "normal share" of investments, as measured by the structure of assets in 1955. These industries were obviously in low standing in the planners' priority scale. Not only did they get a minuscule share of the new capital, but their gains in employment were less than average. The branches that absorbed a disproportionately high share of new employment were the machine-building, lumber, chemicals, and building materials industries, the first two accounting for over half of the growth in new employment. Investments in these branches, with the notable exception of the chemical industry, were relatively small. Two general observations may be culled from this analysis:

1. Disparities in factor proportions that formerly existed among industries were, in general, accentuated by the investment and employment policies of the early 1950's. The capital-to-labor ratios of industries that were relatively capital intensive, such as power, petroleum mining, and nonferrous metals, tended to rise. The capital-to-labor ratios of labor-intensive industries, such as machine building, lumber, and textiles, fell even below their previous levels.

2. If we look simultaneously at the allocation of capital and labor, we observe that branches of industry capable of yielding large amounts of foreign exchange — for example, petroleum, lumber, building materials, and nonferrous metals, including uranium mining — were given preference in the allocation of new resources over industries traditionally associated with a development strategy of a Soviet type — such as

[98] It is reasonable to assume that investments in 1954 and 1955 had a relatively minor effect on the structure of assets.

machine building and ferrous metallurgy. This point emerges even more clearly if we compare the allocation of investments in this period with that in the early 1960's when the metallurgical and machine-building industries, having risen in the priority scale, received a higher share of total investment funds than a decade earlier.[99] The fact that the industries carrying the brunt of the export program fared rather better than average in the allocation process suggests that the government's policy may have been less autarkic during this first part of the Five-Year Plan than it became after 1958. Withal, we should also consider that the Soviet-Rumanian joint companies, which controlled a substantial proportion of the production capacities in the petroleum, metalworking, lumber, and nonferrous metals industries, were in a better position to carry out investments and to employ additional labor than industries working for the home market. Even in the machine-building sector, efforts were made to produce goods with an export market, such as drilling equipment and boats, although expansion along lines paralleling production already existing in the Soviet bloc also developed rapidly during this period, for example, in electric motors, metal-cutting equipment, railroad cars, and agricultural machinery. (This parallelism, incidentally, was usually rooted in imports of complete plants, mainly from the Soviet Union and Czechoslovakia, which duplicated facilities in operation in these countries.) Finally, it may be argued that a concentration of efforts on building up the output of products capable of generating foreign exchange may have been the only feasible way of paying for the fast-rising imports of raw materials required by industries at all echelons of the priority scale.

Data available for the textile industry from 1948 to 1955 shed light on the contribution of greater utilization of capacity to the expansion of output, which was especially important prior to 1950 (Table 1.11).

The remarkable growth in the output of the principal semifabricates of the textile industry between 1948 and 1955 cannot be explained satisfactorily through the expansion of productive capacity except in the case of cotton yarn, whose output was expanded more rapidly than that of cotton fabrics in order to reduce yarn imports. In point of fact, the number of wool-weaving looms declined during the entire period, while the capacities of the wool-spinning, cotton- and silk-weaving industries stayed more or less what they were in 1948.[100] Greater utilization of capacity, thanks to improved supplies of raw materials, and

[99] See pp. 54–55.

[100] Note that investments in the textile industry in 1954 and 1955 were stepped up, so that the capacity situation in 1955 was probably slightly better than what it was in 1953, the end year of our first industrialization period.

TABLE 1.11. SELECTED CAPACITY INDICATORS FOR THE TEXTILE INDUSTRY FOR 1948, 1950, AND 1955

	1948	1950	1955
Cotton Spinning			
Number of spindles (thousands)	290	309	410
Percentage of utilization	80.7	88.5	100
Number of shifts	n.a.	3	3
Output of yarn (1948 = 100)	100	136	213
Cotton Weaving			
Number of looms	13,252	13,208	13,408
Percentage of utilization	42.8	68.1	97
Number of shifts	n.a.	2.1	2.9
Output of cotton cloth (1948 = 100)	100	162	268
Wool Spinning			
Number of spindles (thousands)	n.a.	125	127
Percentage of utilization	n.a.	93	97
Number of shifts	n.a.	2.3	2.9
Output of wool yarn (1948 = 100)	100	157	217
Wool Weaving			
Number of looms	2,835	2,687	2,270
Percentage of utilization	25.7	49.4	93
Number of shifts	n.a.	1.5	2.8
Output of woolen fabrics (1948 = 100)	100	193	266
Silk Weaving			
Number of looms	1,680	1,530	1,783
Percentage of utilization	28.9	49.9	95
Number of shifts	n.a.	1.5	2.9
Output of silk fabrics (1948 = 100)	100	154	251

Sources: Dezvoltarea industriei socialiste în R.P.R. (Bucharest, 1959), pp. 387 ff. and 403; *Dezvoltarea industriei R.P.R.* (Bucharest, 1964), p. 356.

the spread of three-shift operations were responsible for most of the growth of textile output.[101] Employment rose naturally along with more intensive utilization of capacity. In light industry as a whole, which includes — in addition to textiles — garment-making, leather and footwear, ceramics, glass, and manufactures of household articles (together accounting for around a quarter of the labor force of this sector in 1950), employment increased from about 100,000 persons in 1948 to 159,051 persons in 1950 and 194,162 persons in 1955.[102] There can

[101] It is suspected also that some quality deterioration occurred in this period.

[102] *Dezvoltarea industriei socialiste . . . , op. cit.*, pp. 388 and 405. These employment figures, being based on an administrative rather than a statistical classification, differ significantly from those in Table 1.10; they are, however, the only ones that can be linked to 1948. The increase from 1950 to 1955, however, is virtually the same for both sets of figures.

hardly be any doubt that the bulk of output gains in the textile industry resulted from the absorption of new manpower and additional raw-material supplies.[103]

The New Course and Its Aftermath: 1953 to 1957

It is commonly said in Eastern Europe that if Stalin had not died in 1953 the pressure of circumstances would soon have wrung a change in the economic course, even from the most "Stalinist" planners. The assumption behind this conjecture is that a continuation of the old course would have caused an intolerable drop in the standard of living of the population, which would have raised insuperable political problems for the Communist leadership in each of the Soviet Union's dependent states. In my opinion, this view is essentially correct for Rumania, at least in the sense that the standard of living could not have been maintained if the planners had persevered in the strategy of development adopted after 1948. Two principal arguments can be adduced to justify this proposition. The first is that the growth of exports would sooner or later have been insufficient to sustain the level of imports of equipment and raw materials required to keep the economy going on the old expansion path. The second is that certain domestic needs that had been seriously neglected in the postwar years would eventually have had to be satisfied at the expense of investments in heavy industry.

With regard to foreign trade, we may recall that petroleum products, lumber, cement, and other raw materials and semifabricates gave the impetus to the expansion of exports, whereas exports of foodstuffs fluctuated around an average that was substantially below the level of 1948. This pattern of expansion was feasible only as long as the production of raw materials and semifabricates kept on growing faster than domestic requirements. By 1953, however, it must have become obvious that petroleum output, despite enormous investments in drilling and exploration, would soon taper off.[104] Timber, on the other hand, was so heavily exploited during the war and in the early postwar period that by the early 1950's the government had found it necessary, in order to conserve this valuable resource, to stop the expansion of output of the coniferous varieties that make up the bulk of production. Hence-

---

[103] On raw-material supplies of domestic origin, see Table 1.7 and Appendix C, pp. 280–281. It may be noted that in the period 1947 to 1950, deliveries of cotton from imports approximately doubled (computed from data in *Dezvoltarea economiei R.P.R. pe drumul socialismului 1948–1957, op. cit.*, p. 175; I. P. Oleinik, *Dezvoltarea industriei Rominiei . . .* , *op. cit.*, pp. 154–155, 157).

[104] See Appendix D, pp. 295–296.

forth, increases in exports of lumber had to be effected chiefly by deflecting supplies from domestic consumption,[105] at the expense, first of all, of construction. The cement that was not used for priority industrial construction was also largely mortgaged for export. Another factor that was soon due to have an adverse impact on foreign trade was the impending necessity of reimbursing credits for machinery and equipment acquired during the great upsurge of these imports that started in 1948. Given the lack of momentum of traditional foreign-exchange earners, such as petroleum, timber, and foodstuffs, and the limited capability of the economy at this turning point in its industrialization program to produce (or to spare) large amounts of manufactures for export, debt repayment would necessarily have been accompanied by the curtailment of certain imports. Since imports of consumer goods were already pared to the bone and imports of raw materials could not be cut without causing unemployment, it is likely that imports of machinery would have been trimmed, even in the absence of a new policy.[106]

On the home front time was also working to break the headlong pace of industrial expansion. We have seen how urbanization progressed without anything like a parallel expansion of the housing supply or of ancillary urban services. But there was a limit to the possibilities of crowding more people into the same space. An increase in residential construction could not be put off much longer. This *reprise* could not fail to have adverse effects on the export program and on "productive investments" competing with housing for timber and cement.

[105] In 1957, after measures of conservation had been in effect a few years, it was discovered that only 14.4 percent of the coniferous and 11.8 percent of the beech timber was at the optimal age for cutting — 60 to 80 years — as against the "normal" 20 percent. This was ascribed to the "predatory exploitation" of capitalist firms (*Dezvoltarea economiei R.P.R. pe drumul socialismului 1948–1957, op. cit.*, p. 283). Actually, the output of coniferous lumber in 1950 was over 50 percent greater than in 1938 and the output of beech lumber over twice as great as in 1938. A candid Czech commentator explained the over-all curtailment of Rumanian lumber exports in the mid-1950's by "the necessity of preventing the overcutting of forests" (D. Machová, *ČSSR v socialistické mezinárodní délbě přece* [Prague, 1962], p. 202).

[106] Ghita Ionescu, whose book on Rumania has already been cited, describes in a chapter titled "The Need for Relaxation, March 1953–February 1956" the troubles besetting the Rumanian economy in 1952–1953 in even darker tones than I have used here. Leaving aside matters of interpretation on which full agreement can hardly be expected, there is one point of his analysis with which I have to take issue: the Soviet Union did not deal a "blow" to the Rumanian economy in 1952 by "virtually" stopping deliveries of iron ore (p. 225). Imports of iron ore from the U.S.S.R. amounted to 350,000 tons in 1951 (91 percent of total ore imports), 476,000 tons in 1952 (94 percent of total), and 488,000 tons in 1953 (91 percent of total). (Gh. Gaston Marin, "Ajutorul URSS în construirea socialisumului în R.P.R.," *Probleme economice*, No. 10 [1957], pp. 122–123.)

Another consequence of urbanization was that, in order just to preserve both rural and urban consumption at existing levels, provision had to be made for a rise in total consumption by reason of the large disparity in average consumption between rural and urban communities. But by 1952–1953 farm production, as it approached prewar averages, no longer showed the same resiliency as it had in 1947–1948 when it was still a long way from recovery. Compulsory deliveries blunted incentives, especially for the better-off peasants who produced the chief potential surpluses and against whom the delivery tariffs were rigged. We have already speculated that farm investments in housing and productive structures must have suffered a decline during the period 1950–1953. Investment in cattle was probably minimal, if not negative, during certain years.[107]

Employees' real wages, as officially estimated, had barely risen from 1950 to 1952,[108] in a period when food production was expanding; the problem of maintaining the consumption standards of a swelling urban population in the face of stagnant food supplies might eventually have proved insuperable, short of a basic change in policy.

In any event, whether Rumania's Party leaders were moved by necessity or by compassion for the masses, they did resolve, at the Party plenum of August 19–20, 1953, to improve the lot of the Rumanian population. The Party recognized that "the rate of industrialization, particularly in the sphere of heavy industry, was excessively accelerated." [109] The rate of accumulation had been boosted too high; too large a part of fixed investments had gone to heavy industry. The redress of these disproportions was set as the task of the next three years.

The concrete resolutions that were meant to accomplish this task were the following: (1) The share of accumulation in national income

---

[107] The number of cows declined after 1950–1951; the number of hogs fattened for the market remained below the 1948–1949 peak between 1950 and 1952, when it stagnated at little more than half of prewar levels (*Dezvoltarea agriculturii R.P.R.* [Bucharest, 1961], pp. 242–243).

[108] The index of real wages based on 1950 stood at 106.3 in 1951 and at 103.1 in 1952. An analysis of retail sales in Bucharest suggests that the poor harvest of 1952 was not wholly responsible for the deterioration in that year; sales of nonfood items declined by nearly 15 percent, while sales of food actually showed a slight increase (*Anuarul statistic al Orașului București 1959*, p. 101). One could argue of course that sales of textiles, shoes, and other industrial products dropped because peasants, who buy some of these items in the larger cities, were impoverished by the poor harvest. My impression is that supplies, rather than demand, fell short. If anything, the monetary reform of 1952 helped to strike a better balance between lower supplies of industrial goods and inflated incomes.

[109] Cited in Ionescu, *op. cit.*, p. 223.

was to be reduced to an average of 27.8 percent for 1953–1955.[110]
(2) The ratio of (fixed) investments to national income was to decline
from about 26 percent in 1953 to 24 percent in 1954 and to 22 percent
in 1955. (3) Investment outlays scheduled for 1953–1955 were to be
scaled down by 15 to 17 billion lei; but an extra 5 billion lei were to
be spent on agriculture, consumer goods, and housing (the *net* "reduction in the accumulation fund" was fixed at 10–12 million lei). (4)
About 1.5 to 2 percent of national income was to be set aside each
year from 1953 to 1955 in order to build up state reserves.[111] (5) Compulsory deliveries of cereals were to be limited to 23 percent of "the
total effectively harvested." [112] (6) Various concessions were to be made
to members of agricultural associations, including the cancellation of
their arrears on deliveries and a 20 percent reduction in their taxes.[113]
(7) Technical cultures, which had been overexpanded, were to relin-
quish acreage in favor of cereals cultivation. Cotton cultivation was to
be abandoned, except in the rare localities where it could be "cultivated profitably." (8) Private farmers, who still accounted for 80 percent of the total value of marketed output, were to be encouraged by
monetary inducements to enter agricultural associations or collectives;
they were not to be bludgeoned into joining collectives as in the past.
(9) Procurement prices of farm products were to be revised to encourage animal husbandry and to raise the output of meat delivered
to the state. (10) The value of sales on the socialist retail market was
to be raised to 22 billion lei for 1954 (compared to 19 billion estimated
for 1953 and to 25 billion lei in 1955).[114]

The managers of the Rumanian economy were successful in fulfilling at least a part of their plans for improving the population's
living standards, although, in order to achieve this aim, they had to

[110] I believe this "reduction" refers not to past rates of accumulation but to the
rates that had been initially stated for 1953–1955 in the Five-Year Plan. For the
opposite interpretation, see the United Nations, Economic Commission for Europe's
"Economic Development in Rumania," in the *Economic Bulletin for Europe*, Vol. 13,
No. 2, p. 63. My conjecture rests on tentative evidence that the rate of accumulation in 1952 must have been significantly *less* than 27.8 percent.

[111] State reserves had probably been scaled down in late 1952 and in 1953 in
order to improve the food situation, which was aggravated by the poor harvest
of 1952.

[112] *Rezoluţii şi hotărîri ale Comitetului Central al P.M.R.*, Vol. II (Bucharest, 1954),
pp. 487–488. According to a later source, the Central Committee decided at that
time that the system of fixed deliveries and its compulsory character did not favor
the development of agricultural production and planned to cancel these obligations
for a few products at the earliest possible date (*Probleme economice*, No. 10 [1957],
p. 136).

[113] *Probleme economice*, No. 6 (1954), p. 11.

[114] *Rezoluţii şi hotărîri . . . , op. cit.*, pp. 490 and 499.

throw more ballast overboard than they had expected. The promise of increased retail sales to the population was fulfilled.[115] State investments in agriculture and in consumer goods industries both doubled from 1953 to 1955, as they had been expected to. About 16 percent more apartments were built by the state in 1954 than in the previous year; twice as much cement and three times as much lumber were sold to the population as in 1953; the housing surface constructed by the population from its own financial means was already a fourth higher in 1954 than in 1953.

On the other hand, total investments, instead of rising from a planned 19 billion lei in 1953 to 20 billion lei in 1954 and to 21 billion lei in 1955,[116] declined by 11 percent from 1953 to 1954. They rose again in 1955 but failed (by a narrow margin) to recover 1953 levels. The value added by the construction sector in the national-income accounts dropped by a quarter from 1953 to 1954. The brunt of planned and unplanned cuts in investment outlays fell on heavy industry, construction, and transportation. The share of heavy industry in total state investments declined from 52.7 percent in 1953 to 48.8 percent in 1955; it never regained in subsequent years the height reached in 1953.

The rate of accumulation must have dropped considerably below the target of 27.8 percent for 1953–1955. It probably went down to roughly 22–23 percent at current prices.[117] National income in 1954 showed a barely perceptible decline in the official computations at constant prices.[118] The following year, however, a good harvest and the recovery of construction activity helped to boost national income 22 percent above the 1953–1954 level. If my estimates of "accumulation" are even approximately correct, it follows that the sum of inventories and state reserves rose less fast than national income from 1953 to 1955.[119] I suspect, in fact, that state reserves actually declined in

---

[115] In current prices the value of retail sales realized was equal to the target in 1954 and somewhat above target in 1955 (28.6 versus 26.0 billion lei). But price increases estimated at 10 percent at least from 1953 to 1955 wipe out the difference between target and fulfillment. (Retail sales in current prices are from *Anuarul statistic al R.P.R. 1965*, p. 409; sales in 1950 prices are from *Probleme economice*, No. 9 [1956], p. 52, and *Dezvoltarea economiei R.P.R. pe drumul socialismului 1948–1957*, p. 348.)

[116] *Rezoluţii şi hotărîri . . .* , *op. cit.*, p. 487.

[117] See *Dezvoltarea complexă şi echilibrată a economiei naţionale, op. cit.*, p. 9. The accumulation rate averaged 24 percent from 1951 to 1955. It presumably exceeded 25 percent from 1951 to 1953. See also Table 1.20.

[118] *Anuarul statistic al R.P.R. 1965*, p. 102.

[119] If national income rose by 22 percent and fixed investments stayed constant, then the ratio of the two should have declined by 18 percent. But the accumulation ratio in comparable prices dropped by some 25 percent. My inference flows from

this period, instead of absorbing $1\frac{1}{2}$–2 percent of national income as the plenum resolutions had envisaged.[120]

The New Course was essentially a period of consolidation, a breathing spell wherein the expansion of former years could be buttressed and new advances could be prepared. Many investment projects that had been started in pell-mell fashion in the early 1950's were now completed.[121] A determined effort was made to raise industrial output via productivity rather than the massive injection of labor, as had been done in many branches of industry prior to 1953. Total employment in the national economy, which had been rising at the rate of 200,000 persons, or by 8–10 percent a year from 1950 to 1953, was limited to an increase of 73,000 persons in 1954 and 60,000 persons in 1955. These increases went almost exclusively to hitherto neglected sectors such as domestic trade, communal economy, and sanitation. The only sector formerly in a priority position to receive substantial new employment was transportation. Employment in construction went down by 10 percent in 1954. (It did not again surpass the 1953 level until 1961!) The manpower available to industry rose by only 3.4 percent in 1954 and 1.5 percent in 1955, compared to the 7–10 percent annual gains registered from 1950 to 1953.[122]

Thanks to above-average gains in labor productivity, industry weathered this period of consolidation and retrenchment surprisingly well. The official index of output rose by 6.5 percent in 1954 and by 13.7 percent in 1955 (versus an average growth of 18.9 percent from 1950 to 1953).[123] Out of twenty-six branches of industry, only the metallurgical industry, with its coking and coal derivatives annex, failed to recover 1953 levels.[124]

Nevertheless, the slowdown in industrial growth of 1954 and 1955 put out of reach the ambitious targets of the Five-Year Plan. Gross industrial output, which was scheduled to rise by 144 percent from 1950 to 1955, was officially estimated to have attained 202 percent of the 1950 level by the last year of the plan. Labor productivity in

---

the difference in these two percentages. I do not believe the range of error in my estimations to be large enough to encompass the difference.

[120] Grain reserves, which must be one of the more important components of state reserves, were so depleted in 1954 and early 1955 that the government had to buy wheat from the Soviet Union at a time when it was especially short of foreign exchange.

[121] The ratio of investment outlays to fixed assets put into operation rose from 81.6 percent in 1953 to 91 percent in 1954; the value of unfinished investments at the end of each of the two years fell by 20 percent (*Revista de statistică*, No. 5 [1958], p. 23).

[122] *Anuarul statistic al R.P.R. 1965*, pp. 114 and 186.

[123] *Ibid.*, p. 148.

[124] *Ibid.*

industry in 1955 reached 149 percent of the 1950 level, compared to the 179 percent target.[125] A comparison of production targets with actual outputs (Table 1.12) shows that there were very large shortfalls both in heavy and in light industry.

TABLE 1.12. PLANNED AND ACTUAL OUTPUT OF KEY INDUSTRIAL PRODUCTS
(*Thousands of Tons, Except Where Indicated*)

	1950 Actual	1955 Plan	1955 Actual
Petroleum	5,047	11,000	10,555
Coal	3,893	9,000	6,104
Electricity[a]	2.1	4.7	4.3
Pig iron	320	800	570
Steel	555	1,252	766
Rolled steel	524	828	498
Sulfuric acid	52	143	92
Cotton cloth[b]	148	266.5	243
Woolen fabrics[b]	23	39.4	31
Sugar	87	278	130

[a] Billions of kilowatt hours.
[b] Millions of square meters.
Sources: Plan figures are from V. A. Karra, *Stroitel'stvo sotsialistickeskoi ekonomiki v Rumynskoi Narodnoi Respublike* (Moscow, 1953), p. 143; and from S. Fischer-Galati, ed., *Romania* (New York and London: Praeger, 1957), pp. 284, 287, 302, and 311; actual production data are from *Anuarul statistic al R.P.R. 1965*, pp. 168–174.

On the pattern of growth from 1953 to 1955 two further points are worth noting: first, that the acceleration in the growth of output of the consumer-goods industries — textiles and food processing in particular — was relatively small, owing presumably to the delays necessary to bring about an increase in output after investment funds had been committed; and second, that certain branches of heavy industry, including machine building and chemicals, kept forging ahead — albeit at a slower pace than in former years. The increase in the machine-building industry's gross output, for example, was officially estimated at 26 percent from 1953 to 1955. This was, of course, far short of the 58 percent rise recorded in the two years preceding Stalin's death, but still quite a respectable performance.

One might have expected that with a smaller labor intake the efficiency of the machine-building industry, measured as output per unit of combined labor and capital inputs, would have materially improved.

[125] United Nations, Economic Commission for Europe, "Economic Development in Rumania," in *Economic Bulletin for Europe*, Vol. 13, No. 2 (1961), p. 64.

Yet available statistics lend no support to this conjecture, at least in the first two years of the New Course. A cursory inspection of the data in Table 1.13 reveals that, for any reasonable weights that might be

TABLE 1.13. INCREASES IN FIXED CAPITAL, EMPLOYMENT, AND OUTPUT IN THE MACHINE-BUILDING AND METALWORKING INDUSTRY FROM 1951 TO 1957 (*Percentages; First Year of Each Period = 100*)

	1951–1953	*1953–1955*	*1955–1957*
Gross output (official index)	158	126	137
Employment	121	103	103
Fixed assets of the industry	141	111	112

Sources: Gross output and employment: *Anuarul statistic al R.P.R. 1965*, pp. 148 and 186; fixed assets: I. P. Oleinik, *Dezvoltarea industriei Romîniei în anii Regimului Democrat-Popular* (Bucharest, 1960), p. 277.

assigned to labor and capital, the ratio of the theoretical output calculated from the growth of inputs to the actual output must have been about the same from 1953 to 1955 as from 1951 to 1953. Significant progress in efficiency was delayed until the period 1955–1957, when output rose 9 percent more than in the preceding period with the aid of virtually the same increases in labor and capital inputs.[126] The delay in the improvement in efficiency may have been due to the transitional difficulties of converting certain plants from armaments production to civilian uses in 1953 and 1954.

In whatever way we explain the continued rise in machine-building output, we need to look into the availability of outlets for these increases. How could investments in fixed capital drop or stagnate from 1953 to 1955 and the output of the machine-building industry continue to expand? One possibility might be that investments in machinery and equipment rose at the expense of investments in structures. This, however, did not prove to be the case: the ratio of investments in machinery to investments in structures hardly deviated from its 1953 value — a little less than a third — in the next two years. Another possibility is that new machinery products were stock-piled pending the construction of new structures to house them. Some machinery were indeed

[126] The scattered data available on the reduction of average unit costs over the period 1951–1953 and 1953–1955 for individual machine products, such as tractors, motors, and mining vehicles, also fail to show more progress in the second than in the first period (see, for example, Oleinik, *op. cit.*, p. 294). For the machine-building industry as a whole, "comparable costs" are said to have fallen by only 18 percent from 1950 to 1956 but by 35 percent from 1956 to 1958 (*Industria Romîniei 1944–1964* [Bucharest, 1964], p. 501).

stored for this purpose.[127] But the principal explanation for the discrepancy between output and investments lies in the drastic curtailment in imports, which made room for the disposal of domestic products. In 1954, outlays on imported equipment fell from 1.6 billion to a little more than one billion lei at 1959 internal prices. Yet outlays on domestic equipment missed the record level of 1953 (2.8 billion lei) by only 22 million. In 1955, outlays on imported equipment rose by less than one percent and outlays on domestic equipment by 15 percent.

In 1954, a part of the difference between a relatively slight increase in machinery output and a constant investment demand for domestic capital goods was accounted for by the larger volume of exports, which reached the unprecedented level of 184 million lei (31 million U.S. dollars) despite the slackening of demand for capital goods in Eastern Europe. The increase in machinery exports of 7 percent over 1953 was apparently directed mainly to the Soviet Union and to Communist China, which began to play a modest role around this time as a buyer of Rumanian oil-drilling equipment.[128]

In 1955, machinery exports dropped by 16 percent, but the revived demand for domestic capital goods on the home market was probably sufficient to absorb most of the approximately 20 percent increase in machinery output for the year, the surplus presumably going into inventory accumulation and into noninvestment uses including military requirements.

The sharp drop in imported equipment in 1954, which was followed by a more moderate but continuous decline lasting until 1958, hit Czechoslovakia, Rumania's chief supplier of equipment from Eastern Europe, especially hard.[129] Exports of corn, wheat, barley, and oil-bearing seeds, which would normally have been used to pay for imports of equipment, fell below 1949–1952 levels, just at a time when

[127] As late as 1958, 4 percent of the economy's total fixed assets (5 percent in industry alone) were being "held in reserve" or were otherwise unutilized (*Studii de economie socialistă* [Bucharest, 1961], p. 76). The total value of these assets, which incidentally were never amortized, may be estimated at some 7–8 billion lei. I suspect that the greater part of these assets was accumulated during the New Course. (In Poland, similarly, the "freezing" of several billion zlotys of machinery and equipment, which had been imported on the basis of pre-1953 orders but had not been installed by 1956–1957, was the subject of severe criticism in the economic press in 1957.) The value of assets held in reserve dropped by 50 percent from 1959 to 1962, when investments were stepped up to very high levels, and the demand for machinery and equipment rose in parallel fashion (*Probleme economice*, No. 10 [1963], p. 6; and No. 7 [1964], pp. 38–39).

[128] Tables 3.8 and 3.16 of Chapter 3.

[129] The decline in Czechoslovak exports of equipment to other developing East European states, including Albania, Poland, and Hungary also created problems for Prague, but the decline was nowhere as pronounced as it was in trade with Rumania.

Czechoslovakia, about to eliminate consumers' rationing, was in acute need of these foodstuffs.[130]

To help raise popular consumption according to the directions of the August 1953 plenum and to pave the way for the abolition of rationing scheduled for December 1954, the government cut back on food exports in 1954 by nearly 20 percent compared to 1953.[131] This was calculated to release food supplies for home consumption over and above the increment in state procurements from the farm sector estimated at 12 percent for the year.[132] This cut in exports, estimated at 65 million lei for 1954, was small, however, compared to the reduction in machinery and equipment imports of 326 million lei, valued at foreign-exchange prices.

To understand the changes that occurred in the structure of trade in 1954, we should have in mind that the over-all balance of commodity trade turned from a deficit of nearly 300 million lei in 1953 to a surplus of 80 million lei in 1954, which was necessary to finance the repayment of Rumanian debts. Thus, when Rumania's exports of foodstuffs to Czechoslovakia fell off, she had to step up her sales of raw materials to her more developed partner, despite the curtailment of her purchases of machinery.[133]

Almost the entire decline of 278 million lei in total Rumanian imports can be accounted for by the machinery group. The decision to keep industry working at or close to capacity, at least in most of its branches, entailed constant or rising imports of raw materials. The government's decision to prevent a drop in industrial output and employment had the effect of thrusting the whole impact of import entrenchments on the machinery and equipment group.[134]

No such retrenchments would have been called for if exports had shown any degree of resiliency. But the slow growth of petroleum output and cuts in the felling of timber hampered exports of raw materials and semifabricates, which might otherwise have been built up in lieu of the foodstuffs earmarked for increases in domestic consumption.[135]

[130] Machová, *op. cit.*, p. 132.

[131] Computed from percentage data in *Economia Romîniei 1944–1959*, p. 577, and from Table 3.9 of Chapter 3.

[132] *Dezvoltarea agriculturii R.P.R.* (Bucharest, 1961), p. 368.

[133] Machová, *op. cit.*, p. 132.

[134] By subtracting imports of machinery and equipment from total imports, we may deduce that the sum of imports of raw materials, semifabricates, foodstuffs, and manufactured consumer goods rose by 5 percent from 1953 to 1954.

[135] An analysis of Rumanian foreign trade by the United Nations Economic Commission for Europe pointed to the apparent correlation between, on the one hand, the deceleration in the growth of petroleum output and the absolute decline in lumber production and, on the other, the stagnation of total exports from 1954 to 1957 (*Economic Bulletin for Europe*, Vol. 11, No. 1 [1959], p. 53). This correlation

As it was, exports in the raw-material group did go up by some 10 percent from 1953 to 1954, but I suspect that this was because of price rises on petroleum and perhaps on other products on the CMEA market rather than because of any expansion of the physical volume of these exports.[136] In 1955, in any event, exports of raw materials and semifabricates probably did not rise at all. Exports of foodstuffs picked up in that year, but a sudden increase in grain *imports* — the delayed consequence of a poor harvest of cereals in 1954 and of the depletion of reserves — reduced the surplus of exports over imports in this commodity group by 20 percent compared to 1953.[137]

How did urban and rural consumers fare as a result of the redeployment of resources ostensibly carried out for their benefit? While information on living standards and consumption is at best fragmentary, the evidence at hand points to a delay of at least one year — caused in part by the poor harvest of 1954 — before the government measures could take effect for most foodstuffs, although a prompt improvement in retail sales of several industrial staple products was already perceptible within the first year of the New Course (Table 1.14).

The very steep increases in the consumption of sugar and meat by peasant families from 1953–1954 to 1957 may be somewhat exaggerated as a result of poor sampling in the official studies of family budgets, but they appear less incongruous if we bear in mind that consumption took off from an extremely low base. In 1954, the consumption of sugar was about 10 percent below 1938 levels, when it was a little over one kilogram per head per year; the consumption of meat and fats, eggs, bread, and cheese was roughly the same as in 1938, when the consumption of these items was generally inferior to the levels attained in the late

---

helps to explain the sluggishness of exports, although the inability or the unwillingness to expand food exports was also responsible for this phenomenon.

[136] On prices in CMEA trade, see Chapter 4, p. 000. The price increases on petroleum products were probably of the order of 20 percent. My estimate is based on the increase in the value of petroleum exports from 1952 to 1954 given in *Economia Romîniei între anii 1944–1959*, p. 577, on the proportion between domestic consumption and exports of petroleum products in 1952 and 1954 (Oleinik, *op. cit.*, p. 222), and on statistics of output of petroleum and refined products in *Anuarul statistic al R.P.R. 1965*, p. 168. Another explanation for the discrepancy between the increase in the tonnage and in the value of exports may be that exports were deflected from the Soviet market — whose share in Rumanian petroleum exports dropped from 84 percent in 1953 to 63 percent in 1955 (Table 3.17 of Chapter 3) — in the direction of outlets in the West, where higher prices prevailed.

[137] See Table 3.9 in Chapter 3. It is my guess that grain was imported in the first part of the year, before the new harvest came in, which turned out to be above average (some grain imports took place in 1956 but on a much lower scale than in 1955).

TABLE 1.14. Selected Indicators of Rumanian Living Standards, 1950–1958 (*1950 = 100, Except Where Indicated*)

	1952	1953	1954	1955	1956	1957	1958
Real incomes of peasants	106.9	143.2	138.5	170.3	141.8	186.8	157.0
Real incomes of urban workers	103.1	108.5	112.7	123.7	133.9	144.1	144.7
Retail sales in state and cooperative shops at 1950 prices	127	160	182	200	226	238	234
Sales on free market (current prices)	n.a.	175	n.a.	164	n.a.	n.a.	185
Meat consumption per capita							
workers	n.a.	n.a.	n.a.	128	148	174	n.a.[a]
peasants[b]	n.a.	100	120.5	128	145	n.a.	184
Sugar consumption per capita							
workers	n.a.	n.a.	n.a.	107	109	117	n.a.
peasants[c]	n.a.	n.a.	100	250	330	n.a.	705
Retail sales in state and cooperative shops							
meat	95	99	96	127	148	148	167
oil	125	166	222	193	199	247	251
cheese	182	185	155	200	221	255	331
sugar	90	95	100	132	135	153	153
lumber (pine)	37	34	110	103	133	169	157
kerosene	92	104	106	105	116	117	116
cotton cloth and garments	98	125	139	116	125	139	136
woolen fabrics and garments	117	114	144	124	136	150	128
leather footwear	112	121	110	122	157	172	154

[a] Employees, 148.   [b] Based on 1953 = 100.   [c] 1954 = 100.

Sources: Real incomes: *Dezvoltarea agriculturii Republicii Populare Romîne* (Bucharest, 1961), p. 370; workers' and peasants' per capita consumption (based on budget studies): *Dezvoltarea economiei R.P.R. pe drumul socialismului 1948–1957* (Bucharest, 1958), p. 422; *Studii de economie socialistă* (Bucharest, 1961), p. 220; *Economia Romîniei între anii 1944–1959* (Bucharest, 1959), p. 622; I. P. Oleinik, *Dezvoltarea industriei Romîniei . . .* (Bucharest, 1960), p. 373; *Probleme economice*, No. 7 (1960), p. 72; *Revista de statistică*, No. 10 (1961), p. 53. Sales on peasant market: *Probleme economice*, No. 9 (1956), p. 72, and *Economia Romîniei între anii 1944–1959*, p. 516. All other data are from *Anuarul statistic al R.P.R. 1965*, pp. 412, 428–429.

1920's.[138] Peasants were consuming an average of only 2,722 calories a day per person in 1955, of which 66.9 percent came from the consump-

[138] Comparisons are based on the index relatives of consumption per peasant from 1938 to 1960 in M. Levente, E. Barat, and M. Bulgaru, *Analiza statistico-economică a agriculturii* (Bucharest, 1961), p. 22, and on the increases from 1955 to 1960 in *Probleme economice*, No. 7 (1962), p. 14, and in other sources cited in Table 1.15. From the data in Table 2.16 of Chapter 2 and from the index of marketings in Levente, Barat, and Bulgaru (*op. cit.*, p. 19), it would appear that rural consumption of meat alone in 1955 was still substantially below prewar levels. There was apparently some substitution of fats for meat in the peasants' diet.

tion of grain alone and only 17.1 percent from the consumption of animal products.[139]

Still, to provide the rural two thirds of the population with increases of the magnitude I have described, while raising urban consumption in significant, though lower, proportion, was a signal achievement. It was, I believe, mainly as a result of the combined effect of the narrowing of urban-rural differentials, particularly for industrially produced foodstuffs, and of the increased urbanization, which offered immigrants from the countryside the opportunity of sharing in the higher consumption of the cities, that average per capita consumption in 1956 for the nation as a whole exceeded 1938 levels for key food products (by 15 percent for wheat and flour products, by 12 percent for meat, by over 100 percent for sugar, and by about 80 percent for oil).[140]

The data in Table 1.15 reveal how low Rumania's per capita consumption of staple products still was compared to other East European countries as late as 1958. With the exception of leather shoes, where it surpassed Bulgaria, Rumania's per capita consumption of the items listed was lower than that of any other East European country represented in the table.

Resuming our chronological survey we note that from 1955 Rumania's balance of payments was strained and her development hampered not only by the repayment of commercial debts to her socialist partners but also by the necessity of compensating the Soviet Union for the liquidation of the joint companies dissolved in September 1954. With the exception of Sovrompetrol, which lasted until December 1955, and Sovromcvarţ, the uranium-mining enterprise, which was terminated in November 1956, all the joint companies wound up their affairs by the end of 1954.

The 1954 agreements stipulated that the ex-enemy countries repurchasing the Soviet shares "shall pay back the value of the shares under favorable terms in several yearly remittances." [141] In addition to

[139] *Probleme economice*, No. 7 (1958), pp. 76 and 77; *Dezvoltarea economiei R.P.R. pe drumul socialismului 1948–1957* (Bucharest, 1958), p. 233. A Rumanian economist pointed out that the share of grains in calorie consumption in 1955 was far higher in Rumania than in Hungary, Czechoslovakia, and East Germany, and was only comparable with Bulgaria's (S. Hartia, in *Probleme economice*, No. 7 [1958], p. 77). This share was about the same in Rumania in 1955 as before World War II (cf. the data in D. Georgescu, *L'alimentation de la population rurale en Roumanie* [Bucharest, 1940], p. 43).

[140] *Dezvoltarea industriei socialiste în R.P.R.* (Bucharest, 1959), p. 475. If my calculations of the level of peasant consumption of meat and fats in 1954–1955, relative to 1938, are correct, then it follows from the consumption increase for the whole population from 1938 to 1956 that urban consumption of meat in 1956 had not yet recovered prewar levels.

[141] Cited in Spulber, *op. cit.*, p. 203.

TABLE 1.15. PER CAPITA CONSUMPTION OF SELECTED CONSUMER GOODS IN RUMANIA, EAST GERMANY, CZECHOSLOVAKIA, HUNGARY, POLAND, AND BULGARIA (*Selected Years*)

	Rumania	East Germany	Czecho- slovakia	Hungary	Poland	Bulgaria
Meat (slaughter- weight, kilo- grams)						
1938	19.0	n.a.	34[a]	33.2[b]	19.6[c]	n.a.
1950	16.1	25.6	28.9[d]	34.3	38.2	n.a.
1958	23.4	50.8	53.9	41.7	47.8	35.9[e]
Butter (kilograms)						
1950	0.3	4.2	2.8[c]	1.0	3.3	n.a.
1958	0.7	9.2	5.6	1.2	5.0	1.4
Sugar (kilograms)						
1938	5.4	n.a.	23.2	10.5[a]	9.6[c]	n.a.
1950	6.9	21.8	22.3[c]	16.3	21.0	n.a.
1958	10.7	30.1	34.9	24.8	28.5	18.6[f]
Cotton cloth (square meters)						
1955	13.9	16.0	18.0[g]	10.4	15.0	n.a.
1960	12.2	20.7	22.4	15.5	17.6	18.8
Woolen fabrics (square meters)						
1955	n.a.	5.9	3.8	2.4	3.5	1.8
1960	1.8	6.8	4.0	2.4	3.3	3.2
Leather shoes (pairs)						
1955	0.8	1.0	1.5	1.0	0.9	0.4
1960	1.0	1.2	1.5	1.3	1.3	0.6

[a] 1936.
[b] 1934–1938 average.
[c] 1933–1937 average.
[d] 1948.
[e] Per member of worker's family.
[f] Including sugar products.
[g] 1956.

Note: For Poland and Czechoslovakia, which publish their statistics of cloth consumption in meters, a conversion factor of 0.91 square meters to one meter has been utilized for 1955. This factor is based on a comparison of 1960 data expressed in the two units in the official yearbooks and in the first source cited.

Sources: All data are from Jiří Novozámský, *Vyrovnávání ekonomické úrovně zemí RVHP* (Prague, 1964), pp. 26–27, with the following exceptions: Rumania: 1938 consumption of meat and sugar: *Enciclopedia Romăniei*, Vol. IV (1943), p. 922; Poland: prewar consumption of meat and sugar and 1956 consumption of cotton cloth: *Rocznik statystyczny 1957* (Warsaw, 1957), p. 226; Hungary: consumption of cotton cloth in *Statistical Yearbook of Hungary 1949–1955* (Budapest, 1957), translation by U.S. Joint Publications Research Service, Washington, D. C. (1958), p. 295; prewar consumption of meat and sugar: *Sztatisztikai évkönyv 1961* (Budapest, 1962), p. 256; Czechoslovakia: 1938 consumption of meat and sugar and 1956 consumption of cloth: *Statistická ročenka Republiky Československé 1959* (Prague, 1959), pp. 375 and 379.

the original German assets seized by the Soviets, which represented the initial Soviet contribution to the companies, each country had to pay for the capital equipment delivered by the U.S.S.R. to the joint companies. The Soviet shares alone would have cost the Rumanians 710 million dollars, if their debts on this account had not been canceled in December 1956. As we shall see in Chapter 3, the equipment ceded by the Soviets also proved to be costly.[142] Indeed, the burden of these various obligations was so onerous that the Rumanians were obliged to request the Soviets for a postponement of their debts in 1956.[143]

The most evident symptom of these difficulties was the further contraction of machinery imports, which had already receded sharply from their 1953 levels in 1954. These imports fell from 647 million lei in 1954 to 579 million lei in 1955 and 431 million lei in 1956. They finally ebbed to a low point in 1957, when they were valued at 406 million lei, or 42 percent of their 1953 record.[144]

In spite of this external impediment, the stagnation in investments might have been overcome — via the substitution of domestic for foreign equipment — if adverse political circumstances had not supervened, which virtually forced the Rumanian Party leaders to continue the New Course in 1956 and 1957.

By late 1955 it seemed as if the post-Stalin lull was coming to an end. The people's democracies were steeling themselves for another round of industrialization at forced draft. State investments in Rumania were already scheduled to rise by 21 percent in 1956, about the same increase as in Czechoslovakia but more than in Hungary or Poland.[145] However, the political events of the second half of 1956 prompted a more cautious progress, and the actual growth of investment outlays was held down to 12 percent. The ambitious character of the program for that year, which inaugurated the Second Five-Year Plan (1956–1960), may be judged by the fact that the value of fixed funds installed was less than 75 percent of the value of investment outlays, the lowest proportion in any year for which figures are available. Correspondingly, the value of investments in process increased by 37 percent, to a record high.[146] It is worth remarking that employment remained virtually

---

[142] Chapter 3, p. 146.

[143] According to the Chairman of the Rumanian Planning Commission, the U.S.S.R. "taking into account various difficulties that had arisen in our balance of payments agreed to postpone by four years the repayment of all credits accorded from 1949 to 1956." (Gh. Gaston Marin, "Ajutorul URSS în construirea socialismului în R.P.R.," *Probleme economice*, No. 1 [1957], p. 124.)

[144] Table 3.8 of Chapter 3.

[145] United Nations, Economic Commission for Europe, *Economic Survey of Europe in 1956*, Chapter 1, p. 13.

[146] *Revista de statistică*, No. 5 (1958), p. 23.

constant, even in heavy industry, no branch of which showed an increase in employment of more than 5 percent for the year. This cautious employment policy was, and remains, a characteristic feature of Rumanian development in later years.

The Rumanian leaders, just as the leaders in the rest of the Soviet bloc, were severely shaken by the Polish and Hungarian events of the summer and fall of 1956. As early as December the Party leaders convened a special plenum of the Central Committee, which resolved on measures to keep the population quiescent. To placate the peasantry, deliveries of all farm products except meat and wool were abolished. (Discrimination in favor of the collective sector was maintained by exempting cooperatives and their members from obligatory deliveries of meat.) To permit a rise in urban living standards, state investments in the 1957 plan were curtailed by 13 percent. Workers and other state employees were granted increases in pay averaging 15 percent. A grain loan was obtained from the Soviet Union to boost reserves depleted in 1956. As a result of these measures, which were happily reinforced in the course of 1957 by a bountiful harvest, there was an appreciable improvement in living conditions. According to the official index, real wages increased by 8 percent and peasants' incomes by over 30 percent from 1956 to 1957.[147] The Rumanian statistical office estimates that the net output of agriculture rose by 42 percent in 1957, while the parity index relating the trend in agricultural prices to the industrial prices paid by peasants shifted by 10 percent in favor of the farm sector. Both relative farm prices and the real incomes of peasants reached a peak in that year, as compared to the entire period 1954 to 1960.[148]

The Take-Off: 1958 to 1965

From 1958 the Rumanian Communist Party no longer hesitated to press ahead with its objective of accelerated industrialization, centering on the priority development of heavy industry. It also found the means of carrying out the "socialist transformation of the countryside," which within four years succeeded in herding almost the entire peasantry into collective farms. These policies were proclaimed at the Party plenum of November 1958, which also marked a turning point in Rumania's relations with her allies in the Soviet bloc. As we shall see in Chapter 4, the Party leaders' decision to aggrandize the iron and steel industry and to press forward with the development of a complex machine-

[147] *Revista de statistică*, No. 5 (1958), pp. 22 and 23.
[148] Levente, Barat, and Bulgaru, *Analiza statistico-economică a agriculturii, op. cit.*, p. 48; *Dezvoltarea agriculturii R.P.R.* (1961), pp. 356 and 370.

building industry, capable of meeting most domestic requirements, helped set off the dispute that divided Rumania from most of her partners in CMEA.

The industrial policies announced in 1958, which set the frame of the Six-Year Plan for 1960 to 1965, tended to promote increased self-reliance and independence from external sources, especially in the provision of ferrous and nonferrous ores, steel, machine-building products, and complex chemicals. Even though the volume of industrial investments rose enough to allow increases in allotments to all branches of mining and industry,[149] the new order of priorities necessarily lowered the relative status of certain sectors. It is significant that the petroleum industry, traditionally the most important foreign-exchange earner, was the one whose relative standing was most adversely affected by the reshuffle. The share of the petroleum industry in total industrial investments, which had reached a high of 35 percent in 1951, had already declined to 25 percent between 1954 and 1958; it dropped to 14 percent between 1960 and 1965. Geological prospecting for iron ores and nonferrous metals rose sharply at the expense of fuels.[150]

The distribution of investments by branch of industry in the Six-Year Plan shown in Table 1.16, does not express fully the impact of the long-run policies for which the Party opted in 1958 and 1960. In particular, the share of metallurgy and machine building shows little increase over 1954–1959, mainly because the great investment project in the Galați steel complex, which was to underpin the expansion of the iron and steel and machine-building industries, was not slated to receive any large amounts of investments until 1963–1964.

The distribution of investments by principal branches of industry in the Six-Year Plan is shown in Table 1.16.

The distribution of investments in the 1960's was marked, as we have seen, by a decline in the importance of fuels but also by a discontinuous increase in the share of the chemical industry in the total. This share,

[149] Total investments in industry were to be 2.1–2.2 times as great as in the period 1954–1959. Note that the share of industry in total state investments, which was set at 58.8 percent, was higher than in the First Five-Year Plan (51 percent) and in the abortive Second Five-Year Plan for 1956–1960 (56 percent). The division of investments between heavy and light industry was about the same as in the Second Five-Year Plan (*Congresul al III-lea al Partidului Muncitoresc Romîn* [Bucharest, 1960], p. 55).

[150] A complaint made at the Third Party Congress in June 1960, which was apparently endorsed by the Party, was that relatively too little had been spent in the past on the discovery of new sources of iron ores, while petroleum prospecting, which was not proceeding very successfully, had been lavishly provided for (*Petrol și gaz*, No. 8 [1960], pp. 331–332).

TABLE 1.16. PERCENTAGE BREAKDOWN OF TOTAL INDUSTRIAL INVESTMENTS
IN FIXED CAPITAL FOR 1954–1959, 1960–1965, AND THE
SIX-YEAR PLAN

	1954–1959 Actual	1960–1965 Plan	1960–1965 Actual
Fuels and electric power	43.8	32	34.9
Metallurgy and machine building	23.2	23	24.5
Chemicals	9.6	20	14.0
Light and food industries	8.6	11	9.6
Other industries	14.8	14	17.0
Total	100.0	100	100.0

Sources: United Nations, Economic Commission for Europe, *Economic Survey of Europe in 1960*, Chapter II, p. 27; *Statistical Pocket Book of the Socialist Republic of Romania, 1966*, p. 203; *Anuarul statistic al R.P.R. 1965*, pp. 348–349.

however, did not turn out to be as large as had been planned, owing presumably to delays in the construction of chemical plants (for fertilizers and ammonia in particular). Among the "other industries," cellulose and paper received an extraordinarily large amount of investments in the 1960's compared to any previous period. (In 1964 alone this industry was allotted 1,163 million lei, or 5.6 percent of all investments, against 1.0–1.5 percent between 1950 and 1957.) Most of these funds were presumably lavished on the processing of Danubian reeds into cellulose at Brăila, a multinational project carried out with the participation of Czechoslovakia, East Germany, and Poland.[151]

The progress made in recent years toward industrialization cannot be attributed entirely to investments. Labor, materials consumption, and various other factors lumped together as "technical progress" also made a substantial contribution to output, as the data in Table 1.17 testify.

The array of growth rates in Table 1.17 conveys an image of a rapidly expanding industry, propelled forward by the injection of increasing allotments of labor, capital, and materials, and by rapid technical progress. For fifteen years, industrial output according to both the official and our own indices has been rising at annual rates fluctuating between 9 percent and 15 percent. During this span of years, employment expanded at 2–7 percent while both fixed assets and the consumption of materials originating outside the industrial sector rose at 7–10 percent. In every period considered, the growth of production

[151] *Dezvoltarea economică a Romîniei 1944–1964*, p. 707.

TABLE 1.17. ANNUAL RATES OF GROWTH OF INDUSTRIAL OUTPUT, INDUSTRIAL EMPLOYMENT, FIXED CAPITAL, EXOGENOUS MATERIALS CONSUMPTION IN INDUSTRY, AND TOTAL FACTOR PRODUCTIVITY IN SELECTED PERIODS (*1950 to 1965*)

	Annual Percentage Rates of Increase				
	1950–1955	1955–1958	1958–1960	1960–1963	1963–1965
Gross industrial output					
Official index	15.1	9.7	13.2	14.0	13.7
Lee-Montias index	10.6	9.5	15.4	12.2	n.a.
Net industrial output	16.9	9.7	13.8	13.1	14.5
Industrial employment	5.9	2.2	4.2	6.9	4.5
Fixed capital in industry	8.9	7.4	7.7	9.2	10.3
Exogenous materials consumed	9.7	7.2	8.6	8.3	n.a.
Index of combined labor and capital inputs (I)	6.9	3.9	5.4	7.8	6.3
Index of combined labor and capital inputs (II)	7.4	4.8	6.0	8.1	7.3
Index of combined capital, labor, and exogenous material inputs (I)	8.5	5.7	7.1	7.9	n.a.
Index of combined capital, labor, and exogenous material inputs (II)	8.6	5.9	7.2	8.2	n.a.
Total factor productivity based on net output					
Index for combined capital and labor inputs (I)	9.3	5.4	8.0	5.0	7.7
Index for combined capital and labor inputs (II)	8.8	4.5	7.4	4.6	6.7
Total factor productivity based on gross output					
Index for capital, labor, and exogenous material inputs (I)					
official index	6.1	3.8	5.6	5.6	n.a.
Lee-Montias index	2.0	3.5	7.7	4.0	n.a.
Index for capital, labor, and exogenous material inputs (II)					
official index	6.1	3.6	5.5	5.4	n.a.
Lee-Montias index	1.9	3.4	7.6	3.8	n.a.

Sources and Methods: Official gross and net-output indices and indices of the value of the capital stock are from *Anuarul statistic al R.P.R. 1965*, pp. 102, 104, 186–187, and *Statistical Pocket Book 1966*, pp. 43, 45, 53, and 71. The Lee-Montias index is from Appendix A. Exogenous materials are either materials delivered to industry by the agricultural sector or imported from abroad. Domestic materials consumed comprise eight foodstuffs procured by industry from agriculture (wheat, meat, milk, sugar beets, vegetables, fruits, grapes, and sunflowers), four textile raw materials (wool, flax, hemp, and cotton), and tobacco, fish, and hides. Statistics of procurement by industry in physical quantities are from *Economia Romîniei între anii 1944–1959* (Bucharest, 1959), p. 319; *Probleme creării și dezvoltării bazei tehnice-materiale a socialismului în R.P.R.* (Bucharest, 1963), p. 189; *Dezvoltarea complexă și echilibrată a economiei naționale* (Bucharest, 1965), p. 59; *Dezvoltarea economică a Romîniei 1944–1964* (Bucharest, 1964), p. 577; *Dezvoltarea agriculturii R.P.R.* (Bucharest, 1961), pp. 368–369. Wherever data for a given year were missing, they were extrapolated on the basis of changes in total state procurements in *Dezvoltarea agriculturii Romîniei: Culegere de date statistice* (Bucharest, 1965), pp. 578–588. All domestic materials were priced in terms of *valută* lei on the basis of Soviet import and export unit values for 1959 (*Vneshniaia torgovlia SSSR za 1959–1963 gody* [Moscow, 1965], *passim*). The sum total of this domestic production was then added to the value of imports of fuels, minerals, metals, chemicals, fertilizers, rubber, and raw materials of agricultural origin (food and nonfood), which are almost exclusively consumed by industry. (The value of these imports in current prices is given in the statistical yearbooks. To make the 1950 data comparable to the data for later years, imports in that year were raised by 20 percent.) The index was based on these values. An alternative index using domestic agricultural prices (from the *Catalogul prețurilor constante* of the Ministry of Agriculture and Forestry) and converting *valută* into domestic lei at a rate of two to one gave results within one percent of the first index. For all years except 1950, the increases in capital are based on arithmetical averages of successive years to make the time coverage correspond more closely to the employment data, which represent yearly averages.

The indices of labor, capital, and exogenous materials were weighted according to alternative methods, denoted (I) and (II) in the table, which differ only in the evaluation of the returns to capital (see below). In both (I) and (II) the returns to labor were estimated on the basis of the wage bill for 1958, computed from an average yearly wage in industry of 8,000 lei per employee and an employment of 1,157,000 persons (*Anuarul statistic al R.P.R. 1965*, p. 115); the value of materials consumed was calculated from the data used in constructing the alternative index of material inputs (based on domestic prices) as explained in the above paragraph.

In (I), capital was assigned a weight proportional to the estimated value of the annual depreciation costs in industry (computed for the construction of the output index in Appendix A) augmented by capital changes equal to 3 percent of the estimated value of the depreciated (net) capital stock. In (II), capital was weighted in proportion to the value of its annual depreciation plus 15 percent of the estimated value of the depreciated capital stock. The official value of the *gross* capital stock in industry in 1958 — the average of the stocks evaluated at December 31, 1957, and December 31, 1958 — is estimated at 45 billion lei on the following basis: In 1965, 901 million lei of fixed assets were used in republican industry for every billion lei of gross output (*Probleme economice*, No. 12 [1966], p. 10). The gross output of republican industry in 1965 may be estimated at 92.7 billion lei (from the gross output of all industry in 1959, estimated by M. Kaser in the unpublished appendix to his article in *Soviet Studies*, Vol. XVIII [July 1966], the official index of gross output from 1959 to 1965, and the ratio of the value of output of republican industry to the output for all industry in *Anuarul statistic al Republicii Socialiste România 1966*, pp. 158–159). The fixed assets of republican industry therefore equaled 83.5 billion lei at the end of 1965. At the end of 1959 they amounted to an estimated 47.2 billion lei (the result obtained after dividing the 1965 estimate by the index of the value of fixed assets in republican industry in *Probleme economice*, No. 11 (1966), p. 29). On the basis of data relating depreciation to labor costs in republican, local, and cooperative industry (*Dezvoltarea industriei R.P.R.: Culegere de date statistice* [Bucharest, 1964], p. 153), it was inferred that republican industry held about 94 percent of all the fixed assets of indus-

(*footnote continued on p. 58*)

outstripped the growth of measured inputs.[152] Both labor and capital productivity, computed in terms of net output per unit of input, increased in all periods, the former growing by about 7.3 percent per year from 1958 to 1963 and the latter by 4.5 percent. From 1963 to 1965, however, the rate of increase of capital productivity slipped down

[152] As I mentioned earlier, even the rates of growth derived from our independent index may be overstated by one or two percentage points.

The rates of growth of fixed capital, based on an official index, are probably the least reliable of the input measures recorded in the table. The official index is based on the value of the capital stock expressed in 1949 replacement prices for assets installed up to 1952 and on the initial value of assets installed after that date. Since prices of construction works declined by 7 percent and of machinery by 10 to 40 percent from 1950–1954 to 1955, assets installed from 1955 on may be undervalued by as much as one fifth in terms of 1949 constant prices (*Revista de statistică*, No. 5 [1958], p. 25). A rough adjustment can be made for this change in prices by adding 20 percent to the official value of increments to the capital stock for all years from 1955 to 1963. Its effect would be to raise the rate of growth of fixed capital by 1.4

---

try. Hence the latter may be evaluated at approximately 50 billion lei. Estimates for December 31, 1957 and 1958 were then derived by dividing this figure by the index of fixed assets in industry in *Anuarul statistic al R.P.R. 1965*, p. 104. The net stock was estimated by subtracting from the gross value of the stock an arbitrary estimate of cumulative depreciation equal to 25 percent of this stock.

The weights derived from these data that were used to combine the labor and capital input indices were the following: (I) labor 0.67, capital 0.33; (II) labor 0.49, capital 0.51; to combine labor, capital, and exogenous materials: (I) labor 0.29, capital 0.15, materials 0.56; (II) labor 0.26, capital 0.24, materials 0.5. Note that if the net value of the capital stock were actually equal to half of the gross, instead of three quarters as I have assumed, then the capital charges included in this set of weights would amount to 4.5 percent of the value of the recalculated net stock, compared to 3 percent of the estimate actually employed at the lower rate of return to capital, and to 23 percent compared to 15 percent at the higher rate. On the other hand, if the 3 and 15 percent rates were applied to the lower estimates of the net stock, this would have the effect of reducing very slightly the growth rates of the combined inputs in all periods and of raising the growth rates of total factor productivity to the same extent. For the period 1950 to 1955, for instance, the change in weights would have a negligible effect on the rate of growth of total factor productivity based on net output for a 3 percent rate of return on capital, while it would increase the rate of productivity from 8.8 to 9.0 percent per year for a 15 percent rate. It is evident that errors and index number problems arising in estimating the indices of net and gross output would exert far more influence on the rate of growth of total factor productivity than even relatively substantial changes in the input weights. This relative insensitivity of indices to changes in weights applies in the case of Rumania to indices of output as well as of inputs. A recomputation of the Lee-Montias index of gross industrial output from the sectoral indices in Appendix A (Table A.2) using value-added weights corresponding to those applied to the input indices yielded virtually the same growth rates in all periods investigated. Thus for the period 1958 to 1963 the addition of a 15 percent capital charge on the net value of the capital stock in each industry (distributed among industrial sectors on the basis of the percentage breakdown of the gross capital stock in Table 1.18) to the depreciation allowances estimated in Appendix A would only lower the index from 188.1 (as given in Appendix A, Table A.2) to 187.6.

approximately to the level of 1955–1958,[153] when the various adverse circumstances we examined in the preceding section held back the expansion of industry.

Total factor productivity, a measure of output per unit of combined inputs reflecting technical progress, improved skills of the labor force, and various other unquantifiable factors, also rose throughout the fifteen-year period of postwar industrialization. The precise rates of increase depend on the measure of output selected and on the decision to include or to exclude exogenous materials as an independent factor of production.[154] For the period 1950 to 1955, the official index of gross output implies a rate of growth of total factor productivity of about 6 percent, our own index a rate of only 2 percent per year. From 1955, however, the rates obtained from these alternative indices are less disparate, especially if we take the period 1958 to 1963 as a whole. We find that gross output per unit of combined factors — labor, capital, and exogenous materials — rose by 3–4 percent from 1955 to 1958 and by 5–6 percent from 1958 to 1963. The evidence based on trends in combined labor and capital inputs for 1963 to 1965 suggests that total factor productivity has continued to increase at approximately the same rates as in the period 1958–1963, an acceleration in the labor-

---

percent per year from 1955 to 1960 and by 0.8 percent per year from 1958 to 1963. The rate of growth of combined labor and capital inputs would be increased by 0.5 percent for the period 1955–1960 and by 0.2 percent for 1958–1963 (for geometric weights corresponding to index I). However, if inventories were included in the capital stock, total capital inputs would grow at rates slightly smaller than those shown in the table. I have chosen not to amend the capital index because the two errors are mutually offsetting and because I have not enough confidence in the correction factors to be sure of their *net* effect on the growth rates of combined inputs and on total factor productivity. (There is no certainty, incidentally, that the statistical office actually failed to correct the capital stock estimates for the price changes of 1955.)

When we are working with such aggregated data, we should also keep in mind the possibility that changes in the structure of inputs or of outputs may have given the appearance of increases in factor productivity without the substance. The disaggregated data by industrial branches discussed on pp. 62–63 do show substantial increases in total factor productivity in almost all sectors — an indication that changes in the structure of output did not cause the apparent improvement in productivity for industry as a whole.

[153] This deceleration in the rate of growth of capital productivity, however, should not be construed as an absolute decline — an increase in the capital-to-output ratio — of the sort that occurred in the early 1960's in several other countries in Eastern Europe, including Czechoslovakia (*Statistická ročenka ČSSR 1964* [Prague, 1965], pp. 45 and 162).

[154] On the theoretical objections that have been raised against the derivation of weights from observed data on wages and fixed assets see the excellent discussion in Michael Bruno's *Estimation of Production Functions and Factor Contribution to Growth Under Structural Disequilibrium*, paper submitted to the European meeting of the Econometric Society, Copenhagen, 1963.

productivity trend more than offsetting the deceleration in capital productivity already referred to.[155]

Besides the favorable trends in factor productivity, there are other indications that accelerated industrial developments during the Six-Year Plan proceeded without special hindrance or impediment. The "comparable costs" of industry declined at a rate officially estimated at 3.9 percent per year from 1959 to 1963, compared to a rate of 2.2 percent per year between 1955 and 1958. An analysis of inventory accumulation also corroborates our other findings. In general, inventories in the East European socialist economies rise faster than production in periods of strain, when poorly coordinated planning causes enterprises to receive materials that are ill-adapted to their production program or induces them to turn out goods for which there is no demand. It is also true that in a short period, when the rate of industrial growth has been cranked up too rapidly, inventories of raw materials and semifabricated products may "melt." But stocks must be rebuilt if the expansion is to be sustained, lest it founder on materials shortages. The value of inventories, goods in transit, and other "circulating capital" increased by 118 percent from 1958 to 1965, while the marketed production of industry went up by 160 percent. All this improvement, incidentally, appears to have taken place before the end of 1963. In 1964 and 1965, as the industrial expansion began to run into obstacles — especially due to the nonfulfillment of investment plans — the aggregate inventory-to-output ratios rose again, thus offsetting a part of the improvement realized in the preceding years.[156]

The fairly comprehensive data at our disposal on the changes in the supply of capital (fixed) assets and labor by individual branches of industry for the years 1959 to 1963 allow us a better insight than in any previous period into the factors that rendered possible the growth of industry. Our main conclusion from this study of more disaggregated data is that recent trends in the ratio of capital to labor in centrally directed ("republican") industry, which accounts for the bulk of manufacturing and mining activity, reproduced the same pattern of growth as had prevailed in the early 1950's: in the course of expansion, the capital-to-labor ratios of industries that were already

[155] Even allowing for possible upward biases in the output index and for a downward bias in the capital input index, I doubt whether the growth of total factor productivity would be reduced below 2 percent for the period 1955–1958 and 3–4 percent for the period 1958–1963.

[156] For 1958 and 1965, data are to be found in *Probleme economice*, No. 12 (1966), p. 13. Note that the ratio of inventories to marketed output declined from 27 percent in 1958 to 16 percent in 1963 (see *Probleme economice*, No. 12 [1962], and the "indicators of speed of rotation of working capital" for 1958 in *Economia Romîniei între anii 1944–1959, op. cit.*, p. 542, and for 1963 in *Dezvoltarea economică a Romîniei 1944–1964* [Bucharest, 1964], p. 314).

above average in the base year rose in the following years, while the ratios that were below average diminished further (Table 1.18).

The phenomenon just described is strikingly evident in the case of capital-intensive industries such as electric power, fuels, chemicals, cellulose, and paper. The capital-to-labor ratios of these industries, which ranged in 1959 from 60 to 70 percent above average (paper and chemicals) to over six times the average (electric power), all rose

TABLE 1.18. PERCENTAGE CHANGES IN CAPITAL-TO-LABOR RATIOS BY BRANCH OF REPUBLICAN INDUSTRY, 1959–1963

	Relative Capital-to-Labor Ratio[a]		Percentage Change from 1959 to 1963			
Republican Industry	1959	1963	Capital	Labor	Ratio of Capital to Labor	Output (official index)
Electric power	6.42	7.78	200.6	148.6	135	207
Fuels	3.49	3.84	128.0	107.0	120	144
Ferrous metallurgy	2.02	2.00	139.5	126.9	110	187
Nonferrous metallurgy	0.91	0.77	154.1	162.5	95	173
Machine building and metalworking	0.59	0.55	142.9	137.0	104	203
Chemicals	1.70	1.97	212.8	163.5	130	251
Building materials	0.96	0.88	133.7	132.0	101	176
Lumber and woodworking	0.32	0.33	135.4	117.9	115	164
Cellulose and paper	1.61	2.21	238.4	156.5	152	202
Glass, porcelain	0.41	0.45	173.7	142.7	122	186
Textiles	0.50	0.41	115.9	126.7	91	159
Leather and hides	0.32	0.27	119.2	128.9	92	164
Food processing	0.89	0.77	151.2	157.2	95	189
Total	1.0	1.0	149	134.2	111	186

[a] The share of an industrial branch in the total fixed assets of republican industry divided by its share in the total labor force of republican industry.

Sources and methods: The source for the breakdown of fixed assets in republican industry and for the labor force by branch of republican industry is *Dezvoltarea industriei Republicii Populare Romîne: Culegere de date statistice* (Bucharest, 1964), pp. 22, 117, 161, 179, 195, 214, 231, 259, 282, 299, 317, 333, 347, 371, and 385. The index of the total fixed assets and of the gross output of republican industry is from *Probleme economice*, No. 11 (1966), p. 29. The assets are measured as of the end of each year, while employment is based on yearly averages. The percentage change in capital of each republican industry was computed on the basis of its share in total fixed assets in 1959 and 1963 and of the percentage increase in the total assets of republican industry between the two dates. The output trend in each republican industry was derived from the output index for the entire industry and from the proportion of republican to total industry in the two years (*ibid.*, pp. 165, 236, 261, 287, 304, 322, 373, and 391). In the case of the glass and ceramics industry, for which a breakdown of output was not given, production was divided between republican and total industry in proportion to their respective labor forces (*ibid.*, p. 335).

by 20 percent or more from 1959 to 1963. On the other hand the capital-to-labor ratios in the building-materials, textiles, leather, and food-processing industries, which were below average to start with, underwent a further decline. There were only two partial exceptions to this trend: ferrous metallurgy, whose capital-to-labor ratio increased by only 10 percent, even though it was twice the average in 1959, and the glass and porcelain industry, whose ratio rose by 19 percent despite the fact that it was one of the lowest on the list at the start of the period.[157] In the case of ferrous metallurgy one should recall that no new steel mills were built during this period and that the progress of the industry was based chiefly on the expansion of existing plants, presumably without major changes in technology. Thus, this particular exception does not invalidate the following tentative explanation for the trends observed in all other branches of industry: The capital-to-labor ratio rose in industries that grew mainly as a consequence of the construction of new capacities, owing to the fact that the up-to-date technology the Rumanians were anxious to implant was relatively more capital intensive than that which prevailed in existing establishments; in low-priority industries, which received just enough capital funds to replace worn-out assets and to finance relatively minor expansions, capital intensity remained constant or diminished, as more labor shifts were introduced to take advantage of increasing supplies of raw materials.[158]

We may combine the percentage increases in capital assets and employment for individual branches of manufacturing and mining, as we did for industry as a whole, by assigning them appropriate weights and then compare this aggregate input measure with the growth of output in these branches. Using weights roughly approximate to the wage and capital costs of the industries in 1959 [159] and combining the two factors geometrically, we find that productivity

[157] The estimated increase in fixed assets for the glass and porcelain industry may be off by a substantial margin, due to its very small share in total assets and to possible rounding errors. It held 0.6 percent of republican industry's total fixed assets in 1959 and 0.7 percent in 1963.

[158] The appreciable increase in fixed assets in the food-processing industry need not imply that a large proportion of output in this industry came from new plants. In fact, a part of this increase was undoubtedly due to the incorporation into republican industry of plants formerly run by local industry (the labor force of food-processing enterprises organized under local state industry declined from 38,000 to 21,000 between 1959 and 1963). Another part stemmed from the long-delayed reconstruction and modernization of old plants.

[159] Total depreciated capital in industry was taken from the sources for Table 1.17. Its breakdown by industry is from the sources in Table 1.18. The wage rates and depreciation allowances for individual industries are those used in weighting industrial sectors in Appendix A. Alternative interest rates of 3 and 15 percent were charged to capital to compute capital costs.

per unit of capital and labor rose significantly in all industries, with the possible exception of cellulose and paper.[160] The highest rates were registered in chemicals (7.5 to 8.5 percent per year, depending on the interest rate adopted), machine building (10 percent), and iron and steel (9 percent); lumber, textiles, and building materials all showed increases ranging between 6 and 8 percent per year; the lowest rates of productivity increase were calculated for electric power (2 to 3 percent), nonferrous metals (2 percent), fuels (4 to 5 percent), and food processing (5 percent).

These estimates, of course, all ignore the contribution of exogenous material inputs to production. This omission is unavoidable for want of an input-output table of material flows.[161] Lacking information on the material factor, we must treat with reservation productivity calculations for material-intensive sectors such as food processing and textiles.[162]

If these strides in productivity overtax the reader's credulity, he should bear in mind the enormous investments that went into each branch of industry during the period, which made it possible to retire much obsolescent or worn-out equipment and to introduce machinery that was much more productive than that previously installed. It is sufficient to observe that 41.3 percent of the machinery on hand in the machine-building and metal-processing industry, including the reparations shops, was less than five years old in 1963; this was better than the average for industry as a whole (38.8 percent), but not by a wide margin.[163]

[160] If high interest (for example, 15 percent) is charged to capital in the cellulose and paper industry, then its relatively large increase in capital assets is given a heavy weight, and the rise in combined inputs exceeds the rise in output. This may well be due to the fact that the Brăila cellulose project was not yet working at its full capacity and efficiency in 1963.

[161] An input-output table has been prepared in Rumania but it has never been published.

[162] The estimates of material inputs based on the agricultural and imported materials consumed in the food-processing industry, prepared in connection with the analysis of aggregated industrial production in Table 1.17, did not indicate that the productivity increase reported in the text (5 percent) was overstated (if anything, material inputs into this branch of industry seem to have risen slightly less than either capital or labor). A recalculation using our independent index of output for the industry also led to productivity increases of the same magnitude.

[163] C. Tuzu, *Industria socialistă: Temelia economiei R.P.R.* (Bucharest, 1964), p. 57. In the same machine-building industry, only 16 percent of the equipment was over twenty years old in 1963. The proportion of equipment less than five years old was larger and that of equipment twenty years old or over was smaller than in 1957 (38.5 and 19.9 percent, respectively, according to a breakdown in *Economia Romîniei între anii, 1944–1959, op. cit.*, p. 193). The 1957 inventory already reflected the results of the intensive modernization and expansion of industry undertaken in the First Five-Year Plan.

That the process of growth was relatively smooth — at least for so rapid an expansion — does not imply that development proceeded precisely according to plan. Both the Second Five-Year Plan (1956–1960), which was quietly abandoned in 1959, and the Six-Year Plan were underfulfilled in some important respects, though the performance of industry, as a whole, came much closer to previsions than did agriculture. We shall limit our comparisons of targets with actual results to the Six-Year Plan, considering that the preceding plan was framed in a period of political and economic flux and that it remained operational for only a short time.[164] Comparisons for the Six-Year Plan are set forth in Table 1.19.

We do not yet have at our disposal data relating to the proportion of increased output contributed by new plants, but the targeted shares give a general idea of the core of the industrialization program during the years 1960–1965: 46 percent of the increase in output of electric power was to come from new plants; in the chemical, rubber, and paper industry, new plants were to give 41 percent of output, in the building-materials industry, 20 percent, in woodworking, 38 percent, and in food processing, 20 percent.[165] Virtually all the increase in the output of metallurgical products planned for 1965 was to stem from the expansion of old mills, particularly from the mill at Hunedoara,[166] whereas the expansion in the production of coke and iron ores was to depend largely on new capacity. While the targets for the chief semifabricates — pig iron and steel — were fulfilled, Rumania's efforts to reduce her dependency on imports for the raw materials in this industry were unsuccessful: both the coke and the iron ore plans, which seemed excessively ambitious to begin with, were seriously underfulfilled. Rumania still covered 45 percent of her metallurgical coke requirements from imports in 1964 and 1965.

The sectors where the greatest shortfalls for individual products occurred (electric power, coke, iron ores, nonferrous metals, mineral fertilizers, synthetic rubber, and plastics) were those where capacity from new plants or new mines was slated to be of decisive importance for the fulfillment of the plan. In both the power and the chemical industries some of the blame for the delays in construction can be laid to foreign suppliers who did not complete their contractual tasks on time. In 1963 Otakar Šimůnek, Czechoslovakia's delegate to CMEA

---

[164] On the agricultural results of the Second Five-Year Plan, see Table 2.8 of Chapter 2.

[165] *Congresul al III-lea al Partidului Muncitoresc Romîn* (Bucharest, 1961), p. 31.

[166] The Galați mill, under construction during the Six-Year Plan, was not scheduled for large-scale production until the Third Five-Year Plan (1966–1970).

TABLE 1.19. TARGETS AND REALIZATIONS IN THE SIX-YEAR PLAN
(1960–1965)

	Target 1965	Realized 1965
Indices (1959 = 100)		
National income	170–180	168
Foreign trade turnover	200	213
Volume of construction	200	224
Gross output of industry	210	225
Labor productivity	160–165	161
Real wages of employees	140–145	135
Sales of goods in socialist trade	200	188
Volume of investments in fixed assets		
(1960–1965, billions of lei)	170–180	211
Output of selected industrial products (thousands of tons, except where indicated)		
Electric power (billions of kilowatt hours)	19	17
Pig iron	2,000	2,019
Crude steel	3,300	3,425
Rolled steel products	2,000	2,347
Metallurgical coke	1,600	1,135
Crude oil	11,500–12,500	12,571
Iron ore	4,000	2,479
Soda ash and caustic soda	500	592
Plastics and synthetic resins	95	75
Cement	6,500	5,406
Paper	374	244
Mineral fertilizers	500	293
Synthetic rubber	50	31
Metal tools for metal working (units)	7,500–8,000	6,943
Tractors (thousands of units)	25	16
Fabrics (all types, millions of square meters)	540–550	431
Shoes (all types, millions of pairs)	45	43
Television sets (thousands of units)	130	101
Meat	610	308
Sugar	460	402

Sources: Targets: *Congresul al III-lea al Partidului Muncitoresc Romîn* (Bucharest, 1961), pp. 28, 55, 63, and 65; realized: *Probleme economice*, No. 3 (1966), pp. 154–155, 157.

and Politbureau member of the Czechoslovak Communist Party, observed that delays in the delivery of Czechoslovak power equipment threatened to cause difficulties to the Rumanian economy.[167] It was also common knowledge in Rumania that chemical plants ordered in Czechoslovakia and the Soviet Union had not been put up on time.

[167] *Život strany*, No. 14 (1963), p. 810.

Still, it is unlikely that the excess of investment funds expended over the amounts budgeted in the Plan was caused only by external difficulties. A number of projects, which were half prepared when the Plan was drafted in the late 1950's, had to be recast in the course of fulfilling the Plan, with the result that actual outlays rose above initially estimated costs, and many projects failed to attain the technical parameters that their designs called for.[168]

Investments went up at a rapid but highly uneven rate throughout the Six-Year Plan. From 1959 to 1962 they rose at the extraordinary rate of 23 percent per year; from 1962 to 1965 the rate of increase decelerated to 9 percent per year. The watershed was the poor harvest of 1961–1962, as a consequence of which the balance-of-payments situation became critical and less foreign exchange could be spared to buy machinery abroad than had been foreseen. The custodians of the Rumanian economy prudently eased the pace of expansion. But, as in the period following Stalin's death, they endeavored to protect domestic suppliers of machinery and equipment from the slackening pace of investments. Investment outlays on equipment produced at home kept on rising swiftly; outlays on imported equipment grew at a much slower pace after 1963. (They actually fell in 1964.) It is too early to say whether this relative contraction in the investment program, following upon a three-year period during which funds were spent in excess of the amounts initially budgeted, was a principal cause of the shortfalls in the completion of the projects that we have already referred to.

A recent speech by Nicolae Ceaușescu suggests that the deviations from the long-term investment program (at first in the upward, later in the downward direction) were imperfectly coordinated and that they were responsible for some of the disproportions the planners had to wrestle with in subsequent years:

As is known, the economic activity in our country proceeded up to now on the basis of the general directives concerning the development of economy for a 5- or 6-year period. In fact, planning work, in practice, was of drawing up annual economic plans. Of course, the annual planning system did not give the possibility of fully bringing to relief the superiority of our planned socialist economy, it determined some negative state of things, shortcomings

[168] Due to the failure to meet their projected technical-economic parameters, 41 projects put into operation between 1963 and 1966 caused a shortfall of 1.4 billion lei in gross output and 400 million lei in profits. Enterprises subordinate to the Ministry of the Chemical Industry accounted for about 45 percent of the shortfall in output and 64 percent of the shortfall in profits (*Probleme economice*, No. 12 [1966], p. 9). Approximate calculations indicate that the shortfall in output in the chemical industry amounted to 10–15 percent of its actual increase in output from 1963 to 1965.

in the fulfillment of the long-term directives. Thus, sight was lost sometimes of ensuring proportionality between some branches, perturbations and lack of evenness in the fulfillment of the plans were manifest. The carrying on of an activity based on annual plans deprived the ministries and enterprises of a clear prospect of their main targets for a longer period as well as of the possibility of ensuring corresponding material means. In these conditions it was possible for some subjectivist manifestations to appear, as well as unjustified changes in the destination of some investments, in the siting of some industrial objectives which bore negatively on the policy of harmonious development, throughout the country, of the productive forces, as well as on the efficiency of economic activity.[169]

Owing to the flexibility of foreign trade, the delays in completing investment projects and the other disproportions referred to by Ceauşescu did not cause substantial lapses from the full utilization of capacity in the processing industries that were to receive the intermediate goods whose production failed to meet schedule. The Rumanians apparently had enough leeway in redeploying their exports to buy abroad the coke, iron ores, and nonferrous metals that were necessary to utilize their metal-processing industries more or less fully when these materials failed to flow on schedule from domestic production. They were able to do this, despite substantial shortfalls in agricultural production, by raising their exports of certain manufactured goods, including wooden furniture and lumber products, above their original target levels, as well as by shunting to the external market foodstuffs and other consumer goods that would otherwise have helped to improve domestic living standards.[170]

If we now compare the Rumanian economy's performance with that of the other nations of CMEA, we find that, over the period 1960 to 1965, both Rumania's industrial output and national income, de-

[169] Nicolae Ceauşescu, "The Five-Year Plan: A New Stage of Progress and Prosperity in the Life of the Romanian People, in the Flourishing of Socialist Romania," speech at the Plenary Meeting of the Central Committee of the Rumanian Communist Party, June 27–28, 1966, *Agerpres* (Supplement), pp. 7–8. The "subjectivist manifestations" also referred to in Alexandru Bîrlădeanu's speech at the Ninth Congress of the Party in July 1965 (*Congresul al IX-lea al Partidului Comunist Român* [Bucharest, 1965], pp. 579–580) were probably meant as a criticism of the high-handedness of G. Gaston Marin, the former chairman of the Planning Commission, who was removed from this job at the time of the Congress.

[170] See Chapter 3, pp. 180–181, and also Appendix C, pp. 286–288. The failure to hit the electric power plan for 1965 (by about 9 percent) could not so readily be made up by increased imports (although power imports, which were only initiated in 1963, did contribute 1.5 percent of total consumption in 1965). I suspect that the impact of the shortfall on industrial consumers, who absorbed 62 percent of total power available in 1964, was softened by reducing exports and by limiting the expansion of public illumination and private uses below their expected levels. (Note that increased power exports were to come mainly from those capacities, furnished by foreign suppliers, that were not installed on schedule.)

spite year-to-year fluctuations in its increments due to alternating superior and inferior harvests, grew appreciably faster than in the other member nations of CMEA with the possible exception of Bulgaria, whose growth was only slightly slower than Rumania's. The official data cited here show the percentage increases in national income and industrial output over the preceding year in the member states of CMEA.[171]

NATIONAL INCOME PRODUCED

	1961	1962	1963	1964	1965
Rumania	10.0	4.4	9.7	11.6	9.6
Hungary	6.2	4.6	5.7	4.0	2.0
Bulgaria	2.8	6.2	7.5	10.0	6.0
East Germany	3.5	2.2	−2.9	4.5	4.7
Poland	8.2	2.1	6.9	6.6	6.0
U.S.S.R.	6.8	5.7	4.1	9.0	6.0
Czechoslovakia	6.5	1.4	−2.2	0.9	3.7

GROSS INDUSTRIAL OUTPUT

	1961	1962	1963	1964	1965
Rumania	14.8	14.3	12.2	14.1	13.1
Hungary	10.6	8.1	7.0	8.9	6.0
Bulgaria	12.5	11.1	11.0	10.1	13.7
East Germany	6.6	6.2	4.9	6.7	6.1
Poland	11.1	8.2	5.5	9.3	9.1
U.S.S.R.	9.0	9.0	8.1	7.1	8.6
Czechoslovakia	8.9	5.9	−0.6	4.1	7.9

Now that we have described the most salient aspects of the rapid expansion of the years 1958 to 1965, it remains for us to take a broader look at the economy to see how additional resources were mobilized, what the effect of this effort was on consumption levels, and how foreign trade was used to mount this successful campaign. Our task,

[171] From *Hospodářské noviny*, No. 16 (1966), p. 10; United Nations, Economic Commission for Europe, *Economic Survey of Europe in 1965* (Geneva, 1966), Chapter 1, p. 2; and *Statistisches Jahrbuch der D.D.R.* (Berlin, 1965), p. 27. The national income data of all the countries listed suffer from the defects mentioned in footnote 77. It is likely that the upward bias is greater in countries where the agricultural sector is large, as in Rumania, than where it is small, as in Czechoslovakia or Hungary. Nevertheless, it is believed that the disparities in rates of growth to the advantage of the less developed economies of Eastern Europe represents a very real and significant phenomenon.

essentially, will be to ascertain how the Rumanian planners were able to boost the nation's aggregate saving, or "rate of accumulation," decisively above New Course levels.

Table 1.20 illustrates the principal trends in national income distributed, in accumulation, and in consumption, which includes, in addition to private consumption, purchases of goods for defense needs, hospitals, schools, and other "social uses."

The rate of accumulation apparently in terms of current prices was said to have averaged 20 percent from 1956 to 1959 and 25 percent from 1960 to 1963 (compared to 24 percent in the period 1951–1955).[172] As can be seen in Table 1.20, however, these averages conceal and obscure the powerful increase in rates of accumulation that took place from 1959 to 1963 (from 20 to 27 percent in comparable prices and from 16.3 to 23.6 percent in current prices).[173] During these four years total accumulation, reckoned in constant prices, nearly doubled, while consumption rose by some 30 percent. The marginal rate of accumulation, calculated as the ratio of the four-year increment in accumulation to the increment in national income distributed for these same years, works out to 44 percent.

The ratio of productive investments to increments in national income seems to have risen significantly in Rumania in recent years, although to a lesser extent than in the more developed socialist countries. This ratio was recently estimated by a Soviet economist to have averaged 1.5 from 1951 to 1955, 2.4 from 1956 to 1960, and 2.7 from 1961 to 1964. (In Czechoslovakia the ratios for corresponding periods were said to equal 0.92, 1.76, and 7.3!)[174] Such increases as did take place in the Rumanian ratio should for the most part be attributed to the agricultural sector, whose capital-to-output ratio has shown a marked tendency to increase in recent years. The relatively abundant supply of unskilled labor and the successful efforts of the government to train skilled workers and technicians have undoubtedly helped to keep aggregate capital-to-output ratios from rising as fast as in the more developed economies of Eastern Europe.

Compared to the first surge of industrialization of the early 1950's, when enormous increases in requirements for inventories absorbed

---

[172] I. Ravar in *Dezvoltarea complexă* . . . , *op. cit.*, p. 9.

[173] The planned rate of accumulation for 1970 was set at 28.5 percent (*Revista de statistică*, No. 12 [1966], p. 85).

[174] M. Usievich, "Nekotorye problemy nakopleniia v stranakh SEV," *Voprosy ekonomiki*, No. 7 (1966), p. 72. Productive investments are defined in this source to include investments in fixed assets in "productive sectors" plus all increases in inventories and reserves. In Rumania, the percentage ratio of productive investments (so defined) to national income was equal to 9.7 in 1950, 17.4 in 1955, 16.7 in 1960, 20.2 in 1961, 20.2 in 1962, and 21.5 percent in 1963 (*ibid.*).

TABLE 1.20. TRENDS IN NATIONAL INCOME, AGGREGATE CONSUMPTION, AND ACCUMULATION; RATES OF ACCUMULATION IN "COMPARABLE" AND IN CURRENT PRICES (*1955, 1957, 1959, 1962, and 1963*)

| | *"Comparable Prices"* | | | *Current Prices* | | | |
	National Income Distributed (1950 = 100)	Consumption (1950 = 100)	Accumulation (1950 = 100)	National Income Distributed (1950 = 100)	Consumption (1950 = 100)	Accumulation (1950 = 100)	Rate of Accumulation (percent)
1955	164	n.a.	n.a.	197	184	300	16.9
1957	203	n.a.	n.a.	237	226	328	15.2
1959	222	179	424	239	225	357	16.3a
1962	289	223	n.a.	322	289	598	20.2
1963	313	230	805	342	294	741	23.6

[a] The planned target for 1959 was 18 percent (*Probleme economice*, No. 6 [1960], p. 4).

Sources and methods: Indexes of national income and indexes of consumption in current prices were computed from the estimates n Table B.8 of Appendix B. Other index numbers are from *Dezvoltarea complexă și echilibrată a economiei naționale* (Bucharest, 1965), pp. 27, 32, and from S. Țaigar, *Veniturile populației și nivelul de trai în R.P.R.* (Bucharest, 1964), p. 86.

capital without adding immediately to output, it is apparent that a greater part of total investment in recent years has been used to build up fixed capital, with beneficial effects on production. From 1960 to 1964 about three quarters of accumulation, exclusive of state reserves, went into fixed assets, as against 50 percent from 1951 to 1955.[175] The information available on total state and cooperative investments and on inventories confirms on the whole this relatively slow rise of inventories. Investments in fixed assets rose by 19 percent per year from 1959 to 1963 — compared to a planned 16 percent — whereas aggregate inventories in all branches of the economy probably did not rise faster than at a rate of 10 percent per year, at least from the end of 1959 to the end of 1962.[176]

How and whence did the government marshal the additional resources that went into investment uses after 1958? To answer this crucial question, we must consider three principal factors: (1) imports of capital goods, (2) labor employed in construction and in the production of capital goods, and (3) the allocation of capital to capital-producing sectors.

As we have seen, imports of machinery and equipment were compressed as much as possible from 1954 to 1957–1958 in order to save scarce foreign exchange for imports of industrial materials necessary to keep industrial capacity fully employed. From 1958 on, for several reasons, including an acceleration of food exports and a reduction in external obligations, the balance-of-payments problems of Rumania were alleviated; enough foreign exchange was earned to permit a sharp rise in imports of capital goods, without cutting into other essential requirements. From 1958 to 1961 investments in imported machinery and equipment went up from 902 million lei to 4,722 million lei.[177] The increment of nearly 4 billion lei amounted to 18 percent of the total rise in investments by state and cooperative enterprises, including collective farms, between these dates. If we consider investments in machinery and equipment alone, then the rise in imports came to 43 percent of the total increment in this category of investments.

It is not difficult to account for the remaining part of the increase in the machinery component of investments, which stemmed from domestic production. The output of the machine-building and metal-processing industry rose by 126 percent from 1958 to 1963 according

[175] *Viața economică*, No. 36 (1965), p. 4; *Probleme economice*, No. 1 (1964), p. 30.

[176] On the planned rate of increase in investments, see *Probleme economice*, No. 1 (1964), p. 5; on increases in total inventories, see *Probleme economice*, No. 12 (1963), p. 178; and No. 10 (1963), p. 6.

[177] *Anuarul statistic al R.P.R. 1965*, p. 345.

to the official index and by 98 percent according to the index computed in the appendix to the present study.

Only about 10–11 percent of the entire production of this branch of industry was exported in the early 1960's,[178] while the rest was allotted to meet rapidly expanding domestic requirements. Besides current domestic production and imports, use was made of still another source of supply of machinery and equipment, namely "fixed funds held in reserve," which declined by 50 percent from 1959 to 1962.[179]

The value of outlays on machinery and equipment represented 38 percent of total investments from 1960 to 1964. Most of the remaining investment outlays were for construction and assembly (46 percent of total).[180] The value of output of this branch of economic activity showed a more pronounced upswing than any other sector during the period after 1958. The statistics in Table 1.21 throw in relief the trans-

TABLE 1.21. Indices of Production, Manpower, and Fixed Assets from 1953 to 1965 in the Construction Sector (*1950 = 100*)

	Production Index	*Employment*	*Fixed Assets*
1953	270	223	n.a.
1954	221	202	n.a.
1955	256	210	396
1956	294	219	383
1957	260	184	420
1958	269	183	461
1959	294	191	480
1960	360	213	477
1961	409	233	517
1962	474	255	570
1963	539	271	653
1964	604	286	716
1965	649	293	791

Sources: *Anuarul statistic al Republicii Socialiste România 1966*, pp. 106 and 398–399.

formation of the construction industry from a stagnant to a dynamic sector, starting with the late 1950's.

It should be noted that in the first two years of the boom, the con-

[178] See Chapter 3, p. 150.

[179] See footnote 127. The value of unutilized fixed assets in republican industry went down from 6.1 percent of the total fixed assets in the industry in 1960 to 1.7 percent in 1965 (*Probleme economice*, No. 12 [1966], p. 9).

[180] "Geological prospecting," including petroleum drilling, absorbed 5 percent of total investments in this period; and miscellaneous other types of investments, 10.7 percent (*Anuarul statistic al R.P.R. 1965*, p. 340).

struction industry's fixed assets, whose growth lagged behind the increase in investments, rose very little; the impulse to production came mostly from the employment side, with an addition of 52,000 workers to the labor force. From 1960 to 1962 capital assets and employment expanded at about the same pace. In the last three years of the Six-Year Plan fixed assets grew more than twice as fast as employment. In the period 1958–1964 labor and capital increased in about the same proportion (57 and 55 percent, respectively), which was a good deal less than the increase in production, officially evaluated at 125 percent. If the official output measure is accurate, productivity per unit of labor and capital combined must have grown by nearly 45 percent in the six years, or by 7.8 percent per year. I suspect that economies of scale — the consequence of concentrating funds on large new projects instead of scattering them over many small undertakings — together with a greater influx of building materials accounted for most of the increase in the apparent productivity of labor and capital. It is significant that the supply of building materials to the construction industry rose relatively more than their output, as a larger part of a rapidly expanding domestic production of these materials was earmarked for internal uses.[181] One of the many tangible benefits the Rumanian economy drew from the upsurge in food exports was that it made possible the diversion of cement, timber, and other materials from exports to investment uses.

We observed in connection with the first postwar industrialization drive that the growth of investments was attended by consumers' rationing, rising peasant market prices, and — the ultimate symptom of inflationary pressures — by a monetary reform, which confiscated the greater part of the population's excess liquidity. The investment program was partly financed by forced private saving, at a time when the government was still incapable of balancing its financial and fiscal accounts without releasing more currency into the hands of the public than was desirable to maintain a given level of prices. How successful were the planners in the second round of rapid industrialization in preserving macroeconomic equilibrium? The answer, as we might expect, is that they did much better; so much better in fact, that the government had enough confidence in the results to publish data on trends in currency in circulation and in individual bank savings — normally highly secret matters in Rumania (Table 1.22).

The sum of currency in circulation plus savings deposits rose from

---

[181] Both production and imports of building materials approximately doubled from 1959 to 1964, while the rise in exports was limited to 65 percent at current *valută* prices (*Anuarul statistic al R.P.R. 1965*, pp. 152 and 438–439).

TABLE 1.22. TRENDS IN HOUSEHOLD INCOMES, EXPENDITURES, AND
MONETARY CIRCULATION (*1959–1964*)

	1959	1960	1961	1962	1963	1964
Cash incomes of households (index)	100	107	116	125	133	143
from socialist sector	100	112	125	138	152	163
Cash expenditures of household (index)	100	106	115	125	132	141
Currency held by households (index)	100	117	133	138	157	159
Savings deposits of households (index)	100	152	211	281	407	544
Estimated currency in circulation (billions of lei)	3.7	4.3	4.9	5.1	5.8	5.9
Estimated savings deposits (billions of lei)	1.14	1.72	2.4	3.2	4.61	6.2
urban	.91	1.38	1.82	2.24	3.22	4.43
rural	.23	.34	.58	.96	1.39	1.77

Note: Currency and savings deposits are evaluated as of December 31 of each year.

Sources and methods: All indices are from V. Dumitriu, "Economiile populaţiei prîn CEC," *Revista de statistică*, No. 8 (1965), pp. 67–70; and M. Vaşilescu, "Schimbări intervenite in cererea de consum a populaţiei," *Revista de statistică*, No. 11 (1965), p. 59. (The indices per capita in the latter source have been recomputed for the entire population.) The estimates of currency in circulation and savings deposits are derived from estimated currency in circulation in 1959 and from the indices and percentages in the sources cited. Currency in circulation in 1959 was calculated as follows: On December 31, 1959, 15.1 percent of the liabilities of the National Bank of Rumania were identified as "other means" (*Probleme economice*, No. 5 [1960], p. 61). From the detailed breakdown in the source, it was evident that "other means" must represent currency in circulation. Furthermore, since total liabilities equal total assets, and assets consisted entirely, or almost entirely, of short-term credits in 1959, an estimate of the latter could be used as a proxy for the former. These credits amounted to 24.6 billion lei on December 31, 1959 (*Probleme economice*, No. 6 [1965], p. 61).

an estimated 4.8 billion in 1959 to 12.1 billion lei in 1964. The question that arises is to what extent this increase was the result of the higher demand for savings, resulting in turn from higher real incomes, and to what extent it was forced upon the public by the government's inability to balance the population's cash incomes against its expenditures without releasing excess liquidity. I incline to the belief that most of the increase was a normal concomitant of the rise in real incomes, which the statistical office estimated at 28 percent for workers and other employees from 1959 to 1964,[182] and of the rise in supplies of durable goods and of construction materials with which to build private houses, both of which must have stimulated private saving.

[182] *Anuarul statistic al R.P.R. 1965*, p. 103.

In this connection, it is instructive to relate the magnitude of the total increase in the population's liquid assets to other critical variables, partially or wholly under the planner's control. Most significant perhaps is the fact that the increase in currency plus savings from 1959 to 1964 equaled little more than one tenth of retail sales in state and cooperative shops in 1964; it amounted to 40 percent, or 2 billion lei, more than the increment in these sales from 1963 to 1964. Suppose that the demand for currency and savings had risen in the same proportion as real incomes — a most modest assumption considering that saving is normally income elastic — then we should expect an increment in demand from this factor alone of one billion lei. In other words, the excess of currency in circulation plus savings deposited amounted to little more than one year's increase in retail sales. This does not seem excessive for a period of five years. Looking at the surplus from a different angle, we may also reckon that if prices had been allowed to rise to absorb the "excess liquidity," as defined here, it would have been sufficient for them to creep up by 2 percent per year more than they actually did. How this maximum required increase compares with the actual evolution of retail prices in state and cooperative shops may be made out from the data in Table 1.23.

TABLE 1.23. IMPLICIT INDICES OF RETAIL PRICES 1959 TO 1964
        (*1959 = 100*)

	1960	1961	1962	1963	1964
Retail Sales of Foodstuffs					
In current prices	108	122	138	155	178
In prices of 1959	108	122	138	152	170
Implicit price index	100	100	100	102	105
Retail Sales of Nonfood Items					
(excluding public catering)					
In current prices	119	135	150	158	167
In prices of 1959	120	138	155	164	174
Implicit price index	99	98	97	96	96

Source: Anuarul statistic al R.P.R. 1965, pp. 411 and 414.

All these arguments notwithstanding, the queues and the informal rationing of certain food staples that occurred in 1962, when rural supplies fell short as a result of a poor agricultural year and the government's excessive procurements from farmers,[183] and the decision

[183] See Chapter 2, p. 121. Note also that the (uncontrolled) prices of agricultural products on the peasant market probably rose substantially during the period 1958–1962. Nevertheless, as will be shown in Chapter 2, the total receipts from

taken in 1964 to raise retail meat prices to restore equilibrium in this market suggest that some monetary overhang existed during part of the period or at least that inventories of consumer goods — whose ratio to retail sales declined from 1959 to 1964 — were not sufficient to withstand unanticipated fluctuations in supply and demand. However, the adjustments in the prices of foodstuffs that became necessary to cure the imbalances were relatively minor. They may even be considered as the normal continuation of the differential trend in the prices of agricultural and of industrial commodities that one would expect in an industrializing country, especially one where prices of industrial goods were exorbitantly high to begin with.

The official claim of rising real incomes for both the urban and the rural population in the period since 1958 is generally consistent with the evidence on per capita consumption of workers and peasants, although one should bear in mind that the 1958 harvest was a poor one and that peasants' real incomes in that year were lower than in 1955 and 1957.[184] The volume of retail sales, which expanded rapidly during the period 1958 to 1965, exaggerates the rise in consumption, owing to the shift from peasants' consumption in kind to purchases from state and cooperative shops, a trend that assumed some importance during this period. Massive residential construction, which deflected building materials and workers from more "productive" uses, should also be counted on the credit side of the development ledger in these years. The pertinent evidence on these points is presented in Table 1.24.

If we may judge by the evidence of Table 1.24, it would seem as if the upsurge in investments of the post-1958 period was accompanied

---

this source stayed more or less constant as the physical volume of these sales declined. There was therefore little or no "unplanned transfer" of purchasing power from the urban to the rural population.

[184] According to the official index, real wages of all employees rose by a yearly average of 6.2 percent from 1958 to 1962 and by 3.9 percent per year from 1962 to 1965. The real incomes of peasants were about 3 percent higher on the average in 1959–1960 than in 1957–1958. In 1961 and 1962, on the basis of fragmentary data on real incomes, one may surmise that they exceeded 1957–1958 levels by about 5 percent. The fact that no statistics on peasants' real incomes have been published in recent years suggests that a deterioration may have set in since 1962. The last published data on rural consumption trends, which refer to 1963, a year when the gross output of agriculture was a little above 1962 and real incomes should normally have risen proportionately, tend to confirm the possibility of such a decline (see Table 1.24). Real wages are regularly published in the statistical yearbooks. The index of real incomes of the rural population for 1950 to 1960 appeared in *Dezvoltarea agriculturii R.P.R. 1961*, p. 370; the next issue of a statistical compendium for agriculture (*Dezvoltarea agriculturii R.P.R.: Culegere de date statistice, 1965*) contained no information on the subject. A 1962 estimate is given in S. Țaigar, *op. cit.*, p. 212.

TABLE 1.24. SELECTED INDICATORS OF URBAN AND RURAL CONSUMPTION, 1958 TO 1964

	1960	1962 (1958 = 100)	1963
Workers' Consumption per Capita			
Bread	100	100	98
Meat	121	121	n.a.
Sugar	100	105	n.a.
Milk	108	120	n.a.
Butter	n.a.	105	114
Eggs	n.a.	113	110
Peasants' Consumption per Capita			
Wheat and rye flour	108	120	115
Meats and animal fats	129	130	128
Sugar	120	135	129
Milk	105	105	95
Eggs	125	115	111
Urban Retail Sales per Urban Resident[a]			
Food[b]	102	127	138
Nonfood	133	171	179
Rural Retail Sales per Rural Resident[a]			
Food[b]	133	184	208
Nonfood	112	139	149

	1953–1958	1959–1964
Urban Residential Construction		
From state funds		
number of dwellings	68,042	209,589
usable area (thousands of square meters)	2,188	6,559
From private funds		
number of dwellings	50,330	49,961
usable area (thousands of square meters)	1,588	1,785
Rural Residential Construction		
From state funds		
number of dwellings	13,945	18,122
usable area (thousands of square meters)	478	588
From private funds		
number of dwellings	363,479	511,593
usable area (thousands of square meters)	10,591	15,659

[a] In comparable prices of 1950. State and cooperative stores only.

[b] Exclusive of public catering.

Sources: Consumption per capita: S. Țaigar, *Veniturile populației și nivelul de trai în R.P.R.* (Bucharest, 1964), pp. 231 and 233; *Economia Romîniei între anii 1944–1959* (Bucharest, 1959), p. 622; *Probleme economice*, No. 4 (1961), p. 28; *Revista de statistică*, No. 4 (1961), p. 41; *Viața economică*, No. 34 (August 21, 1964), p. 5. Other data: *Anuarul statistic al R.P.R. 1965*, pp. 65, 370–371, and 413.

by rising consumption, at least until 1962. This average rise was due both to the improvement of workers' and peasants' levels of consumption and to the migration from low consumption rural areas to urban communities.[185] These gains could not have been achieved without an improvement in the agricultural situation and without an expanding output of industrial consumer goods, which deflected some of the demand released by higher incomes away from foodstuffs (which might otherwise have been in very short supply, inasmuch as a sizable proportion of state procurements were earmarked for export).

While we are on the subject, we may note that peasants' consumption in the early 1960's, according to official estimates, was higher than before the war for most basic food products. Calculated per person engaged in agriculture, the consumption of cheese products in 1960 was said to be 36 percent higher than in 1938, that of meat and fats and eggs to be roughly twice as great as in 1938, while the consumption of sugar, the only industrial product for which we have information, was 7.6 times as great as in 1938.[186] The consumption of milk and cereal products, whose income elasticity is lower than that of the products just cited, was probably only slightly higher than before World War II.

Unfortunately, no data whatsoever have been published on urban consumption after the war, and only the most approximate calculations of trends in real wages can be invoked to help fill this gap. While no precise data on wages and salaries either in the prewar or in the postwar period have been released, we have it on the authority of Simon Ţaigar, one of Rumania's prominent specialists in the field of wages and social welfare, that the average wage of Rumanian workers in 1938, expressed in prewar lei, was approximately 1.9 times as great as the average wage of 1963 in current lei.[187] Ţaigar also estimates that prices were 4.4

[185] According to the Six-Year Plan, out of a total increase in employment of one million persons, 400,000–500,000 persons were to be "absorbed from rural areas." From 1960 to 1964 alone, 500,000 persons were drawn from rural areas to urban employment (*Dezvoltarea complexă . . .* , *op. cit.*, p. 140).

[186] Levente, Barat, and Bulgaru, *Analiza statistico-economică a agriculturii*, *op. cit.*, p. 22. Note, however, that peasants' consumption of meat, exclusive of fats, was much less than twice as great as in 1938. (Cf. the data in Table 2.16 of Chapter 2 and the calculations in note 140.)

[187] Ţaigar, *op. cit.*, p. 98. The average monthly wage of workers in 1963 was a little below 1,000 lei. Applying the Ţaigar index relative to the rounded figure, we obtain an estimate of the average prewar wage of 1,900 lei per month. On the basis of the monthly wage data published in *Buletinul muncii* (Vol. XIX, September–December 1939, pp. 661, 668, and 808), I am inclined to accept this figure as correct at least until more detailed data are published. Note that Ţaigar's study was apparently based on a far wider sample of workers' wages, taken mainly from the records of enterprises in manufacturing industries, than those published in *Buletinul muncii*.

times as high in 1938 as in 1963; hence real wages were 132 percent higher at the latter date.[188] His index relative of prices, however, seems greatly overstated.[189]

If and when a systematic study of the evolution of real wages is ever undertaken, my guess is that their increase between 1938 and 1963 will turn out to be somewhere between 30 and 80 percent, depending on the quantity weights used in constructing the price index and on the adjustments made for quality differences between the two dates. These putative gains in real wages, it should be stressed, refer to workers only. The situation of salaried employees, particularly of functionaries and professionals, evolved much less favorably, and a deterioration for at least some categories of employees is by no means to be excluded.

Present and Future: 1965 to 1970

Despite the perceptible deceleration in the rate of expansion of the economy that occurred after 1962, the planners are confident that they have achieved self-sustained growth and that there will be no more "slowdowns" of the sort that held back progress in 1954–1955 or in 1957. They believe that the forward momentum of the economy *can* be maintained in the next five years, although they envisage some reduction in the rates of growth of the principal sectors as compared to the Six-Year Plan. Their initial draft of the Five-Year Plan for 1966–1970, officially approved in mid-1965, called for a growth rate of 10.5 percent a year in the gross output of industry, compared to an officially achieved rate of 14.5 percent from 1959 to 1965; they set a 7 percent a year target for the growth of national income, compared to the 9.1 percent rate recorded for 1959–1965, and a 3.5 percent rate for

[188] *Ibid.*, p. 99.
[189] White bread cost 2.3 times as much in 1938 as in 1962, black bread 3.6 times, meat and eggs 1.5 times, sugar 3.6 times, oil 3 times, coffee twice, and milk and butter roughly 2.7 times. Shoes were roughly two to three times as expensive in 1938 as in 1962, men's socks three to four times, and shirts four to five times (but probably of superior quality at the earlier date). Rent was, of course, disproportionately higher in 1938. The relative importance in workers' budgets of food (28 percent of total expenditures, including services, in workers' budgets in 1963), rent (2 percent in 1963), and industrial goods excluding processed foods (40 to 50 percent in 1963) differed substantially from the shares of these groups in workers' expenditures in 1938. One would have to assign a disproportionately high weight to rent, utilities, and other items of consumption whose relative prices have greatly declined to arrive at Țaigar's index relative. (Bucharest 1938 prices are from *Anuarul statistic al Romaniei 1938 și 1940* [Bucharest, 1940], pp. 635–639. Prices of 1962 are based on the author's notes in 1962. The shares of rent and of food and nonfood industrial commodities in workers' total expenditures are based on calculations from data in Țaigar, *op. cit.*, p. 223, and *Dezvoltarea economică a Rominiei 1944–1964, op. cit.*, pp. 3 and 643.)

TABLE 1.25. FIVE-YEAR PLAN TARGETS FOR THE RUMANIAN ECONOMY,
1965 TO 1970

	Initial Targets (percentage increase 1965–1970)	Average Rate of Growth	Revised Targets (percentage increase 1965–1970)	Average Rate of Growth
Gross output of industry	65	10.5	73	11.6
Producer goods (Group A)	70	11	70–77	11.2–12.1
Consumer goods (Group B)	60	10	60–65	9.9–10.5
Gross output of agriculture (five-year averages)	20	3.5	26–32	4.7– 5.7
Transportation of goods	55–60	9–10	n.a.	n.a.
National income	40	7	50	8.5
Consumption fund	30	5.5	40	7.0
Centralized state investments (increase in 1966–1970 over 1961–1965)	50	—	66	10.7
Retail sales	50–55	8.5–9.0	55–59	9.2– 9.7
Numbers of employees in national economy (increase 1965–1970)	900,000	180,000	900,000	180,000
Labor productivity (per employee)				
Industry	40	7	40–45	7.0– 7.7
Construction	30	5.5	30–35	5.4– 6.2
Transportation	28	5	28–29	5.1– 5.2
Reduction of costs				
Industry	10	2	10	2.0
Transportation	14	2.5	14.5	2.7
Real wages of employees	20–25	4.0–4.5	25	4.6
Peasants' real incomes	20–25	4.0–4.5	20–25	3.8– 4.6
Volume of external trade	over 40	over 7	50–55	8.5– 9.2

Sources: Initial targets: *Congresul al IX-lea al Partidului Comunist Român* (Bucharest, 1965), p. 756; all revised targets except for increase in consumption fund: "Legea pentru adoptarea planului de stat de dezvoltare a economiei naţionale pe anii 1966–1970," *Scînteia* (July 1, 1966), p. 7; increase in consumption fund: *Scînteia* (July 1, 1966), p. 4.

the gross output of agriculture, compared to the 2 percent yearly growth of 1959–1965. A year later they decided the economy could develop at an even faster pace. They revised the yearly growth rate of industry for 1960–1970 to 11.6 percent, of national income to 8.4 percent, and of agriculture to 5.9 percent (Table 1.25).[190]

[190] The upward revision was prompted, at least in part, by the encouraging performance of the farm sector in 1965 — particularly by the excellent wheat harvest for that year — and by the overfulfillment of the plan of industrial output in the first half of 1966, which yielded an unanticipated windfall of 1.8 billion lei in industrial production. Cf. the article on the new plan by Mihai Marinescu, Minister of the Machine-building Industry, in *Scînteia* (July 14, 1966), pp. 1–2.

Were the original targets internally consistent? Do the revisions, which raised the agricultural target to a greater extent than the industrial growth rate, make the plan more or less coherent? I have no clear-cut answers to these questions. What I can do, by way of an answer, is to speculate on the conditions that would have to be met for the economy to achieve growth rates of the magnitude envisioned in the plans and on the chances of their being realized.

From an analysis of foreign trade targets, which will be set forth in detail in Chapter 3, one may deduce that the revised targets for 1970 hinge on an extraordinary expansion of exports of machinery and chemicals rather than on the development of agricultural exports, which contributed decisively to the economic boom of the late 1950's and early 1960's. The upward revision in agricultural output seems to be aimed instead at raising living standards beyond initial expectations. (This is reflected, for instance, in the increase in the consumption fund target for 1970 from 30 percent above 1965, in the original draft, to 40 percent.) If this is true, then the repercussions in the industrial sector of a shortfall in the fulfillment of the agricultural plan are not likely to be so damaging as in the period of the Six-Year Plan, when additional supplies of farm products were counted on to finance imports of machinery and industrial raw materials. For reasons that will be made explicit in Chapter 3, I believe that the fulfillment of the export plan will depend on the willingness of CMEA countries, and particularly of the Soviet Union, to buy more machinery and chemicals from Rumania than they sell to her in return. (The alternative of selling manufactures en masse in Western Europe and in the developing countries would seem to hold only dim prospects.) If the assumptions on which the export plan are founded are not realized, then agriculture will have to fill the breach — at the expense of consumption.

The Rumanians' ability to sustain their previous record of rapid growth will depend in part on whether their industry will be capable of supplying the material and capital inputs needed for a healthy expansion of agriculture,[191] which will in turn provide leverage to boost exports and to pay for the imports needed to keep the economy running. It is in this sense that growth will have to be balanced in the short run, each sector lending support to the other by providing it, directly or indirectly, with its required inputs. For the economy to break out of this interdependency, industrial production would have to become a great deal more efficient. This could be done in several ways, all yielding direct benefits: (1) material inputs could be pared down, with

[191] This assumes, of course, that the collectivized sector will be capable of using these inputs effectively.

a concomitant abatement of the pressure on the balance of payments, either via increased exports or via reduced imports; (2) less labor might be used per unit of output: this would trim the demand for wage goods, particularly for foodstuffs; (3) less capital might be required to achieve a given gain in output, thus lessening the need for investments.

If the Ministry of Foreign Trade could acquire manufactures at substantially lower cost and could sell them abroad at the prices these goods normally fetch on foreign markets, then these goods would afford the government an additional source of "financial accumulation," which would help to finance investments, in addition to their direct contribution to the acquisition of foreign exchange. For the time being, it would seem as if agricultural and petroleum exports are the only ones to achieve both aims at once.[192] In any event, for cost reductions to have a decisive impact on the balance between accumulation and consumption or on Rumania's balance of payments, much more would have to be done than the compression of industrial costs by 10 percent over five years as stipulated in both the original and the revised draft of the Second Five-Year Plan.[193]

One is tempted to predict that the "extensive" development of Rumanian industry oriented toward the production of a steadily increasing number of new and technologically advanced products, geared mainly to the satisfaction of a relatively narrow domestic market, will eventually run into the problems that the other, more advanced economies of Eastern Europe have already encountered after following a similar strategy for a number of years. Rumania's industry, which is heavily dependent on imported raw materials, must participate more deeply in the international division of labor, specializing in the lines of production in which it can secure a large enough market to take full advantage of the economies of scale inherent in modern capital-intensive technologies, or allow its imports to be financed from the foreign-exchange earnings of the agricultural sector, insofar as this sector will remain capable of generating large surpluses for export.

It might also be argued that the eventual disadvantages of industrialization centered on the domestic market will not be felt for many years. At this point in their industrialization, the Rumanians may still count on appreciable productivity gains from mastering technological processes and from "learning by doing" before the limitations of the

[192] Petroleum products, whether consumed domestically or not, pay turnover taxes, which contribute significantly to accumulation. On the inference of low purchase prices for agricultural products processed for export, see Chapter 3, p. 150.

[193] In the revised draft, however, the cost-reduction target was said to be a minimum objective.

market become restrictive. To the extent that productivity gains *are* achieved and real income per head rises, the market will widen and justify production on a larger scale. I doubt whether the Rumanian planners themselves are in a position to know whether these sources of productivity increases can offset the disadvantages of a steadily widening nomenclature, and if so, for how long.

So much for balanced growth in the short and in the medium run. Now it is opportune to write about the organic structure of the Rumanian economy from a wider standpoint than has been done so far. We have seen how investments have been concentrated in heavy industry ever since Soviet-style planning was introduced in the country. Did this single-minded attention to priority sectors create a lopsided infrastructure? Are there neglected sectors that need to be bolstered if future development is not to be hamstrung?

For a country with a relatively advanced industry, capable by now of exporting a greater value of machinery and equipment than of petroleum products, Rumania does have an extraordinary distribution of resources. In 1964 only 18.2 percent of the active population was engaged in industry and mining; this minority of the labor force was equipped with 54.9 percent of all productive fixed assets of the country. On the other hand, 58 percent of the labor force and 23 percent of total productive assets (not including land) were employed in agriculture.

The share of total fixed assets attached to transportation and communications diminished from 17.7 percent in 1950 (probably less than before the war) to 13.3 percent in 1964.[194] Even though the railroad network only increased by 985 kilometers from 1938 to 1964 (from a density of 42.1 kilometers to one of 46.3 kilometers per 1,000 square kilometers of territory), it was made to carry nearly five times the prewar merchandise traffic (measured in ton-kilometers per year). Railroad transportation accounted for 70 percent of all the merchandise traffic of the country, while transportation by trucks, which was confined mainly to very short hauls (averaging eleven miles per trip!) accounted for only 5.8 percent of all ton-kilometers transported in 1965.[195] In the last eight years great progress has been made in the modernization of the road system, starting out from a very low base: in 1956 only 3,625 kilometers of road were "of a modern type" — that is, hard-cover, all-weather roads. This network had grown to 8,462 kilometers in 1964, which was still flagrantly inadequate for a country of 237,500 square kilometers. In the winter and early spring of 1962,

---

[194] *Anuarul statistic al R.P.R. 1965*, pp. 105 and 113.
[195] *Statistical Pocket Book, 1966*, p. 213. For planned development, see note 195.

as the present writer can testify, truck traffic was thin or nonexistent even on the roads connecting large cities.

Rumania's economy, viewed in its spatial dimensions, is still largely rural and agricultural, although focuses of intense industrial activity, linked with each other by a heavily burdened railroad system, are interspersed throughout the land. These industrial islands are privileged, in a number of respects, in comparison with the surrounding countryside: their labor force is still much better off than the peasant population;[196] they are endowed with a great deal more capital per person employed; and they are the vehicles of technical progress, the receptacles of "human capital," on which most of the solicitude of the state in these domains, up to very recently, has been lavished.

This last point may be supported by data (see Table 1.26) showing that the overwhelming proportion of the graduates from professional schools went into industry, mining, and construction, until efforts were deployed in the last two or three years to redress the lack of balance that had come about in the "structure of human capital," as more students were encouraged to pursue agricultural careers.

The neglect of agriculture aside, we cannot fail to be impressed by the progress made in technical education in the postwar years of industrialization. We must also recognize the flexibility of the educational

[196] In 1964, urban communities, which held a third of Rumania's population, accounted for over three quarters of total sales in state and cooperative shops. We should, however, take into consideration that 35 to 40 percent of peasants' purchases are normally made in the cities (*Economia Romîniei între anii 1944–1959, op. cit.*, p. 519) and that peasants' consumption in kind makes up a large part of their food consumption. Taking these factors into account, we find that rural consumption per head, estimated at retail prices for purchases and at average sales prices for consumption in kind, cannot be far in excess of one half of that of urban inhabitants. (Consumption in kind may be estimated from its percentage relation to retail sales in state and cooperative shops in Ţaigar, *op. cit.*, p. 86; sales data, broken down by urban and rural areas, are to be found in *Anuarul statistic al R.P.R. 1965*, p. 411.) The disparity in consumption levels between rural and urban inhabitants, as well as between inhabitants of the capital and of provincial cities, are reflected in data on Bucharest retail sales. Selecting only industrially produced commodities, we find that Bucharest, with 7 percent of the country's population, accounted for the following shares of total retail sales in 1962: sugar and sugar products, 14 percent; beer, 18 percent; refrigerators, 45 percent; televisions, 43 percent; sewing machines, 15 percent; kitchen ranges, 20 percent; textiles and footwear, 17 percent; and furniture, 20 percent. The last two items are based on the value of retail sales at current prices, all the others on quantities sold. (Sources: *Anuarul statistic al Orașului București 1963*, pp. 147–148, and *Anuarul statistic al R.P.R. 1965*, p. 411.)

Spontaneous migration from the farm to the city is discouraged by administrative controls, both at the source of the migration and at the receiving end. In principle, no one may move into a city who does not have a job and assured lodgings. Some exceptions are allowed, for example, in favor of rural inhabitants hiring themselves out as construction workers for a season. Many of these squat on the outskirts of large cities.

TABLE 1.26. GRADUATES OF PROFESSIONAL SCHOOLS BY BRANCH OF ACTIVITY AND LEVEL OF EDUCATION IN VARIOUS ECONOMIC SECTORS *(1949–1964)*

	Graduates 1949–1961 *(thousands)*	Graduates 1962–1964 *(thousands)*	Persons with Middle-Level Education 1964 *(thousands)*	Percent Increase Since 1958	Persons with Higher Education June 1964 *(thousands)*	Percent Increase Since 1958
Industry and mining	221.0	89.5	108	73.9	34	21.4
Construction	37.2	18.6	25	67.3	11	23.2
Transportation[a]	21.7	5.8	20	20.0	4	31.2
Trade	15.1	10.2	39	55.5	12	33.7
Agriculture	52.7[b]	36.9[b]	17	43.3	14	98.2

[a] Including telecommunications.
[b] Including forestry.

Sources: Dezvoltarea complexă și echilibrată a economiei naționale (Bucharest, 1965), p. 157; *Anuarul statistic al R.P.R. 1965*, pp. 470–471.

system, which permitted the Rumanian planners to double in the space of a few years the number of students registered in professional schools of agriculture and forestry — whose graduates helped to fill the gap in the cadres required for the collectivization of the farm sector and for the management of state farms a short while after the need was felt.

This flexibility goes far beyond technical education. Thanks to the industrial potential they have built up, the custodians of the Rumanian economy are now in a much better position than fifteen years ago to bring up lagging sectors and to mend the holes in the country's infrastructure.[197] This does not mean that industrialization *à outrance* has been the most judicious means of extricating Rumania from its state of economic backwardness. Other strategies, relying on a more balanced growth of agriculture, industry, and services, might have achieved a comparable growth of national income without compelling the population to forgo as much consumption as it did, at least in the early 1950's. Industrial development need not have been so capital

[197] How quickly some of these holes may be mended is illustrated by the target on transportation by motor vehicles in the plan for 1970. In terms of ton-kilometers, the share of such vehicles in total mechandise traffic will rise from 5.8 percent in 1965 to 37.9 percent in 1970 (*Viața economică*, No. 27 [July 8, 1961], p. 2). To achieve this goal, 2,900 kilometers of roads will be "modernized" for intense traffic and 5,000 kilometers will be asphalted for lighter traffic (*Scînteia* [July 1, 1966], p. 7). If these goals are realized, this will spell a substantial improvement in the country's transportation system.

intensive; more resources could have been spent to improve light industry — particularly food processing and furniture making — to make its products competitive on foreign markets. More could have been done to modernize agriculture and to reduce the gulf between the techniques used in this traditional sector and in the industrial enclave. The benefits of different policies might have been greater or better distributed in time. But it would be futile to deny that both the regime and the nation as a whole have quite a lot to show for their labors.

CHAPTER TWO

AGRICULTURE

Introduction

In 1965, agriculture still employed 56.5 percent of the total labor force of Rumania. Food sales, including public catering, made up about half of the total receipts of socialist trade. Over a third of all exports originated in the agricultural and forestry sectors.[1] This is sufficient evidence to justify a prominent position for agriculture in any survey of the Rumanian economy, even though the *relative* standing of the sector has been declining through time and stands to decline further as industrialization proceeds. It so happens, also, that published statistics are more abundant and more comprehensive here than elsewhere; because they cover, at least in part, both the inputs going into the sector and the outputs delivered to the rest of the economy, they provide more insight into the problems faced by the Rumanian planners than those of any other sector except foreign trade.

My plan in this chapter is first to trace the history of collectivization, then to describe trends in farm output — separately for crop and animal products — and compare achievements during the last decade with the targets set in the long-term plans for 1956–1960 and 1960–1965. Next I discuss trends in land and labor productivity and the sources of such increases in productivity as have occurred on the various types of farms. A section is given to a systematic description of farm marketings, both in the aggregate and in terms of individual crops. Finally, in the last section, I try to weld together the evidence from the previous sections to appraise the agricultural policy of the regime and to limn some likely prospects for the next few years.

First a few words may be interposed about the quality of the crop statistics for individual products. The information published by the Central Direction of Statistics on the farm output of different crops, cultivated acreage, animal herds, and animal products covers these subjects adequately. It is difficult to determine the precision of these

[1] *Anuarul statistic al Republicii Socialiste România 1966* (Bucharest, 1966), pp. 115, 443, and 472.

87

data, particularly of the harvest yields. We do know that sometime around 1958 the estimates of the corn harvests of 1954 and 1955 were scaled down by 17.5 and 20 percent, respectively, and that the same percentage reduction was applied to the yields of all categories of farms (state, cooperative, and private). If these adjustments had been due to a redefinition of output — for example, from biological to barn yields — based on data collected according to both the old and the new definition, the reductions would hardly have been proportional (harvesting losses do not represent the same percentage of total yields on state and on private farms). Furthermore, the 1955 estimate of the combined harvest of wheat and rye was also revised downwards — by 14 percent — but in this case only the yields of private farms were affected. This suggests again that no redefinition was involved, since a redefinition of yields would presumably have necessitated adjustment on state units and cooperatives as well as on private farms.[2] I suspect rather that the studies of peasant budgets and on-farm consumption that were made about this time showed that the quantities of produce retained by farmers for self-consumption and for cattle feed could not have been as large as they had been estimated by deducting the amounts marketed from the recorded harvest yields. The latter, therefore, had to be pared down.

According to a 1956 vade mecum for agricultural statisticians, barn yields were computed for the private sector from biological yields minus harvest losses; but the book does not make clear whether these barn yields were the estimates actually published. For the socialist sector, it states specifically that all agricultural plans and economic calculations are based on the recorded barn yields.[3]

In general, statistics of state procurement and of marketed output are much harder to come by than those of total yields. Here possible error stems not only from shortcomings in the original data but from difficulties in reconstructing the official estimates from percentages and from occasionally released absolute figures.

Agricultural Cooperation in Retrospect

In the immediate postwar period, the Communist Party of Rumania called for land reform, not for collectivization. In 1945, nearly 1.5

[2] M. Stancu, "Problema producţiei agricole marfă," *Probleme agricole*, No. 1 (1957), pp. 12–13. Central Direction of Statistics, *Dezvoltarea agriculturii R.P.R.* (Bucharest, 1961), pp. 185–186 (henceforth referred to as *Dezvoltarea agriculturii 1961*).

[3] E. Barat and M. Bulgaru, *Evidenţa şi statistica producţiei agricole vegetale* (Bucharest, 1956), p. 62.

million hectares of land, or about 10 percent of the total agricultural land area of the country, were confiscated from owners of estates and from farmers of German origin.[4] Of these, a little more than one million hectares were distributed to 918,000 farmers.[5] As a result of the reform, 400,000 new farms were created, and about 500,000 small holders added small parcels to their previous holdings. The breakup of estates and larger farms after World War II completed the work done in the land redistribution of 1917–1921 when 5.8 million hectares had been parceled out among 1.4 million farmers.[6]

The next step taken by the Party in waging the class struggle in the countryside was to "liquidate the kulaks as a class." This expendable class was made up of peasants who owned more land than average (usually over 15 hectares), hired labor, or rented out a part of their holdings. They were harassed by steeply progressive rates of compulsory deliveries and by other discriminatory measures.[7] While the taxes and compulsory deliveries imposed on the "medium" and "poor" peasants were relatively lighter than on the kulaks, they were also hard pressed to fulfill delivery quotas. As we already had occasion to remark in the first chapter, these exactions left the peasants little incentive to invest in and improve their farms. The threat of forced collectivization, when it finally materialized, was only the last in a series of onerous demands laid by the government on the rural population.

The "socialist transformation of agriculture" was not resolved until the Central Committee plenum of the Rumanian Workers' Party of March 3 to 5, 1949. By the end of 1950, 1,027 collectives (*cooperative agricole de producţie*, or C.A.P.),[8] had been formed, in most respects identical with Soviet artels. They grouped together 67,719 households occupying 288,900 hectares of land, or 2.6 percent of the country's total agricultural land area.[9] The opposition of the peasants, despite "long sieges laid against entire regions," proved too strong to pursue

---

[4] An average of only eleven hectares were confiscated per owner.

[5] *Agricultura Romîniei 1944–1964* (Bucharest, 1964), p. 25. In addition, in 1948 and 1949, some 940,000 hectares of agricultural land were confiscated from "kulaks" and former owners of estates, but these were turned over to state and collective farms rather than divided among the peasantry.

[6] S. Fischer-Galati, ed., *Romania* (New York, 1956), p. 203.

[7] For a schedule of surcharges on deliveries according to size of farm, see Fl. Balaure and C. Grigorescu, "Infăptuirea politicii P.M.R. de lichidare a chiaburimii ca clasă," *Probleme economice*, No. 7 (1961), p. 9.

[8] At first called *Gospodării agricole colective*, or G.A.C. The new name of the collectives has been used throughout this chapter.

[9] Institute of Economic Research of the Academy of R.P.R., *Economia Romîniei între anii 1944–1959* (Bucharest, 1959), p. 429 (cited henceforth as *Economia Romîniei 1944–1959*).

the campaign.[10] No progress was made toward collectivization during 1951. On September 18 of that year, the Central Committee of the Party decided to promote a looser form of collective, the agricultural association (intovărăşire), which was meant to serve as a transition to the higher stage of socialization represented by the C.A.P.[11] The members of these associations, similar to the Soviet T.O.Z. of the late 1920's, retained ownership in their land, animals, and equipment but worked a part or all of their arable land in common, usually with the aid of government-operated machine-tractor stations (M.T.S.). The remuneration of their members depended on the amount of land they contributed as well as on the labor they performed.

By the end of 1952, 1,834 associations occupying about 2 percent of the country's land area had been formed. In 1952 the creation of collectives was resumed, the number of families collectivized and their land area increasing threefold during the course of the year.[12] Various measures of discrimination against richer peasants ("kulaks") were also introduced. The Party Central Committee plenums of February, March, and May 1952 laid the blame for the failure to carry out the directives of 1949 on the Minister of Finance Vasile Luca, as well as on Politbureau member Ana Pauker and on T. Georgescu, who was at that time Minister of the Interior. The charges included various right-wing deviations, such as "softness" toward kulaks and toward peasants in arrears on their compulsory deliveries, but also bore down on the left-wing deviation consisting in the failure "to respect strictly the principle of free consent in attracting working peasants to socialism." [13] According to a recent source, Luca and Pauker had attacked the creation of the associations as a right-wing deviation and as a "danger for the future of socialism in the countryside." [14]

A New Course in the Party's economic policy was launched at the

[10] Ghita Ionescu, Communism in Rumania, 1944–1962 (London, New York, and Toronto: Oxford University Press, 1964), p. 200. According to Ionescu, "in the winter of 1949 and the spring of 1950 . . . the peasants fought pitched battles against the forces of the government."

[11] As late as the summer of 1952, after the campaign to form new associations had been started, there were only 800 of them, grouping 36,000 peasant families (V. A. Karra, Stroitel'stvo sotsialisticheskoi ekonomiki v Rumynskoi narodnoi Respubliki [Moscow, 1953], p. 174).

[12] Economia Rominiei 1944–1959, pp. 427–428.

[13] Economia Rominiei 1944–1959, p. 429. The plenum of February 29–March 1, 1952 noted that one million peasants had been exonerated from paying state taxes "without any justification whatsoever." It also castigated the Minister of Finance for setting the number of kulak households at 50–60,000 as against the estimate of 150,000 pronounced at the March 1949 plenum (Karra, op. cit., p. 172). Yet according to data published in later years, the number of kulak farms had fallen from 170,000 in 1948 to 103,700 in 1951 (Dezvoltarea agriculturii 1961, p 41)

[14] Probleme economice, No. 8 (1964), p. 67.

August 1953 plenum, shortly after the death of Stalin. Compulsory deliveries were reduced. The principle of free consent in collectivization was reaffirmed. In conjunction with the announced policy of containing rather than liquidating the kulaks as a class, the Party decided that it was "in the interest of the national economy that kulak farms should produce important quantities of agricultural products, that they should deliver quotas to the state, and that they should supply goods to the [free] market."[15] More resources were to be assigned to agriculture, including tractors, fertilizers, and building materials.

The measures of clemency introduced by the New Course resulted in a second slowdown in collectivization. In the first few months after the plenum the number of households in collectives and associations declined from 280,000 families in the spring of 1953 to 271,000 families at the end of the year.[16] This breathing spell lasted little more than a year. The Second Party Congress in December 1955 marked the end of the softer line on collectivization. Local Party organs were blamed for letting the socialist transformation of agriculture "take its own course." The Congress called for "an intensification of efforts" toward the goal of establishing socialist relations in the countryside. Slow but steady progress was made in the next two years, in contrast to the situation that prevailed in other East European countries where a large number of collectives were allowed to disband (as in Poland and Hungary) or where their number stagnated (as in Czechoslovakia). Nevertheless, by 1958 the collectives still held only 17.5 percent of the country's arable land. In that year a full-scale collectivization campaign got under way. Efforts were kept up until the formal completion of collectivization in April 1962.

Simultaneously, from 1958, pressure was applied on the associations to move up to a higher stage of cooperation — that is, to transform themselves into C.A.P.'s. Out of the combined acreages of arable lands under collectives and associations, 42 percent belonged to the full-fledged collectives and 58 percent to the associations in 1957; by 1960 the proportions were 62 and 38 percent. As can be seen from Table 2.1, the share of the associations dwindled to a negligible fraction in the next three years.

The agricultural state units (*unități agricole de stat*), whose share in the country's total arable land is shown in Table 2.1, are of two types: (1) the state farms proper (*gospodării agricole de stat*, or G.A.S.), and (2) other state agricultural units belonging to national committees (local

---

[15] Fl. Balaure and C. Grigorescu, *op. cit.*, p. 7.
[16] Karra, *op. cit.*, p. 176; and *Economia Romîniei 1944–1959*, *op. cit.*, p. 429.

TABLE 2.1. Percentage Distribution of Total Arable Land Area by Type of Farm (*1957–1965*)

End of Year	Private Farms	Associations	Collective Farms[a]	State Agricultural Units	
				Total	State Farms
1957	52.0	20.2	14.5	13.3	9.3
1958	44.7	24.3	17.5	13.5	10.4
1959	26.0	30.3	27.3	16.4	12.9
1960	15.7	25.3	41.8	17.2	13.7
1961	13.1	15.9	53.5	17.5	13.8
1962	3.5	1.5	77.4	17.6	13.9
1963	3.4	1.5	76.0[b]	19.1	15.3
1964	4.5	0.3	75.3	19.9	16.1
1965	4.6	0.1	75.3	20.0	16.6

[a] Including members' private plots.

[b] In 1963, 8.0 percent of the total arable land area was held by members of collective farms for their private use.

Sources: Anuarul statistic 1965, pp. 222–224; *Statistical Pocket Book of the Socialist Republic of Rumania, 1966*, p. 132.

soviets) as well as to industrial and transportation enterprises, which serve as auxiliary sources of supply for canteens or directly for the employees of these organizations.

Finally, Table 2.2 recapitulates the entire process of collectivization in terms of the numbers and percentages of peasant households in each category of farm (excepting the families of employees of state farms, who are considered as proletarians).

Table 2.3 traces the evolution of the collectivization campaign of 1958 to 1962 in the various regions of Rumania.

How are we to account for the substantial disparities among regions in the proportion of land collectivized at the outset of the campaign and in the pace of collectivization in subsequent years? The data of Table 2.3 suggest that the mountainous regions were fully collectivized later than the flat, cereal-growing districts of the country, where mechanization could be introduced most easily. It was Party policy "to give priority to the extension of machine-tractor stations (M.T.S.)[17] in zones in which soil, contours, and the specialization of crops permitted the most rapid introduction of mechanization." [18] The spread of the M.T.S. was of course bound up with the extension of the collectives. By 1959,

[17] Machine-tractor stations were not abolished in Rumania in 1958 as they were in the Soviet Union and are still in custody of all the tractors, combines, and other mechanical equipment servicing cooperatives.

[18] Institute of Economic Research of the Academy of R.P.R., *Probleme ale dezvoltării și consolidării agriculturii socialiste* (Bucharest, 1961), p. 608.

TABLE 2.2. NUMBERS AND PERCENTAGES OF HOUSEHOLDS ENGAGED IN
PRIVATE AND COOPERATIVE FARMING (*Thousands of
Households, 1950–1963*)

End of Year	Number of Private Farms	Percentage of All Peasant Households	Number of Households in Collective Farms	Percentage of All Peasant Households	Number of Households in Associations	Percentage of All Peasant Households
1950	3142	97.9	68	2.1	—	—
1951	3129	97.7	75	2.3	—	—
1952	2982	92.3	166	5.1	84	2.6
1953	2982	91.7	169	5.2	102	3.1
1954	2987	90.4	179	5.4	139	4.2
1955	2990	88.5	183	5.4	206	6.1
1956	2763	80.2	232	6.7	452	13.1
1957	2063	58.7	380	10.8	1074	30.5
1958	1716	47.9	469	13.1	1400	39.0
1959	987	27.4	851	23.6	1767	49.0
1960	716	19.4	1420	38.4	1564	42.3
1961	618	16.5	2051	54.7	1081	28.8
1962	263	6.9	3295	86.7	242	6.4
1963	265	6.9	3346	86.9	239	6.2
1964	450	14.1	3381	86.6	70	1.8

Note: The total numbers of households for 1961, 1962, 1963, and 1964 have
been estimated from the total for 1960 augmented by 50,000 per year, the average
rate of increase of previous years.

Sources: Dezvoltarea agriculturii R.P.R. 1961, p. 41; *Anuarul statistic al R.P.R. 1963,*
pp. 206–207; *Rumanian Statistical Pocket Book 1964,* p. 107; *Dezvoltarea agriculturii
Republicii Populare Române: Culegere de date statistice,* p. 39.

the four principal cereal-producing regions (Bucureşti, Dobrogea,
Galaţi, and Timişoara), which held 40 percent of the arable area, were
endowed with 68 percent of the M.T.S.'s tractors. The official Rumanian claim is that by the middle of 1960 most of the 680,000 households
still uncollectivized, which accounted for 1,800,000 hectares of land,
were to be found in mountain areas.

Another factor determining the relative progress of collectivization
may have been the proportion of minorities in each region. Between
1958 and 1960, collectivization proceeded more slowly in regions where
Hungarians and other minorities were heavily concentrated (for instance, Cluj, Crişana, Maramureş, and Mureş Hungarian Autonomous
Region). While these regions were also more mountainous than average, a detailed statistical analysis indicated that the minorities factor
exerted an independent effect on the uneven progress of collectivization.

The capacity of the machine-tractor stations to service the newly

TABLE 2.3. PERCENTAGE OF ARABLE LAND COLLECTIVIZED[a] IN EACH
REGION (*1958, 1960, 1962*)

Region	1958	1960	1962
Argeş	4.0	35.8	91.1
Bacău	3.4	12.3	95.2
Banat	42.3	76.4	89.2
Braşov	22.3	38.0	94.3
Bucureşti	16.0	94.5	99.9
Cluj	8.0	36.8	86.7
Crişana	8.4	28.9	88.5
Dobrogea	89.6	96.9	99.6
Galaţi	51.5	72.2	97.3
Hunedoara	6.5	32.7	73.6
Iaşi	8.3	38.3	99.6
Maramureş	9.4	34.6	86.9
Mureş Hungarian Autonomous Region	11.5	33.1	92.6
Oltenia	6.6	32.7	94.0
Ploieşti	6.6	18.9	94.1
Suceava	3.1	13.7	96.3
Total for Rumania	20.0	50.3	93.9

[a] Percentages based on total "collectivizable land," that is, excluding land held
by state units. The arable land of the collectives includes members' plots.
Source: Direcţia centrală de statistică, *Dezvoltarea agriculturii Republicii Populare
Române: Culegere de date statistice* (Bucharest, 1965), pp. 42–44.

formed collectives is an important indicator bearing on our assessment
of the success of the 1958–1962 collectivization campaign. A measure
of this capacity is given by the available statistics on the mechanization of farm tasks in collectives, as compared to state farms, in Table 2.4.

The statistics on the percentage of various tasks performed by
mechanized means on the state farms and on the collectives show a
remarkable stability during the collectivization drive. It would seem
that the equipment allotted each year to the M.T.S. was sufficient to
maintain about the same degree of mechanization on the enormous
new parcels collectivized during the year as on the already established
collectives. If so, this was a signal achievement.[19]

[19] This performance is not, on the face of it, entirely consistent with the estimates
on the arable area of collectives per M.T.S. tractor, which show a marked increase,
whereas the work performed per tractor was approximately stable. It is conceivable
that a moderate decrease in the degree of mechanization — perhaps of the order
of 15 to 20 percent — has been obscured by optimistic reporting of work performed
at the local level. Even this lag, given the rate of increase in the supply of tractors
to agriculture maintained in recent years, was probably bridged in 1963 or 1964
when the area under collectives increased much more slowly than in the recent
past (collectivization being virtually completed by that date).

TABLE 2.4. MECHANIZATION OF COLLECTIVE FARMS AND STATE FARMS (*1955, 1958, 1960, 1962*)

	1955	1958	1960	1962
Collective Farms				
Hectares of arable area in C.A.P. serviced per				
M.T.S. tractor (15 hp equivalent)	75	87	115	138
Percentage of area ploughed by tractor-drawn				
ploughs	85.8	87.4	85.9	85.8
Percentage of area sown mechanically	48.5	60.2	57.6	66.4
Percentage of harvested area harvested me-				
chanically (cereals only)	49.2	49.7	41.8	44.1
Average work performed per M.T.S. tractor				
(15 hp equivalent) in hectares per year	n.a.	240	243	249
State Farms				
Hectares of arable area per tractor (15 hp				
equivalent)	81	58	57	56
Percentage of area ploughed by tractor-drawn				
ploughs	96.0	98.0	98.9	99.8
Percentage of area sown mechanically	86.5	96.4	96.1	96.1
Percentage of harvested area harvested me-				
chanically (cereals)	86.0	91.6	95.3	98.7

Sources: Anuarul statistic 1963, pp. 206–207, 230–231; Direcţia centrală de statistică, *Dezvoltarea agriculturii R.P.R.: Culegere de date statistice* (Bucharest, 1965), pp. 73, 416–417.

Methods: To estimate the number of M.T.S. tractors servicing the C.A.P., the total number of M.T.S. tractors of 15 hp equivalent has been reduced in proportion to the share of all M.T.S. work (ploughing, sowing, harvesting, and so on) performed on behalf of the collectives (*Anuarul statistic 1963*, pp. 226–227). This proportion came to 60 percent in 1955, 86 percent in 1958, 90 percent in 1960, and 93.2 percent in 1962. Our independently calculated estimate of hectares of arable land per tractor (15 hp equivalent) on state farms nearly coincides with the official statistics in *Dezvoltarea agriculturii Republicii Populare Române: Culegere de date statistice* (Bucharest, 1965), p. 73.

As in the Soviet Union and elsewhere in Eastern Europe, the collective farmers were allowed to keep a small plot of land and a few domestic animals for their private use. The contribution of these plots to total farm output — shown in Table 2.5 — was vastly in excess of their share in the arable area of the collectives.

Between 1958 and 1962 there took place a significant increase in the size of the private plots and in their contribution to the output of plant products. This was offset, however, by a decline in the relative importance of animal herds still in the possession of C.A.P. members. What happened apparently is that the collectives bought up members' cattle with accumulated funds from their earnings and from state loans. In the years 1960–1962, they utilized loans amounting to 1.5

TABLE 2.5. PRIVATE PLOTS AND THEIR SHARE IN THE TOTAL OUTPUT OF
COLLECTIVE FARMS (C.A.P.)

	Total Arable Area of Private Plots (hectares)	Percent of Total Arable Area of C.A.P.[a]	Size of Plot per Family (hectares)	Percentage Share of Plots in C.A.P. Output[a] for		
				Cereals	Legumes	Potatoes and Vegetables
1955	31,900	3.9	0.17	3.3	5.4	27.8
1958	78,600	4.6	0.17	7.0	25.2	29.1
1960	276,000	7.4	0.19	6.3	6.4	39.8
1962	771,500	10.2	0.23	9.4	12.9	39.7
1964	788,800	10.7	0.23	9.8	12.9	36.6
1965	800,000	10.8	0.23	8.9	10.7	39.4

[a] Including the private plots.
Source: Anuarul statistic 1966, pp. 264, 285, 292–303.

billion lei — 65 percent of the credits they received from the state —
to build up their animal herds. In 1961 alone, they purchased 99,000
cows and heifers, 220,000 calves, 330,000 sheep, and 31,000 sows. Over
three quarters of these animals were bought with the help of state
credits. The plan for 1962, which was overfulfilled, called for purchases
on at least as large a scale.[20]

Prices paid to private farmers for the animals they owned in excess
of the maximum number they were permitted to keep as C.A.P. members — one cow, eight sheep, one sow, ten chickens — were reported
to be about as high as on the open market.[21]

Despite these transfers, the private plots continued to play an important role in meat and milk production. In 1964, for instance, the
meat output of C.A.P. members was 478,000 tons — 40 percent of
Rumania's total output — as against only 243,000 tons for the collectives themselves; milk output was 10.3 million hectoliters for members
— 39 percent of total output — versus 6.7 million hectoliters for the
collectives.[22]

All in all, the orderly and relatively mild character of the Rumanian
collectivization campaign of 1958 to 1962 contrasts happily with the
Soviet experience of the early 1930's and even with Rumania's earlier
attempts to dragoon farmers into collectives in the early 1950's. The

[20] *Probleme agricole*, No. 12 (1962), p. 20.
[21] Rumanian peasants I talked with in April 1962 confessed that they were not
happy about having had to join a collective but nevertheless conceded that they
had unloaded their "surplus" animals at favorable prices.
[22] Direcţia centrală de statistică, *Dezvoltarea agriculturii R.P.R.: Culegere de date
statistice* (Bucharest, 1965), pp. 519 and 523 (hereafter referred to as *Dezvoltarea
agriculturii 1965*).

facilities given to the C.A.P.'s to buy cattle from members, instead of confiscating it outright, helped to mollify recalcitrant joiners.[23] At the very least, this enlightened policy averted the mass slaughtering of members' cattle, which plagued the Soviet Union in the early 1930's.

Farm Output

The gross output of plant crops in Rumanian agriculture first recovered its 1938 level in 1953 and then oscillated around this mark for the next three years. This slow recovery is all the more remarkable when we consider that per-acre yields of staple crops in the 1930's were lower than they had been before World War I. (The wheat yield averaged 11 quintals per hectare from 1906 to 1910 and 9 quintals from 1933 to 1939; the respective averages for corn were 11.6 and 9.8 quintals.)[24] The gross output of animal products had nearly recovered its 1938 level in 1950–1951 but did not rise decisively beyond this mark until 1954. The stagnation of the intervening years apparently resulted from the disincentive effects of the government's repressive policy vis-à-vis the peasantry — the fear of collectivization, the steepness of compulsory deliveries of farm products to the state, and the low prices paid by the state for its procurements all tending to hold back farmers' investments in animal breeding. The manifest improvement in the next four years in both plant and animal output must be attributed at least in part to the beneficial influence of the New Course. Peasants were encouraged to farm their holdings more intensively as the immediate threat of collectivization receded, prices of products acquired by the government on contract were lifted,[25] and compulsory deliveries were reduced or abolished.

[23] According to Ionescu (*op. cit.*, p. 335), after 1958 "depression spread in the countryside where harassment and chicanery was the lot of each individual farmer visited by the hordes of activists, propagandists and controllers." However that may be, the absence of massive uprisings and the maintenance of the size of herds testify to the absence of desperation among farmers.

[24] Ministerul agriculturii şi silviculturii, *Dezvoltarea agriculturii în R.P.R.* (Bucharest, 1958), p. 21. The declines in yields have been attributed to the effects of the extensive land reform of the early 1920's. The undercapitalized farms created as a result of the reform could not fight land erosion; neither could they make use of improved seed imported from other regions nor, in general, carry on most of the capital-absorbing activities that the former landlords had deployed to maintain or increase yields. Another explanation of the decline in yields in the interwar period is that the acreage under crops was rapidly expanded, thus bringing marginal, low-yield lands into cultivation. (I am indebted to Dr. Harry Trend for this observation.)

[25] A measure of the rise in agricultural prices in 1953–1954 is given by the deflator of the net output of agriculture in the national income accounts. According to this index, as I was able to reconstruct it approximately, prices of agricultural products rose by over 70 percent from 1952 to 1954 (see Appendix B, Table B.7).

The recovery of net farm output lagged behind that of gross output throughout the postwar period. Since 1961 the spread between the two has been growing wider, as the increases in over-all farm output tapered off and material costs continued to rise. If we take four-year averages, we find that the net-output index grew by 10 percent and the gross-output index by 14 percent between 1955–1958 and 1959–1962. Between 1957–1960 and 1961–1964, the net index rose by only four percent, compared to a rise of 8.2 percent in gross output (Table 2.6).

Divergences can also be observed in the trends in crop and in animal production. The gross outputs of crop and animal products expanded by 5.5 percent and 13.7 percent, respectively, from 1957–1960 to 1961–1964. Since the consumption of fodder and litter, the principal material inputs into animal products, hardly increased between the two periods, one may assume that the net increases in animal production were at least as great as the gross. If this is correct, then it can be shown that the net output of crop products must have declined between the first and the second of these four-year periods.[26]

Finally, it is of some interest to note that gross animal production reached its record level in 1961. We shall have occasion to comment on the reasons for the decline that ensued when we come to discuss the fodder-supply situation.

From now on, due to the lack of detailed data on material expenditures by type of farms and by product, we shall be dealing almost exclusively with gross-output statistics, which, as we have just seen, make the over-all performance of the farm sector look better than it really was, taking into account rising outlays on material and capital inputs. The use of gross crop and animal production statistics is not so misleading, however, as it might appear at first glance. Most Rumanian farm products are easily exportable, whereas the inputs into agriculture may have relatively low opportunity costs in terms of foreign exchange. Thus Rumanian-made tractors and other farm implements,

[26] If we assume that all other material inputs but fodder and litter were used in crop production, then calculations based on Table 2.12 and on the original source from which this table was taken indicate that inputs into crop production went up by 30 percent between 1957–1960 and 1961–1964 (as against 14 percent for all material inputs including fodder). It may also be estimated that material expenditures were about 23 percent of crop output in the period 1957–1960. From these data and from the increase in crop output of 5.5 percent between the two four-year periods, we can infer that net crop output must have declined by 1 or 2 percent. Net animal output, on the other hand, must have risen a good deal more than by 13.7 percent. Note, however, that the gains in gross output of crop and animal products are sensitive to the benchmark years chosen. The rise in the gross output of crop products from 1958–1961 to 1962–1965 equaled 7.6 percent and that of animal products 6.2 percent.

TABLE 2.6. INDICES OF THE GROSS AND NET OUTPUT OF RUMANIAN AGRICULTURE, 1950, 1953–1965 (*1938 = 100*)

| Year | Gross Output | | | Net Output of Agriculture |
	Total	Crop	Animal	
1938	100.0	100.0	100.0	100.0
1950	74.0	65.1	94.4	70.2
1953	100.3	101.2	98.2	93.8
1954	101.5	97.8	110.1	90.3
1955	120.1	118.8	123.3	115.7
1956	96.8	88.6	115.8	79.8
1957	120.4	119.7	122.1	113.4
1958	104.1	95.0	125.2	94.0
1959	124.4	120.1	134.2	120.6
1960	126.2	118.2	144.5	120.6
1961	132.6	121.4	158.6	123.8
1962	121.5	110.4	146.9	110.0
1963	125.9	121.3	136.4	114.8
1964	134.1	124.7	156.0	119.0
1965	140	132	158	123.0[a]

[a] Estimate based on the increase from 1964 to 1965 in the net output of agriculture and forestry combined.

Note: The index of gross output is based on the evaluation of crops and annual production at 1955 current prices. For state agricultural units these prices are equal to delivery prices for marketed output and to production costs for production retained on the farm. For collectives and for the products of the private plots of their members, as well as for individual farms, the prices are the averages of the prices obtained for all output marketed (including compulsory deliveries, contracts, and the peasant market) weighted by the quantities sold on each market. The deductions from gross output to obtain net output include seed, chemical fertilizers, insecticides, fuels and lubricants, current repairs to agricultural equipment and structures, amortization of fixed funds, animal feed and litters, eggs for incubation, medicine, and administrative costs. (Central Direction of Statistics, *Studii de statistică: Lucrările consfătuirii științifice de statistică*, November 27–29, 1961 [Bucharest, 1962], pp. 305–306.) The U.S. Department of Agriculture has constructed an independent index of Rumanian gross agricultural output from production statistics for crop and livestock products, weighted in terms of 1957–1959 average West European producer or wholesale prices. This index, based on an average of 1957–1959, diverges from the Rumanian index by less than one percent for 1963, 1964, and 1965 (see U.S. Department of Agriculture, Economic Research Service, *The USSR and Eastern Europe Agricultural Situation* [Washington, D. C., 1966], p. 2).

Sources: Dezvoltarea agriculturii R.P.R. 1965, pp. 563, 574–575; *Statistical Pocket Book 1966*, p. 182.

whose depreciation enters into material costs, may have a limited market abroad, at least over and above certain quotas. This is all the more true of the labor and materials that went into the repairs and maintenance costs on this equipment, which amounted to about 5 percent of total material costs. One could also argue that hay and other similar fodder cannot easily be exported, so that increasing expenditures on this account would have hardly any impact on the net contribution of the sector to foreign trade.

We can gain some insight into the growth of the farm sector by disaggregating the gross output series in Table 2.6 according to the main categories of produce and according to the contributions of the main types of farms. Data relating to the former are contained in Table 2.7.

TABLE 2.7. INDICES OF GROSS OUTPUT OF CHIEF GROUPS OF CROP AND ANIMAL PRODUCTS, 1938, 1950, 1953, 1955, 1958, 1960, 1962, 1964 (*1938* = *100*)

	1950	1953	1955	1958	1960	1962	1964
Crop Production							
Grain cereals	57	94	116	83	114	110	131
Textile plants	195	375	212	114	129	121	91
Oil-bearing plants	106	189	156	170	314	220	260
Industrial crops[a]	135	261	359	346	484	394	642
Potatoes and vegetables	151	224	232	221	256	216	233
Fodder crops	64	86	95	95	187	178	204
Grapes and vines	58	61	99	104	78	93	81
Fruits	28	53	65	69	62	52	49
Animal Products							
Beef	114	113	133	141	156	154	156
Pork	66	76	123	96	115	126	143
Cow's milk	102	101	122	134	163	159	151
Wool	103	123	137	129	144	159	163
Eggs	81	103	114	148	174	190	181

[a] Chiefly sugar beet and tobacco.

Sources and methods: Data for 1938 to 1960 are from *Dezvoltarea agriculturii 1961*, pp. 358 and 363; data for 1962 and 1964 were computed from the indices of gross output for plant and animal products and from the composition of output in these groups in respective years in *Dezvoltarea agriculturii R.P.R. 1965*, pp. 518, 563, and 569.

It should first be observed that the increases in crop output recorded in Table 2.7 were not accomplished through any extension of total acreage. In contrast to the prewar period when acreage expanded rapidly, the total area under crops rose only from 9.4 million hectares in 1938 to 9.8 million hectares in 1964. For some crops, gains in output resulted from improved yields, for others from increases in sown area pre-empted from other crops. Grains belong to the first category. (Due mainly to a sharp curtailment in the cultivation of oats and barley, the area under grain crops actually shrank by 18 percent between

1938 and 1964.) On the other hand, the area sown to oil-bearing plants, consisting mainly of sunflowers, grew fourfold and that under vegetables and fodder crops more than doubled: constant or declining yields per hectare characterized this group of crops.

The sharp fluctuations in the harvests of textile crops were entirely due to the vicissitudes of cotton production. The planting of cotton, virtually an unknown crop in the 1930's, was pushed vigorously in the late 1940's and early 1950's; then, from 1954 on, this very expensive autarkic policy was gradually abandoned. Plantings were cut back drastically between 1954 and 1958. By 1964 the area under cotton had been reduced to a surface even smaller than that which it had occupied before World War II.

The drop in the output of vineyards was caused by a collapse in yields during the war and its aftermath; after some improvement in the mid-1950's, yields deteriorated again in the 1960's.

The striking regression in fruit crops apparently resulted from the combined effect of fewer trees and lower yields per tree. (Most of the damage was done before 1948; it was slowly repaired in the 1950's. As in the case of grapes, retrogression set in anew around 1959.)[27]

The output of animal products generally surpassed the growth of herds, with the exception of pork, whose average yield per animal was depressed by a disproportionate increase in the number of piglets and young hogs. The 50 percent increase in pork output (liveweight plus slaughterings) between 1958 and 1964 was in marked contrast with the virtual stagnation of beef production in this period. The disparity in the two trends may be attributed in large part to the reduced demand for draft oxen, due to the spreading mechanization of farm work. The number of these animals fell by nearly two thirds between the two dates. However, one would have expected the number of cows, heifers, and calves to rise *pari passu* with the decline in the number of draft animals as the barn space, straw, and fodder formerly assigned to the latter became available. There was indeed a moderate increase in the number of calves, but this was offset by a gradual diminution in the number of cows in more recent years (between January 1961 and January 1965).

Two broad conclusions flow from this analysis of output trends. The first is that crops serving as inputs for industry, such as sunflowers and sugar beets, have undergone an enormous extension since before the war. They have made their contribution to the improvement in the balance of payments, at first by replacing imports and, in more recent years, by generating surpluses for export. The second is that the output

[27] See *Dezvoltarea agriculturii 1965*, pp. 378–385, 399–401.

of agricultural products requiring a long production cycle — fruits, grapes, and beef — has lagged seriously behind that of short-cycle products like annual crops, pork, and eggs, particularly in the last decade. An identical phenomenon would have been observed in a free market system, *ceteris paribus*, if the interest rates paid by farmers on bank credits had risen steeply. In the Rumanian context, the shortening of the average production cycle of farm produce, which seems especially marked since the onset of the last collectivization campaign, may represent the farmers' response to the increased risk and uncertainty of tying up resources in slow-maturing investments (for example, in fruit trees, vineyards, and large-horned cattle).[28]

Although the (gross) output gains registered in the last decade do not compare unfavorably with the mediocre performance of the farm sector in other socialist countries (and in quite a few capitalist countries as well), one cannot gloss over the fact that the progress made fell far short of plans. In 1960 and again in 1965 the harvest of most crops and the output of animal products failed to come within striking distance of the targets set for these terminal years for the Five-Year Plan and the Six-Year Plan, respectively (as can be seen in Table 2.8).

These shortfalls from targets, as we shall see in greater detail in the last section of this chapter, had serious consequences for foreign trade, and also, due to the necessity of fulfilling export obligations for corn that had been contracted on the basis of excessively optimistic forecasts, had adverse effects on animal husbandry, the fodder base for which depends in large part on the availability of coarse grains.

The responsibility for the shortfalls can be laid, for the most part, on the excessive optimism of the planners. Even if the industrial inputs earmarked for the farm sector had actually been supplied, their effect on output could not have been as great as had been foreseen. The "socialization of agriculture" must have been expected to exert a favorable impact on output by virtue of its inherent superiority. This superiority did not materialize. It would have been helpful, of course, if the inputs assigned to agriculture had been delivered on schedule. It was too early at the time of writing to lay bare all the shortcomings in this domain. We know for sure, however, that the supply of ferti-

---

[28] Notice that the decline in yields per fruit tree may have been caused by the neglect to maintain old investments (for example, the failure to prune or to graft trees). Higher risk may affect output long before the full production cycle of bringing trees from saplings to maturity has run its course.

It cannot be argued that the fears and apprehensions of individual farmers became irrelevant after collectivization had taken over most of the privately held land, inasmuch as a majority of domestic animals and fruit trees, and about a third of the country's vines, remained in private possession throughout the campaign.

TABLE 2.8. TARGETS AND ACHIEVEMENTS IN THE SECOND FIVE-YEAR PLAN AND IN THE SIX-YEAR PLAN

	Targeted in the Five-Year Plan 1960	Actual 1960	Targeted in the Six-Year Plan 1965	Actual 1965
Total production of cereals (millions of tons)	15.0	9.8[a]	n.a.	12.6[b]
Wheat and rye	5.5	3.6[a]	5.0–5.4	6.1[b]
Corn	8.0–9.0	5.5[a]	8.0–9.0	5.9[b]
Potatoes	n.a.	3.0[a]	4.5–5.0	2.2[b]
Vegetables	n.a.	1.8[a]	3.3	1.7[b]
Index of the gross output of agriculture (year preceding onset of plan = 100)	n.a.	105	170–180	113
Meat output (liveweight, millions of tons)	1.3	.97	1.7–1.8	1.1
Cow's milk output[c] (millions of hectoliters)	25	22.9	50[d]	26.0[d]

[a] 1960–1961 averages in millions of tons: cereals 10.2, wheat-rye 3.8, corn 5.6, potatoes 2.9, vegetables 1.8.

[b] 1964–1965 averages in million of tons: cereals 11.9, wheat-rye 5.0, corn 6.3, potatoes 2.7, vegetables 1.7.

[c] Excluding milk drunk by calves.

[d] Includes sheep and goat's milk.

Sources: For data on the Second Five-Year Plan: Ministerul agriculturii şi silviculturii, *Dezvoltarea agriculturii în R.P.R.* (Bucharest, 1958), pp. 322–323; on the Six-Year Plan: M. Levente, E. Barat, and M. Bulgaru, *Analiza statistico-economică a agriculturii* (Bucharest, 1961), pp. 258–260. Actual production data are from *Dezvoltarea aariculturii: Culegere de date statistice* (Bucharest, 1965), pp. 314, 322, 518, and 563; *Statistical Pocket Book 1966*, pp. 161, 181–182.

lizers and the irrigation program lagged seriously behind plan: the output of mineral fertilizers reached 293,000 tons by 1965, compared to a plan target of half a million tons (expressed in mineral nutrients). The irrigated area extended over only 230,000 hectares in 1965 — when 800,000 hectares were supposed to be ready for irrigation by this date.[29] Finally, the supply of machinery available to state and collective farms — including tractors, sowers, and combines — also lagged behind schedule, and labor was tied up in manual operations when it could have been released to tend cattle or to "intensify" crop production.

[29] Plan data are contained in Levente, Barat, and Bulgaru, *op. cit.*, pp. 256–257. The actual surface prepared for irrigation is from *Anuarul statistic al Republicii Socialiste România 1966*, p. 233.

Inputs, Outputs, and Efficiency

In this section we shall study the relation between the output of agricultural products and key inputs, including land, labor, and fertilizers. To begin with, we shall endeavor to find out whether factor productivity was seriously influenced by the institutional transformation associated with collectivization. We can reconstruct statistics measuring the changes in productivity per hectare for each type of farm over time, as well as the relative yields of the different farms in

TABLE 2.9. PERCENTAGE SHARES OF STATE AGRICULTURAL UNITS, AGRICULTURAL COOPERATIVES, ASSOCIATIONS, PERSONAL HOLDINGS OF COOPERATIVE MEMBERS, AND INDIVIDUAL FARMS IN CROP AND ANIMAL OUTPUT (*1950, 1953, 1955, 1958, 1960, 1962, 1964*)

	1950	1953	1955	1958	1960	1962	1964
	Crop Output						
State agricultural units	8.8	13.2	12.4	12.7	16.5	19.6	20.0
State farms	5.7	5.8	5.8	8.8	12.3	16.0	18.0
Agricultural cooperatives (C.A.P.)	0.5	6.9	6.6	12.9	28.4	60.2	60.9
Associations	—	2.0	3.0	15.5	26.4	0.8	1.2
Personal holdings of C.A.P. members	0.1	0.6	0.7	1.9	4.7	14.8	13.6
Individual farms	90.6	77.3	77.3	57.0	24.0	4.6	4.3
Total	100.0	100.0	100.0	100.0	100.0	100.0	100.0
	Animal Output						
State agricultural units	6.0	10.7	7.1	8.7	10.6	14.9	18.6
State farms	2.7	3.8	2.4	6.2	9.5	13.5	16.9
Agricultural cooperatives	0.2	1.0	1.4	3.0	9.3	19.5	19.5
Associations	—	—	—	0.2	0.4	0.2	0.1
Personal holdings of C.A.P. members	0.1	3.8	4.3	9.7	22.8	45.3	46.2
Individual farms	93.7	84.5	87.2	78.4	56.9	20.1	15.6
Total	100.0	100.0	100.0	100.0	100.0	100.0	100.0

Source: Dezvoltarea agriculturii R.P.R. 1965, pp. 566–567.

terms of gross output per unit of land area. The data in Table 2.9 constitute the basis for these calculations.

From these statistics and from gross output trends for crop and animal production we can construct indices of output for the different types of farms. By dividing the resulting relatives by an index of the arable area under each type of farm we obtain an index of the output per unit of area. The results are reproduced in Table 2.10.

TABLE 2.10. Trends in Productivity per Unit of Area on Different Types of Farms (*1953* = *100*)

	1955	1958	1960	1962	1964
Index of gross crop output (all farms)	117.5	94.9	116.9	109.1	123.2
State agricultural units					
Index of gross output	110.3	91.3	146.0	162.0	186.6
Index of arable area	96.2	95.8	122.8	127.0	142.0
Index of productivity per unit of area	114.7	95.3	118.9	127.6	131.4
State farms					
Index of gross crop output	117.5	178.2	247.9	301.0	382.3
Index of productivity per unit of area	88.9	115.7	122.2	144.5	159.4
Agricultural cooperatives					
Index of gross crop output	112.4	177.2	481.2	951.8	1,087.4
Index of arable area	109.0	233.3	547.8	989.5	947.1
Index of productivity per unit of area	103.1	76.0	87.8	96.2	114.8
Private plots of C.A.P. members					
Index of gross crop output	137.1	300.8	915.3	2,694.8	2,791.6
Index of arable area	113.9	280.7	985.7	2755.3	2817.2
Index of productivity per unit of area	120.0	107.2	92.8	97.8	99.1
Private farms					
Index of gross crop output	117.5	69.9	36.2	6.5	6.9
Index of arable area	100.4	61.2	21.7	4.8	6.2
Index of productivity per unit of area	117.0	114.2	166.8	135.4	111.3

Source: Computed from percentage shares and indices in *Dezvoltarea agriculturii R.P.R.: Culegere de date statistice* (Bucharest, 1965), pp. 100–103, 563, and 566–571.

Alternatively, we may consider all farms excepting the state agricultural units as one group and construct a productivity index for this aggregate. Between 1958 and 1964, the crucial years of the final collectivization campaign, productivity per unit of area rose by 27.2 percent for this entire group (including the agricultural associations omitted from Table 2.10). If, instead, we compare two-year averages — 1963–1964 with 1957–1958 — the productivity improvement is reduced to 7.5 percent.

Before commenting on these trends, something must be said about the *relative* productivity per unit of area of the different types of farms, which may be evaluated by comparing their share in output with their share in the country's arable area. Collective farms, for example, contributed 12.9 percent of crop output in 1958, with 16.7 percent of the arable area, and 61 percent of crop output in 1964, with 67 percent of the area, from which we may infer that the value of output per acre was smaller than average in both years, but more so in the former than in the latter — a relative improvement of some significance. In the early 1960's, the private plots of C.A.P. members and individual farms produced 14 to 15 percent of plant output with 8 percent of the arable area. Individual farms were also more productive than average in most years. Their share in output was 57 percent in 1958 with 45 percent of the arable area; in 1963 and 1964, however, their relative superiority had been virtually wiped out. (They held about 4 percent of the arable area, mainly in mountainous regions, and contributed about the same proportion of output.) State farms, whose productivity per acre had been below average until 1961, could boast of slightly larger shares of total output than of total arable area after 1962.

The lower than average productivity per unit of area of the collective farms may appear surprising in view of the fact that yields per hectare for the great majority of crops — both in the nation as a whole and in individual regions — were higher on the collectives than on private farms and on the plots of C.A.P. members. Thus the yield of wheat, measured in quintals per hectare, was 13.5 in 1960 on the collectives and 8.6 on individual farms and private plots combined (for Rumania as a whole). For corn the yields were 15.2 and 10.1 quintals per hectare, respectively. The apparent contradiction is resolved when we consider that the collectives allotted a smaller proportion of their arable area to the more valuable, labor-intensive crops than did the private sector. In 1960, for instance, the C.A.P.'s allotted 2.7 percent of their arable area to potatoes and vegetables, as against 13.2 percent for the private farms and C.A.P. members' plots combined.[30]

Differences in the availability of labor in the several types of farms help to explain disparities in productivity per unit of area, although one may question whether the published statistics covering the distribution of the labor force among the various farm types are accurate enough to support any firm conclusions, at least for the years when the agricultural associations still played a major intermediate role in the process of collectivization. It is hard to believe, for instance, that in 1958 the members of these associations could have made up 36 percent of the total agricultural labor force and yet have contributed only 15.5 percent of crop output.[31] According to this method of reckoning, all other types of farms contributed more to crop output than their share in the labor force. At that time the collectives comprised 9 per-

[30] *Dezvoltarea agriculturii 1965*, pp. 197–198.

[31] *Ibid.*, pp. 81 and 567. Since the statistics on employment are estimated at the end of the year, I have used means of successive years to represent average employment during the course of each year.

cent of the labor force in agriculture but were responsible for 14.8 percent of the crop output including that from members' plots;[32] the contribution of private farms to crop output was 57 percent, with 51 percent of the labor force. If we assume, however, that statistical errors may have arisen in determining the relative share of private farms and associations in the labor force, we may combine the two. We then find that with 88 percent of the labor force they supplied only 73 percent of output. It is more than likely that this relative inferiority of private farms and associations can be explained by their higher than average ratio of labor to land and by their low degree of "capitalization" when compared to state farms and collectives.

Turning back to the statistics of Table 2.10, we observe that if the collectives' gross productivity per hectare had not improved markedly from 1958 to 1964, collectivization would have had a very deleterious effect on output. This follows from the lower productivity per acre of the C.A.P.'s compared to private farms at the inception of the campaign and from their increased share in the total arable area in the following years. Of course, what facilitated this improvement was that the labor-to-land ratio increased in the course of the transformation of agriculture — from 0.61 able-bodied collective farmers per hectare in 1959 to 0.79 in 1964 — as the more densely settled private farms were incorporated into the collectivized sector.

On the other hand, the increased labor-to-land ratio, in the absence of vigorous technical progress or of increased supplies of other co-operant factors to offset this change in factor proportions, might have been expected to cause a decline in labor productivity on the collectives. In point of fact, productivity per "participant in collective work" did fall by roughly 8 percent between 1956–1957 and 1958–1959.[33] Computed per collective farmer of working age productivity again slipped by at least 5 percent from 1959–1960 to 1961–1962. After these initial reverses, labor productivity rose again sharply after 1962. It is alleged to have increased by 20.4 percent from 1962 to 1964 and by another 8 percent from 1964 to 1965.[34] In any case, labor productivity on the collective farms probably did not decline to the level of private farms and associations combined. We can infer this from the fact that

[32] There is, of course, no way to divide up the labor force on the C.A.P.'s between private plots and collectivized land. The breakdown of the agricultural labor force on which the C.A.P.'s share is based is contained in *Dezvoltarea agriculturii 1965*, p. 81. The farm labor force in question comprises the personnel of M.T.S., which, however, represented less than 0.5 percent of the total.

[33] *Dezvoltarea agriculturii 1961*, p. 335.

[34] The decline from 1959–1960 to 1961–1962 is inferred from data in *Dezvoltarea agriculturii 1965*, pp. 554, 563, and 565. For the period 1962 to 1965, the data are from *Probleme economice*, No. 5 (1966), p. 22.

gross crop output on all farms except state holdings increased by almost 5 percent from 1955–1958 to 1961–1964 despite a drop of at least 10 percent in the labor force on these farms.

All available data on labor productivity are expressed in terms of output per man-year. The possibility must be kept in mind, however, that as the number of persons on the farm declined, those who remained may have been induced to work a greater number of days. We may conjecture that this was the case from a recent analysis of the number of work days performed in different regions of the country. Compared to a national average of 131 work days per year, peasants contributed an average of 200 work days per year to the collective farms of the Banat and Brașov regions in 1964. These two regions are relatively industrialized and have the lowest density of agricultural population per 100 hectares of agricultural area of the country. In Argeș, Iași, Oltenia, and Suceava, less industrialized areas with an above-average density of agricultural population, peasants labored an average of 117 work days per year. As industrialization proceeded, the average number of days worked per year probably went up in conformance with the interregional pattern.[35] (The great differences in the number of days worked on the collective farms among regions suggests that there is still a good deal of underemployed labor left in the poorer regions, which can eventually be tapped for the needs of industry and other sectors.)

So far, in seeking to explain observable differences in the productivity per acre of collective and private farms, we have taken into account only one complementary factor of production, namely labor. Yet productivity must have been influenced by other forces affecting differences in yields both among farm types and through time, if we consider that average crop productivity per acre on all farms outside the state sector rose by 5 or 6 percent between 1955–1958 and 1961–1964, even though, as we mentioned before, their labor force went down by at least 10 percent.

The answer must be sought either in changes in the supply of other complementary inputs or in improvements in "total factor productivity" due to technical progress or greater efficiency. Could changes in the supply of fixed capital have brought about the improvement in

[35] Work days, like the Soviet *Trudodni*, are calculated from the calendar days actually worked by collective farm members by weighting them according to the relative importance of the work done and/or by the qualifications of the individual concerned. In Rumania, according to an official interviewed in 1962, the work day is said to come very close, on the average, to an actual calendar day. The data in the text are from the important article by C. Grigorescu, "Rolul utilizării forței de muncă în repartizarea teritorială a industriei," *Probleme economice*, No. 10 (1966), pp. 37 and 45.

labor productivity? From the end of 1957 to the end of 1962, the gross fixed assets of agriculture and forestry rose by only 13 percent. Most, if not all, of this increase must have been vested in the state farms, whose assets approximately doubled during this period. This relatively small increase in total agricultural capital is consistent with the rapid progress made toward the mechanization of basic farm tasks, since tractors, combines, and other farm implements displaced work animals, the value of which must have represented an important part of the assets of private farms. Because this intracapital substitution was labor saving, it may have helped to raise labor productivity on the private and collective farm sectors, irrespective of its effect on the net total supply of capital.

Another factor to consider would be fertilizers, which, under favorable circumstances, may exert a decisive impact on yields per acre. If we looked only at the supply of mineral fertilizers, we might be satisfied with the conclusion that this was one of the causes of the rise in over-all yields as well as of the disparity in yields among farms. But a simultaneous examination of the situation with respect to organic (natural) fertilizers leads to a radically different appraisal (see Table 2.11).

TABLE 2.11. Organic and Mineral Fertilizers Used on State Farms, Collectives, and All Other Farms (*1958, 1960, 1962, and 1964*)

	1958	1960	1962	1964
State Farms				
Organic fertilizers (thousands of tons)	1,657	2,300	2,401	2,992
Per hectare of arable land (kilograms)	1,765	1,745	1,779	1,951
Mineral fertilizers (thousands of tons)	92	238	279	427
Per hectare of arable land (kilograms)	98	180	207	278
Collective Farms (C.A.P.)				
Organic fertilizers (thousands of tons)	3,248	8,400	11,165	11,132
Per hectare of arable land (kilograms)	2,144	2,803	1,592	1,609
Mineral fertilizers (thousands of tons)	24	96	122	280
Per hectare of arable land (kilograms)	16	32	17	41
All Other Farms[a]				
Organic fertilizers (thousands of tons)	28,126	22,400	5,285	7,800
Per hectare of arable land (kilograms)	3,800	4,800	3,210	4,780
Mineral fertilizers (thousands of tons)	56	36	20	36
Per hectare of arable land (kilograms)	8	10	12	22

[a] Individual farms, state agricultural units not organized under "Gostat," private plots of C.A.P. members, associations.

Source: Dezvoltarea agriculturii R.P.R.: Culegere de date statistice (Bucharest, 1965), pp. 416–417.

The total use of organic fertilizers by all farms declined drastically — from a peak of 33 million tons in 1958 to 22 million tons in 1964. Until 1962, private farms used about twice as much natural fertilizer per hectare as did collective farms; thereafter the transformation of private into collective farms failed to raise the average application of natural fertilizers on the collectives, which, if anything, applied them even more sparingly than before.

We can form an approximate notion of the total supply of all fertilizers by converting natural fertilizers into artificial-fertilizer equivalents, using the ratio of 35 to 40 kilograms of the former to 1 kilogram of the latter, as suggested in several Rumanian sources.[36] From this calculation we learn that the aggregate supply of plant nutrients on all farms dropped from the equivalent of 1.2–1.3 million tons of mineral fertilizers in 1958 to 0.9–1.0 million tons in 1962; it then went up again to 1.3–1.4 million tons in 1964, surpassing the level prior to the great collectivization drive of 1959–1960. Because of the highly uneven distribution of mineral fertilizers — the state farms getting far more than their proportionate share of the total amount available — the combined supply of organic and mineral fertilizers on private and collective farms failed to recover the 1958 levels after the initial decline of 1960 and 1962. (Their supply equaled 900,000–1,000,000 tons in 1958, 550,000–600,000 tons in 1962, and 800,000–850,000 tons in 1964.)

During the entire period 1958 to 1964 the aggregate supply of fertilizers was highest on state farms and lowest on collectives. In 1958, the state farms applied the equivalent of 140–150 kilograms of mineral fertilizers per hectare, the collectives 70–75 kilograms, and all other farms (chiefly private holdings and associations) 100–110 kilograms. In 1962, the respective figures were 250–255 kilograms on state farms, 57–62 kilograms on the C.A.P., and 90–100 kilograms on all others.

We conclude, therefore, that changes in the total supply of fertilizers cannot explain why average productivity per hectare rose on private and collective lands combined, in spite of declining labor inputs.

Without being able to measure their differential impact on yields, I can cite four more or less quantifiable factors that must to some extent have contributed to the rise in productivity:

1. The quality of seeds planted was improved systematically after 1958. Out of the total area sown with corn, for example, hybrid varieties occupied 20 per cent in 1960, 40 percent in 1962, and 100 percent

---

[36] See, in particular, *Probleme ale dezvoltării și consolidării agriculturii socialiste* (Institutul de cercetări economice Academia R.P.R., Bucharest, 1960), p. 310 (referred to henceforth as *Probleme ale dezvoltării*).

in 1964; by 1963 all wheat planted was said to be from improved seeds.[37]

2. The total area prepared for irrigation doubled from 1958 to 1964, reaching 213,800 hectares in 1964, or 2.2 percent of the arable area of the country.[38] Since over half of this irrigable surface was planted with vegetables, rice, and other high-yield crops, its contribution to gross output must have been greater than its share in the total arable area would indicate.

3. Work on soil conservation, particularly to combat the effects of soil erosion, was greatly intensified after 1958. From 13,100 hectares in 1958, the surface on which conservations measures were undertaken increased to 165,600 hectares in 1964.[39]

4. Deep ploughing on certain types of soils in dry areas may have contributed to raise yields or at least to reduce fluctuations from year to year (37.4 percent of the total arable area of the country was ploughed by tractor-drawn ploughs in 1958 and 84.6 percent in 1964).[40]

My guess would be that the provision of better seed had a greater effect on raising yields than the other three sources of improvement cited.

Finally, I cannot omit to mention the possibility that gross crop output per unit of area may have been raised partly at the expense of animal yields, which have shown if anything a tendency to regress in recent years. As a result of collectivization, it is likely that some labor that had formerly been expended on the care of animals was switched to work on crops.

We can compute animal productivity by the same method as we used in the case of crop output, except for one additional difficulty: we have no way of aggregating our inputs — animals — into a simple measure with which to compare our outputs (as we compared total crop output to arable area). We must therefore match trends in output with the separate trends in the stocks of the various types of animals contributing to output, as I shall now illustrate. From 1958 to 1964, the total animal output of collective farms rose an estimated 8.1 times; the value of cow's milk produced rose 16.2 times, of beef (liveweight) 7.6 times, sheep and goat's milk 3.8 times, sheep and goat meat 4.2 times, pork 7.1 times, wool 5.2 times, and eggs 18.4 times. During this same period the collectives' holdings of cows and heifers increased

[37] *Agricultura Romîniei 1944–1964* (Bucharest, 1964), p. 147; and *Dezvoltarea economică a Romîniei 1944–1964* (Bucharest, 1964), p. 479.

[38] *Dezvoltarea agriculturii 1965*, p. 413.

[39] *Ibid.*

[40] *Ibid.*, pp. 563, 566, 572, 573.

18.1 times, all large-horned cattle 17.4 times, hogs 11 times, sheep 5.3 times, and poultry 18.6 times.[41] It is manifest that productivity for all the types of farm animals listed, with the exception of poultry where it remained constant, must have declined. This deterioration can also be measured in physical terms. For example, the collectives' milk production per cow, one of the key indexes of productivity in the animal sector, fell off from 1,360 liters in 1958–1959 to 1,220 liters in 1964–1965.[42]

One cannot even argue that productivity diminished because the low-productivity collectivized sector absorbed animals from the high-productivity private sector, inasmuch as the differences in productivity per animal between the two sectors were small or nonexistent in 1958 and actually developed during the course of collectivization.

The mediocre results obtained in animal breeding can be attributed in part to the shortage of fodder, a problem that will be studied in the last section of this chapter. But it was also due to the inadequate provision of barns and other structures in the C.A.P.'s, as well as to insufficient expenditure of labor on the care of the animals (which may in turn be explained by the lack of incentives to breed animals, given the relative prices of animal and plant products competing for resources on the farm).

The effects of collectivization on the performance of the farm sector may be summarized in the following points. Productivity in terms of gross crop output per unit of area was lower to begin with on collectives than on individual farms. This inferiority can be attributed only partly to lower labor inputs per hectare. Thanks to the provision of better seed, to increased supplies of mineral fertilizers, to deeper ploughing, and to various other improvements, the deterioration in output that might have taken place as a result of the "socialization" of the higher productivity sector was averted. The rapid expansion of production and the rise in productivity per hectare on the state farms helped to raise the value of gross output of the entire farm sector in the early 1960's decisively above precollectivization levels. Over-all performance in crop output would have been better if a sharp reduction had not occurred in the application of organic fertilizers, espe-

[41] *Ibid.*, pp. 428–429. The herds are evaluated at the beginning of the year in the source. To obtain midyear averages, I have taken the means of two successive years.

[42] Note that the indexes used were based on the value of these products, but virtually the same results are obtained from indexes based on quantities produced. This coincidence may be due to the fact that the gross output computations are themselves built up from physical series that do not take fully into account quality differences within given product categories (for example, milk of varying fat content, meat from animals of different weights and ages, and so on).

cially to soils planted with cereals. Since animal herds increased during the period, the potential supply of these fertilizers should not have declined. It is probable that collectivization as such, or apprehensions of it, affected the use — or nonuse — of this valuable resource.

In general, animal breeding fared worse than crop output. While the size of herds continued to expand (with the exception of cows, which numbered less in 1965 then in 1958), this increase was accomplished largely by reducing the slaughter of young animals. The yearly increment in weight of animals must have been a good deal less than satisfactory. In the light of these considerations, one may question whether the most judicious use of resources consisted in building up herds at the expense of productivity per animal.

For an over-all appraisal of the relative performances of the private, collective, and state sectors, we ought to analyze trends in *net* output for each type of farm. To do this we should have detailed information on all inputs, not only labor and land but also expenditures on materials and depreciation. It is regrettable that the only indexes of material expenditures published refer to Rumanian agriculture as a whole and conceal the disparities in the structure and the level of material inputs consumed by the highly capitalized state farms and by other farms.[43] Nevertheless, some useful observations may be culled from these official data (see Table 2.12).

TABLE 2.12. INDEXES OF MATERIAL EXPENDITURES IN RUMANIAN AGRICULTURE (*1953 = 100*)

	1950	1955	1958	1960	1962	1963	1964
Total material expenditures	72.4	114.8	109.3	122.1	127.0	130.5	144.2
Seed	82.8	101.7	92.1	104.9	93.2	98.3	99.8
Fodder and litter	68.3	114.8	102.5	109.1	110.4	105.9	123.6
Fertilizers (mineral)	82.4	120.0	150.2	169.4	139.8	198.4	187.8
Fuels and lubricants	53.0	153.5	189.6	238.7	276.1	326.1	345.7
Current repairs	75.6	141.4	135.3	137.7	209.9	199.7	172.0
Depreciation of fixed funds	89.3	118.2	131.3	153.1	162.8	181.7	181.4
Chemical products	78.9	193.1	235.3	235.3	349.4	328.3	473.4

Source: Dezvoltarea agriculturii R.P.R.: Culegere de date statistice (Bucharest, 1965), pp. 574–575.

The fast-rising items of expenditure during the last decade were fertilizers, fuels, repairs, depreciation, and chemicals. Together these five

[43] In 1964, for example, 52.4 percent of the material costs of state farms consisted of inputs from the industrial sector, as against only 33.1 percent for Rumanian agriculture as a whole (*Dezvoltarea complexă . . .* , *op. cit.,* p. 70).

inputs rose by 40 percent compared to 19 percent for fodder and seed. Outlays on fertilizers increased from 3.5 percent of total expenditures in 1953 to 4.6 percent in 1964, fuels and lubricants from 1.5 to 3.5 percent, repairs from 3.6 to 4.3 percent, depreciation from 10.5 to 13.2 percent, and chemical products from 0.5 to 1.5 percent. These five inputs still amounted to only 27.1 percent in 1964, as against 56.8 percent for fodder and litter alone.[44] It is remarkable that the inputs whose relative importance increased were all of industrial provenance, while fodder and seeds produced within the farm sector declined relatively. In this connection one should note that the fast-growing expenditures on fuels, repairs, and depreciation arising from the use of M.T.S. machinery ought to be subtracted from the gross output of the collective farms, since the M.T.S. worked chiefly for the latter. (In 1958, when the collectives covered 27 percent of the total arable land excluding state agricultural units, 63 percent of the work executed by the M.T.S. — measured in area ploughed, sown, cultivated, or harvested — was carried out for the benefit of the collectives.)[45] We can surmise that a comparison of the productivity per acre of the private and collectivized farms in terms of *net* output must have been even less favorable to the latter than comparisons based on *gross* output, if depreciation on the capital of the machine-tractor stations was added to the material costs of collective farms.

Farm Output and Marketings

For a country like Rumania, where the necessity of industrialization takes precedence over all other economic goals, agriculture may be treated as an intermediate sector receiving industrial and other inputs from the outside and delivering produce to other sectors. (Some of the industrial inputs may be directly productive, such as fertilizers; others may be consumed by the farm population but may stimulate output through their incentive effects on the labor force.) Viewed from this vantage point, it should be the object of government policy, within a given political context defining the minimum tolerable consumption of the peasantry, to allocate industrial inputs to agriculture up to the point where the last unit allotted makes a contribution to marketings equal to its cost.

The state in Soviet-type economies, through its monopsonistic position as sole central buyer of farm produce, is able to manipulate the terms of trade between industrial and agricultural products. However,

---

[44] *Dezvoltarea agriculturii 1965*, pp. 574–575.
[45] *Dezvoltarea agriculturii 1965*, p. 549.

if the authorities are mindful of the positive incentive effects of allowing peasants to keep a greater part of their output or to sell it at advantageous terms on the free market, they should not try to extract too high a proportion of output by compulsory deliveries or by "acquisitions" at lower than free market prices. In the short run, of course, they may be impelled to squeeze more than the optimal quantities in order to meet export commitments, or for other pressing reasons. Indeed, such immediate considerations must have played a role in the decision taken by the Rumanian government in the 1960's to step up procurements in the face of slowly rising output.

In Rumania, the marketing of agricultural products is carried out either by state agencies or directly through sale on the "unorganized" or "peasant" market. Produce bought or collected by the state enters the "state fund," which draws on four principal sources of procurement: (1) collections from state farms and other "state units," (2) compulsory deliveries from private and cooperative farms, (3) acquisitions and contracts, and (4) payments in kind by individual farmers and cooperatives to machine-tractor stations, flour mills, and other state-run agencies. The second have greatly diminished in importance since 1953, when quotas were reduced, and 1956, when they were abolished for all products except meat and wool. The third type of procurement refers to sales by private and cooperative farms to the state, which in principle are voluntary.[46]

A portion of the state fund is redistributed to the farm sector in the form of seeds, fodder, and other agricultural inputs. Little information is available on this feedback, all procurement statistics being expressed in terms of gross rather than net produce.

In Table 2.13 and in the discussion that follows, I have tried to separate the output and the marketings of state units from the rest of the farm sector in order to get a sharper picture of the impact of state procurement policies on the private and cooperative sectors. The inclusion of the capital-intensive, dynamic state sector, which sells a much higher proportion of its output to the state than does any other type of farm, would otherwise tend to distort the analysis of these policies.[47]

[46] "Acquisitions" are purchases made on the spot; "contracts" for future delivery at predetermined prices are settled a season or more in advance of delivery by the producer.

[47] From 1959 to 1963, for example, the state farms marketed produce valued at 4,776 million lei out of a gross output of 6,704 million lei (*Agricultura Romîniei 1944–1964* [Bucharest, 1964], p. 269). The ratio of these two magnitudes — 71.3 percent — may be compared with the corresponding ratio for private and cooperative farms, estimated at 36 percent in 1959 and 52 percent in 1964 (Table 2.13). The procurement-to-output ratio for all farms, including state units, would be approximately 40 percent in 1959 and 57 percent in 1964.

TABLE 2.13. Selected Indexes of Output and Marketings of Private and Cooperative Farm Sectors (*Comparable Prices*)

	1955	1958	1959	1960	1962	1963	1964
Gross agricultural output (private and cooperative farms)	100	86.1	102.1	100.7	93.1	96.1	100.7
Peasants' consumption in kind	100	n.a.	92.8	n.a.	98.0	93.8	n.a.
Total procurements from private and cooperative farms	100	121.3	134.9	150.1	170.6	176.8	191.1
Share of procurements to gross output (private and cooperative farms)	27	38	36	41	50	51	52
Share of private and cooperative farms in total procurements	86	84	80	79	77	76	75
Total procurements from all farms	100	124.8	145.8	164.6	192.5	200.0	220.9
Crop products	100	129.7	155.8	175.7	199.0	217.6	233.1
Animal products	100	183.0	195.3	212.3	287.2	295.0	344.1
Animals	100	97.2	112.5	130.4	150.2	139.1	159.3

Sources and methods: Gross agricultural output: computed from data on total agricultural output and on the share of all farms, excluding state units, in these totals in *Dezvoltarea agriculturii R.P.R.: Culegere de date statistice* (Bucharest, 1965), pp. 576–577; peasants' consumption in kind: data in current prices may be estimated from the percentage breakdown of the consumption fund in S. Ţaigar, *Veniturile populaţiei şi nivelul de trai în R.P.R.* (Bucharest, 1964), p. 86; and *Dezvoltarea complexă şi echilibrată a economiei naţionale* (Bucharest, 1965), p. 37. The current prices in which consumption in kind is expressed are a weighted average of prices paid by the state for its procurements and of peasant market prices (*Studii de statistică: Lucrările celei de-a treia consfătuiri ştiinţifice de statistică, 5–7 December 1963* [Bucharest, 1964], p. 706). An index of these prices, derived from national income data in Appendix B, Table B.7, was used to deflate consumption in current prices. Procurements from private and cooperative farms: The share of state units in total procurements of individual crops is given in *Dezvoltarea agriculturii 1965*, pp. 583–589; an average share for 1959 was calculated by weighting the shares for individual crops by their proportion in gross output (*ibid.*, p. 567). The resulting aggregate shares of state units in total state procurements were 20.6 percent for crop products and 18.8 percent for animal products. The over-all share was exactly 20 percent. Trends in total procurements from all farms and in procurements from state units being available (*Dezvoltarea agriculturii 1965*, p. 576), an index of procurements from all but state units was easily computed with the aid of the 1959 proportion. Share of procurements to gross output: Data on the average gross output and marketings of state farms from 1959 to 1963 are given in *Agricultura României 1944–1964* (Bucharest, 1964), p. 264. An index of marketings of state farms in *Revista de statistică*, No. 6 (1963), p. 7, yielded marketings in individual years. Total gross output from all farms was obtained from the gross value of output of cooperative farms in 1962 (*Probleme economice*, No. 12 [1966], p. 95) and from their share in the total gross output of all farms in *Dezvoltarea agriculturii 1965*, p. 567. Total procurements from all state units were calculated from procurements from state farms alone on the assumption that the procurements-to-output ratio for state units was 97 percent of that for state farms alone, the average obtained from a comparison of the ratio pertaining to the two types of farms for wheat, corn, meat, milk, and wool. Total procurements from all farms were then computed by dividing procurements from state units by 0.2, the share of these units in total procurements estimated above. Procurements from state units sub-

The data in Table 2.13 show that procurements by the state from the private and cooperative sectors rose much faster than their output (which stagnated), so much so in fact that the ratio of procurements to output nearly doubled from 1955 to 1964. Nevertheless, the share of private and cooperative farms in total procurements fell because procurements from state farms rose still faster than those from all other sectors.

State procurements from private and collective farms rose at the expense of peasants' consumption in kind, sales on the peasant market, and output retained for productive uses. Since the state collected into the fund and then redistributed appreciable amounts of seed and fodder, the net volume of agricultural produce remaining at the disposal of the agricultural sector was larger than the residual obtained by subtracting total procurements from total output. Very rough calculations indicate that these feedbacks may have amounted in 1963 to as much as 2 billion lei at 1955 prices. The value of "other disposals," after taking redistributions into account, is calculated in the following table.[48]

OUTPUT AND DISPOSALS OF FARM PRODUCTS BY PRIVATE AND
COLLECTIVE FARMS
(Billions of Lei at 1955 Prices)

	1955	1959	1962	1963
State procurements	11	15	19	20
Other disposals	30	27	20	21
Total disposals	41	42	39	41
Minus redistributions from the state fund (for seed and fodder)	—	−0.3	−1	−2
Gross output	41	42	38	39

[48] Data on procurements and output are derived from the same sources and by the methods used for Table B.13. "Other disposals" include consumption in kind, sales on the peasant market, and output retained for productive uses (by private and collective farms). The estimate of redistributions from the state fund in 1963 is based on the assumption that the state sold about 0.5 to 0.7 billion lei of hybrid seeds to farmers, 0.5 to 0.8 billion lei of corn for fodder, and 0.5 to 1 billion lei of

(footnote continued on p. 118)

tracted from total procurements yielded procurements by private and cooperative farms in 1959. Once a ratio of procurements to output had been calculated for private and cooperative farms in one year, the indices of gross output and procurements for these farms made it possible to arrive at the ratios for all other years. Procurements from all farms by types of products collected: *Dezvoltarea agriculturii 1965*, p. 576.

Between 1955 and 1962–1963 peasants' consumption declined by about 5 percent (Table B.13) and the output retained by private collective farms for productive uses probably fell by less than 10 percent.[49] The brunt of the contraction in "other disposals" must have fallen on peasant market sales.

Since the statistics available on peasant market sales in current prices do not reveal any marked decline,[50] our inference of a steep drop in their physical volume leads to the conclusion that prices on the peasant market must have risen a great deal — even more than the index of average farm prices calculated in Table B.7 of the Appendix.[51]

As we have already observed, only a moderate decline set in after 1955 in the volume of produce retained on the farm for productive purposes, thanks in part to redistributions from the state fund. Hybrid seed acquired more widespread use during the period under study; this seed must have been sold, lent, or given out of the state fund, mainly to state and collective farms, thus freeing farmers from the necessity of holding back a part of their crop for seeding. Similarly, the state distributed concentrated feeds — often in exchange for produce — as an incentive for peasants to sell their animals for slaughter. These feeds would otherwise have had to be grown and retained on the farm. In spite of this greater degree of specialization, we still find

---

byproducts of the food-processing industry for fodder, including bran and molasses (see *Lupta de clasă*, No. 5 [1965], p. 34, and *Probleme economice*, No. 12 [1960], p. 80).

[49] The trend in output retained for productive uses by all farms can be inferred from indices of seed and fodder expenditures in *Dezvoltarea agriculturii 1965*, pp. 574–575. Seed expenditures went down by 5 percent and fodder by 6 percent from 1955 to 1962–1963 (averaged). Note that the choice of 1955 as a base year, which happens to be convenient owing to the availability of data for that year, gives an unjustifiably poor image of trends in output and consumption since that date. In interpreting these trends, one should remember that the gross output of 1955 was nearly 20 percent above the level of 1954 and 25 percent above that of 1956.

[50] Peasant market sales were officially estimated at about 7.4 billion lei in 1959, 6.5 billion in 1962, and between 6 and 7 billion lei in 1963. These estimates were reconstructed from the proportion they bore to socialist retail trade in Țaigar, *op. cit.*, p. 86, and *Dezvoltarea complexă și echilibrată a economiei naționale* (Bucharest, 1965), p. 37. See also *Probleme economice*, No. 8 (1964), p. 138.

[51] There is also a strong possibility that the Central Direction of Statistics has incorrectly estimated peasant market sales in the different years. The value of sales in the official sample, based on 59 urban centers, represented only 16 percent of the total value of peasant market sales as estimated from the balance of the supply and disposals of agricultural products in an unspecified but apparently fairly recent year (S. Bugeanu and A. Făinaru, "Probleme metodologice privind observarea statistică a pieței țărănești," in *Studii de statistică: Lucrările celei de-a treia consfătuiri științifice de statistică, 5–7 Decembrie 1963* [Bucharest, 1964], p. 627). From this same source, it is apparent that the evaluations made from the sample, due in part to the omission of a number of products sold intermittently whose aggregate importance is appreciable, are difficult to reconcile with the data derived from the agricultural balances.

that total farm expenses for seed, reckoned in fixed prices, never regained their 1955 level from 1956 to 1964 — fluctuating at a level 5 to 10 percent below that peak — and that outlays for fodder and litter, which represented two thirds of total material expenses in 1955, were a few percent below their 1954–1955 levels in 1958 and 1959, and again in 1962 and 1963.[52] How little seed and fodder must have been retained in the regions where they were produced if this reduction in net supplies occurred, notwithstanding the government's redistributions![53]

Four factors must have contributed to the steep increase in the "marketability" of Rumanian agriculture during the period of collectivization: (1) the collectives, by virtue of their relatively greater labor productivity, needed to retain a smaller proportion of their output for the purpose of feeding their members;[54] (2) a successful campaign was launched to sow technical crops — mainly sunflowers and sugar beets — the bulk of which was sold to the state; (3) the exodus from rural areas reduced the need for consumption in kind; (4) collective farms consumed relatively more off-farm inputs — the services of M.T.S. tractors, fodder bought from the state, gasoline for trucks, and so on — than private farms, and were therefore impelled to market a greater share of their produce; and (5) peasants acquired an increasing share of their food consumption from rural state and cooperative shops.

We shall now move to a lower level of aggregation and consider the marketing of the individual crops that played a preponderant role in production, consumption, and foreign trade.

The statistics in Table 2.14 reveal that state procurements did not begin to outstrip production until after the inception of the final collectivization drive; from that point on, however, the pressure on deliveries intensified rapidly. That these differential trends could not have been due to random harvest fluctuations can be shown by comparing successive pairs of years, thus ironing out the greater part of these fluctuations. In the case of grains, for instance, the average of the 1960 and 1961 harvests exceeded 1958–1959 output by 7 percent for wheat and by 15 percent for corn, while procurements in 1960–1961 were, respectively, 26 and 89 percent higher than in 1958–1959. Again in 1962–1963 the wheat and corn harvests were 2 and 5 percent greater

---

[52] See Table 2.12.

[53] Note that while the total number of large-horned cattle was about the same in 1955 and 1962–1963, the size of other animal herds — hogs, sheep, and goats — had increased, thus putting even more pressure on the diminished supply of fodder in the trough years.

[54] Note that produce distributed in kind to members is not counted as part of marketed production (*Revista de statistică*, No. 10 [1961], p. 7).

TABLE 2.14. Trends in Output, Deliveries to State Fund, and Marketings of Wheat-Rye, Corn, Legumes, Sunflowers, Sugar Beets, and Potatoes in 1955, 1958–1964 (*Indices, 1959 = 100*)

	1955–1956	1958	1959	1960	1961	1962	1963	1964
Wheat-Rye								
Total harvest (average)	70.1	73.6	100	86.0	99.2	100.0	93.9	94.8
Deliveries to state fund	78.1	79.4	100	106.8	119.5	137.2	133.6	139.6
Total marketed	n.a.	n.a.	100	105.6	105.1	n.a.	n.a.	126.7
Sold on peasant market	n.a.	n.a.	100	n.a.	n.a.	103.5	n.a.	n.a.
Corn								
Total harvest	86.3	64.4	100	97.4	101.0	86.8	106.0	117.8
Deliveries to state fund	104.5	86.7	100	167.6	184.6	199.6	274.9	234.9
Total marketed	n.a.	n.a.	100	145.4	141.1	n.a.	n.a.	219.7
Sold on peasant market	n.a.	n.a.	100	n.a.	n.a.	85.0	n.a.	n.a.
Legumes								
Total harvest	128.8	82.3	100	162.7	156.2	139.7	141.6	117.9
Deliveries to state fund	511.0	165.8	100	200.0	329.2	348.4	475.2	452.8
Sunflowers								
Total harvest	47.3	54.1	100	98.6	91.0	84.9	95.6	97.9
Deliveries to state fund	52.4	50.5	100	126.8	123.3	120.4	133.3	136.0
Sugar Beets								
Total harvest	51.1	50.3	100	98.6	84.5	63.3	66.7	106.4
Deliveries to state fund	49.2	49.0	100	110.1	95.8	68.5	75.6	113.6
Total marketings	n.a.	n.a.	100	110.1	n.a.	n.a.	n.a.	75.6
Potatoes								
Total harvest	91.2	95.9	100	103.9	99.3	89.7	92.9	90.4
Deliveries to state fund	104.1	120.6	100	115.1	135.1	127.1	156.0	166.6
Sales on peasant market	n.a.	n.a.	100	n.a.	n.a.	91.0	n.a.	n.a.

Sources: Dezvoltarea agriculturii R.P.R.: Culegere de date statistice (Bucharest, 1965), pp. 304–323 and 578; *Probleme economice*, No. 11 (1963), p. 78; M. Levente, E. Barat, and M. Bulgaru, *Analiza statistico-economică a agriculturii* (Bucharest, 1961), p. 19; *Dezvoltarea complexă și echilibrată a economiei naționale* (Bucharest, 1965), p. 71; *Probleme ale creării și dezvoltării bazei tehnice-materiale a socialismului în R.P.R.* (Bucharest, 1963), p. 25.

than in 1960–1961, whereas collections were 19 and 34 percent higher. The share of the output of legumes (chiefly peas and dried beans) supplied to the state seems to have dropped appreciably from 1955–1956 to 1958–1959 and then to have risen again, as it did for the other crops shown in the table (sunflowers, sugar beets, and potatoes).

Even though our data on total marketings, including both state procurements and sales on the peasant market, are less complete, they still suggest that the stagnation or decline in peasant market sales offset only partially the trends in procurements (with the exception of sugar beets and possibly of potatoes). The official estimates for 1964 show that total marketings of wheat, including sales to the peasant market, were almost 27 percent higher than in 1959, compared to a 5 percent decrease in the harvest; the corresponding increase in corn marketings was 120 percent over the five-year period, compared to an 18 percent rise in the harvest.[55]

An examination of grain output and procurements in absolute quantities (see Table 2.15) shows that the effects of the pressure on procurements were not as drastic as the differential trends might suggest.

What happened, essentially, was that the state bought up, or collected through the collectives' payments in kind to the machine-tractor stations, little more than the *increments* in the harvests of wheat and corn, leaving private and collective farms only slightly reduced supplies for human consumption. The reduction in the volume of wheat and rye left to private and state farms — from an average of about 2 million tons in 1958–1959 to 1.6 million tons in 1963–1964 — was also mitigated by the decline in the farm population.

In 1962, however, combined supplies of wheat and corn left on the farm must have fallen below minimum safety levels. There was not enough grain in the villages to meet the demand for bread, which had to be informally rationed.[56] The shortage of corn was serious enough to cause an absolute drop in the output of meat in 1962–1963. That procurements were not scaled down in the face of these difficulties may be explained by the necessity of meeting export commitments "at any cost." (As it was, the government had to dip into state reserves in order to make good on its export obligations.)[57]

Even in a good year like 1964, the amount of corn left for animal fodder and for human consumption on private and collective farms — together estimated at 4 million tons — was much below that anticipated for the end of the Six-Year Plan. Since human consumption on the farm must have amounted to a minimum of 500,000 tons, at most 3.5 million tons were left for animal fodder.[58] According to one Rumanian agricultural economist writing in 1960, the amount of corn fed to

[55] By 1963, the peasant market accounted for less than 5 percent of wheat and corn marketings. An order of magnitude for 1959 would be 10 percent for wheat and 12–15 percent for corn.

[56] In April 1962 I saw many peasants on the road and in the outskirts of Rumanian cities returning to their villages with bags of bread bought in urban bakeries. It is said that in some localities bread could be purchased only with tickets, but I had no direct evidence of this.

[57] Interview material.

[58] This assumes (1) that all the corn seed used was delivered from the state fund, and (2) that sales on the free market approximately offset redistributions of corn from the state fund for fodder uses.

TABLE 2.15. PROCUREMENTS AND RESIDUALS OF WHEAT-RYE AND CORN IN STATE AGRICULTURAL UNITS AND ALL OTHER FARMS (*Thousands of Tons*)

	1955–1956	1958	1959	1960	1961	1962	1963	1964
Wheat-Rye								
Total harvest	2,896	3,037	4,129	3,553	4,095	4,129	3,877	3,916
State agricultural units	280	444	637	745	820	952	747	958
All other farms	2,616	2,593	3,492	2,808	3,275	3,177	3,130	2,958
Total state procurements	1,247	1,268	1,596	1,704	1,908	2,190	2,134	2,228
State agricultural units	182	372	560	636	695	863	636	838
All other farms	1,065	896	1,036	1,068	1,213	1,327	1,498	1,390
Residual left to all but state units	1,551	1,697	2,456	1,740	2,062	1,850	1,633	1,568
Percentage ratio of state procurements to harvest								
All farms	43.1	41.7	38.7	48.0	46.6	53.0	55.0	56.9
All but state units	40.7	34.6	29.7	38.1	37.0	41.8	47.8	46.9
Corn								
Total harvest	4,904	3,657	5,680	5,531	5,740	4,932	6,023	6,692
State agricultural units	296	367	567	694	822	779	1,341	1,420
All other farms	4,608	3,290	5,113	4,837	4,918	4,153	4,682	5,272
Total state procurements	811	673	776	1,300	1,433	1,552	2,132	1,820
State agricultural units	5	11	104	296	339	299	646	520
All other farms	806	662	672	1,004	1,094	1,253	1,486	1,300
Residual left to all but state units	3,802	2,628	4,441	3,833	3,824	2,900	3,196	3,972
Ratio of procurements to harvest								
All farms	16.5	17.4	13.7	23.5	25.0	31.5	35.4	27.2
All but state units	17.5	20.1	13.1	20.8	22.2	30.2	31.7	24.7

Sources and methods: Crop outputs are from *Dezvoltarea agriculturii 1965*, pp. 304–322. Procurements of wheat and rye: Deliveries of state farms (G.A.S.) in 1955 are given in *Economia Romîniei 1944–1959* (Bucharest, 1959), p. 413; the percentage of G.A.S. in total deliveries in that year was 12.5 percent (*Probleme ale dezvoltării și consolidării agriculturii socialiste* [Bucharest, 1960], p. 29). The ratio of these two figures yielded total procurements in 1955. Data for all other years are based on the indices and percentage shares in *Dezvoltarea agriculturii R.P.R.* (Bucharest, 1965), pp. 579 and 583. Procurements of corn: Total G.A.S. deliveries to the state fund between 1959 and 1963 are given in *Agricultura Romîniei 1944–1964* (Bucharest, 1964), p. 269. From the percentages of G.A.S. in total deliveries for each year and the index of total deliveries from 1959 to 1963, it is possible by elementary algebra to estimate the actual volume of deliveries in every year.

animals in the form of grain was to reach 7.8–8.3 million tons by 1965, or more than twice as much as I have estimated for 1964.[59] To make matters worse, the crop of corn harvested green for silo, which was slated to contribute as much nutritive substance ("feed units") as corn harvested in the form of grain, came to only 5.3 million tons in 1964, an eighth or less of the 42–48 million tons targeted for the end of the plan period.[60] The fact that less than 500,000 hectares were sown with corn for silo in 1964 (compared to a target of 1.2 million hectares), while the acreage of corn harvested for grain was larger than plan, indicates that the fodder-expansion program was sacrificed to help meet minimum requirements for marketed grains — for export and for urban consumption.[61]

The data in Table 2.15 cast light not only on the fodder problem but on the role played by the various types of farms in increasing marketings faster than output.

According to my computations, state agricultural units contributed 36 percent and 41 percent of the increments in wheat and corn procurements, respectively, between 1958–1959 and 1963–1964. The share of state units in total wheat procurements rose from about 15 percent in 1955–1956 to 31 percent in 1958–1959; it finally reached 37 percent between 1961 and 1964. Their share of corn procurements was negligible up to 1958; in 1959, a year of intense collectivization, it rose to 13.4 percent; by 1963–1964 state units were delivering about a third of total procurements of this coarse grain. Their very substantial if not decisive contribution to increased marketings of grain can be traced partly to increases in the acreage under wheat and corn and partly to higher yields, caused in turn by wider use of hybrid seeds and by relatively lavish applications of mineral fertilizers.[62]

Nevertheless, farms outside the state sector also increased the share of their grain output after the onset of the final collectivization cam-

---

[59] S. Stoian, "Creşterea producţiei de cereale — temelia dezvoltării agriculturii şi a îmbunătăţirii aprovizionării populaţiei," *Probleme economice*, No. 12 (1960), p. 80.

[60] Corn harvested both for grain and for silo represents about 50 percent of the fodder base. Sugar beets, sunflower seeds, potatoes, hay, bran from milled grains, and natural pastures make up most of the rest. There is evidence that the quantities of sugar beets and sunflowers left to farmers were reduced after 1960. Moreover, according to a Rumanian informant, the transfer of cattle into the dry plain areas of the south, away from the pasture lands of the more mountainous regions, led to a poorer utilization of natural supplies. Hay and natural pastures contributed about 18 percent of the available nutrients in 1962 (*Probleme economice*, No. 12 [1963], p. 59).

[61] The target for sowings is from Stoian, *op. cit.*, p. 81. The actual average sown in 1964 is given in *Dezvoltarea agriculturii 1965*, p. 191.

[62] State agricultural units delivered an average of 8.8 quintals of wheat per hectare sown between 1955 and 1958 and 16.8 quintals between 1961 and 1964.

paign. With respect to wheat, the procurement-to-output ratio of private and collective farms at first dropped from 40.7 percent in 1955–1956 to 32 percent in 1958–1959, then approximately recovered in the next two years, and finally by 1962, surpassed precollectivization levels, reaching 47 percent in 1963–1964. For corn, it rose from an average of 18 percent for 1958–1960 to nearly 29 percent for 1962–1964.

In view of the deterioration in the fodder base, the successful pressure on farms to market a greater proportion of their produce was a mixed blessing. One may speculate, however, that in face of the failure of grain output to rise according to plan, there was no other choice open to the government but to extract as much as possible from the newly formed collectives in order to meet its most urgent needs.

The adverse consequences of this policy were twofold. On the one hand, the size of herds grew much less than had been contemplated when the Six-Year Plan had been framed: the number of cows and heifers declined steadily after 1960, and only the number of piglets and young hogs fattened for slaughter showed any substantial increase. (The 1965 targets for the size of herds were missed by a wide margin. In January of that year the census tally for large-horned cattle was 4,935,000, compared to a target of 5.8 million, with the entire shortfall accounted for by the stagnation of cow herds. The number of hogs reached 5.4 million, or 2.1 million short of target.)[63] On the other hand, the increase in the liveweight of herds, as officially estimated, was exceedingly small; it was never large enough to permit an increase in marketings after 1960, the first year of the plan. The central fund, as can be seen in Table 2.16, grew only at the expense of the peasant market, whose share in total marketings went down from 10–15 percent in the early 1960's to a negligible fraction by 1964.

The increase in deliveries to the central fund, such as it was, came entirely from state agricultural units, whose share in the fund rose from 12 percent in 1955–1956 to 34 percent in 1963–1964. Deliveries by all other farms stagnated after 1958. If we add to the deliveries of the "other farms" our estimates of free markets sales (on the assumption that the state farms sold virtually all their marketable output to the state), we come to the conclusion that marketings from farms outside the state sector must have dropped appreciably, from perhaps 460,000–480,000 tons in 1959–1960 to 360,000 tons in 1964.

The data on slaughterings released for the first time in 1966 allow us to gauge the effects of the fodder crises following the crops harvested

---

[63] The plan figures are from Levente, Barat, and Bulgaru, *op. cit.*, p. 260; the actual estimates of the size of herds are from *Dezvoltarea agriculturii 1965*, p. 426. There was a decline of nearly 700,000 hogs from January 1965 to January 1966.

TABLE 2.16. Livestock Numbers, Meat Production, Slaughterings, Marketings, Deliveries to the State Fund, Procurements by the Meat Industry, Industrial Meat Output, and Retail Sales, 1955, 1958, 1960, 1962–1965 (*Thousands of Animals for Livestock Numbers and Thousands of Tons for All Output Data*)

	1955	1958	1960	1962	1963	1964	1965
Livestock numbers							
Large-horned cattle	4,715	4,432	4,490	4,636	4,601	4,696	4,845
Pigs	4,660	3,628	4,300	4,591	4,588	5,346	5,699
Meat production (offspring plus increase in weight of herds)	886	852	969	1,036	910	1,102	1,116
Slaughterings for consumption (liveweight)	787	839	943	1,068	841	984	1,047
Meat marketings (liveweight)	n.a.	567[a]	601	677	n.a.	554	n.a.
Deliveries to central fund (liveweight)	440	462	542	567	501	551	n.a.
Meat procurement by food industry (liveweight)	461	458	527	520	n.a.	549	n.a.
Industrial meat output[b]	221	226	270	297	265	284	308
Retail sales of meat in socialist trade	96	127	139	144	134	146	157

[a] 1959.

[b] Not including lard.

Methods: The average quantity of meat marketed for the years 1957 to 1961 was computed from data on the share of marketings to total meat output in *Probleme economice*, No. 4 (1964), p. 108. Index numbers of meat marketed for 1959 to 1961 were published in M. Levente, E. Barat, and M. Bulgaru, *Analiza statistico-economică a agriculturii* (Bucharest, 1961), p. 19; and in *Probleme ale creării și dezvoltării bazei tehnice-materiale a socialismului în R.P.R.* (Bucharest, 1963), p. 251. The links for 1957 and 1958 were estimated from changes in the total fund in these years. From these data, it was possible to deduce the approximate estimates of marketings in 1960 and 1961 shown in the table. Marketings in 1964 are based on index numbers in *Dezvoltarea complexă și echilibrată a economiei naționale* (Bucharest, 1965), pp. 59 and 71. The deliveries of meat to the state fund in 1955 are estimated as follows: deliveries of state farms to the fund for 1955 are given in *Economia Romîniei între anii 1944–1959*, p. 413; the percentage of these deliveries to the total meat fund is to be found in *Probleme ale dezvoltării agriculturii și consolidării agriculturii socialiste* (Bucharest, 1960), p. 29. From these two statistics, the total meat fund for 1955 can be calculated. Data for other years are based on the index of meat deliveries to the state fund in *Dezvoltarea agriculturii 1965*, p. 587.

Other sources: Anuarul statistic al R.P.R. 1965, pp. 175, 327, and 425; *Anuarul statistic al Republicii Socialiste România 1966* (Bucharest, 1966), pp. 181, 357 and 459; *Economia Romîniei între anii 1944–1959* (Bucharest, 1959), p. 319; *Probleme ale creări și dezvoltării bazei tehnice-materiale a socialismului în R.P.R.* (Bucharest, 1963), p. 189; *Studii de economie socialistă* (Bucharest, 1961), p. 258; *Probleme economice*, No. 3 (1964), pp. 15, 23; No. 4 (1964), p. 107; *Probleme ale dezvoltării agriculturii și consolidării agriculturii socialiste* (Bucharest, 1960), p. 103; *Dezvoltarea economică a Romîniei 1944–1964* (Bucharest, 1964), p. 577.

in 1952, 1956, and 1962. The pattern was virtually identical in the three cases: a poor corn crop, followed by heavy slaughterings in the autumn of the harvest year, and a subsequent reduction in cattle herds and in slaughterings starting the following year. The years 1952, 1956, and 1962 are the only ones since 1950 when the weight of animals slaughtered for consumption exceeded meat output (offsprings plus the estimated increase in the weight of herds). Comparing the animal censuses of January 1956 and 1957, we observe a greater than average decline in the number of oxen and an unprecedented drop of over one million animals in pig herds (chiefly accounted for by the number of piglets). The total number of pigs did not rise again to the January 1956 level until 1964–1965. The January 1963 census showed a 23 percent drop in the number of oxen compared to 1962; the decline in pig herds, however, was limited this time to less than 150,000 animals. From 1963 to 1965, efforts were made to rebuild herds — especially in the state and collective sectors. By 1965, slaughterings, which were kept substantially below output in the intervening years, had not yet recovered the level reached in 1962.

The replacement of work animals — chiefly oxen and horses — by tractors and other farm implements cushioned the impact of failures in the corn harvest, inasmuch as these animals could more easily be sacrificed when there was not enough fodder to go around.[64] But so few oxen and work horses are now left — 273,000 of the former and 318,000 of the latter as of January 1966 — that this buffer cannot be counted on to relieve the severity of any future crises in fodder supplies.

When I considered earlier the relation between the size of herds and meat output, I questioned the wisdom of increasing the relative number of young animals at a time when the fodder situation was fraught with uncertainty.[65] The continued growth in the size of pig herds not only restricted the possibility of bringing the animals up to a proper weight for slaughter but also competed for a limited supply of fodder with milk cows, whose milk yield necessarily suffered. Indeed, the output of cow's milk, after reaching a peak in 1961, declined for two years in a row in the wake of the 1962 harvest failure and was still 4 percent short of the 1961 record in 1965.[66]

---

[64] Note, however, that there is an additional loss of organic fertilizers when the oxen are slaughtered, which must be made up by the increased provision of mineral fertilizers.

[65] Pig herds rose from 4,658,000 in January 1964 to 6,034,000 in January 1965 and then, in consequence of a mediocre corn harvest, were trimmed to 5,365,000 by January 1966. Almost the entire fluctuation can be accounted for by variations in the number of piglets.

[66] *Anuarul statistic al Republicii Socialiste România 1966* (Bucharest, 1966), p. 357.

The relation between the number of cows, milk production, and marketings is brought out in Table 2.17.

The apparent stability of milk yields in recent years, judging from

TABLE 2.17. Number of Cows, Milk Production, Deliveries of Milk to the State Fund, Milk Procurement by Food Industry, Trends in Total Milk Marketings, Industrial Output of Milk and Butter, and Retail Sales

	1950	1955	1958	1960	1961	1962	1963	1964
Cows and buffalo cows (millions of heads)	2.15	1.93	2.04	2.2	2.19	2.09	1.99	1.93
Total production of cow's milk[a] (millions of hectoliters)	14.7	17.6	19.3	22.9	24.2	23.3	21.2	20.5
Deliveries to state fund (millions of hectoliters)	0.6	3.0	4.6	5.4	6.7	7.6	7.8	9.1
Index of total milk marketings[b] (1938 = 100)	n.a.	n.a.	200.5[c]	212.0	208.4	n.a.	n.a.	215.9
Procurement by food industry[b] (millions of hectoliters)	1.2	2.7	5.4	6.1	n.a.	7.8	n.a.	9.4
Industrial milk output[d] (millions of hectoliters)	0.4	0.9	1.2	1.3	1.7	2.1	2.3	2.4
Industrial butter output (thousands of tons)	2.3	6.9	10.2	12.6	14.3	14.7	16.2	19.0
Retail sales of milk[e] (millions of hectoliters)	0.4	0.9	1.1	1.2	1.5	1.9	2.0	2.3

[a] Excluding milk consumed by calves. In 1960 the difference between the output estimates including and excluding milk drunk by calves was equal to 8.8 million hectoliters.

[b] Including sheep and goat's milk. In 1958 deliveries of sheep and goat's milk to the state fund came to an estimated 700,000 hectoliters or 13 percent of the total state milk fund.

[c] 1959.

[d] Including powdered milk.

[e] Socialized retail network only.

Note: The number of cows and buffalo cows for each year represent the average of the census figures for January 1 of that year and January 1 of the next year.

Sources and methods: Deliveries of cow's milk to the central fund in 1955 are based on deliveries by state farms (*Economia Romîniei 1944–1959*, p. 413) and on the percentage of these deliveries in the fund (*Probleme ale dezvoltării și consolidării agriculturii socialiste* [Bucharest, 1960], p. 29). Data for other years were computed from the index numbers in *Dezvoltarea agriculturii 1965*, p. 587. Other data are from *Anuarul statistic al R.P.R. 1965*, pp. 175, 327, and 427; M. Levente, E. Barat, and M. Bulgaru, *Analiza statistico-economică a agriculturii* (Bucharest, 1961), p. 19; *Dezvoltarea complexă si echilibrată a economiei naționale* (Bucharest, 1965), pp. 59 and 71; *Dezvoltarea economică a Romîniei 1944–1964* (Bucharest, 1964), p. 577; *Probleme ale creării și dezvoltării bazei technice-materiale a socialismului în R.P.R.* (Bucharest, 1963), p. 189.

the ratio of milk output to the number of cows (as shown in Table 2.17), conceals diverging trends in state farms and in the rest of the farm sector. If we take out all state units, we find that milk output per cow on remaining farms fell by 5 percent from 1960 to 1964.

It was not possible to estimate total marketings as distinguished from deliveries to the state fund alone. However, there can be no doubt that sales on the peasant market dwindled as state procurements were stepped up. As a result of these opposite trends, total marketings remained approximately at their 1960 levels.[67] From 1960 to 1964, the total amount of milk retained by peasants for their consumption must have fallen by more than 10 percent. If we estimate the decrease in agricultural population to have been on the order of 4 percent between these dates,[68] consumption *in kind* of cow's milk per head of agricultural population must have gone down by at least 5 percent; this was partly but not wholly compensated by an increase in peasants' purchases of milk from state and cooperative shops.[69]

We may summarize our findings in this section as follows. From 1958 to 1962, the state bought or collected all, or nearly all, the increments in crop output. In a poor harvest year like 1962 the farmers were left with less produce than in the mid-1950's. Sales on the free market collapsed. After 1960, fodder supplies were barely sufficient to prevent a drastic drop in meat and milk production, let alone to raise output to the ambitious levels set in the 1965 targets. State procurement policy with respect to animal products had to reconcile itself to the stagnation of meat and milk output. Although the state took over quantities formerly sold on the free market, the share of animal products marketed, including free sales, stayed more or less constant. Enough young animals were left on the farms after meeting deliveries to the state to permit a slow expansion in the size of herds. This policy must have assumed that an improvement in the fodder situation, such as would permit the animals kept on the farm to be brought up to an adequate weight for slaughter, was in the offing. The immediate consequence was that the calves, heifers, and piglets consumed fodder that would otherwise have been fed to cows. The adverse effects of this allocation on milk production were appreciable. Nevertheless, it is too early to

[67] Between 1959 and 1962, sales of milk on the peasant market went down by 8 percent (*Probleme economice*, No. 11 [1963], p. 78). They must have dropped a great deal more between 1962 and 1964.

[68] From 1960 to 1962, the agricultural labor force diminished by about 1 percent per year (*Dezvoltarea economică a Romîniei 1944–1964* [Bucharest, 1964], p. 203). The projection of this trend to 1964 rests on the percentage data in *Anuarul statistic al R.P.R. 1964*, p. 113.

[69] Statistics based on family budgets in farm households actually show a drop of around 5 percent in milk consumption per head from 1958 to 1963 (see Table 1.24).

tell whether the future increments in meat deliveries that will eventually result from this policy will make the gamble pay off.

A Synthesis

The recovery of Rumanian agriculture to prewar levels was delayed until 1953–1954. The New Course introduced about that time was grounded on the expectation that a policy stressing incentives rather than coercion would prod farmers to raise output and marketings decisively above the prewar mark. Collectivization was postponed. Prices paid by the state for procurements were raised substantially. Compulsory deliveries were abolished for all products except meat and wool. The terms of trade relating prices of agricultural products sold by peasants to the prices of the industrial products that they bought from the state retail network improved by nearly 30 percent between 1954 and 1957.[70] Agricultural taxes fell. The new policy was successful to the extent that it coaxed out more produce from the farms at what must have been a moderate cost in terms of the additional industrial consumer and producer goods sold to the rural population.[71] The official index of the real incomes of peasants based on 1950 rose from an average of 154.4 in 1953–1954 to 164.3 in 1955–1956 and then to 170.5 in 1957–1958.[72] State investments in agriculture rose sharply from 1953 to 1954, then remained constant from 1955 to 1957; they represented at that time only 12 percent of the total investment fund.[73]

The collectivization drive of 1958–1959 inaugurated a sharp new turn in agricultural policy. State prices for agricultural produce ceased to rise; the terms of trade began to turn against the peasants, who lost about a third of the 1954–1957 improvement in the parity index.[74] State procurements of crop products now expanded at the expense of free market sales and of fodder supplies, as the state resorted to administrative measures in preference to market incentives to achieve its goals.

The government's strategy from 1958 was to advance simultaneously

[70] *Revista de statistică*, No. 5–6 (1960), p. 23. The index of the terms of trade (based on 1954) stood at 99.7 in 1955, 112.3 in 1956, 128.9 in 1957, and 126.4 in 1958.

[71] From 1955 to 1958, sales of industrial goods through the village retail network increased by 21 percent — from 4.6 to 5.6 billion lei. Sales of these same goods in the urban network rose by 31 percent, from 9.5 to 12.5 billion lei (*Economia Romîniei între anii 1944–1959*, p. 519).

[72] *Dezvoltarea agriculturii 1961*, p. 370.

[73] *Anuarul statistic al R.P.R. 1965*, pp. 344–345.

[74] Levente, Barat, and Bulgaru, *op. cit.*, p. 48. The index of the terms of trade fell from a high of 128.9 in 1957 to 119 in 1960.

on two fronts: (1) to raise production and marketings in the collectivized sector, which was slated to absorb virtually all the individual farms capable of yielding a marketable surplus; and (2) to build up the state farms in case of failure on the collectivized front. Both campaigns were costly to the state in terms of investments, which nearly tripled from 1957 to 1961, reaching a high in this latter year of 17.8 percent of total investments from state funds; but only the second, I believe, really paid off in terms of production. Gross output rose only slightly outside the state sector. Such increases as were achieved were due mainly to improved seeds, irrigation, and conservation measures, which might have been carried out just as well, or nearly as well, in the framework of private farming. (The reader will recall that collectivization had an adverse effect on the total supply of plant nutrients from fertilizers due to the declining application of organic fertilizers.) Whether or not the great expansion of sugar beet and sunflower cultivation that was launched after 1958 could have taken place under private auspices is a moot point. One must observe, in any event, that if so much labor had not been expended on these intensive cultures more could have been lavished on the care of animals and on the tending of orchards and vines, which were neglected in this period. Instead of striving for self-sufficiency in sugar and vegetable oils, the state might have exported more animal products and more fruit. We do not have sufficient information to calculate which would have been the more profitable alternative.

After 1958, marketings of crop products from farms outside the state sector did increase, as procurements skimmed off the increments in output; but this policy had the disadvantage of depriving the collectives and the members' private plots of the corn and other fodder that they needed to feed their cattle. The government's allotments of feeds, redistributed from the state fund, did not fully offset these extractions.

If we disregard the substantial cost of the inputs that were allotted to state farms — half of the total investments in agriculture from state funds and half of the mineral fertilizers delivered to agriculture from 1958 to 1960, when they occupied less than 15 percent of the arable land of Rumania — the state sector seems to have done better in most respects than the collectives. With 15 percent of the country's arable area, they contributed 30–35 percent of the total deliveries of wheat and rye to the state fund in the early 1960's; their share in deliveries of corn was 20–25 percent, of meat 20–30 percent, and of cow's milk 40–50 percent. Their per-acre yields and marketings rose apace. They were allowed to keep enough fodder to increase the amount of milk obtained per cow and to build up their herds. Their net output seems to have risen, while it stagnated or declined in the collectivized sector.

From July 1963 the government again resorted to monetary incentives to stimulate lagging meat production. Prices of beef and pork were raised, and various other measures were taken to encourage the breeding of hogs and steers for the market. In 1965, to combat declining yields of milk, procurement prices for cow's milk were raised by 31 percent; at the same time producers were promised that they would be able to buy certain quantities of feed concentrates for every hectoliter of milk delivered. Collective farmers were also offered the possibility of buying limited amounts of corn to fatten the animals they had contracted to sell to the state.[75]

The twists and turns in official agricultural policy since 1958 make better sense when we consider simultaneously the goals the authorities had set for agriculture in the Six-Year Plan and the measures they had to improvise in the face of the plan's apparent failure after 1962. The planners had counted on a decisive improvement in the performance of the farm sector as a result of collectivization and the consolidation of the state sector. They had made provision for shifting acreage from corn, whose yields per acre were to rise substantially, to sunflowers, sugar beets, and fodder crops. The size of cattle herds was to expand in step with increasing supplies of coarse grains and other feeds. Exports of foodstuffs to both East and West were slated to expand at a rapid pace. When the agricultural sector failed to grow according to plan (in part because of the failure of industry to provide it with the necessary inputs), the state was compelled to trim its program according to its priority scale. Exports were to suffer as little as possible, so as not to affect imports of investment goods and raw materials needed for continued industrialization. The expansion of herds and of meat output, which were essential to achieve a real improvement in consumers' living standards, had to be postponed. A conspicuous symptom of this policy was the decision to raise retail meat prices in 1964. Another was that the acreage planted to corn for grain, which had fallen in 1962 in favor of corn for silo, rose again in 1963 and 1964.

The counterproductive effects of excessively ambitious targets in the long-term plans for 1956–1960 and 1960–1965 apparently discouraged the planners from repeating the experience in fixing their targets for 1970.

The initial targets approved at the Ninth Congress of the Communist Party in July 1965 called for only a 20 percent rise in gross farm output from 1965 to 1970. However, as we saw in the last chapter, the planners were moved to raise their sights after studying the results of the above-

[75] *Probleme economice*, No. 6 (1965), pp. 55–57.

average 1965 harvest. The final target — calling for a 36 percent increase in output — seems somewhat optimistic, at least in view of the poor record achieved in the previous decade. Doubts also arise from the fact that the investments allotted to agriculture in order to meet these higher goals appear to be exactly the same as in the initial version of the plan — 35.7 billion lei over five years, or 66 percent more than in the period 1961–1965.[76] The targets for individual crops and animal products, before and after the revision, are shown in Table 2.18.

TABLE 2.18. INITIAL AND REVISED TARGETS FOR INDIVIDUAL CROPS AND ANIMAL PRODUCTS (*Thousands of Tons*)

	1961–1965 Average Realized	1966–1970 Average Initial Targets	1966–1970 Average Revised Targets
Wheat-rye	4,416	4,800	4,975–5,200
Corn	5,853	7,600	7,600–7,785
Sugar beets	2,867	4,000	4,015–4,130
Sunflower seeds	504	620–670	670–705
Potatoes	2,595	2,900	3,130–3,490
Vegetables	1,657	2,500	2,560–2,887
Fruits and grapes	1,800	2,600	2,640–2,690
Meat	1,044	1,150	1,150–1,216
Milk[a]	25,700	28,500	30,400–33,000
Wool	24,000	28,500	29,200–29,900

[a] Thousands of hectoliters; excludes milk drunk by calves.

Sources: Statistical Pocket Book of the Socialist Republic of Romania, 1966, pp. 160–161, 181; *Congresul al IX-lea al Partidului Comunist Român* (Bucharest, 1965), p. 768; *Scînteia* (July 1, 1966), p. 7.

To help achieve their targets of crop output the planners have called for a production of fertilizers in 1970 equal to more than four times the actual 1965 output. (This ambitious target, incidentally, was already incorporated in the initial plan.) On the basis of past performance it is legitimate to question (1) whether this target will be fulfilled (given that 1965 output fell short of plan by a wide margin), and (2) if it is fulfilled, whether, in view of the present organization of the farm sector, the farms will be capable of utilizing efficiently anything like the quantities of fertilizer foreseen in the plan.[77]

With regard to the output of animal products, even the revised

[76] *Scînteia* (July 1, 1966), p. 7. The share of agriculture in total investments will be about the same in 1966–1970 as in 1961–1965.

[77] According to the initial plan, 1.1 million tons out of a total of 1.3 million tons in 1970 were to be delivered to the farm sector (*Congresul al IX-lea al Partidului Comunist Român, op. cit.,* p. 768).

targets show that the Planning Commission has abandoned the "teleological" precepts that guided the setting of goals in earlier days. The meat target for 1970 of around 1.2 million tons falls slightly short of the target for 1960 in the Second Five-Year Plan and is much inferior to the 1.7–1.8 million tons slated for 1965 in the Six-Year Plan. The milk target for 1970 comes to less than 70 percent of the goal set in the Six-Year Plan.[78] These relatively modest goals suggest that the planners have given up their earlier hopes of finding a radical solution to the fodder problem in the foreseeable future.

If progress in the current plan is realized, where will Rumania's agriculture stand relative to that of other Communist countries? Yields of wheat, corn, and sugar beets per hectare in 1966–1970 will be on a level with what they were in Poland and Hungary a decade earlier (circa 15–17 quintals for wheat, 23–24 quintals for corn, and 215–220 quintals for sugar beets). They will be higher than they were in 1956–1960 in the Soviet Union (10.4, 17.6, and 183 quintals, respectively) but still a good deal lower than in Czechoslovakia. Potato yields will be somewhat higher than in Hungary and 15 percent lower than in Poland in this earlier period.[79] Since no decisive change is anticipated in the structure of crops and in the ratio of animal to crop output in Rumania, it is probable that the value of output per hectare will still be inferior to that of Poland and Hungary. Labor productivity will remain at a low level by the standards of most European countries. (Although 400,000 laborers will be shifted from agriculture to other occupations from 1966 to 1970, 50 percent of the labor force will still be working on the farm in 1970,[80] compared to 30 percent in Hungary in 1965.)

While the progress realized in the last few years and the advances mapped out for the future are not spectacular, the willingness of the leaders to inject much greater resources into the sector than they did in the late 1940's and in the 1950's demonstrates at least their understanding of the pivotal role that agriculture must play if the growth of the economy is to be maintained simultaneously with the continuous improvement of living standards. The gamble they are taking, it seems to me, is not so much in depriving the farm sector of the resources needed for its expansion but in maintaining an institutional framework

[78] See Table 2.8.

[79] Average yields in Eastern Europe for the period 1956–1960 are given in J. Lipták, *Mezinárodní dělba práce v zemědělství zemí RVHP* (Prague, 1965), p. 41. I have computed yields planned in Rumania for the period 1966–1970 by assuming that the entire increase in the average harvest targeted for the period could be attributed to an increase in yields.

[80] *Scînteia* (July 1, 1966), p. 7.

that may not be favorable to the efficient absorption of these resources. The slow growth of *net* agricultural output per person employed in the farm sector in recent years suggests that newly injected inputs have not been used very efficiently. Whether the collectives, to which the great majority of agricultural households belong, will be capable of mobilizing the potential resources, the initiative, and the intelligence of an increasingly schooled population will be decisive in determining the extent to which the traditional backwardness of Rumanian agriculture will be overcome.

CHAPTER THREE

FOREIGN TRADE

The Importance of Foreign Trade

When the central planners in an economy constricted by a limited range of natural resources and by a narrow domestic market face up to the task of balancing their country's external accounts, they must cling to a severely realistic appraisal of future prospects. For unless a sober reckoning has been made of foreign-exchange earning resources, the planners risk having to switch exportables from domestic consumption to foreign markets at a moment's notice during the course of the year and thus inflict serious damage on the economy. Ritualistic optimism, slogans, and exhortations — useful as they may be to mobilize the economy's domestic forces — are likely to be worse than useless when imports and external services must be paid for on time and loans must be reimbursed.

The possibility of trading with the outside world, while it imposes constraints on the planners, also provides them with greater flexibility for solving the internal problems of the economy. These problems are often easier for an outside observer to detect from a study of foreign trade returns than from the highly selective statistics published on internal economic activity. Minor domestic impediments often trigger off perceptible changes in imports or exports, although their effects could not be detected at all in internal statistics. In Rumania, as we shall see, the consequences of the New Course were much more severe (and evident) on imports of machinery and equipment than they were on domestic output. In the late 1950's and early 1960's, moderate fluctuations in agricultural production exerted a profound influence on the balance of trade and, via imports, on the entire development program of the country. Finally, the value of imports and exports in Soviet-type economies is generally expressed in units of account that are approximately proportional to world prices, and this lends to foreign trade statistics a solidity and significance as a basis for analyzing the state of the economy which aggregate measures of domestic development cannot match.

135

In this chapter I attempt to describe and to analyze the organic relation between structural trends in external trade and in the rest of the economy. Since I had to reconstruct most of the statistics I needed to establish these links, much space is taken up with estimating procedures and manipulations that many readers will find fastidious. I have also introduced a profusion of details on exchanges in specific commodity groups and subgroups that will be of interest, if at all, only to a few specialists. But if these laborious exercises provide even partial insight into the problems that Rumania's planners have had to contend with during the last two decades, I believe that consigning them to print will not have been totally in vain.

"Old" and *"Revised"* Statistics of Foreign Trade

In 1960, for the first time in the postwar period, the Central Statistical Office of the Rumanian Republic released data on the country's foreign trade in its official statistical yearbook.

The coverage of the statistics given out at this time was highly selective. It comprised only the total value of imports and exports in "foreign-currency lei" in 1958, index numbers linking these data to 1950 and 1955, a geographical breakdown of trade by countries for 1958, and the volume of imports and exports of the "principal commodities" traded in that year. From 1961 to 1963, these figures were brought up to date each year, but no additional information was given out. In the 1964 yearbook there appeared a breakdown of imports and exports by commodity groups (nine in all) covering the years 1950, 1955, and 1959 to 1963. While these published statistics were extremely valuable in themselves, they did not supply an adequate basis for an understanding of the most important trends in postwar trade, including the trade expansion associated with the first period of intensive industrialization from 1949 to 1953, the three- or four-year stagnation period that followed the introduction of the New Course in mid-1953, and the major restructuring of Rumania's trade relations between its Comecon partners and Western markets after 1958, which is only imperfectly reflected in the geographical distribution of imports and exports in recent years.

The problem is complicated by the fact that all the scattered data published before 1959 refer to statistical series that do not accord with those that were finally released.

A basic revision in the methodology of reporting foreign trade returns must have taken place. To some extent at least this revision must have been prompted by the recommendations of the statistical committee of the Council on Mutual Economic Assistance, which early in 1959 issued a set of uniform rules for recording foreign trade accounts. Yet

it is most unlikely that the large differences that can be observed between the "old" and the "revised" values of trade turnover in 1955,
1956, and 1957 are due to any minor changes in statistical methodology.
Thanks to data on Rumanian trade released in Czech, Slovak, Hungarian, and Soviet sources, we can get some notion of the nature of
this revision.

Table 3.1 brings together all the available statistics of trade since

TABLE 3.1. THE VALUE OF IMPORTS, EXPORTS, AND TRADE TURNOVER IN
CURRENT PRICES FROM 1946 TO 1965 (*Millions of Foreign-Currency Lei*)

	Old Series			Revised Series		
	Imports	Exports	Total Trade	Imports	Exports	Total Trade
1946	130	135	265			
1947	389	252	641	(368)[a]	(205)[a]	(573)[a]
1948	749	904	1,653	n.a.	n.a.	1,611
1949	1,153	1,166	2,319			
1950	1,460	1,274	2,734	1,460	1,274	2,734
1951	1,636	1,580	3,216			
1952	1,996	1,827	3,823			
1953	2,340	2,083	4,423			
1954	2,062	2,142	4,204			
1955	2,335	2,389	4,724	2,771	2,530	5,301
1956	2,101	2,401	4,502	n.a.	n.a.	5,076
1957	2,589	2,217	4,806	n.a.	n.a.	5,417
1958				2,890	2,810	5,700
1959				3,012	3,135	6,147
1960				3,887	4,302	8,189
1961				4,888	4,755	9,643
1962				5,647	4,908	10,555
1963				6,132	5,490	11,622
1964				7,009	6,000	13,009
1965				6,463	6,609	13,072

[a] The 1947 data are from V. Karra's *Stroitel'stvo sotsialisticheskoi ekonomiki v R.N.R.*
(Moscow, 1953), p. 88. They are cited from an official Rumanian government
report for 1948. The statistical methodology on which they are based differs from
the "old series," but it of course antedates the elaboration of the revised series.

Sources: Old series; 1950 to 1957; Imre Vajda, *Nemzetközi kereskedelem* (Budapest,
1959), p. 231; for 1946–1949 the figures were derived with the aid of indexes in
Economia Romîniei între anii 1944–1959 (Bucharest, 1959), p. 570, and *Geografia
economică a R.P.R.*, M. Haşeganu, ed. (Bucharest, 1957), p. 303.

Revised series; 1950, 1955, 1958–1964: *Anuarul statistic al R.P.R. (1964 and 1965);*
1965: *Statistical Pocket Book of the Socialist Republic of Romania, 1966*, p. 240; 1956
and 1957: A. Apró, *A szocialista országok gazdasági együttműködésének időszerű kérdései*
(Budapest, 1964), p. 107; 1948: based on a link to 1963 in *Rumania in the International
Trade 1944–1964* (Bucharest, 1964), p. 48.

1946 according to both the "old" and the "revised" series.[1] The aggregate values of imports and exports in the table are expressed in *valută lei* (foreign-currency lei), officially valued at six to the U.S. dollar.[2] Insofar as trade between Rumania and its partners, both within and without the Communist bloc, was conducted at some approximation to "world prices," this official exchange rate is economically valid, in the sense that trade values expressed in foreign-currency lei can be treated as dollar values multiplied by a constant factor of six. The true extent of the rise in imports and exports in the table is of course distorted to the extent that world prices fluctuated during the postwar period.[3]

Four plausible hypotheses may be put forward to account for the differences between the two series.

1. The revised series include recurrent items, such as gold, uranium ores, armaments, reparations, or deliveries to Soviet forces stationed in Rumania, that were not formerly included in trade.

2. The basis for recording trade was changed, for example, to include or to exclude transportation costs into or out of Rumania.

3. Trade statistics were originally recorded on the basis of preliminary price agreements, which were later revised.

4. The original data for 1955, 1956, and 1957 were adjusted for certain nonrecurrent items that arose in earlier years (for example, reparation payments) or from special actions taken within the period 1955–1957.

To narrow down the possible reasons for the revision, I proceed as follows. I first disaggregate the old and the revised statistics by broad commodity groups for the year 1955, then break down imports and exports by trading areas for the years 1955, 1956, and 1957 (Table 3.3). Finally, for 1955 I attempt to reconstruct trade by region and by com-

---

[1] All statistics in Table 3.1 refer to "commercial trade" only, exclusive of exports on reparations account. In my article "Background and Origins of the Rumanian Dispute with Comecon," *Soviet Studies* (October 1964), I mistakenly assumed that the balance of trade for the years 1946 to 1948 reflected the volume of reparations. The data at my disposal, however, referred only to "commercial trade."

[2] Except where indicated, all data in this chapter are in foreign-currency lei.

[3] No indices of Rumanian foreign trade prices have been released. Dr. Maurice Ernst, using an average of the indices of import prices for Bulgaria, Czechoslovakia, and Poland deflated Rumanian (revised) imports with the following results (on a 1955 base): for 1950, 54 (compared to 53 in current prices); for 1960, 148 (140 in current prices); for 1964, 272 (253 in current prices). According to Ernst, the 1950 volume of imports in constant prices was 12 percent greater than the 1938 volume. The source is Ernst's "Postwar Economic Growth in Eastern Europe (A Comparison with Western Europe)," in *New Directions in the Soviet Economy*, Part IV, Joint Economic Committee, 89th Congress (Washington, 1966), p. 899.

TABLE 3.2. COMMODITY COMPOSITION OF IMPORTS AND EXPORTS IN 1955

	Old Series		Revised Series	
	Percentage of Total	Value (millions of lei)	Percentage of Total	Value (millions of lei)
Imports				
Machinery and equipment	24.8	579	37.2	1,032
Raw materials and semi-fabricates	56.5	1,319	46.6	1,291
Foodstuffs and live animals	13.7	320	12.0	332
Manufactured consumer goods	5.0	117	4.2	116
Total imports	100	2,335	100	2,771
Exports				
Machinery and equipment	6.5	155	6.1	155
Raw materials and semi-fabricates	68.0	1,625	69.7	1,764
Foodstuffs and live animals	23.1	552	22.9	579
Manufactured consumer goods	2.4	57	1.3	32
Total exports	100	2,389	100	2,530

Sources: Total imports and exports in both series are taken from Table 3.1. Old series: the percentage of machinery and equipment imports is from I. P. Oleinik, *Razvitie promyshlennosti Rumynii v usloviakh narodnogo demokraticheskogo stroia* (Moscow, 1959), p. 299. The value of machinery and equipment exports is given in Imre Vajda, *Nemzetközi kereskedelem* (Budapest, 1959), p. 260. Except for trade in manufactured consumer goods, all the other percentages are from Vajda, *op. cit.*, pp. 257 and 262. Imports and exports of manufactured consumer goods are derived as residuals. New series: *Anuarul statistic al R.P.R. 1965*, pp. 438–439.

modity groups simultaneously to ascertain how Rumanian exports of raw materials and imports of machinery products, whose values were significantly revised, were divided between the Soviet Union, the European people's democracies, and the rest of the world. This exercise, without revealing a unique reason for the revision, helps to bring it into sharper focus.

Much can be learned about the revision by studying the commodity composition of trade in the two series, according to the standard four-group classification in use at the time among the countries of CMEA.[4] Just enough data have been released in Soviet and Hungarian sources to make this comparison possible in Table 3.2.

[4] A fifth group, live animals, is usually included with foodstuffs in published statistics; I have followed this practice throughout, even in the few cases where separate statistics for this group were available.

By far the largest difference between the two series occurs in machinery and equipment imports, where the upward revision amounts to 453 million lei, a 78 percent increase over the initial figure. The only other item that adds significantly to the total discrepancy is the increase in raw-material exports from 1,625 million lei in the old series to 1,764 million lei in the new, an increment of 8.5 percent. The other differences are so small that it is not certain whether they are due to minor changes in the definition of the groups, to rounding errors, or to slight inaccuracies in the sources from which the old series have been computed.[5]

Let us first consider the various items of trade that might have been omitted from the statistics prior to 1959 and included thereafter. Armaments provide the only recurrent item that could conceivably account for the large discrepancy between the old and the revised data for machinery and equipment imports. This hypothesis can be largely discounted. For one thing, the estimate of machinery imports for 1950 was not affected by the revision. For another, the trade classification published by the CMEA secretariat omits armaments from what appears to be a complete nomenclature.[6]

[5] The upward revision in the exports of foodstuffs is almost exactly matched by a negative revision in the exports of consumer goods, which were derived as a residual. The reclassification of certain items between the two groups probably accounts for this coincidence.

[6] "Products of the armaments industry" may, however, have been included in trade prior to the revision of 1959. In 1953 Czechoslovakia's exports to Rumania were so conspicuously large that a Czech economist was moved to explain that "special circumstances" had caused "an extraordinary upsurge in the export of products of the machine-building and armaments industries" (D. Machová, ČSSR v socialistické mezinárodní dělbě práce [Prague, 1962], p. 127). In that same year the share of machinery and equipment in total Czechoslovak exports to Rumania was 87.9 percent. In view of this high proportion, and the fact that the breakdown of trade into five groups according to the CMEA commodity classification was exhaustive in the source from which this information was taken, it is clear that armaments could not have been concealed anywhere but in the machinery group. In that same year, according to another Czech source, 58.4 percent of total Rumanian imports of machinery and equipment came from Czechoslovakia (B. Malý, "Hospodářská spolupráce zemí socialistického tábora," Nová mysl, No. 10 [1956], p. 1012). These total machinery imports can be estimated from the old series at 973 million lei. (According to a breakdown of Rumanian imports for 1953 the machinery group represented 41.6 percent of total imports; see Probleme economice, No. 5 [1958], pp. 98–99.) Hence, machinery and equipment imports from Czechoslovakia should have amounted to 568 million lei. Czechoslovakia's exports of these items to Rumania may be estimated from Czech statistics at 582 million lei, which is quite close to this last figure, considering the errors involved in working with percentages. On the other hand, as pointed out in the text, it can be shown that the value of machinery imports for 1950, when imports of armaments presumably occurred, was not affected by the revision (cf. the revised data in Anuarul statistic al R.P.R. 1965 [Bucharest, 1965], p. 439; and the old percentages in I. P. Oleinik, Razvitie promyshlennosti Rumynii v usloviakh narodnogo demokraticheskogo stroia [Moscow, 1959],

On the basis of Table 3.2, we can also assert with some confidence that deliveries to Soviet forces stationed in Rumania were not involved in the revision. Such deliveries would have consisted to a large extent of foodstuffs and consumer goods; but it happens that the sum of these two groups was virtually identical in the two series.

The upward revision in raw-material exports, however, was most probably due to the inclusion in the new series of gold and uranium ores, especially of the latter. I infer this from the fact that the percentage increases in exports of other staple items in this group — petroleum products, building materials, chemicals, and lumber — were almost identical in the old and in the revised series.[7] This near coincidence also suggests that retroactive price concessions (hypothesis 3) were not a significant factor in the revision, for primary exports would have been leading candidates for price adjustments after the "price stop" of the Korean War.[8]

Reparations were not covered in the old series, where trade was defined as "commercial" only. Their inclusion in the revised series would have raised the value of 1950 trade, when they were still at a significant level. The totals for 1950 being the same in both series, I infer that reparations were excluded from trade statistics in the revised series.

The second hypothesis, involving a redefinition of the basis for recording imports or exports, may be tested by comparing the value of Rumania's trade with individual countries as recorded in Rumanian statistics with the value of this trade as recorded in the statistics of her trading partners, before and after the revision.

We first note that if a change had been made from a c.i.f. to the present f.o.b. basis for recording trade,[9] this would have had virtually no effect on statistics of trade with the Soviet Union, Hungary, Yugoslavia, or Bulgaria, with which Rumania has common borders. It should have had a definite impact on trade with "socialist Asian

---

p. 299). The question cannot be resolved at this time. In any case, it should be observed that if armaments were included prior to the revision and excluded thereafter, this would be reflected in a reduction rather than in an increase in the value of machinery imports.

[7] The percentage increases in the old series are from *Information Bulletin of the Chamber of Commerce of the Rumanian People's Republic*, No. 7 (1956), p. 8. For the new series, see *Anuarul statistic al R.P.R. 1965*, p. 438, and for lumber exports, *Valorificarea superioară a resurselor naturale* (Bucharest, 1965), p. 170.

[8] Cf. Chapter 4, pp. 188–189.

[9] The value of both imports and exports at present includes transportation, insurance, and all other expenses up to the border of Rumania for exports and of the supplying country for imports (*Revista de statistică*, No. 10 [1964], p. 83). This source contains the most detailed description available of the contents and valuation of foreign trade statistics.

countries" and with capitalist countries, which are all far distant from Rumania. The statistics for 1955 in Table 3.3 show that trade with these regions was not seriously affected by the revision; they lend no support, therefore, to the hypothesis of a redefinition.

A detailed analysis of trade returns with individual members of CMEA (see Table 3.4) reveals that the value of trade turnover (imports plus

TABLE 3.3. ALTERNATIVE ESTIMATES OF RUMANIA'S TRADE TURNOVER BY REGION, 1955 TO 1957 (*Millions of Lei*)

			Trading Partners			
	Soviet Union	People's Democ- racies	Total CMEA	Socialist Coun- tries Outside CMEA	Capi- talist Coun- tries[a]	All Coun- tries
1955						
Old series	2,319	1,299	3,618	127	979	4,724
Revised series	n.a.	n.a.	4,209	127	965	5,301
Trading partners' statistics	2,865	1,358	4,223	n.a.	1,158	n.a.
1956						
Old series	2,143	1,103	3,246	221	1,035	4,502
Revised series	n.a.	n.a.	3,816	n.a.	n.a.	5,076
Trading partners' statistics	2,684	1,203	3,887	n.a.	1,132	n.a.
1957						
Old series	n.a.	n.a.	n.a.	n.a.	n.a.	4,806
Revised series	2,674	1,238	3,912	310	1,195	5,417
Trading partners' statistics	2,645	1,171	3,816	n.a.	1,218	n.a.

[a] Including Yugoslavia.

Sources and methods: Old series: M. Haşeganu, ed., *Geografia economică a R.P.R.* (Bucharest, 1957), p. 305; *Dezvoltare economiei R.P.R. pe drumul socialismului 1948–1957* (Bucharest, 1958), p. 397. For the revised series, the 1955 data are based on J. Košnár, *RVHP: Výsledky a problémy* (Bratislava, 1964), p. 122; the 1956 and 1957 estimates of trade turnover with CMEA are from *Vŭnshna tŭrgovia* (Sofia), No. 7 (1960), p. 3; the 1957 estimate for the Soviet Union was calculated from an index of Rumanian-Soviet trade turnover with a link to 1958, for which published data are available (*Probleme economice*, No. 8 [1959], p. 137). An analysis of the index shows that it must correspond to the revised series. Total trade with "socialist" and with "capitalist" countries was derived from percentages in *Economia Romîniei între anii 1944–1959* (Bucharest, 1959), p. 580. Judging from the 1955 data in the same table and from other indirect evidence, it may be surmised that these 1957 percentages belong to the revised series. Trading partners' statistics were taken, in the case of Communist countries, from the official statistical yearbooks of the individual countries; for the rest of the world, use was made of the United Nations' *Statistical Papers*, Series T, *Direction of International Trade*, Vol. XI, No. 9 (1958).

TABLE 3.4. Rumania's Trade Turnover (Imports plus Exports) with Principal Partners in CMEA According to Official Rumanian Statistics and to Statistics of Its Trading Partners (*Millions of Lei*)

Country and Origin of Statistic	1955	1956	1957	1958	1959	1960	1961	1962
Soviet Union								
Soviet	2,865	2,684	2,645	2,864	2,884	3,243	3,800	4,335
Rumanian	2,319	2,143	n.a.	2,935	2,909	3,284	3,900	4,283
Difference	+546	+541	n.a.	−71	−25	−41	−100	+52
Czechoslovakia								
Czechoslovak	475	381	391	361	619	768	786	889
Rumanian	411	301	330	370	505	759	798	882
Difference	+64	+80	+61	−9	+114	+9	−12	+7
Hungary								
Hungarian	224	150	174	173	245	404	317	453
Rumanian	231	149	176	174	247	407	327	449
Difference	−7	+1	−2	−1	−2	−3	−10	+4
Bulgaria								
Bulgarian	121	113	75	47	69	105	128	177
Rumanian	113	116	n.a.	48	70	107	139	173
Difference	+8	−3	n.a.	−1	−1	−2	−11	+4
Poland								
Polish	146	200	195	156	233	262	340	452
Rumanian	146	189	127	152	239	264	339	451
Difference	0	+11	+68	+4	−6	−2	+1	+1
East Germany								
East German	376	346	330	387	485	632	687	622
Rumanian	383	350	n.a.	398	482	635	670	614
Difference	−7	−4	n.a.	−11	+3	−3	+17	+8
Total People's Democracies[a]								
Partners' statistics	1,342	1,190	1,165	1,124	1,651	2,171	2,258	2,593
Rumanian	1,284	1,105	n.a.	1,142	1,543	2,172	2,273	2,569
Difference	+58	+85	n.a.	−18	+108	−1	−15	+24

[a] Except Albania.

Note: All Rumanian statistics in 1955 and 1956 are based on percentages of total trade turnover pertaining to the "old series."

Sources: Rumanian statistics, 1955: All statistics are based on M. Haşeganu, ed., *Geografia economică a R.P.R.* (Bucharest, 1957), p. 304–305; 1956: derived from percentages in *Dezvoltare economiei R.P.R. pe drumul socialismului 1948–1957*, Institutul de cercetari economice, Academia R.P.R. (Bucharest, 1958), p. 397; 1958–1962: Rumania; *Anuarul statistic R.P.R. 1964 and 1965;* Soviet Union: *Vneshniaia torgovlia SSSR za 1956, 1958, 1960, 1962;* for other socialist countries: official statistical yearbooks for corresponding years. Trade with Hungary in 1957, according to Rumanian statistics, was computed from a percentage increase from 1956 to 1957 in *Razvitie ekonomiki stran narodnoi demokratii: Obzor za 1957* (Moscow, 1958), p. 527. Trade with Czechoslovakia and Poland in 1957 was derived from the published Rumanian statistics for 1958 and from the percentage increases for the year in *Dve mirovye sistemy khoziaistva* (Moscow, 1961), p. 325.

exports) with Rumania recorded in official statistics by Hungary, Poland, Bulgaria, and East Germany nearly coincided with the value given in Rumanian statistics corresponding to the old series, for the years 1955 to 1957, and to the revised series for subsequent years. Since the coincidence between turnovers, as recorded from both sides, goes back at least to 1955, it seems as if the revision did not affect the Rumanian basis for valuation, at least in trade with these countries.

In 1955, 1956, and 1957 there were large disparities between Soviet and Czechoslovak statistics of trade turnover with Rumania, on the one hand, and Rumanian statistics of trade with these partners, on the other. These disparities dwindled to insignificant amounts from 1958 on, with the exception of Czech-Rumanian trade in the year 1959 when an appreciable gap opened up again for no apparent reason.

Turning again to Table 3.3 we note that the differences between the "old" and the "revised" estimates of turnover with CMEA in 1955 and 1956 come very close to the total discrepancies recorded between the old and the revised series for these two years. For 1955 the difference in CMEA trade comes to 591 million lei as against 577 million for the entire discrepancy between the two series; for 1956 the gaps between the two series are virtually identical — 570 million for CMEA trade and 574 million lei for the entire trade of the country. The remaining unexplained divergencies may arise from a revision of trade with the rest of the world, from small discrepancies in the statistical returns of trading partners, such as can be observed between 1958 and 1962, and from errors in the percentages used to estimated the data on the Rumanian side.

Finally, we observe that the estimates of the revised series that we have been able to reconstruct are in fairly close accord with the data derived from the statistics of Rumania's East European partners. The evidence tentatively suggests that these partners' data can be used as proxy for the revised series wherever the latter cannot be reconstructed directly.

So far we have deduced that the revision of the 1955 accounts affected mainly machinery imports and raw-material exports and that it was almost entirely confined to trade with the Soviet Union and Czechoslovakia. There remains the task of assigning to each country its share in the discrepancies observed in the two groups (see Table 3.5).

The main result of the calculations in Table 3.5 is that the discrepancy in raw-material exports arose more or less exclusively in trade with the Soviet Union, whereas the upward revision in machinery imports was accounted for by one or more of the people's democracies as well as by the Soviet Union. It may be conjectured, on the basis of

TABLE 3.5. ESTIMATED BREAKDOWN OF RUMANIAN IMPORTS AND EXPORTS IN 1955 BY REGIONS AND COMMODITY GROUPS (*Millions of Lei*)

	Old Series			Revised Series		
	Total CMEA	People's Democ- racies	Soviet Union	Total CMEA	People's Democ- racies	Soviet Union
	Imports					
Machinery and equipment	550	185	365	1,003	219	784
Raw materials, fuels, and semifabricates	914	276	638	886	268	618
Foodstuffs and consumer goods	318	120	198	330	126	204
Total	1,782	581	1,201	2,219	613	1,606
	Exports					
Machinery and equipment	122	35	87	122	35	87
Raw materials, fuels, and semifabricates	1,243	418	825	1,383	417	966
Foodstuffs and consumer goods	485	279	206	485	279	206
Total	1,850	732	1,118	1,990	731	1,259

Sources and methods: The following assumptions underlie the construction of the table: (1) Soviet statistics of total imports from and exports to Rumania are close enough to the revised values of Rumanian trade to act as a proxy for the latter. (2) The breakdown of imports in the revised series is based on the assumption that in the official Soviet trade statistics the itemized Soviet exports to Rumania in the groups "raw materials, fuels, and semifabricates," "foodstuffs," and "manufactured consumer goods" are all complete and that their sums are true representations of Soviet exports to Rumania in these three groups. From this assumption it follows that virtually the entire gap between the old and the revised figure of imports from the Soviet Union is filled by a discrepancy in the machinery group alone. (3) In the official Soviet statistics for 1955 there is a gap of 182.5 million lei between the sum of itemized exports and the total recorded value of exports to Rumania. This gap amounts to 14 percent of total exports. It was estimated on the basis of 1956 data that the food and consumer goods component was underestimated by 20 percent, or 32 million lei. The rest, or 150 million lei, was assigned to the raw materials group. (4) Trade with CMEA accounts for the entire difference between the old and the revised series for (*a*) raw materials, fuels, and semifabricates, and (*b*) foodstuffs and consumer goods, as it does for imports of machinery and equipment for which the old and the revised estimates were calculated independently (see sources listed). (5) The relatively small discrepancies between the old and the revised estimates for imports of raw materials and of foodstuffs and consumer goods were divided between the Soviet Union and the people's democracies in proportion to the shares of these two areas in CMEA trade in these two consolidated groups.

The estimates are based on the following sources. For machinery and equip-

our previous analysis of trade turnovers, that Czechoslovakia was the people's democracy involved.

One possible explanation for the revision in the machinery group appears more convincing than any other conjecture. When the Soviets, in 1954, chose to liquidate most of the "joint companies" they had formed with the Rumanians after 1945, they at first sold to the Rumanians the "former German assets" they had initially contributed and also their share in the equipment they had invested in these companies until 1954. In 1956 the remaining joint companies were dissolved. In December of that year the U.S.S.R. absolved the Rumanians from payment for the original assets, which were estimated at approximately 4.3 billion lei (710 million dollars). Rumania, however, still had to compensate the Soviet Union for its share of the investments carried out.[10] I suspect that the equipment invested by the Soviet Union in the joint companies was not originally included in Soviet export statistics.[11] When the equipment was ceded to Rumania, the Soviet Union may have included in the statistics at least that portion of the equipment that had been manufactured in the Soviet Union. They may have

[10] *15 let svobodnoi Rumynii* (Moscow, 1958), p. 242.
[11] A similar omission was made in the case of Soviet investments in Soviet-Hungarian joint companies in the early postwar period (interview material).

ment: (1) Old series: Imports from CMEA and from the Soviet Union are based on percentages of total machinery imports in *Probleme economice*, No. 12 (1957), p. 20; exports to CMEA are from Imre Vajda, *Nemzetközi kereskedelem* (Budapest, 1959), p. 200. (2) Revised series: Imports from CMEA are based on the latter's share in total imports of machinery and equipment in J. Novozámský, *Otázky vyrovnávání ekonomické úrovně evropských socialistických zemí* (candidate dissertation, Prague, July 1962), p. 124; exports of machinery to CMEA are assumed to be the same as in the old series; exports to the Soviet Union are from *Vneshniaia torgovlia SSSR za 1956 god* (Moscow, 1958), p. 85. Raw materials, fuels, and semifabricates: Imports from and exports to CMEA in the revised series are from J. Novozámský, *Vyrovnávání ekonomické úrovně zemí RVHP* (Prague, 1964), p. 109. Total revised exports to CMEA are based on the share of machinery exports in total exports to CMEA in *Czechoslovak Foreign Trade*, No. 5 (1964), p. 11. Total revised imports from CMEA are derived as the difference between revised turnover in Table 3.3 and revised exports. Imports from and exports to CMEA of foodstuffs and consumer goods were then obtained as residuals. Imports and exports in the raw material group and in the combined foodstuffs and consumer goods groups of the old series in trade with CMEA were estimated by subtracting the algebraic difference between the old and the revised series in each corresponding group (from Table 3.2) from the revised data already obtained. Total imports from and exports to the Soviet Union in the revised series are from *Vneshniaia torgovlia SSSR za 1956 god*, pp. 84–85. Total turnover with the Soviet Union in the old series is from Table 3.3. All other data are estimated according to the methods and assumptions in these notes or as residuals. It will be noted that total imports and exports in "old series" trade with CMEA were obtained independently of the data in Table 3.3. The discrepancy between the two totals (3,618 in Table 3.3 and 3,632 in Table 3.5) is due to the inaccuracy of working from percentages and to possible errors in the assumptions.

recorded these sales as exports along with Rumanian payments scheduled over several years.[12] When the Rumanian Statistical Office prepared its foreign trade statistics for publication, it presumably adjusted its previous accounts to conform with Soviet records, which included these extraordinary exports. It would stand to reason that the additional imports from the people's democracies in the revised series corresponded to the part of the Soviet contribution that came from Eastern Europe rather than from the Soviet Union itself and therefore could not properly be incorporated into Soviet exports.

Foreign Trade and the National Economy

The most revealing measure of the degree of participation of an economy in foreign trade is the relation of imports and exports to national product. As far as I know, information of this type has never been made public in postwar Rumania.

On the basis of the analysis of export-to-production ratios for industry, which was said to account for 80 percent of deliveries for exports to the foreign trade sector, the ratio of exports to national (material) product may have amounted to 14 percent in 1960.[13] In 1964 exports were valued at almost exactly one billion U.S. dollars, or $53 per capita. In that same year, a Czechoslovak study estimated Rumania's national income at $423 per capita. The export ratio was therefore 12.5 percent, a figure consistent with the estimate given for 1960. Rumania's export-to-national-income ratio in the first part of the 1960's was substantially lower than that of Bulgaria, Hungary, and East Germany, a little lower than that of Poland, and considerably above that of the U.S.S.R. Given the size of her population — 60 percent of Poland's — the extent of Rumania's integration in world trade was below average in Eastern

[12] According to the Soviet economist I. P. Oleinik, the Rumanians had to compensate the U.S.S.R. "only for the part of the value of the assets of the mixed companies which was supplied directly from the U.S.S.R. (*nepostredstvenno iz SSSR*) in the form of raw materials, material and equipment." Compensation was to be carried out over the course of several years in Rumanian lei (*Razvitie promyshlennosti Rumynii v usloviakh narodnogo demokraticheskogo stroia, op. cit.*, p. 165).

[13] The ratio of industrial exports to gross industrial output exclusive of turnover taxes is estimated at 13.5 percent, for reasons set out later (p. 150). The gross output of industry in 1960 may be evaluated at approximately 81.1 billion lei (my calculations on this point agree with those of M. C. Kaser in his note on Rumanian national accounts in *Soviet Studies*, July 1966). Therefore, the absolute value of industrial exports at domestic prices should be 10.95 billion lei. If industrial deliveries came to four fifths of all exports, then the latter equaled 13.7 billion lei. National product in 1960 may be estimated at 96 billion lei (Table B.10, Appendix B), hence the ratio in the text.

Europe.[14] Ratios of this magnitude were observed before the war, when they varied greatly from year to year in response to harvest fluctuations.[15]

The ratio of trade to income was subject to moderate fluctuations from 1950 to 1965, judging from the trends in the numerator and denominator of this proportion in Table 3.6.

TABLE 3.6. TRENDS IN IMPORTS AND EXPORTS AND IN NATIONAL INCOME (*Indices, 1950 = 100*)

	1950	1953	1955	1958	1960	1962	1964	1965
National income at "comparable prices"	100	158	192	214	268	308	377	411
Imports in current *valută* lei	100	160	190	198	266	387	480	442
Exports in current *valută* lei	100	164	199	221	338	385	471	519
Trade turnover in current *valută* lei	100	162	194	208	299	386	476	478

Sources: Anuarul statistic 1965, pp. 102, 433; and *Statistical Pocket Book, 1966*, pp. 39, 239.

From 1950 to 1953 trade grew at about the same rate as the official estimates of national income. Then, during the period of trade stagnation from 1955 to 1958, the rise in income was somewhat faster than trade turnover (especially, faster than imports). After 1958, the boom in investments and industrial production, which battened on imported equipment and materials, was a powerful stimulant to imports. Through what might be described as an acceleration process, trade soon outpaced the growth of the domestic forces that propelled it. The tendency for imports to rise faster than national income came to an end in 1962. In the next two years, imports, exports, and national income all grew at approximately the same rate of 10–11 percent per year. In 1965, the ratio of foreign trade turnover to national income declined, as imports fell and exports just kept up with the growth of income.

On the relation of trade to output for individual branches of industry, we have at least indirect evidence to go on since the publication of the interesting data in Table 3.7.

[14] National income per head — material product only — as estimated by Czechoslovak statisticians for the countries cited, is given in Chapter 4, p. 190, note 13.

[15] The ratio of exports to national income including services, was equal to 13 percent in 1937 and 8 percent in 1938. National income is from *Enciclopedia României*, Vol. IV (1943), p. 964; exports are from *Probleme economice*, No. 3 (1965), p. 62. If we exclude "public services" we get a ratio of 15 percent for 1937 and 9 percent for 1938.

TABLE 3.7. SHARES OF VARIOUS BRANCHES OF INDUSTRY IN GROSS
INDUSTRIAL OUTPUT AND IN DELIVERIES FOR EXPORT
IN 1960 AND 1964 (*Percentages*)

	Gross Output of Industry		Deliveries for Export		Imports for Industrial Uses	
	1960	1964	1960	1964	1960	1964
Ministry of Metallurgical Industry	8.0	7.0	8.0	9.0	38.9	35.9
Ministry of Machine-Building Industry	17.0	21.0	14.2	18.6	5.3	6.2
Ministry of Petroleum	7.0	6.0	28.0	16.7	1.5	1.4
Ministry of Chemical Industry	7.0	10.0	3.3	6.8	13.8	16.5
Ministry of Forest Economy	5.0	6.0	15.9	18.1	0.7	0.9
Ministry of Mines	2.0	2.0	2.4	1.8	0.9	0.1
Ministry of Food Industry	16.0	14.0	3.5	4.2	15.8	10.1
Ministry of Light Industry	15.0	14.0	10.0	8.3	2.4	2.5
Total of ministries listed	77.0	80.0	85.3	83.5	79.3	73.6
All industry	100.0	100.0	100.0	100.0	100.0	100.0

Source: A. Crăciun, Gh. Pozderie, and I. Olteanu, "Întărirea colaborării dintre industrie şi comerţul exterior în realizarea sarcinilor de export," *Probleme economice*, No. 12 (1965), p. 73.

From the discussion of these figures and from a comparison with gross output breakdowns in the official statistical yearbook, it is apparent that all percentage shares in the table are derived from data expressed in internal prices exclusive of turnover taxes.[16]

Now it is obvious from these data that if the Ministry of the Metallurgical Industry contributed 8 percent to both output and deliveries to exports in 1960 its ratio of exports to output must have been exactly equal to the average for all industry. In general we may compute the *relative* ratio of the industry by dividing its share in exports by its share in output. Thus the ratio for the Machine-Building Ministry was 84 percent of average in 1960 and 89 percent in 1964; for the Petroleum Ministry, it was 400 percent of average in 1960 and only 278 percent in 1964; for the Ministry of the Chemical Industry, 47 percent of average in 1960 and 68 percent in 1964; for the Ministry of Forest Economy, 318 percent of average in 1960 and 302 percent in 1964; for the Ministry of Mines, 120 percent of average in 1960 and 90 percent

[16] Because imports include both equipment and raw materials, the exclusion from the ministries listed of the power industry, which contributed very little to exports but consumed a significant portion of equipment imports, reduces the total of the shares accounted for on the import side compared to the deliveries for export.

in 1964; for the Ministry of the Food Industry, 22 percent of average in 1960 and 30 percent in 1964; and finally, for the Ministry of Light Industry, 67 percent of average in 1960 and 59 percent in 1964. Noteworthy are the very high but diminishing ratios for the ministries of petroleum and forest economy and the low ratios for the ministries of food and light industry. If we consider that manufactured foodstuffs alone made up 11.8 percent of all exports in 1960 at *valută* prices and 12.7 percent in 1964, whereas the Ministry of the Food Industry, which must be responsible for most of these processed-food exports, contributed only 3.5 and 4.2 percent, respectively, to export deliveries in *domestic* prices, it is apparent that the ratio of domestic to foreign prices must have been very low in this branch of industry.

If we had a single reliable ratio of exports to output for any of the ministries listed in the table, we should be able to compute an average for all industry as well as industrial ratios for all other ministries. It is regrettable that the ratios we do have for the machine-building and chemical industries are derived from data whose coverage does not coincide with the administrative breakdown of Table 3.7.[17]

For the machine-building industry, the ratio of exports to output for 1960 given in a Czechoslovak source was 11.3 percent.[18] For chemicals, the ratio for 1959 was 8.7 percent;[19] given the increase in the gross output of the industry and of exports in foreign currency from 1959 to 1960, the ratio for the latter year must have risen to nearly 10 percent. These two percentages, used in conjunction with the data in Table 3.7 to compute average export-to-output ratios for manufacturing industry as a whole, yield widely disparate results — 13.5 and 20.4 percent, respectively, for 1960 — either through a lack of congruence in the classifications on which the two sets of percentages are based or through errors in the estimates of the export-to-output ratios for the industries concerned. On the basis of the export ratio for machinery products, the ratio for the Petroleum Ministry turns out to be 54 percent; if we start our calculation from the chemical industry's ratio, it rises to 82 percent. The first of these ratios seems approximately correct, the second much too high.[20] Since, moreover, an export ratio of

---

[17] These two ratios refer to the total output and deliveries for export of the entire industry, irrespective of the administrative subordination of producing plants. For machine building, this definition of output gives rise to a larger proportion of total industrial output than the administrative definition. The converse is true for the chemical industry. In 1960, the output of machine building and processed metal products came to 24 percent of total industrial output, compared to the ministry's 17 percent. For chemicals, the corresponding proportions were 6.1 and 7 percent.

[18] J. Novozámský, *Vyrovnávání ekonomické úrovně zemí RVHP* (Prague, 1965), p. 104.

[19] *Dezvoltarea complexă şi echilibrată a economiei naţionale* (Bucharest, 1965), p. 291.

[20] See the data in Table A.3.

TABLE 3.8. TRADE IN MACHINERY AND EQUIPMENT IN 1946, 1948, AND 1950–1965

	Total Machinery and Equipment Imports (millions of valută lei)	Percentage of Total Imports	Investments in Imported Equipment at 1959 Prices (millions of lei)	Total Machinery and Equipment Exports (millions of valută lei)	Percentage of Total Exports
1946	30	23.1	n.a.	n.a.	n.a.
1948	184	24.5	n.a.	7	0.8
1950	542	37.1	1,001	53	4.2
1951	484	29.6	1,192	n.a.	n.a.
1952	786	39.4	1,440	75	4.1
1953	973	41.6	1,613	173	8.3
1954	647	31.4	1,018	180	8.4
1955	579[a]	24.8	1,099	155	6.5
1956	431	20.5	991	242	10.1
1957	406	14.7	825	234	10.6
1958	756	26.2	902	333	11.8
1959	977	32.4	1,267	469	15.0
1960	1,263	32.5	2,022	716	16.6
1961	1,978	40.5	3,642	763	16.0
1962	2,450	43.4	4,318	884	18.0
1963	2,563	41.8	4,772	904	16.4
1964	2,749	39.2	4,365	1,094	18.2
1965	2,517	39.0	4,987	1,223	18.5

[a] Revised: 1,032 million lei.

Note: All data for 1955 to 1957 refer to the "old series."

Sources: Imports: Total machinery imports in *valută* lei from 1948 to 1957 are based on percentages in I. P. Oleinik, *Dezvoltarea industriei Romîniei în anii Regimului Democrat-Popular* (Bucharest, 1960), p. 178; and on the import statistics in Table 3.1 (old series). 1958 imports are based on I. V. Dudinskii's *Mirovaia sistema sotsializma* (Moscow, 1961), p. 166. Data for 1959 to 1964 are from *Anuarul statistic al R.P.R.* (1965), pp. 438–439. Investments in imported machines and equipment are derived by subtraction between total investments in machinery and equipment and that part of the latter that was domestically produced (*Anuarul statistic al R.P.R.* [1965], pp. 344–345). Exports: 1953 and 1956 are based on percentages of total exports in *Probleme economice,* No. 12 (1957), p. 33; percentage links to 1953 and 1956 in *Information Bulletin of the Chamber of Commerce of the R.P.R.,* No. 12 (1957), p. 17, can be used to prove that exports in 1950 in the old series were exactly equal to the figures in the revised statistics in *Anuarul statistic al R.P.R. 1965,* p. 438. The estimates for the years 1952, 1954, 1957, and 1958 are based on the index numbers in *Economia Romîniei între anii 1944–1959* (Bucharest, 1959), p. 577; and *Ekonomicheskoe sotrudnichestvo i vzaimopomoshch' sotsialisticheskikh stran,* A. D. Stupov, ed. (Moscow, 1962), p. 257. These indexes are consistent with each other and with the data for machinery exports in *Anuarul statistic al Republicii Socialiste România, 1966,* pp. 472–473, from which the estimates in the table for all other years were taken.

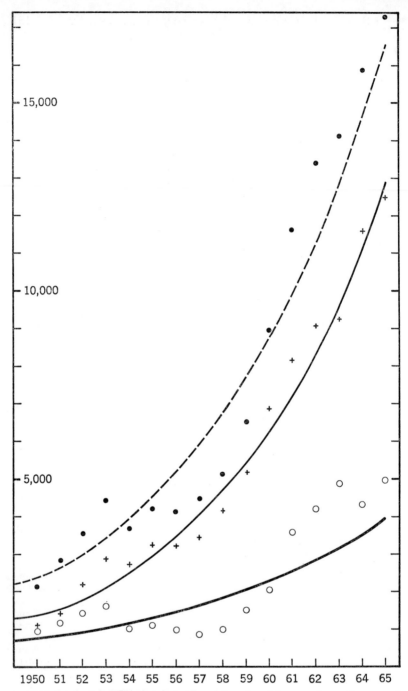

FIGURE 3.1. Trends in domestically produced and imported machinery and equipment, 1950–1965 (millions of lei at 1959 prices). See key to figure on facing page.

48 percent for the Ministry of Forest Economy, derived from the lower of the two ratios for industry as a whole, is consistent with other information,[21] I am disposed to accept this lower average ratio for industry — 13.5 percent — as a first approximation, although bearing in mind that it may be understated.

It may also be pointed out that, in the early 1960's, 15 percent of the value of all minerals and fuels produced was exported, while imports of these goods represented 10 percent of domestic consumption. The degree of integration of Rumania's extractive industries in world trade appears to have been substantially smaller at the time than it was in Hungary and Bulgaria but somewhat greater than in Poland.[22]

To supplement this discussion of export ratios for entire branches of industry, I have tried to estimate in Appendix C the dependency of domestic production on exports and of consumption on imports for key products in textiles, metallurgy, petroleum mining and refining, and a few other branches of industry. For the machine-building industry, however, which plays such a pivotal role in discussions on specialization among the members of the Council for Mutual Economic Assistance, I shall present in the following pages such evidence as I have been able to collect.

Machinery imports, shown in Table 3.8 and in Figure 3.1, followed the same general trend as imports as a whole but with amplified fluctuations: they went up sharply in the early 1950's, fell from 1953 to

---

[21] See Appendix C, p. 286.

[22] The corresponding export and import ratios for minerals and fuels were 20 and 27 percent for Hungary, 34 and 15 percent for Bulgaria, and 8 and 11 percent for Poland (*Mirovaia ekonomika i mezhdunarodnye otnosheniia*, No. 5 [1966], p. 18).

Key to Figure 3.1, page 152:

Identification of Observed Points

● = total investment in machinery and equipment
+ = investment in domestically produced machinery and equipment
O = investment in imported machinery and equipment

Equations of Trend Lines

```
---- Log I  = 3.31 + .057X
———— Log P  = 3.10 + .064X
———— Log M  = 2.85 + .047X
```

Symbols Used

I = total investments in machinery and equipment
P = investments in domestically produced machinery and equipment
M = investments in imported machinery and equipment
X = any year from 1950 to 1965

1957, and rose again at a fast rate from 1958 to 1963.[23] Nevertheless, due to the government's systematic policy of building up a domestic machine-building industry capable of supplying all the more common types of equipment hitherto imported, the share of imports in total investments in machinery and equipment did not move in close harmony with the import cycle itself. During 1950 to 1953, for example, although investments in imported machinery were increasing rapidly, their share in total investments in equipment fell from 49.2 to 36.5 percent. It continued to fall when imports were declining, reaching a low point of 18.6 percent in 1958. Investments went up so fast in the next four years that domestic machine-building capacity could not keep pace with the demand, and the share of imported equipment in investments increased again (to 34 percent in 1963). From 1963 to 1964, imports dropped as the investment boom lost its momentum: the share of imported equipment fell back to 27.5 percent.[24]

Imports of "equipment and matériel for complete enterprises" (in Russian *komplektnoe oborudovanie*) must have fluctuated even more in response to changes in total investments than did total machine imports. For instance, Soviet exports of these items to Rumania in 1953 amounted to 377 million lei and Czech exports to 46 million lei; by 1956 the former had fallen to 46 million and the latter to 5.5 million.[25] In recent years imports of these complete assemblies have again been running at high levels. They rose from 166 million lei in 1958 to 1,045 million lei in 1963, or from 22 to 41 percent of total imports of machinery and equipment.[26]

From a very low base, Rumanian exports of machines and equipment have risen a good deal faster in the last fifteen years than have

[23] See also Tables 3.15 and 3.16 and the discussion later in this chapter. In Figure 3.1, the official statistics of total machinery investments, investments in domestic machinery, and investments in imported machinery, are plotted with the logarithmic trend line for each of these variables. While the fits are fairly good, there is a clear tendency for the observed points to lie above the trend line up to 1953, below the line from 1954 to 1958 or 1959, and above the line thereafter. The greatest deviations from the trend line are shown by the investments in imported machinery.

[24] All these data are from *Anuarul statistic al R.P.R. 1965*, pp. 344–345.

[25] The Soviet data are from *Ekonomicheskoe sotrudnichestvo i vzaimopomoshch' sotsialisticheskikh stran* (Moscow, 1962), p. 250. Czech data for exports of investment assemblies to every socialist country from 1950 to 1956 are contained in V. Kaigl, "Mesto Chekhoslovakii v razdelenii truda," in *Mirovaia sotsialisticheskaia sistema khoziaistva* (Moscow, 1958), p. 266.

[26] *Rumania in the International Trade 1944–1964* (Chamber of Commerce of the R.P.R., Bucharest, 1964), p. 70, and Table 3.8. It may be estimated that from 1948 to 1958 the proportion of complete assemblies to total machinery imports was approximately 25 percent (cf. the cumulative value of such imports until 1958 in *Economia Romîniei între anii 1944–1959* [Bucharest, 1959], p. 579).

imports in this group. This rise has been fairly continuous, escaping the serious recession that pulled imports down from 1953 to 1957. (Exports doubled from 1953 to 1958 while imports fell by 23 percent.) Exports of equipment have also become much more diversified. While the Soviet Union, for example, purchased mainly boats and trawlers from Rumania up to 1958, in more recent years its petroleum equipment and other specialized machinery imports from that country have become at least as important as those of the more traditional items. In 1963, the shares in the total machinery exports of Rumania of the most important group of products were the following: boats and trawlers 8.5 percent, motor vehicles 12 percent, chemical equipment 16.8 percent, petroleum equipment 21.3 percent, agricultural equipment (chiefly tractors) 11 percent, machine tools 1.9 percent, ball bearings 3 percent, and electrochemical products 6.5 percent.[27]

Despite the great expansion of machinery exports in recent years, their share in total machine-building production, as we have previously mentioned, reached only 11.3 percent in 1960, compared to 18.4 percent in Czechoslovakia and 18.5 percent in Bulgaria.[28] The Rumanian share could only have decreased since that time, if we consider that Rumania's machine-building output went up, according to the official index, by 119 percent from 1960 to 1965, while her exports of machine products rose by only 71 percent in the same period.[29]

For a few products in which Rumania specializes within the framework of CMEA, the ratio of exports to output has been far higher than this average. For petroleum equipment, which represented about one fifth of total machinery exports, this ratio varied between 30 and 60 percent in recent years (it reached 80 percent for deep-drilling equipment alone). In 1958, 47 percent of the output of corn combines and 92 percent of all self-loading cars for the transportation of ores and coal were exported.[30] The export-to-output ratio for railroad cars in the early 1960's fluctuated around 35 to 45 percent and for tractors around 25 to 30 percent. For lathes it rose from 13.2 percent in 1960 to 21 percent in 1962.[31]

On the other hand, electrical engineering products, including motors, power transformers, and other electrical equipment, were mostly con-

[27] *Industria Romîniei 1944–1964* (Bucharest, 1964), p. 504.

[28] Novozámský, *Vyrovnávání* . . . , *op. cit.*, p. 104. These percentages are based in principle on a comparison of exports with total output, both measured in domestic prices.

[29] Table 3.16 and *Statistical Pocket Book, 1966*, pp. 82–83.

[30] *Ekonomicheskoe sotrudnichestvo i vzaimopomoshch' sotsialisticheskikh stran, op. cit.*, p. 258; and *Revista de statistică*, No. 10 (1963), p. 48.

[31] *Rumania in the International Trade 1944–1964* (Chamber of Commerce of the R.P.R.), pp. 67–68.

sumed at home. The export ratio for this branch was only 5.6 percent in 1958; it could hardly have exceeded 10 percent in 1963.[32]

The structure of exports, however, has not been as "favorable" as it might have been from a purely mercantilistic point of view. The relative importance of metal-intensive products such as railroad cars, radiators, trailers, and other heavy equipment has tended to depress the average value in foreign currency obtained per ton of machinery exported, while purchases of "technically progressive" advanced equipment have tended to raise the unit value of imports. In 1964, it has recently been disclosed, the price per ton of machinery and equipment exported was "2.3 times lower" than the price per ton of machinery imported.[33]

We now turn to the trade statistics for other commodity groups, for the years 1948 to 1965, which are shown in Table 3.9.

The evolution of the commodity composition of Rumania's trade has been marked by the dominant position in both imports and exports of raw materials, fuels, and semifabricates, which alone made up about half of total imports and exports in 1965. In the case of imports, this proportion was about average for the entire period from 1950 to 1965, while for exports it showed a regression from the still higher ratios — 68 to 70 percent — recorded in 1950 and 1955.

Imports of raw materials, unlike imports of machinery and equipment, which fluctuated widely, followed a steady advance from 1948 to 1964. They kept on rising, albeit at a slower pace than in previous years, from 1953 to 1956, when imports of machinery plummeted. There is no question but that raw-material imports were quite closely correlated with the level of industrial output, whose rate of growth declined, but never became negative, during the years of the New Course.[34]

Exports of raw materials, fuels, and semifabricates expanded somewhat more rapidly than imports in this group from 1948 to 1955. A deceleration set in that year (or possibly in 1954), due largely to the stagnation of petroleum and lumber exports. After World War II imports of manufactured consumer goods were relatively much less impor-

[32] The percentage ratio for 1958 is from the *Information Bulletin of the Rumanian Chamber of Commerce* (April 1959), p. 8. According to this source, the ratio was scheduled to rise to 6.7 percent in 1959. Assuming that this planned ratio was realized, and using the output and export indices for 1959 in *Rumania in the International Trade* (*op. cit.*, pp. 65–66), we obtain the percentage in the text.

[33] *Probleme economice*, No. 12 (1965), p. 79.

[34] There is no evident explanation for the decline in imports of raw materials in 1965, despite a 9 percent growth in industrial production during the year. It is possible, of course, that inventories and reserves of imported materials were temporarily scaled down during the year.

TABLE 3.9. Imports and Exports of Raw Materials, Fuels, Semifabricates, Animals, Foodstuffs, and Manufactured Consumer Goods in Selected Years (*Millions of Lei*)

IMPORTS

	Raw Materials, Fuels, and Semifabricates		Animals and Foodstuffs	Manufactured Consumer Goods
	Total	Chemical Products		
1948	473	n.a.	36	57
1950	764 (757)	n.a. (13)	16 (13)	138 (149)
1951	1,015	n.a.	88	49
1953	1,227	n.a.	63	77
1955	1,319 (1,291)	n.a. (147)	320 (332)	117 (116)
1956	1,433	n.a.	145	92
1958	1,739	n.a.	229	163
1960	2,227	289	196	201
1961	2,475	320	156	280
1962	2,721	333	178	298
1963	2,915	414	236	419
1964	3,457	418	392	411
1965	3,311	407	202	434

EXPORTS

	Raw Materials, Fuels, and Semifabricates			Animals and Foodstuffs	Manufactured Consumer Goods
	Total	Petroleum Products	Chemical Products		
1948	455	n.a.	n.a.	440	2
1950	880 (885)	383 (383)	21 (21)	284 (318)	57 (17)
1951	964	461	n.a.	400	n.a.
1953	1,475	729[a]	31[a]	349	87
1955	1,625 (1,764)	912 (912)	33 (33)	552 (579)	57 (32)
1956	1,503	1,058	n.a.	571	84
1958	1,929	n.a.	56	418	130
1960	2,443	1,045	94	894	249
1961	2,618	1,026	135	1,075	300
1962	2,623	961	154	1,077	324
1963	2,880	963	222	1,273	433
1964	3,063	951	341	1,329	514
1965	3,252	835	425	1,405	729

[a] Average of 1952 and 1954.

Note: All data for 1950, 1955, and 1956 refer to the old series. Revised series data, where available, are shown in parentheses.

Sources and methods: All revised data for 1950, 1955, and 1960 to 1965 are from

tant than in the 1930's, when they accounted for more than half of the value of imports; they never exceeded a tenth of total imports during the postwar period, a proportion that they reached in 1950. The Korean War forced serious retrenchments in these imports. It is worth noting that as early as 1953 Rumania exported more manufactured consumer goods — mainly in the form of textiles — than she imported. This surplus turned into a temporary deficit during the years of the New Course — as imports were stepped up and exports were trimmed to add to domestic supplies — but after 1959 a surplus again accrued to Rumania on this account.

Despite the large amounts of foreign currency the Rumanians had to expend to fuel their industrial expansion, they succeeded in raising their imports of manufactured consumer goods by 166 percent between 1958 and 1965, with noticeable effects on the size and the variety of the fund of consumer goods available to the population.

The breakdowns by broad commodity groups just discussed, along with a product-by-product analysis of the relation between imports and consumption and exports and production,[35] allow us to draw some conclusions about the relation of foreign trade to trends in the domestic economy. The inability to raise food exports substantially, starting in 1948, forced the Rumanian planners to step up petroleum, cement, and timber exports at the expense of the domestic market. This policy made it possible to buy enough machines and raw materials to meet the minimal requirements of industrial development during the First

[35] In Appendix B.

Anuarul statistic al Republicii Socialiste România, 1966, pp. 472–473; data for 1951 are based on index relatives linked to 1955 (old series) in *Geografia economică a R.P.R.* (Bucharest, 1957), pp. 303–304. Except for petroleum products and chemicals, all "old series" estimates for 1950 are derived from percentages in Imre Vajda, *Nemzetközi kereskedelem* (Budapest, 1959), pp. 257 and 262, and for 1955 are taken from Table 3.2. Index relatives for exports of petroleum products and chemicals from 1950 to 1955 in the *Information Bulletin of the Chamber of Commerce of the R.P.R.,* No. 7 (1956), p. 8, were so close to the increases that can be computed from the revised data that it was surmised no revision had taken place in these data. This assumption made it possible to estimate 1951 and 1956 exports of petroleum products, for which percentage links with 1950 and 1955 are to be found in the same *Information Bulletin,* No. 3 (1956), p. 8; and No. 10 (1958), p. 5. For 1952 and 1954, which were averaged to obtain a rough estimate for 1953, indices in *Economia Romîniei între anii 1944–1959* (Bucharest, 1959), p. 577, were used. A percentage breakdown of imports and exports by commodity groups in *Probleme economice,* No. 12 (1957), served to estimate all data for 1948, 1953, and 1956 in the table. All data for 1958 stem from percentages in I. V. Dudinskii, *Mirovaia sistema sotsializma* (Moscow, 1961), p. 166. Except for errors due to rounding, they are consistent with the absolute figures on trade in machinery and raw materials given for that year in J. Novozámský, *Vyrovnávání ekonomické úrovně zemí RVHP* (Prague, 1964), pp. 103–109.

Five-Year Plan. However, it left little leeway to improve the population's living standards, which were still below prewar levels in the early 1950's. In the mid-1950's the export drive had to be intensified to meet various financial obligations to Rumania's allies. The extra timber, cement, and petroleum that had to be sold abroad cut into allocations to industry and construction. Investments stagnated, and the economy could not take off for lack of a free supply of foreign exchange to finance the imports that were required for a massive advance.

From 1959–1960, however, external obligations no longer placed such a heavy burden on the economy. Increased agricultural procurements made it possible simultaneously to raise domestic consumption by moderate amounts and to expand food exports. This in turn released petroleum products, cement, and timber for domestic uses, providing material support for a renewed industrial drive. Without question, the "valorification" of Rumanian staple products — imparting to these products greater per-unit value by processing them into semifinished and finished products — facilitated this strategy. Thanks to this policy, the Rumanians could earmark a greater share of unprocessed output for domestic consumption without jeopardizing exports. It is remarkable, nevertheless, that the export-to-output ratio fell for the petroleum industry as a whole after 1960, as domestic consumption expanded even faster than "valorification" could proceed.

The persistent drive toward self-sufficiency in light and food-processing industries (wool, flax and hemp, edible oils, sugar, and hides), in metallurgy (iron ores, coke, and copper), and in chemicals (dyes and pharmaceuticals) has spared foreign exchange resources for other "indispensable uses," that is, for commodities that cannot be produced at home for lack of domestic raw materials — nickel, natural rubber, and cocoa — or because their production would be patently inefficient — as would be the case for cotton and various types of machinery and equipment required in small quantities on the Rumanian market.

From this examination of trends in imports and exports by commodity groups since 1948, we can advance the following generalizations:

1. The diversification of industrial exports, the policy of exporting products in as highly processed a form as possible, and the displacement of imports of manufactures by domestic production went on during the entire period under consideration. These trends were even more pronounced during the 1958–1965 boom than in the first period of rapid expansion of 1948–1953.

2. The relative shares of foodstuffs and of raw materials in exports were to some extent inversely correlated. During periods of high investments and rapid growth, exports of foodstuffs were stepped up, while certain quantities of petroleum products, cement, and lumber that otherwise would have been exported were retained at home as material support for the expansion. During the slowdown of 1953–1957, exports of foodstuffs were kept fairly low, while exports of raw materials and semifabricates were intensified to bridge the gap.

3. All export trends were sensitive to changes in domestic production: the stagnation of petroleum and lumber output from the mid-1950's and the sudden rise in state procurements of agricultural products in the late 1950's had a decisive influence on the planners' willingness and ability to substitute agricultural products for raw materials in the export program.

The Regional Distribution of Trade

Available statistics on trade by region are scanty and difficult to interpret prior to the publication in the official yearbooks of complete breakdowns for the year 1958. What we do have is confined almost exclusively to turnover statistics. Up to 1950, the members of the Council for Mutual Economic Assistance comprised the entire noncapitalist world; thereafter trade with Communist China and eventually with the Asiatic Communist states widened the sphere of exchanges with "socialist countries" beyond CMEA. (Until 1953, exchanges with Communist China came to less than 1 percent of Rumania's turnover, but by 1956 China already made up 4.2 percent of total trade.)[36]

From the estimates of trade turnover with the Soviet Union and with CMEA as a whole that correspond to the "old series" presented in Table 3.10, it can be seen that the European people's democracies accounted for a fairly steady 27 to 28 percent of trade turnover in most years, or only a little more than half the Soviet share. The share of trade turnover with capitalist countries was about 20 percent in 1951 and as low as 16 percent in 1953; it then rose again to 20.5 percent in 1955 and

[36] Based on the percentages and index numbers in *Dezvoltarea economiei R.P.R. pe drumul socialismului 1948–1957* (Bucharest, 1958), p. 397; and *Geografia economică a R.P.R.* (Bucharest, 1957), p. 305. The following index numbers (1952 = 100) show the rapid growth of Rumania's trade with Communist China: in 1953 the index of total turnover stood at 338, in 1954 at 374, and in 1956 at 1,125 (*Information Bulletin of the Chamber of Commerce of the R.P.R.*, No. 11 [1955], p. 4, and previous source listed).

TABLE 3.10. TRADE TURNOVER WITH THE SOVIET UNION AND WITH CMEA, 1947–1956 (*Millions of Lei and Percentages*)

	Soviet Union			CMEA		
	Index (1948 = 100)	Value (millions of lei)	Percent of Total Turnover	Index (1948 = 100)	Value (millions of lei)	Percent of Total Turnover
1947	46	329	51	42	483	75.4
1948	150	714	45	100	1,163	72.8
1949	n.a.	n.a.	n.a.	163	1,897	81.8
1950	192	1,368	50	196	2,279	83.3
1951	230	1,640	51	222	2,570	79.8
1952	278	1,988	58	274	3,186	83.3
1953	374	2,477	56.0	316	3,674	83.1
1954	n.a.	n.a.	n.a.	287	3,338	79.4
1955	325	2,319	49.1	311[a]	3,618	77.1
1956	300	2,143	47.6	279	3,246	72.1

[a] 313 according to the index in *Mezinárodní socialistická dělba práce* cited in *Sources and methods* below.

Note: All statistics in the table correspond to the "old series."

Sources and methods: All data on trade with the Soviet Union are based on percentages of total turnover corresponding to the "old series" of Table 3.1. The sources for these percentages are, for 1947: I. Oleinik, *Razvitie promyshlennosti Rumynii* . . . (Moscow, 1959), p. 157; for 1948, 1951, 1952, and 1953: B. Zotov, *Vneshniaia torgovlia evropeiskikh stran narodnoi demokratii* (Moscow, 1958), p. 99; for 1955 and 1956: see sources to Table 3.3. Trade with CMEA: for 1947: computed from percentages in I. Oleinik, *op. cit.*, p. 157; for 1949 and 1950: from percentages in *Revista de statistică*, No. 4 (1956), p. 130. Data for all other years were reconstructed using an index of trade turnover with CMEA in *Mezinárodní socialistická dělba práce*, V. Wacker and B. Malý, eds. (Prague, 1964), p. 80, which was linked to the estimate for 1950 obtained from a percentage of total trade. Data for 1955 and 1956 are from the sources indicated in Tables 3.3 and 3.4.

to 23.3 percent in 1956 — a significant recovery from the low point reached in 1953.[37]

Such fragments of information as we possess on the geographic composition of imports and exports suggest that trade with individual regions was far from balanced, although, as can be judged from the statistics in Table 3.1, total imports from all countries did not differ so much from total exports in most years. There was a large deficit in trade with the capitalist world, imports from this group amounting to about twice as much as exports from 1950 to 1953. There is no ready

[37] Calculations based on an index of trade with the Soviet Union published in September 1959 indicate that statistics of trade with the Soviet Union were revised upward in conjunction with the general revision of 1959 (cf. Table 3.3).

explanation for these deficits, although it is conceivable that a part of
the exports to socialist countries might have been paid in convertible
currencies and used to purchase goods from Western Europe. (During
the Korean War, neither credits nor invisible earnings from the West
were likely to have been large enough to finance deficits of this magnitude.) Although trade with socialist countries was more or less balanced, at least from 1949, it is remarkable that exports to the Soviet

TABLE 3.11. IMPORTS FROM AND EXPORTS TO SOCIALIST COUNTRIES AND THE
REST OF THE WORLD IN SELECTED YEARS, 1947–1956
(*Millions of Lei*)

	Socialist Countries		Rest of the World		Total	
	Imports	Exports	Imports	Exports	Imports	Exports
1947	258	186	110	19	368	205
1948	472	758	277	146	749	904
1949	922	977	231	189	1,153	1,166
1950	1,153	1,134	307	140	1,460	1,274
1952	1,557	1,699	439	128	1,996	1,827
1953	1,878	1,824	432	222	2,310	2,046
1955	1,839	1,921	496	468	2,335	2,389
1956	1,658	1,958	443	689	2,101	2,401

Note: All data correspond to the "old series."
Sources and methods: 1947: I. P. Oleinik, *Dezvoltarea industriei Romîniei în anii
regimului democrat-popular* (Bucharest, 1960), p. 156. 1948: V. A. Karra, *Stroitel'stvo
sotsialisticheskoi ekonomiki v R.N.R.* (Moscow, 1953), p. 188. 1949, 1950 and 1952:
based on percentages in *Zahzaniční obchod*, No. 6 (1962), p. 31. 1953: United Nations, Economic Commission for Europe, *Economic Bulletin for Europe*, Vol. 11,
No. 1 (Geneva, 1959), p. A.21. 1955: data on trade with CMEA are contained in
Table 3.5; in addition, imports from and exports to socialist countries other than
CMEA are evaluated in Imre Vajda, *Nemzetközi kereskedelem* (Budapest, 1959), p. 254.
1956: trade with capitalist countries was estimated from the United Nations,
Direction of International Trade, Series T, Vol. IX, No. 10 (New York, 1958), pp.
175–176; trade with socialist countries was derived as a residual.

Union were greatly in excess of imports, while the converse was true
for the people's democracies. In 1953, for instance, imports from the
people's democracies are estimated to have been about twice as great
as exports (mainly due to large deliveries on credit from Czechoslovakia).[38] If this contention is correct, it follows from the statistics in
Table 3.11 that exports to the Soviet Union exceeded imports by 60

[38] Calculated from the official trade statistics of Czechoslovakia, East Germany,
and Hungary, which accounted for the bulk of trade with Rumania in 1953.

to 70 percent.[39] These imbalances may be linked to the operation of the Soviet-Rumanian joint companies. The Soviet Union obtained imports of petroleum and of other products, corresponding to its share in the proceeds of these enterprises, without having to compensate for these acquisitions by supplying goods or services to Rumania in return.

In 1955, after most of the mixed companies had been liquidated, a change occurred in this pattern of exchanges. The old series for 1955 show that Rumania's trade accounts were approximately balanced with the people's democracies, while a moderate deficit developed in trade with the Soviet Union.[40]

The capitalist states, from 1959 on, increased their share of trade at the expense of the Soviet Union and of the Asian Communist states[41] (Table 3.12). Virtually the entire shift took place between 1959 and 1961, during which period the share of the non-Communist nations went up from a fifth to nearly a third of Rumania's trade. Imports from and exports to the capitalist world both rose by nearly 80 percent from 1959 to 1960; the respective increases were 56 and 22 percent in the following year. The chief gainers were France and Western Germany, imports from which rose by nearly 150 percent in 1960, but Austria, Great Britain, Italy, Switzerland, Yugoslavia, and the United States (starting virtually from scratch) also shared in the expansion. Imports from Japan rose from a negligible level before 1960 to 110 million lei by 1964, when they accounted for some 5 percent of imports from all capitalist states (Table 3.13).

Rumania's trade with the developing countries kept up with her total level of trade but failed to match the spectacular upsurge in exchanges with Western Europe and the United States. Their share in total Rumanian exports reached 6.4 percent in 1965, compared to 4.4 percent in 1956 and 5.3 percent in 1959.[42] Owing to the fact that a

---

[39] The Economic Commission for Europe observed the same pattern of trade, but its estimates, prepared in 1959, show much smaller disparities. According to this source, exports to the people's democracies in 1953 were 672 million lei and imports 924 million lei; exports to the Soviet Union were 1,134 million lei and imports 918 million lei (*Economic Bulletin for Europe*, Vol. 11, No. 1 [Geneva, 1959], p. A.21).

[40] See Table 3.5.

[41] Exports to Communist China dropped from 177 million lei in 1959 to a low of 13 million in 1962, then gradually recovered, reaching 159.8 million lei in 1965. It is believed that petroleum products and machinery make up the bulk of these exports. Imports from China declined less drastically — from 180 million in 1959 to a low of 62 million in 1962 — but lagged in their recovery, reaching 131 million lei in 1965.

[42] Table 3.13, and *Dezvoltarea economiei pe drumul socialismului, 1948–1957, op. cit.*, p. 404.

TABLE 3.12. REGIONAL DISTRIBUTION OF RUMANIAN IMPORTS AND EXPORTS, 1958 TO 1965 (*Millions of Lei*)

	1958	1959	1960	1961	1962	1963	1964	1965
Imports from								
Soviet Union	1,523	1,408	1,596	1,793	2,223	2,396	2,958	2,437
Percent of total imports	*52.7*	*46.7*	*41.0*	*36.7*	*39.4*	*39.0*	*42.2*	*37.7*
Other CMEA[a]	640	813	1,043	1,265	1,401	1,531	1,580	1,269
Percent	*22.0*	*27.0*	*26.8*	*25.9*	*24.8*	*25.0*	*22.5*	*19.6*
Other socialist countries[b]	107	192	174	157	131	207	168	180
Percent	*3.7*	*6.4*	*4.5*	*3.2*	*2.3*	*3.4*	*2.4*	*2.8*
Capitalist countries[c]	621	598	1,074	1,674	1,892	1,998	2,303	2,577
Percent	*21.5*	*19.9*	*27.6*	*34.2*	*33.5*	*32.6 6*	*32.9*	*39.9*
Total imports	2,890	3,012	3,887	4,888	5,647	6,132	7,009	6,463
Exports to								
Soviet Union	1,412	1,500	1,689	2,107	2,060	2,477	2,531	2,631
Percent of total exports	*50.2*	*47.8*	*39.3*	*44.3*	*42.0*	*45.1*	*42.2*	*39.8*
Other CMEA[a]	521	738	1,143	1,019	1,174	1,075	1,345	1,563
Percent	*18.5*	*23.5*	*26.6*	*21.4*	*23.9*	*19.6*	*22.4*	*23.7*
Other socialist countries[b]	178	219	260	158	99	232	191	243
Percent	*6.3*	*7.0*	*6.0*	*3.3*	*2.0*	*4.2*	*3.2*	*3.7*
Capitalist countries[c]	698	677	1,210	1,472	1,576	1,706	1,933	2,171
Percent	*24.9*	*21.7*	*28.1*	*31.0*	*32.1*	*31.1*	*32.2*	*32.8*
Total exports	2,810	3,135	4,302	4,755	4,908	5,490	6,000	6,609

[a] Bulgaria, Czechoslovakia, East Germany, Hungary, Poland, and Albania until 1961. These same countries minus Albania plus Mongolia thereafter.

[b] Albania, Mainland China, Cuba, North Vietnam, North Korea, and Mongolia until 1961. These same countries minus Mongolia plus Albania thereafter. Trade relations with Cuba were initiated in 1961.

[c] Including Yugoslavia.

Sources: Anuarul Statistic al R.P.R. 1961, pp. 315–316; and *1965*, pp. 433–437; *Statistical Pocket Book of the Socialist Republic of Romania, 1966*, pp. 240–247.

considerable part of these exports was on credit, Rumania's balance of trade with respect to most of her customers in the underdeveloped world was strongly positive.

Was the Westward shift in Rumania's trade foreseen when the Six-Year Plan (1960 to 1965) was drafted, or was this new policy improvised after the long-term plan had been approved? From the

TABLE 3.13. Trade with Selected Western European Countries, Yugoslavia, the United States, Japan, and the Developing Nations, 1958–1965 (*Millions of Lei*)

	1958	1959	1960	1961	1962	1963	1964	1965
Imports from								
Federal Republic of								
Germany	134.2	112.5	276.6	380.4	479.8	458.2	526.8	662.8
Italy	48.7	53.5	98.1	144.0	279.8	293.7	289.5	311.6
France	94.3	60.6	149.0	152.2	124.1	142.5	272.2	295.3
Great Britain	44.6	64.5	106.5	308.0	263.9	299.7	250.0	263.4
Austria	34.2	30.7	59.2	87.7	108.9	106.9	152.9	143.2
Japan	—	0.1	—	10.3	34.6	49.9	111.5	106.0
Yugoslavia	21.3	10.2	29.1	74.6	50.1	33.0	61.6	74.5
Switzerland	15.9	48.9	51.4	85.6	82.5	91.2	73.8	72.4
United States	4.1	5.7	37.8	24.1	12.8	5.2	31.2	54.8
Developing nations[a]	130.8	125.7	136.1	234.4	270.6	300.2	290.5	352.8
Exports to								
Federal Republic of								
Germany	157.7	143.9	262.6	300.1	309.8	322.5	321.7	379.4
Italy	66.5	56.3	153.7	173.2	184.8	283.8	295.4	395.7
France	92.4	84.3	116.9	130.8	167.7	193.0	157.6	131.2
Great Britain	39.0	52.0	89.5	137.7	130.9	145.1	189.9	183.2
Austria	35.7	39.5	94.2	101.4	88.7	133.9	145.2	145.8
Japan	—	—	—	29.0	24.7	35.5	55.4	83.5
Yugoslavia	30.1	24.3	47.4	53.8	24.4	52.9	60.3	98.6
Switzerland	37.7	24.9	66.7	98.0	49.4	41.5	71.4	56.6
United States	3.9	4.4	3.8	4.9	7.8	5.5	11.1	15.8
Developing nations[a]	155.3	166.6	244.1	249.1	351.2	294.7	384.5	419.7

[a] Listed separately in the statistical yearbooks. Countries omitted are of negligible importance for Rumanian trade.

Sources: Anuarul statistic al R.P.R. 1961, pp. 315–316; *Anuarul statistic al R.P.R. 1965*, pp. 433–437.

fragmentary statistics available, it would appear that the new strategy *was* reflected in the plan, although the new pattern of exchanges that eventually emerged showed rather large discrepancies from the targets set for 1965. Trade turnover was slated to double from 1959 to 1965, while exchanges with CMEA were to rise by only 83 percent (see Table 3.14). These figures imply a planned increase of 181 percent in trade with capitalist countries and Asiatic Communist states. In actuality, this increase was already achieved by 1964, despite the drop in trade with China after 1960. By 1965 trade turnover with all non-CMEA countries had risen to threefold its 1959 level.

The data in Table 3.14 show the targets for trade with individual

TABLE 3.14. The Six-Year Plan in Foreign Trade: Imports from
and Exports to CMEA Members in 1959 and 1965 and
in the 1965 Plan (*Millions of Lei*)

			1965 (*Plan*)	
	1959	1965	Total	Comprised in Long-Term Agreements
Imports from				
U.S.S.R.	1,408	2,437	2,100	1,837
Albania	2	15	11	11
Bulgaria	30	78	127	107
Czechoslovakia	295	418	600	513
East Germany	269	375	480	161
Hungary	110	169	219	126
Poland	107	222	270	159
Total	2,221	3,714	3,807	2,914
Exports to				
U.S.S.R.	1,500	2,631	2,400	2,102
Albania	7	19	19	12
Bulgaria	40	55	98	68
Czechoslovakia	210	572	675	553
East Germany	213	430	480	159
Hungary	137	231	225	147
Poland	132	270	259	156
Total	2,239	4,208	4,156	3,197

Sources: Data for 1959 are from *Anuarul statistic al R.P.R. 1965*, pp. 433–435;
for 1965: from the *Statistical Pocket Book, 1966*, pp. 240–243; planned targets are
from J. Novozámský, *Otázky vyrovnávání ekonomické úrovně evropscýkh socialistických
zemí* (candidate dissertation, Prague, 1962), p. 137.

members of CMEA in 1965 in conjunction with the published trade
returns for 1959 and 1965.

The most striking discrepancy between target and performance for
1965, the end year of the plan, occurred in trade with the Soviet Union,
both imports from which and exports to which exceeded forecasts (by
16 and 10 percent, respectively). This was probably due to the failure
to program raw-material requirements correctly. Nevertheless, imports from CMEA as a whole fell short of the targets set for 1965, due to
the failure to reach the planned level of imports from Bulgaria, Czechoslovakia, East Germany, Hungary, and Poland, the combined shortfall
for these five countries amounting to about 25 percent. (Exports to
CMEA countries excepting the Soviet Union were about 10 percent

below target in 1965.) It is interesting that instead of being approximately balanced as the plan foresaw, Rumania's trade with these countries showed a surplus of 300 million lei, amounting to nearly one fifth of exports. This suggests that the shortfall on the import side affected chiefly machinery and equipment: for at least a part of these purchases would normally have been made on credit, which would have tended to offset the repayment of Rumanian debts to these countries, thus making for a closer balance between imports and exports than actually occurred.

The Geographic Distribution of Trade by Commodity Groups

We have already seen that imports of machinery and equipment were stepped up to very high levels during the first three years of the Five-Year Plan (1951–1955). Nine tenths of the machinery purchased abroad during the entire Five-Year Plan was imported from socialist countries,[43] with the Soviet Union contributing one half to two thirds of these imports, chiefly in the form of complete factories and assemblies. As can be seen in Table 3.15, capitalist countries played a major role in the more recent expansion in total machinery and equipment imports, starting in 1958.

As late as 1958, 89 percent of machinery and equipment imports originated in CMEA countries; from 1962, the share of these countries in the Rumanian market fluctuated between 60 and 70 percent. If we consider that machinery prices in the Communist bloc were somewhat higher on the average than in the world market at the time, this share, by 1965, may have fallen as low as 50 percent on a comparable evaluation (compared to 62 percent on the basis of actual foreign-trade prices).[44]

[43] *Ekonomicheskoe sotrudnichestvo i vzaimopomoshch sotsialisticheskikh stran, op. cit.,* p. 249.

[44] Although the situation, from the viewpoint of machinery suppliers in the Communist bloc, cannot be termed satisfactory, it is not as bad as some observers make out. For example, the Czech economist Novozámský, in a book published in 1964, showed that Rumania's trade in machinery and equipment with CMEA countries had risen by only 20 percent between 1955 and 1960. This increase, which he contrasted with comparable data from other CMEA countries, was ostensibly the smallest in the bloc. (Poland, the next lowest on the list, registered a 65 percent increase in machinery trade with CMEA.) Rumania's 20 percent increase also lagged behind the rise in its own domestic machine building, to a greater extent than any other listed country (J. Novozámský, *Vyrovnávání ekonomické úrovně zemí RVHP* [Prague, 1964], p. 113). These results could be obtained only by computing the increase on the basis of the revised machinery imports for 1955, which were nearly double the original evaluation. Starting with the original statistics, we find that Rumania's trade turnover with CMEA in these five years increased slightly more than twofold, as compared to an 80 percent increase for Czechoslovakia and East Germany.

TABLE 3.15. RUMANIAN IMPORTS OF MACHINERY AND EQUIPMENT:
REGIONAL DISTRIBUTION IN SELECTED YEARS,
1950 TO 1965 (*Millions of Lei*)

	Soviet Union	East Germany	Czechoslovakia	CMEA Total	Capitalist Countries	Total Imports
1950	238	9*	n.a.	428	114	542
1953	n.a.	163	234	n.a.	n.a.	973
1955ᵃ	365	n.a.	145	550	29	579
1956	205	n.a.	82	401	30	431
1958	302	100*	n.a.	676	75	759
1960	373*	n.a.	177*	939	226*	1,263
1961	393*	n.a.	n.a.	1,280	582*	1,978
1962	800	210	266	1,500	731*	2,450
1964	513*	n.a.	n.a.	1,936	693*	2,749
1965	n.a.	n.a.	n.a.	1,568	875*	2,517

ᵃ Data for 1955 are from the "old series."

Note: All data derived from partners' trade statistics are marked with an asterisk.

Sources and methods: Imports from the Soviet Union and CMEA: for 1950, 1955, and 1956, *Probleme economice*, No. 12 (1957), p. 20; for 1958, *Dezvoltarea industriei socialiste în R.P.R.* (Bucharest, 1959), p. 218, and L. Ciamaga, *Od wspôłpracy do integracji* (Warsaw, 1965), p. 171; for 1962, *Rumania in the International Trade 1944–1964* (Bucharest, 1964), pp. 161–162, and *Dezvoltarea economică a Romîniei 1944–1964* (Bucharest, 1964), p. 703. Imports from CMEA in 1960 were computed from exports in that year (see the notes and sources to Table 3.16) and from the surplus of imports over exports as given in G. M. Sorokin, ed., *Stroitel'stvo kommunizma v SSSR* (Moscow, 1962), p. 110; for 1961 they were computed by subtracting exports, estimated in Table 3.16, from total turnover in machinery products, obtained from an index in *Mezinárodní socialistická dělba práce* (Prague, 1964), p. 246. (If exports to CMEA in 1961 were 75 percent, instead of 80 percent as estimated in Table 3.16, machinery imports from CMEA for that year would be raised by 3 percent.) Soviet imports in 1960 and 1961 are from *Vneshniaia torgovlia SSSR za 1959–1963 gody* (Moscow, 1965), p. 279; for 1964, they are from *Vneshniaia torgovlia SSSR za 1964 god* (Moscow, 1965), p. 167. Imports from Czechoslovakia in 1953, 1955, and 1956 are based on percentages of total Rumanian machinery imports in J. Vaněk, *Ekonomický a politický význam vývozu strojírenských výrobků z Č.S.S.R.* (Prague, 1960), p. 197. Imports from East Germany are derived from East German export statistics in *Wirtschaftswissenschaftliche Informationen* (East Berlin), Nos. 4 and 5 (1958), p. 74; machinery imports from Czechoslovakia and from East Germany in 1962 were computed from percentages of total Rumanian imports from these countries in *Rumania in the International Trade 1944–1964*, pp. 161–162. Imports from "capitalist countries" are based on the export data of Western European states, together with Canada and the United States, in O.E.C.D. *Statistical Bulletins*, Series C, *Trade by Commodities*, Annual Supplements for January–December 1960, 1961, 1962, and 1964 (Paris, 1960, 1961, 1962, and 1964). Imports from CMEA in 1964 are derived from the estimate of exports to CMEA in Table 3.16 and from the percentage relation of imports to exports in machinery trade with the region given in *Mirovaia ekonomika i mezhdunarodnye otnosheniia*, No. 5 (1966), p. 22. Imports from CMEA in 1965: based on the share of machinery and equipment in total imports from CMEA in *Plánované hospodářství*, No. 12 (1966), p. 63.

Why did the Rumanians look to the West for the procurement of such a large portion of their increased requirements of machinery and equipment? The answer lies partly in the dissatisfaction of the Rumanian leaders with CMEA, specifically in their impatience with the efforts of the more industrialized members of the Council, including Czechoslovakia and East Germany, to promote bloc-wide specialization agreements that might have crippled Rumanian plans to industrialize along a wide front.[45] But there were also more concrete reasons for the reorientation. Western Europe had the equipment the Rumanians wanted for their industrial program while their East European partners either did not have it or could not meet the technical specifications the Rumanians insisted on. This was especially the case for chemical installations — hardware in short supply throughout the bloc[46] — for plants that were supposed to represent the highest level of world technology.

The geographical distribution of Rumanian purchases within CMEA also underwent marked changes. The position of Czechoslovakia, which used to be the main purveyor of equipment and of armaments to Rumania about the time of Stalin's death, weakened relative to that of both the Soviet Union and East Germany. (Czechoslovakia supplied 24 percent of Rumania's machinery imports in 1953, 19 percent in 1956, and 11 percent in 1962.)[47] One reason for this decline is that Czechoslovakia was reluctant to buy equipment from Rumania in partial compensation for her sales of equipment to that country, whereas East Germany and the Soviet Union showed considerably more good will in negotiating this *quid pro quo*. In the end Rumania gave her preference to suppliers willing to accommodate her in this regard.

The trends in Rumania's total machinery exports and in their geographic distribution are traced in the statistics in Table 3.16.

Considering now the distribution of Rumanian machinery exports by region in Table 3.16, we find, in contrast to the situation on the import side, that the share of CMEA has actually risen in recent years from an average of 61 percent for 1955 to 1958 to an average of 83

[45] See Chapter 4, pp. 189–198 and *passim*.

[46] According to J. Novozámský, around 1960 about two thirds of CMEA's imports of chemical equipment came from capitalist states (*Otázky vyrovnávání . . . , op. cit.*, p. 194).

[47] According to B. Malý (*Nová mysl*, No. 10 [1956], p. 1012), the share of Czechoslovakia in total Rumanian imports of machinery and equipment was as high as 58 percent in 1953. If Malý's figure includes armaments, it is not fully comparable with data for later years cited by Vaněk and with the percentage for 1962 that was computed from *Rumania in the International Trade 1944–1964* (Bucharest, 1964), p. 162.

TABLE 3.16. Rumanian Exports of Machinery and Equipment:
Geographical Distribution in Selected Years,
1950 to 1964 (*Millions of Lei*)

	Soviet Union	East Germany	Czechoslovakia	CMEA Total	Other Countries	Total Exports
1950	51	—	—	53	—	53
1952	64	—	—	n.a.	n.a.	75
1953	n.a.	3 *a	19	n.a.	n.a.	173
1955	87	n.a.	n.a.	122	33	155
1956	89	n.a.	n.a.	133	129	242
1957	73 *	25 *	n.a.	162	72	234
1958	60	n.a.	n.a.	169	164	333
1960	142 *	135 *	75 *	455	261	716
1961	266 *	n.a.	n.a.	610	153	763
1962	350	118	115	769	117 b	884
1964	382 *	n.a.	n.a.	892	202 b	1,094
1965	n.a.	n.a.	n.a.	1,028	195	1,223

a 1954.

b Of which 65 million lei to Communist nations outside CMEA in 1962 and 76 million in 1964.

Note: All data derived from partners' trade statistics are marked with an asterisk.

Sources and methods: Total exports of machinery and equipment: 1953 and 1956, based on percentages of total exports in *Probleme economice*, No. 12 (1957), p. 33; for other years, *Anuarul statistic al R.P.R. 1964*, pp. 437–439; and the index relatives in *Ekonomicheskoe sotrudnichestvo i vzaimopomoshch' sotsialisticheskikh stran* (Moscow, 1962), p. 257 (this index is consistent with published data of total machinery exports for 1950, 1958, 1959, and 1960). Exports to the Soviet Union in 1955, 1957, 1960, and 1961 are from *Vneshniaia torgovlia SSSR za 1958–1963 gody* (Moscow, 1965), pp. 134–135; for 1964 they are from *Vneshniaia torgovlia SSSR za 1964 god* (Moscow, 1965), p. 171; for 1950, 1956, and 1958, they are based on percentages of total machinery exports in *Probleme economice*, No. 12 (1957), p. 35; and No. 8 (1959), p. 137; and *Information Bulletin* (Chamber of Commerce of the R.P.R., November 1958), p. 4. Exports to CMEA in 1955, 1956, and 1957 are taken from Imre Vajda, *Nemzetközi kereskedelem* (Budapest, 1959), p. 260; in 1958, from L. Ciamaga, *Od współpracy do integracji* (Warsaw, 1965), p. 171; in 1960 and 1964 they are based on percentages in *Czechoslovak Foreign Trade*, No. 10 (1965), p. 5; in 1962, on a percentage in *ibid.*, No. 5 (1964), p. 11. Exports to CMEA countries in 1961 were assumed to represent 80 percent of total machinery exports, compared to 64 percent in 1960 and 87 percent in 1962. Czechoslovakia's machinery imports from Rumania in 1953 were computed from D. Machová, *ČSSR v socialistické mezinárodní dělbe práce* (Prague, 1962), p. 210. (This source indicates that 1953 was the first year when Rumania exported a significant volume of machinery to Czechoslovakia.) Exports to East Germany in 1960 are based on percentages in *Der Aussenhandel*, Nos. 16–17 (1960), p. 20. (Imports in 1950 and 1952 were negligible.) Exports to the Soviet Union, Czechoslovakia, and East Germany in 1960, 1962, and 1964 are from the same sources as those indicated for these years and countries in Table 3.15. Exports to Communist nations not members of CMEA were calculated by subtracting exports to CMEA in 1962 and 1964 from exports to all "socialist countries" in those years, which were themselves estimated from percentages in *Dezvoltarea economică a Romîniei 1944–1964* (Bucharest, 1964), p. 705; and *Documents, Articles and Information on Romania* (Agerpres), No. 19 (1965), p. 4. Exports to CMEA in 1965 are derived from the percentage of machinery and equipment in total Rumanian exports to CMEA in *Hospodářské noviny*, No. 29 (1966), p. 3.

percent for 1961 to 1965. This has been due mainly to the recession in trade with China, which absorbed at least a quarter of Rumania's equipment exports in 1956[48] but less than 7 percent in 1964. Still, it is worth noting that exports to less developed countries now represent a smaller share of total machinery exports than in 1956, while exports to industrialized Western nations were, and have remained, at relatively insignificant levels.

The interest of traditional exporters of equipment in the Soviet bloc (such as Czechoslovakia and East Germany) in the Rumanian market depends not so much on the value of the machinery, equipment, and manufactured consumer goods they export to Rumania as on the surplus of their exports over their imports of these goods in their trade with Rumania. Given the bilateral nature of trading relations in the bloc and the shortage of convertible Western currencies, the size of these surpluses determines how much Rumanian oil, timber, minerals, and foodstuffs these industrialized nations are able to buy. Czechoslovakia and East Germany must be especially concerned over the very slow growth in their surpluses in trade with Rumania at a time when Rumania's machinery purchases from the capitalist world — at least from Western Europe, its chief supplying area — have been almost entirely paid for by sales of raw materials and foodstuffs. From 1958 to 1962 Rumania's deficit in machinery trade with CMEA members other than the Soviet Union only increased from 265 to 281 million lei, or by 6 percent. This was hardly commensurate with the gains East European exporters might have expected from a more than three-fold increase in total Rumanian machinery imports in these four years, accompanied by a rise in the net deficits in this group from 426 million lei in 1958 to 1,566 million lei (261 million dollars) in 1962.[49] In point of fact, the widening of the Rumanian market chiefly benefited West European exporting nations and the Soviet Union. Western Europe's surplus in machinery trade with Rumania rose from about 75 million lei in 1958 to something like 800 million lei in 1962 and 1964. The Soviet Union's surplus nearly doubled during this period.[50] In 1965,

[48] *Probleme economice*, No. 12 (1957), pp. 35–36.

[49] In my article, "The Background and Origins of the Rumanian Dispute with Comecon" (*op. cit.*), I speculated that the Rumanian upsurge in machinery imports after 1958 had removed one of the causes of tension in its relation to CMEA (pp. 137–138). I did not then realize how little this profited the traditional machinery exporters in the Communist bloc.

[50] Between 1962 and 1964, the Soviet Union's surplus in the machinery group seems to have dropped appreciably. Fluctuations in this surplus may be attributed in part to changes in the balance of foodstuffs between the Soviet Union and Rumania. When Rumania sells grain to the Soviet Union, as it did in 1961, 1962, and 1963, it buys machinery in return. But when it imports grain from the Soviet

which may have been an atypical year, Rumania's deficit in machinery trade with CMEA as a whole fell to a lower level than in 1958 while her deficit with the rest of the world rose to a record high.[51]

The Regional Distribution of Trade in Raw Materials, Semifabricates, Foodstuffs, and Consumer Goods

In the early 1950's, as can be seen in Table 3.17, the Rumanians were predominantly dependent on the Soviet Union for the provision of their raw-material imports. During the same period, the Soviets

TABLE 3.17. SHARE OF THE U.S.S.R. IN TOTAL IMPORTS AND EXPORTS OF SELECTED RUMANIAN COMMODITY GROUPS, 1950 TO 1956 (*Percentages*)

	1950	1951	1952	1953	1954	1955	1956
				Exports			
Petroleum products	86	80	84	84	69	63	63
Foodstuffs	41	24	23	17	19	31	25
Machines, equipment	96	89	86	58	66	57	37
Construction materials	50	54	65	59	39	32	47
				Imports			
Steel and rolled steel products	65	74	49	47	84	69	63
Nonferrous metals	82	62	37	60	86	79	81
Iron ores	86	91	94	91	93	82	85
Coke	52	41	60	58	70	58	57
Cotton	97	80	95	89	85	84	69

Source: Gh. Gaston Marin, "Ajutorul URSS în construirea socialismului în R.P.R.," *Probleme economice*, No. 10 (1957), pp. 122–123.

bought a very large share of Rumania's export staples. The degree of Rumanian dependence on the Soviet Union as a source of supply and as a market diminished during the New Course, as trade with the West picked up from the trough into which it had fallen prior to Stalin's death. By 1955 no more than half of Rumanian trade in raw materials and semifabricates was conducted with the Soviet Union. The European people's democracies accounted for about one fifth of the imports

Union, as it did in 1964, it must reduce its purchases of machinery and equipment, and increase its sales of these items to keep total trade in balance, thus causing the deficit to shrink. (This was pointed out to me by a Rumanian economist.)

[51] The total deficit with CMEA rose from 507 million lei in 1958 to 731 million in 1962 and 1,044 million in 1964; it then dropped to some 479 million lei in 1965 (Tables 3.15 and 3.16).

in this same group and slightly more than a quarter of the exports.[52] The share of CMEA as a whole in raw-material imports remained approximately the same from 1955 to 1958 while its share of exports declined from 76 to 70 percent.

The trends in the regional distribution of trade by commodity groups after 1958 can be perceived most clearly against the general background of development in the years immediately preceding and following 1958 (the benchmark year marking the resumption of the rapid industrial advance that had been interrupted by the New Course).

How were the Rumanians able to pay for these vastly increased imports?

The answer to this question is bound up in the evolution of Rumanian foreign trade prior to the upsurge in trade of the late 1950's. From 1948 to 1958 exports of foodstuffs fluctuated, without a clear upward trend, between 400 and 600 million lei. Exports of petroleum products, which had increased by nearly 140 percent from 1950 to 1955, were no longer growing by the late 1950's. Consumer goods and chemicals contributed only marginally to the export program (5 and 2 percent of exports, respectively, in 1958). Although exports of ships, trawlers, and oil-drilling equipment were beginning to earn foreign exchange, most branches of the machine-building industry were still incapable of marketing abroad products that would meet foreign competition. Finally, the volume of imports was held down by a severe balance-of-payments crisis, arising from the repayment of Soviet and Czechoslovak credits and from obligations linked with the liquidation of the joint Soviet-Rumanian companies.[53]

The situation improved on most of these counts after 1958. New credits from the Soviet Union, Czechoslovakia, and from Western Europe made it possible to defer payments on imports of plants and equipment for the new industrialization drive.[54] Tourism flourished,

[52] Computed from the statistics in the "old series" in Table 3.2.

[53] See the statement by Gh. Gaston Marin, cited in Chapter 1, p. 52, note 143. The crisis is also alluded to in several Czechoslovak sources, including D. Machová, *op. cit.*, p. 201. Gheorghiu-Dej mentioned in his report to the Central Committee of November 26, 1958, that a rise in exports had made it possible to equilibrate the balance of payments in 1958, with a clear implication that it had not been in equilibrium previously (*Economia Romîniei între anii 1944–1959* [Bucharest, 1959], p. 577).

[54] On Rumania's credits from the Soviet Union and Czechoslovakia, see Čestmír Konečný, *Socialistický mezinárodní úvěr* (Prague, 1964), pp. 193, 237, and 240. While Rumania obtained some credits from Western Europe, it also incurred new obligations as a result of the signing of compensation agreements. It was not until 1961 that the balance of trade with Western countries began to show a deficit.

as resort facilities on the Black Sea were expanded and modernized.[55] Exports of raw materials and semifabricates rose fairly rapidly, despite continued stagnation in the output and export of petroleum products. Gold shipments abroad, based on newly discovered deposits, began to contribute to the credit side of the balance of payments.[56] The most dramatic upturn, and the one most productive of foreign exchange, however, occurred in the agricultural sector. Thanks partly to a rise in the output of state farms and partly to the increased marketability of key export products such as corn from the collectivized sector, state procurements of all farm products rose by two thirds from 1958 to 1964. (Procurements of cereals actually doubled.) With these additional supplies on hand, the government was able to triple exports of food products during this period.

The data in Table 3.18 should be appraised in the light of an essential distinction made in CMEA parlance between "hard" and "soft" goods. Hard goods are those that tend to be in short supply on the CMEA market. They include most raw materials and foodstuffs.[57] The soft goods are those in relatively abundant supply that exporters try to foist on their partners so that they can obtain the hard goods they wish to acquire. Machines and equipment, especially of the technologically standard types produced in large numbers by several members of the socialist common market, belong to this category, as do most manufactured consumer goods. When we amalgamate raw materials and foodstuffs, the two groups in Table 3.18 that comprise mainly hard goods, we find that exports to CMEA rose by 30 percent from 1958 to 1960 and by only 19 percent from 1960 to 1965, whereas exports to the "rest of the world" — that is, mainly to the Western industrialized nations — rose by 72 percent in the first period and by 80 percent in the second.

[55] The number of foreign tourists visiting Rumania increased from 5,000 in 1956 to 30,000 in 1958 and 134,000 in 1961. It reached 162,000 in 1963. The number of Rumanian tourists going abroad increased fifteenfold from 1956 to 1963, but this was still less than half the relative increase in incoming tourists (*Revista de statistică*, No. 10 [1965]).

[56] According to M. Dyner, writing in the Polish economic weekly *Życie gospodarcze*, "the value of gold extracted [in Rumania] is evaluated by Western circles at 30 to 40 million dollars a year" ("Rumunia-kraj nafty i słońca," *Życie gospodarcze*, No. 34 [1964], p. 11). I have not come across any such estimate in Western sources, and I am inclined to believe that Dyner's figures are of Rumanian origin.

[57] An additional reason for the term "hard" is that most of these goods can be used to acquire "hard currencies" in Western markets. The existence of "hard" and "soft" goods testifies to the failure of prices in transactions among CMEA members to equate supply and demand. The world market prices in use in CMEA probably understate the relative scarcity of raw materials and foodstuffs and overstate that of manufactured goods in the CMEA market (cf. the debate on CMEA prices in Chapter 4, p. 224).

TABLE 3.18. Exports by Commodity Groups to CMEA Countries and to the Rest of the World in 1958, 1960, 1962–1965 (*Millions of Lei*)

	1958			*1960*		
	CMEA	Rest of the World	All Coun-tries	CMEA	Rest of the World	All Coun-tries
Machinery and equipment	169	164	333	455	261	716
Manufactured consumer goods	91	39	130	199	50	249
Raw materials and semi-fabricates	1,345	584	1,929			2,443
				2,178	1,159	
Foodstuffs	328	90	418			894
Total	1,933	877	2,810	2,832	1,470	4,302

	1962			*1963*		
	CMEA	Rest of the World	All Coun-tries	CMEA	Rest of the World	All Coun-tries
Machinery and equipment	769	115	884	762	142	904
Manufactured consumer goods	259	65	324	334	99	433
Raw materials, semi-fabricates, and foodstuffs	2,207	1,493	3,700	2,456	1,696	4,152
Total	3,234	1,674	4,908	3,552	1,937	5,489

	1964			*1965*		
	CMEA	Rest of the World	All Coun-tries	CMEA	Rest of the World	All Coun-tries
Machinery and equipment	892	202	1,094	1,028	195	1,223
Manufactured consumer goods	411	103	514	583	146	729
Raw materials and semi-fabricates	1,933	1,130	3,063			3,252
				2,583	2,074	
Foodstuffs	640	689	1,329			1,405
Total	3,876	2,124	6,000	4,194	2,415	6,609

Notes to table are given on p. 176.

The trend in the two remaining groups, which account for the bulk of the soft goods, are in marked contrast to those we have just looked at. Exports to CMEA of machinery and manufactured consumer goods more than doubled from 1958 to 1960, rose by 57 percent from 1960 to 1962, and by another 27 percent from 1962 to 1964; exports in these groups to the rest of the world went up by roughly 50 percent in the first two years and then fell sharply between 1960 and 1962, mainly as a result of the collapse of trade with China.

The data of Table 3.18 indicate that the reorientation of Rumanian exports toward the West, which deflected from the Soviet bloc chiefly hard goods in deficit supply in those markets, made its greatest headway from 1958 to 1960, decelerated in the next two years, and virtually came to a halt between 1962 and 1964, when Rumania's dispute with CMEA was moving toward its climax. It made some further progress in 1965, a year, however, that may have been off trend.

For 1958 and 1964 we have disaggregated data[58] which show that

[58] Although these particular data are liable to a greater percentage error than those cited, they are, I believe, sufficiently accurate to bear out the general tendency described in the text.

Notes to Table 3.18, p. 175. CMEA includes Albania and excludes Mongolia in 1958 and 1960 and conversely in 1962–1965.

Sources and methods: Total exports in all commodity groups are from Tables 3.8 and 3.9. Raw-material exports to CMEA in 1958 are from J. Novozámský, *Vyrovnávání ekonomické úrovně zemí RVHP* (Prague, 1964), p. 109. Exports of manufactured consumer goods to CMEA in that year were derived as the sum of exports to the Soviet Union (*Vneshniaia torgovlia SSSR za 1958–1963 gody* [Moscow, 1965], p. 290) and of exports to the European people's democracies. These latter were estimated on the assumption that they represented the same percentage of exports in this group as in 1956, or 14 percent (N. I. Ivanov, *Razvitie ekonomicheskikh sviazei evropeiskikh stran narodnoi demokratii* [Moscow, 1959], p. 161). Raw-material exports in 1964 are based on percentages in *Czechoslovak Foreign Trade*, No. 10 (1965), pp. 5 and 7. Machinery exports to CMEA in all years except 1963 are from Table 3.16. For 1963, they are derived as a residual after subtracting exports in all other groups from total exports to CMEA. Exports of raw materials, semifabricates, and foodstuffs in 1963 were calculated from percentage data relating to trade with capitalist countries in J. Kovács and V. Vékony, *A Szocialista országok gazdasági együttműködése* (Budapest, 1965), p. 82, after adjusting these data roughly to encompass trade with non-CMEA socialist countries. Exports of manufactured consumer goods to CMEA were based on the assumption that they made up the same share as in 1962, or 80 percent (computed from a percentage in *Dezvoltarea economică a Rominiei 1944–1964* [Bucharest, 1964], p. 706). The same assumption was made for 1960, 1964, and 1965. Note that even substantial errors in the regional division of trade in this group, which made up 5.8 percent of exports in 1960, would have a relatively small effect on the distribution of trade in raw materials and foodstuffs between CMEA and other countries, where exports to CMEA in these groups are obtained as residuals. Thus if consumer goods exports to CMEA were 90 percent rather than 80 percent of total exports in this group in 1960 and 1965, this would only cause a reduction in the raw materials and foodstuffs residual of 1 and 3 percent, respectively.

foodstuffs contributed far more to the reorientation of exports than raw materials and semifabricates. While the share of CMEA members in total exports of raw materials and semifabricates fell only from an estimated 69 to 63 percent, their share in the exports of foodstuffs dropped from 78 to 48 percent. There is a strong likelihood that the brunt of the decline in CMEA's share in food exports fell on the people's democracies and not on the Soviet Union.[59]

For the year 1964 we can break down the raw-materials group into its four principal components: (1) fuels, minerals, and semifabricated metals; (2) chemical products, rubber, and fertilizers; (3) building materials; and (4) raw materials of agricultural origin, excluding foodstuffs. It is remarkable that CMEA's share exceeded 50 percent in all but the fourth subgroup, which consisted almost entirely of lumber and lumber products.[60] CMEA made up 72.5, 71.6, 58.6, and 43.0 percent of the exports in these respective groups.[61]

It may be calculated from these statistics that exports of agricultural products, counting both food and nonfood products, made up 56 percent of all Rumanian exports to countries other than CMEA members in 1964, as compared to only 26 percent in exports to the CMEA bloc. Among foodstuffs, exports to the West concentrated on a few staples, including chiefly corn, meat, oil seeds, butter, eggs, and concentrated feeds. On the average from 1958 to 1962, three quarters of Rumania's corn exports, half of her meat exports, and virtually all of her exports of butter, eggs, and oil seeds went to countries outside CMEA.[62] On the other hand, in the last two or three years, 96 percent of Rumania's vegetable and fruit exports have been sold on the CMEA market.[63]

Among the nonagricultural commodities that the Rumanians shunted away from their traditional outlets in the Soviet bloc, petro-

[59] Itemized exports of foodstuffs to the Soviet Union increased from 44 million lei in 1958 to 253 million in 1962 (*Vneshniaia torgovlia SSSR za 1964 god* [Moscow, 1965], p. 173). If the itemized foodstuffs represented even approximately the same fraction of the total in the group in the two years, the relative loss in the importance of the people's democracies is manifest.

[60] In 1960, exports of furniture, which made up 9.6 percent of total lumber exports, were evaluated at 61.9 million foreign exchange lei (*Valorificarea superioară . . .* , *op. cit.*, p. 170, and *Anuarul statistic 1965*, p. 441). Hence the total value of lumber exports was about 644 million foreign-exchange lei. The value of all exports of vegetable and animal origin, excepting foodstuffs, was equal in that year to 648.5 million lei (*Anuarul statistic 1965*, p. 438).

[61] These data are based on a percentage breakdown of raw-materials exports to CMEA in *Czechoslovak Foreign Trade*, No. 10 (1965), p. 7.

[62] Juliús Lipták, *Mezinárodní dělba práce v zemědělství zemí RVHP* (Prague, 1965), p. 178; and the same author's "Podminky mezinárodní socialistické dělby práce v zemědělství," in *Výzkumne práce* (Výzkumný ústav národohospodářského plánování), No. 52 (Prague, 1963), pp. 54–55.

[63] *Politická ekonomie*, No. 5 (1965), p. 446.

leum and rolled-steel products deserve special mention. In contrast to 1955, when Rumania sold her petroleum products more or less exclusively to the Soviet Union and to the people's democracies, about 40–45 percent of the tonnage exported in 1961 was being shipped to the West and to Asian Communist countries.[64] Exports of rolled-steel products underwent a similar evolution. Whereas as late as 1959 CMEA was the only outlet for these items, in 1960 two thirds of rolled steel exports, computed by tonnage, went to other countries, and in 1961, 42 percent.[65]

This is about all that can be said on the basis of published information about the structure of exports by commodity groups and about their repartition between CMEA and other markets. Still less is known, unfortunately, about the regional origin of imports by commodity groups. Without at least a rudimentary knowledge of the situation on the import side we cannot be sure about the nature of the Westward shift in Rumania's trade. If it happened, for example, that increased sales of raw materials and foodstuffs to Western Europe had been matched by increased purchases of goods in the same groups from outside CMEA, then the balance between soft and hard goods in exports to CMEA and in exports to the West might have remained unaltered. This in fact would seem to be most unlikely, if only because, as we have already seen, Rumania's deficit in trade in machinery products with the West rose much faster than her deficit in these products with her traditional suppliers in CMEA. Nevertheless, this outside possibility can only be eliminated by examining the balance for each commodity group separately, as I have attempted to do for selected years from 1958 to 1965 (see Table 3.19).

From 1958 to 1960 the balance of trade with CMEA turned from a deficit of 229 million lei to a surplus of 193 million lei. The Rumanians repaid their debts by increasing their surplus in raw-material trade with CMEA by approximately 100 million lei and their surplus in food-

[64] Calculated as the difference between the total tonnage exported of the five principal oil products and exports to the Soviet Union (*Vneshniaia torgovlia SSSR za 1958–1963 gody* [Moscow, 1965], pp. 287–288) and to the people's democracies (J. Košnár, *RVHP: Výsledky a problémy* [Bratislava, 1964], p. 152). Petroleum exports to Western Europe were estimated in O.E.C.D. statistics at the equivalent in U.S. dollars of 204 million lei in 1960, 277 million lei in 1962, and 310 million lei in 1963, at which time they represented nearly 30 percent of the total value of Rumanian petroleum exports (O.E.C.D. *Statistical Bulletin*, Series C, *Trade by Commodities, Annual Supplement* for January–December 1960, 1962, and 1963 [Paris, 1960, 1962, and 1963]).

[65] The tonnages involved were far from negligible by East European standards: in 1960, 203,400 out of 318,600 tons were sold outside CMEA, and in 1961, 157,800 out of 381,400 tons (Imre Vajda, *Magyarország és a világ kereskedelme* [Budapest, 1965], pp. 190–191).

TABLE 3.19. RUMANIAN SURPLUSES (+) AND DEFICITS (−) IN TRADE BY COMMODITY GROUPS AND BY REGION, 1958, 1960, 1962, AND 1965 (*Millions of Lei*)

	1958			1960		
	CMEA	Rest of the World	All Countries	CMEA	Rest of the World	All Countries
Machinery and equipment	−507	+ 81	− 426	−484	− 63	− 547
Manufactured consumer goods	− 20	− 13	− 33	+ 51	− 3	+ 48
Raw materials and semi-fabricates	+121	+ 69	+ 190	+219	− 3	+ 216
Foodstuffs	+177	+ 12	+ 189	+392	+306	+ 698
Total	−229	+149	− 80	+193[a]	+222	+ 415

	1962			1965		
	CMEA	Rest of the World	All Countries	CMEA	Rest of the World	All Countries
Machinery and equipment	−731	−835	−1,566	−540	−753	−1,293
Manufactured consumer goods	+ 25	—	+25	+354	− 59	+ 295
Raw materials and semi-fabricates			− 98			− 59
	+316	+486		+674	+470	
Foodstuffs			+ 900			+1,203
Total	−390	−349	− 739	+488	−342	+ 146

[a] The algebraic sum of the surpluses and deficits with CMEA for 1960 equals 178 million lei, compared to a recorded 193 million lei in Rumanian statistics. The difference is presumably due to a small error in the Soviet source from which the surpluses and deficits by commodity groups were taken.

Note: CMEA includes Albania and excludes Mongolia in 1958 and 1960, and conversely in 1962 and 1965.

Sources and methods: Total exports and imports in all groups for all four years are from Tables 3.8 and 3.9. Exports and imports of machinery in trade with CMEA are from Tables 3.15 and 3.18. The surplus in raw-materials trade in 1958 is based on J. Novozámský, *Vyrovnávání ekonomické úrovně zemí RVHP* (Prague, 1964), p. 109. All data for 1960 are from G. M. Sorokin, ed., *Stroitel'stvo kommunizma v SSSR* (Moscow, 1962), p. 110. The surplus in foodstuffs with CMEA in 1958 was estimated as follows: The surplus so defined, averaged over the years 1958 to 1960, is given in J. Lipták, *Mezinárodní dělba práce v zemědělství zemí RVHP* (Prague, 1965), p. 161. For 1960 alone, it is published in G. M. Sorokin, ed., *Stroitel'stvo kommunizma v SSSR* (Moscow, 1962), p. 110. The 1960 surplus was subtracted from the average for 1958–1960 to arrive at an average for 1958–1959. The surplus with CMEA for 1958 was finally calculated on the assumption that it bore the same relation to the 1959 surplus with CMEA as the total surplus in foodstuffs in 1958 did to the

stuffs trade by 215 million lei, while they kept their deficit in the machinery group with this same area approximately constant. In trade with the West and with Communist Asia they ran a large enough surplus in foodstuffs not only to finance their deficit in machinery trade but also to settle some of their obligations to Western Europe and to expand credits to less developed countries. From 1960 to 1962 the surpluses in total trade turned into sizable deficits with both East and West, which widened further in 1963 and 1964. The deficit in total trade with CMEA in 1962 was large enough for Rumania to afford an increase in net imports of machinery and equipment and simultaneously to allow a nearly 50 percent reduction in her surplus in hard goods — raw materials and foodstuffs — with this region. In trade with the rest of the world, however, the surplus in hard goods rose from 81 million in 1958 to a peak of 486 million lei in 1962, then dropped to 355 million lei in 1964 and finally rebounded to within a a few million lei of the 1962 level in 1965.[66] After 1962 an appreciable increase in the share of non-CMEA countries in total imports of raw materials and foodstuffs seems to have been chiefly responsible for Rumania's failure to increase her surplus of hard goods to the West.

Separate balances for foodstuffs and raw materials in 1962 may be reconstructed very approximately. From these estimates it would appear that the old surplus in raw-materials trade with CMEA had vanished by 1962 and been replaced by a deficit of perhaps 150 million lei, due mainly to increased imports from the Soviet Union. Trade in raw materials with the other countries remained approximately balanced. From 1960 to 1962 the surplus in foodstuffs rose with respect to both regions, although somewhat more markedly in trade with the West.[67]

The following figures highlight the post-1958 reorientation of Ru-

[66] The calculations for 1964 (not shown in Table 3.19) are based on the breakdown of exports in Table 3.18, on imports of machinery from CMEA in Table 3.15, and on the assumption that the share of CMEA in imports of consumer goods was the same as in 1965 (see sources and methods for Table 3.19).

[67] These guesses are founded on Soviet trade data and on the relation between surpluses and deficits with the Soviet Union and with other CMEA members based on partial information for 1960.

total surplus in this group in 1959. All data for 1960 are computed from Sorokin, ed., *op. cit.* For 1962, it was assumed that the deficit in trade in consumer goods with non-CMEA countries was balanced, as it was approximately in 1960. All other surpluses and deficits for the years 1958, 1960, and 1962 were obtained as residuals. For 1965, imports of raw materials and foodstuffs can be precisely estimated from the share of these two groups in total imports from CMEA (*Hospodářské noviny*, No. 29 [1966], p. 3). Imports of consumer goods come out as a residual. Surpluses and deficits can then be derived by subtracting imports algebraically from the export data for 1965 in Table 3.18.

manian trade. The share of CMEA in the combined surpluses in raw materials and foodstuffs was cut in half — from nearly 80 percent in 1958 to 39 percent in 1962; it then made a partial recovery, reaching 59 percent in 1965, when the total surplus in trade with CMEA was unusually high. In 1958 the net deficit with CMEA in machinery and consumer goods combined had been partially offset by a small surplus vis-à-vis the rest of the world; in 1960 CMEA only made up 86 percent of the combined deficit with both East and West; by 1962 CMEA's share was down to 46 percent. In 1965 Rumania's deficit in the two groups reached slightly over one billion lei, to which the CMEA countries contributed less than 200 million lei and the rest of the world — chiefly Western Europe — about 800 million lei. This transformation in the commodity distribution of Rumania's trade by region is especially impressive when we consider that CMEA's share in total exports declined only from 69 to 64 percent between 1958 and 1965 and its share in total imports from 75 to 57 percent. The explanation for this apparent disagreement between the relatively moderate declines in trade with CMEA and the sharp drops in surpluses and deficits with that area is that trade by commodity groups became more balanced in exchanges with CMEA, while it became more imbalanced in exchanges with the rest of the world.

The question now arises whether similar shifts in trade by commodity groups occurred in Rumanian trade *within* CMEA, in particular between the Soviet Union and the people's democracies of Eastern Europe. If we take the period 1958 to 1962 as a whole, we fail to detect any spectacular changes in surpluses and deficits for the aggregated "hard" and "soft" groups that we have distinguished so far in our analysis. If anything, the deficit in soft goods with the people's democracies increased slightly more than with the Soviet Union, because in trade with the latter the Rumanian surplus in consumer goods partially compensated for the growing deficit in machinery, whereas in trade with the remaining members of CMEA the deficit in consumer goods trade reinforced the deficit in machinery products. The Rumanian surplus in raw materials and foodstuffs did grow by about 30 percent in trade with the Soviet Union, while it fell by some 10 percent in trade with the people's democracies,[68] but the absolute differences are not large — of the order of 20 to 30 million lei — and could easily have been caused by crop variations or other chance events.

It is interesting that the share of the Soviet Union in Rumania's

[68] These calculations are based on the estimates of machinery imports and exports in Tables 3.15 and 3.16 and on trade in consumer goods as given in official Soviet statistics. The other two combined groups are derived as residuals.

trade in raw materials was not much lower in 1962 than it had been in 1955. It could hardly have been below 43–45 percent of imports and exports in this group in 1962, compared to roughly 50 percent in 1955. In 1962 the Soviet Union supplied 73 percent of all Rumanian rolled steel imports (compared to 69 percent of all steel products, including raw steel, in 1955), 61 percent of her iron ore imports (82 percent in 1955), 60 percent of her coke imports (58 percent in 1955), and 44 percent of her cotton imports (84 percent in 1955). The Soviet Union absorbed 71 percent of Rumanian gasoline exports (and smaller fractions of the other petroleum products), 55 percent of her cement exports, and a third of her exports of rolled steel products.[69] One could hardly dispute the assertion that, as a consequence of her "heavy industrialization," Rumania's economy has become highly complementary with that of Russia. The somewhat less than cordial relations that have developed in Rumania's relations with CMEA have not significantly altered that dependence, which is grounded on economic rather than on political necessity.

Conclusions and Prospects

In summary, we may distinguish three characteristic periods in Rumania's trade during the last dozen years, each of which reflects the specific situation of the national economy at the time. The first, from 1954 to 1957, was marked by the virtual stagnation of trade. Current imports of machinery and equipment were depressed by low levels of domestic investment and by the substitution of Rumanian for foreign products. Exports of foodstuffs were limited by the failure to expand output and by the political necessity of at least maintaining home consumption. Such agricultural and raw-material surpluses as the government disposed of were largely mortgaged to the Soviet Union and to the people's democracies to pay for current raw-material imports and to meet various financial obligations, including the reimbursement of loans and the acquisition of the Soviet share of the joint companies. From 1958 to 1962, investments rose at a rapid pace, propelling imports of capital goods. Surpluses of foodstuffs and forest products were now generated that were sufficient to pay for expanded raw-material imports, leaving a sizable margin to finance pur-

---

[69] Computed from *Vneshniaia torgovlia SSSR za 1958–1963 gody*, pp. 282–288; and *Anuarul statistic al R.P.R. 1964*, pp. 439–441. Note that the percentages for 1955 and 1962 are not fully comparable. The former refer to value aggregates and the latter to tonnage. However, for small, relatively homogeneous groups of commodities such as "iron ore" or "coke" the two methods of computing the Soviet share should give very similar results.

chases of equipment. Rumania's balance of payments with CMEA countries was strengthened by her newly acquired ability to export a large
volume of equipment and consumer goods to these countries, chiefly
from the output of plants whose construction had been started in the
first round of postwar industrialization prior to 1953; her payments
situation with respect to the Soviet Union and to her more industrialized partners in CMEA was also eased by new borrowings, which,
after 1960, more than offset the reverse capital flow due to the settlement of previously incurred obligations. These various ameliorations
left Rumania a good deal of leeway to redirect her imports toward
Western Europe, particularly to acquire high-quality, technically
advanced equipment for her industrialization program. From 1962,
the costs of her protracted industrial boom in terms of increased raw-
materials requirements began to exceed the benefits flowing from new
surpluses of manufactures available for export. The situation was
aggravated by the recession of petroleum exports and by sharp fluctuations in state procurements of foodstuffs, which no longer grew as
fast as in the period 1958 to 1962. The extra margin in hard goods that
was needed to keep switching trade toward the West was no longer
at hand.[70]

In the next few years, the volume and orientation of trade will
depend chiefly on five factors: (1) the performance of the farm sector; (2) the pace of industrial expansion, which will be the determining
influence on the volume of investments in imported machinery and on
imports of raw materials and semifabricates; (3) the ability of the
Rumanian planners to utilize the machines and equipment imported
in the last few years to generate exports of industrial goods that can be
sold in the West or to produce acceptable substitutes for imports; (4)
the balance between new credits from East and West and the repayment of old debts; and finally (5) political-economic relations with
CMEA (in particular the continued willingness of the Soviet Union to
deliver vast amounts of "hard" raw materials against payment partly
in the form of consumer goods and other "soft" articles).

The official foreign trade targets for 1970, which were revised upward
in July 1966, have been published only in aggregated terms, but some
insight into the planners' detailed forecasts may be gained from addi-

[70] The trade returns for 1965, as we have seen, indicate a new shift toward the
West in purchases of machinery and equipment. Nevertheless, the surplus of exports of raw materials and foodstuffs over imports in Rumania's trade with the
"rest of the world" was no higher in 1965 than in 1962. This would suggest that
this most recent switch must have been financed by the extension of new credits
by the West rather than by any further reorientation of Rumania's surpluses in
hard goods away from CMEA.

tional details disclosed at the time the plan was presented to the Rumanian legislative assembly (*Marea Adunare Naţională*). Import and export targets for 1970, by commodity groups, have been tentatively reconstructed in Table 3.20.

TABLE 3.20. A RECONSTRUCTION OF OFFICIAL IMPORT AND EXPORT FORECASTS BY COMMODITY GROUPS FOR 1970
(*Billions of Foreign-Exchange Lei*)

	Imports		Exports	
	1965	1970	1965	1970
Machinery and equipment	2.5	4.1	1.2	2.9
Raw materials and semifabricates	3.3	4.7	3.3	4.6
Foodstuffs	.2		1.4	
		1.0		2.9
Manufactured consumer goods	.4		.7	
Total	6.4	9.8	6.6	10.4

Sources and methods: For 1965: Tables 3.8 and 3.9. For 1970: total imports and exports were computed from percentage increases over 1965 in *Viaţa economică*, No. 29 (July 22, 1966), p. 13. Imports of machinery and equipment are based on the increase in domestic investments for 1966–1970, on the assumption that machinery and equipment will make up the same proportion of total investments in 1970 as in 1965. (One third of the total investment outlays in machinery will be on imported equipment, according to *Scînteia* [July 14, 1966], p. 2.) The sum of imports of consumer goods and of foodstuffs was estimated as a residual on the basis of a statement by Ion Maurer to the effect that imports of raw materials and machinery would make up "almost 90 percent" of total imports in 1970 (*Agerpres, Documents, Articles and Information on Romania* [July 15, 1966], p. 10). Machinery and equipment: based on their targeted share in total imports in 1970 in *Scînteia* (July 1, 1966), p. 6. Raw materials and semifabricates: all the components of this group were projected from their trends since 1961, except for exports of chemicals, which were derived from their projected share (15 percent) in exports in 1970 (*Scînteia* [July 1, 1966], p. 6). Exports of consumer goods and of foodstuffs were obtained as a residual.

It is manifest from the data that the planners cannot be counting on any great upswing in agricultural exports, such as occurred after 1958. In fact, any significant increase in targeted exports of consumer goods, continuing the trend of recent years, would imply that the planners had provided for virtually no expansion of exports of foodstuffs.[71] From this we may conclude that a further reorientation of trade toward the West, predicated as it was in the late 1950's and early 1960's on the

[71] Given the official forecasts for agricultural production, the targeted increases in real incomes would, in any case, be inconsistent with any large rise in exports in this group.

availability of additional supplies of foodstuffs for export, is not in the offing.

Another interesting feature of the plan, as we are able to reconstruct it, is that exports of machinery are expected by 1970 to represent as much as 70 percent of the value of imports in this group. Now if we suppose that 40 percent of imports will still come from the West, as they did in 1964, and that 20 percent of those imports at most will be offset by exports of machinery *to* the West, then it follows that more machinery will be sold to CMEA members than will be bought from them by the target date (that is, exports to CMEA will be approximately 2.6 billion lei and imports 2.5 billion lei). This state of affairs would represent an extraordinary change from that prevailing until 1964, when exports of machinery and equipment to CMEA offset only about half the value of imports in this group. It is hard to believe that the traditional exporters of equipment, such as Czechoslovakia and East Germany, could have been induced to underwrite this transformation by ordering more equipment from Rumania than they sold to her. Only the Soviets could have agreed to sell materials in exchange for machinery on such a large scale. If so, this has been a signal diplomatic accomplishment on the part of the Rumanians.[72]

It is interesting that the targeted increase in raw-material imports for 1970, insofar as I have correctly estimated it, corresponds to the level that would have been projected if the correlation between the rise in these imports and the rise in gross industrial output from 1959 to 1965 had been assumed to hold for the next five years as well.[73] Actually, however, the fitting of actual requirements to this trend was not a mechanical task. Studies were apparently made, after the first version of the plan was published in 1965, to find out whether the consumption of imported materials could be reduced. As a result, the requirements initially estimated for the years 1967–1970 were trimmed by 280 million foreign-exchange lei. Maxim Berghianu, the new chairman of the State Planning Commission, blamed these excessive demands on the "tendency" to apply for imports without studying the possibility of producing domestically the products solicited.[74] One is entitled to ask whether this official policy of import substitution rests on sound economic calculation or whether it is inspired by straightforward autarkic considerations.

[72] It is, of course, possible that the Rumanians are counting on a much greater penetration of Western, and possibly of non-CMEA Communist markets, than they have achieved to date. But to rely on such a chancy prospect would be imprudent.

[73] The percentage increase in raw-material imports from 1959 to 1965 came to 84 percent of the increase in gross industrial output for these years.

[74] *Scînteia* (July 1, 1966), p. 6.

My over-all impression of the foreign trade plan, as it was revised in 1966, is (1) that it is ambitious and taut, both on the import and on the export side, and (2) that it relies on the continuation of friendly economic relations with CMEA and, more particularly, with the Soviet Union in its capacity as a supplier of raw materials and as a purchaser of Rumanian manufactures. If the policy of banking on the good will of her CMEA allies appears unduly risky, it should not be forgotten that Rumania is holding back a major asset in case the assumptions on which the plan was built happen to collapse. If worse comes to worse, consumers may be denied a part of, or all, the increases in living standards they have been promised. Additional agricultural produce might then be extracted from the economy and sold on the world market. If the Soviet Union decided unilaterally to reduce exports of raw materials to its southern neighbor, Ceaușescu and his colleagues could easily justify the abandonment of projected improvements in living standards and the introduction of austerity measures by invoking this crisis in Rumania's external relations and by appealing to the nationalistic feelings of their compatriots.

CHAPTER FOUR

RUMANIA AND THE ECONOMIC INTEGRATION OF EASTERN EUROPE

Background

The antecedents, or "causes," of an event that has already occurred can often be traced with ease, even though it would not have been possible to pick out the relevant factors beforehand and to predict the event itself. Anyone investigating the background of the rift among the members of the Council for Mutual Economic Assistance will find, scattered through the postwar period, telltale signs of the future estrangement. One cannot, of course, infer from these more or less overt symptoms of discord that a dispute was inevitable or that eventually it had to flare in the open. Some of the divergences among specialists on foreign trade in the Soviet bloc may have reflected their private opinions rather than the attitude of their respective governments toward the problems of specialization in the "camp of peace."

Nevertheless, it may be proper at this time to record all the available evidence pointing in the direction of the future dispute, even if some of it is liable to prove coincidental or irrelevant when all the facts are in. It will take more than the evidence presently at hand to tell what is relevant from what is not. The interpretation of the facts can be only tentative at this stage.

In searching through the past for signs of rift, I found it useful to distinguish three kinds of evidence: (1) conflicts of interests among CMEA members arising from their economic relations; (2) theoretical disagreements that tended to reflect underlying conflicts of interests; (3) extraneous sources of discord that aggravated the first two types of antagonism. I shall concentrate on conflicts of interests and theoretical disagreements, even though I am well aware that political issues probably strained Rumania's relations with the Soviet Union more seriously than did any economic factors. The annexation of Bessarabia in 1940, the imposition of a heavy reparation burden on a country that considered herself an ally of the Soviet Union in the last nine months of World War II, the exploitation of Rumanian resources by the mixed companies, the stinting aid given to Rumania for her industrialization,[1] and the humiliating political subservience imposed by their Soviet mentors could hardly be expected to induce the Rumanian leaders to strive for a perfectly harmonious settlement of outstanding economic issues. In any event, political friction arising from this burdensome legacy began to manifest itself only at a comparatively late stage in Rumania's dispute with CMEA.

Let us begin then with sources of conflict in the economic realm between Rumania and Czechoslovakia, which was to take the lead in pressing for a greater degree of specialization among socialist countries.

Preliminaries: 1950 to 1958

For nearly a decade after the end of World War II, Rumania's exports to the Soviet bloc consisted almost exclusively of raw materials, semifabricates, and foodstuffs, while nearly half of her imports were made up of machinery and manufactured consumer goods, which she bought mostly from Czechoslovakia, East Germany, and the U.S.S.R.[2] Trade between socialist countries was conducted "at world prices" until the end of 1950, at which time it was decided to prevent the "speculative rise" in world prices of raw materials from exerting its full impact on the socialist market. "Stop prices" were then agreed on, which, if they did not completely eliminate the influence of the Korean War inflation, at least delayed and mitigated its effects.[3] G. Radulescu, who was later to become a member of the Rumanian Politbureau, wrote in 1958 that if Czechoslovakia had been compelled to buy her raw materials from capitalist countries from 1951 to 1953 instead of at fixed pre-Korean War prices, she would have had to disburse an extra one billion dollars. (This would have added approximately one third to the cost of her imports between these dates.)[4] It appears clearly from the structure of Rumania's trade with her developed partners that she stood to lose, on balance, from this agreement to "stop prices."

---

[1] According to G. S. Garnett and M. H. Crawford in "The Scope and Distribution of Soviet Economic Aid," in *Dimensions of Soviet Power*, Joint Economic Committee, 87th Congress (1962), p. 474, Soviet aid to Rumania from 1945 to 1962 came to $10 per head, as against $73 for Bulgaria, $38 for Hungary, $33 for Poland, and $78 for East Germany.

[2] See Chapter 3, p. 168.

[3] J. Mervart, *Význam a vývoj cen v mezinárodním obchodě* (Prague, 1960), pp. 181–183.

[4] G. Radulescu and I. Burştein, "Insemnătatea ajutorului URSS în sistemul relaţiilor economice dintre ţarile socialiste," *Probleme economice*, No. 12 (1958), p. 59.

In a paper delivered at a trade conference in Moscow in 1957,[5] V. Kaigl, director of the Institute of Economics of the Czechoslovak Academy of Sciences, pointed out that Czechoslovakia had not succeeded in negotiating long-term trade agreements with Rumania and Hungary in the period 1949 to 1953. Lack of planned cooperation, he wrote, had "adverse consequences" both for these countries and for their partners. The former strove to develop all branches of the national economy, including those for which they had an inadequate raw-material base. On the other hand, Czechoslovakia, once she had adopted the structure of output of her machine-building industry to serve the needs of her less developed clients, was left, after 1953, with surplus capacities on hand in certain lines of production when "disproportions were corrected" in the economies of her partner states.[6]

The "correction of disproportions" alluded to by Kaigl was linked to the New Course that was introduced after Stalin's death in March 1953 to avert popular unrest. For a time, heavy industry lost its top-priority status. Investments were scaled down, or they failed to rise as they had in former years. In the less developed countries of the region, including Rumania, exports of foodstuffs and other primary commodities were cut back to increase domestic consumption. Imports of machinery and equipment fell drastically, by reason of the reduced availability of foreign exchange (due to decreased export earnings) and the slowdown in investments directly consequent on the New Course.[7] The termination of the Korean War, superimposed on these other events, caused a reduction in the demand for armaments, which had been furnished in large part by Czechoslovakia. The total exports of machinery and equipment from Czechoslovakia to Rumania, apparently including armaments, went down by four fifths from 1953 to 1956.[8] (The magnitude of this decline between these two particular years was extraordinary, but the data correctly illustrate the general downward trend that took place in the years of the New Course in Czechoslovak exports not only to Rumania but also to Hungary, Bulgaria, Albania, and Poland.)

Confronted with these difficulties in marketing the heavy industrial products in which the country had specialized, the Communist Party

[5] I have read and taken notes from a mimeographed copy of this paper, the full text of which was never published. What appears to be a revision of the paper appeared in *Voprosy ekonomiki*, No. 10 (1957), pp. 32–41. (Critical references about individual socialist countries were omitted.)

[6] V. Kaigl, mimeographed "Referat" (in Russian), Institute of Economics of the Academy of Sciences of the U.S.S.R. (Moscow, 1957), p. 28.

[7] See Chapter 1, p. 46, and Chapter 3, p. 154.

[8] Jan Vaněk, *Ekonomický a politický význam vývozu strojírenských výrobků z ČSSR* (Prague, 1960), p. 197.

of Czechoslovakia, ostensibly for the sake of aiding the industrialization of her less developed partners,[9] issued a directive in February 1956
calling for the scientific study of the "political economy of the division
of labor among the countries of the socialist camp."[10] A series of articles
followed, by V. Kaigl, D. Machová, B. Malý, and J. Mervart, which
for the first time aired in public the crucial problems hindering trade
in the bloc and dividing the CMEA countries. Although few of the published articles I have found criticized any socialist country by name,
they left little doubt that most of the less developed members of CMEA
were implicated. It is not surprising that the first controversial article
by a Rumanian economist on theoretical problems of specialization
should have singled out one of these Czech economists as a foil for his
counterarguments.[11]

These Czech writings were all aimed at promoting greater multilateral cooperation among socialist countries under the auspices of
CMEA. A few words of background on the previous record of this in-
stitution may be in order at this point.

Although the Council for Mutual Economic Assistance had been
founded in 1949, it is generally admitted that, up to 1955, it more or
less confined its role to the registration of bilateral commercial agreements between its members. It was not until late 1955 and early 1956
that it got down to work on a pattern of specialization among its members and began to draw up balances of key materials to harmonize
the total supply and demand for these materials in the entire bloc.[12]
The conflicting interests between the more developed economies — East
Germany and Czechoslovakia — and the less developed economies —
Albania, Rumania, and Bulgaria — with Poland and Hungary closer
to the latter than to the former,[13] flared up already at the seventh
session of CMEA in May 1956 where specialization in machine products
was discussed. According to a Czech author, specialization could have

---

[9] Kaigl, *op. cit.*, p. 16.

[10] *Politická ekonomie*, No. 4 (1956), p. 247.

[11] See p. 194.

[12] Frederic L. Pryor, *The Communist Foreign Trade System* (Cambridge, Mass.:
The M.I.T. Press, 1963), p. 32.

[13] According to an unpublished Czechoslovak computation, national income per
head in 1958 was $238 in Albania, $340 in Rumania, $470 in Bulgaria, $551 in
Poland, $640 in Hungary, $795 in East Germany, and $833 in Czechoslovakia. A
more recent set of estimates based on a country-by-country comparison of a sample
of physical outputs for each sector set national income per head in 1964 at $423 in
Rumania, $469 in Bulgaria, $498 in Poland, $513 in Hungary, $844 in East Germany, $813 in Czechoslovakia, and $630 in the U.S.S.R. (*Politická ekonomie*, No. 8
(1966), p. 731). The earlier of the two sets of estimates involves a conversion of
national currencies into dollars at the tourist (noncommercial) exchange rate, which
overvalues some of the national currencies, including that of Poland.

been carried further if it had not been for the "narrow outlook of certain economic officials." He did warn, however, that "it would be wrong to see obstacles in the way of specialization only from the less industrialized countries." There were also some officials from the more developed countries, including Czechoslovakia, who did not sufficiently understand the necessity of transferring the production of certain machinery products to the less developed countries, especially products requiring a less complicated technology.[14] There, already, was the crux of the problem. Items such as tractors, trucks, roller bearings, lathes, and combines, which generate significant economies of scale when produced in large quantities, present relatively simple technological problems;[15] they can be taken over profitably by the underdeveloped countries, leaving the less profitable large-scale manufacture of complex equipment for the metallurgical, mining, chemical, and paper-making industries to their more advanced partners. The unwillingness of the industrialized nations to yield standardized, apparently highly profitable, manufacturing activities to the less developed countries was one of the prime causes of the friction in CMEA.[16]

Another bone of contention in CMEA discussions was the problem of prices in transactions within the socialist camp. In 1953 and 1954, the pre-Korean War "stop prices" that had been in effect hitherto had already been adjusted in trade agreements among several CMEA countries to bring them closer into line with world levels. This was done, allegedly, "to avert differences in the profitability of trading on socialist and capitalist markets for individual countries."[17] By that time the world prices of primary commodities, which had increased sharply during the first two years of the Korean War, had subsided; and it is not clear whether it was any longer to the advantage of the CMEA exporters of these commodities to adapt prices in intrabloc trade to the new price relations on the world market. In mid-1956, the price problem was discussed at a Moscow meeting of CMEA, as a result of which "the majority of members adopted the use of contemporary world prices."[18]

The conflict of interests over prices was reflected in the theoretical

[14] Vaněk, *op. cit.*, p. 228.

[15] Cf. "Węzłowe problemy współpracy," *Życie Gospodarcze*, No. 46 (1963), p. 3.

[16] These goods, given the price structure in effect in the less developed countries, may appear to be very profitable, at least in relation to other manufactures. It is not so certain whether, in the light of the strong comparative advantage of these economies in foodstuffs and other unprocessed products, they are so profitable compared to all other potential exportables.

[17] J. Mervart, "Ceny na světovém socialistickém trhu," *Nová mysl*, No. 9 (1958), p. 829.

[18] J. Mervart, *Význam a vývoj cen v mezinarodním obchodě, op. cit.*, p. 186.

problem of "unequivalent exchange," the potential disadvantage incurred by less developed countries in trading with industrially mature economies — due to the fact that the former must expend more labor time to produce a unit of value at world prices than their advanced partners who produce their exports with a higher labor productivity. The authoritative Soviet textbook on political economy had laid down the principle that "in the socialist camp there does not exist and cannot exist unequivalent exchange."[19] The Czechs who addressed themselves to this problem contended that trade conducted at world prices would be equivalent as long as these prices were free of monopolistic elements or other deviations from "world value."[20] "Although unequivalency may occur in any one year," wrote J. Tauchman, one of the more influential Czech economists in this domain, "the total exchange of goods between Czechoslovakia and all other socialist countries between 1950 and 1956 has been fully equivalent."[21] Tauchman categorically rejected the idea, urged by "some authors" and also put forward in the course of certain economic negotiations, of applying a double price system, which would oblige the more developed countries to extend to their less developed clients more favorable terms of trade than those prevailing on the world market. In the long run, Tauchman argued, such a scheme would work to the disadvantage of the less developed countries, apparently because it would induce the industrialized nations to buy their raw materials and to sell their machinery and equipment on the capitalist market.[22]

In 1961, a Bulgarian economist revealed that the equivalency problem had been debated at the ninth session of CMEA in Bucharest in May 1958, at which it had been decided to study the means whereby the socialist market might switch from world prices to "its own price basis." According to this source, V. Černiánský and J. Mervart, both members of the Czechoslovak delegation, had opposed this switch, arguing that any other price system would "inhibit trade among socialist countries and cause the disintegration of the world socialist market." "Experience," the Bulgarian claimed, "has essentially refuted this point of view" (in the sense that prices have deviated in many instances from world price relations without disrupting trade).[23] It is

[19] Cited by D. Machová in *Nová mysl*, No. 1 (1958), p. 47.

[20] See in particular, J. Mervart, "Některé otázky působení zákona hodnoty na světovém socialistickém trhu," *Politická ekonomie*, No. 7 (1957), pp. 514–515.

[21] Comment on Kaigl's paper in *Mezinárodní dělba práce v socialistické světové soustavě* (Prague, 1958), p. 96.

[22] *Ibid.*, p. 17.

[23] Mikhail Savov, "O tovarnykh otnosheniakh mezhdu sotsialisticheskimi stranami," in *Dve mirovye sistemy* (Moscow, 1961), p. 160.

believed that the Rumanian delegation sided with the Bulgarians against the Czechoslovaks on this issue.

Three other themes, all of an "internationalist" character, frequently crop up in Czech literature of the period. (1) Autarkic tendencies are "directly contrary to the laws of development of the world socialist system" because they tend to weaken the socialist camp; they are hence profoundly harmful to the interests of all socialist countries.[24] The less developed countries are not islands unto themselves; their protectionist measures harm them if they are injurious to the cause of socialism. (2) International specialization is the best way to remove existing differences in levels of development among socialist countries.[25] (3) The principle according to which the output of the means of production (Marx's sector I) must grow faster than the output of consumer goods (sector II) need not operate in each separate country although it must apply to the socialist camp as a whole. "It may be much more advantageous for a less developed country to use its resources for the faster expansion of production in branches of sector II and exchange a part of its production for the instruments of production needed for the priority development of its first sector."[26] Needless to say, the representatives of Czechoslovakia were arguing *pro domo sua*.

The Rumanians Respond

The Rumanians, as we have seen, sharply curtailed their imports of machinery and equipment after 1953. In the face of a severe balance-of-payments crisis, they pursued the industrialization of the country with a stress on the heavy branches of industry. Official propaganda

[24] V. Kaigl, "Bratskoe sotrudnichestvo . . . ," *Voprosy ekonomiki*, No. 10 (1957), p. 36.

[25] *Ibid.*, p. 39.

[26] V. Kaigl's address to a conference in Liblice, December 12–14, 1957, published in V. Wacker and B. Malý, eds., *Mezinárodní dělba práce v socialistické světové soustavě* (Prague, 1958), p. 37. For a later and more moderate statement of the same theme, see Willi Kunz, "Zu einigen Grundproblemen der Internationalen Arbeitsteilung im sozialistischen Weltsystem" in *Probleme der Politischen Okonomie*, Vol. III, (Berlin, 1960), p. 191. D. Machová argued in *Nová mysl*, No. 1 (1958), p. 48, that the principle of the priority expansion of sector I in individual countries should not be interpreted in the narrow context of the growth of output of instruments of production (that is, machines and equipment) but of all means of production, including raw materials, which are in short supply in the socialist camp. The Rumanian economist Anghel, in his comments at the Liblice conference, had already objected to the excessive use of the "law of value" as a regulator of trade among socialist countries (see J. P. Saltiel, "L'attitude de la Roumanie vis-à-vis d'une planification supranationale," *Cahiers de l'ISEA* (Economie Planifiée, Paris, December 1965), p. 71).

was not called upon to justify this policy, which was very much in line with the doctrine in vogue in the Soviet bloc up to that time.[27] There is some truth to the claim, recently made by a Rumanian specialist on foreign trade in an interview with the author, that "other socialist countries" deviated from the generally accepted line while the Rumanians continued to adhere to it, although this argument glosses over the fact that the received doctrine on specialization and comparative advantage was too vague to be a guide to the solution of concrete problems. The Czechs, and later the East Germans, could also contend that they were hewing close to the old line: they were interpreting the doctrine in a broad "integrationist" way for the sake of ensuring the healthy, proportional development of the socialist camp as a whole.

Probably the earliest statement of a protectionist point of view that later became officially sanctioned in Rumanian pronouncements appeared in an article by T. Pavel on profitability criteria in foreign trade. The author argued at the time that even though profitability calculations in foreign trade may be useful to avoid certain deficit operations they must not have the effect of holding back industrialization: "It is evident that if the profitability coefficient were decisive, a country with a weakly developed industry would find that the importation of finished products was more advantageous than their production. Such a conclusion would be tantamount to forsaking industrialization."[28]

In an article published in April 1958, M. Horovitz introduced a number of the protectionist arguments that were to be played up in Rumanian writings in the subsequent years:[29]

1. Trade among socialist countries, which is carried on at world prices, involves an equivalent exchange from the viewpoint of international value and an unequivalent exchange from the viewpoint of the domestic value of goods whose content is based on socially necessary costs. "International value" is determined not by average conditions of production in the world but by the conditions obtaining in the country, or countries, producing or exporting the bulk of a given type of output.[30] National value is determined by socially necessary (labor)

---

[27] For an unequivocal early statement of the policy of industrialization with special emphasis on the development of the machine-building industry, see Gh. Badrus, "Colaborarea economică dintre ţările lagărului democratic" in *Studii şi referate economice* (Bucharest: Academia R.P.R., 1954), pp. 24–25.

[28] *Probleme economice*, No. 6 (1957), cited by Saltiel, *op. cit.*, p. 71.

[29] M. Horovitz, "Despre unele particularitaţi şi limite ale acţiune legii valorii în comerţ exterior socialist," *Probleme economice*, No. 4 (1958), pp. 10–20.

[30] Horovitz at this point polemicizes with the article already cited by J. Mervart, in which the latter had asserted that international values were determined in effect by average world costs.

costs in each country. Countries that have a centuries-old lead in developing skills and in raising their labor productivity are in a favorable trading position because they do not have to sell at prices below world market levels and are able therefore to export goods whose international value exceeds their national value. In underdeveloped countries, on the other hand, national value (except in the case of extractive industries) is in excess of international value. Only the elimination of disparities in the development of the socialist nations can do away with this "unfavorable situation." [31]

2. If the criterion of economizing social labor time were to be made the basis for the international division of labor (that is, if specialization were determined by relative labor costs), "this would tend to perpetuate the backwardness of underdeveloped countries and to conserve the old economic structure inherited from the domination of monopolistic trusts." [32]

3. Strict respect for the principle of specialization on the basis of production costs must be replaced by an analysis of natural endowment and of specific national conditions, which may give rise to greater future profitability. [33]

4. A country may manufacture products with higher social costs than those of other countries for three basic reasons: first, because of its industrialization policy, which will eventually make these goods profitable on an international scale; second, because of discrimination on the part of the capitalist world; third, because of foreign-exchange shortages that make it impossible for the country to import these goods. [34]

We have here, barely cloaked in Marxist terminology, the basic arsenal of protectionism in underdeveloped countries, from infant-industry arguments to balance-of-payments appeals. It could hardly be denied, at any rate, that Horovitz's arguments were geared to Rumania's special conditions and that they were consonant with the protectionist policy she had been pursuing since the onset of her acute balance-of-payments problem after 1953.

M. Manoilescu, the Rumanian economist, whose advocacy of protectionist policy exercised so much influence on agrarian countries before World War II, had already advanced similar ideas in the late

[31] Horovitz, *op. cit.*, pp. 11 and 12.
[32] *Ibid.*, p. 15. Here Horovitz may be referring to Rumanian specialization in petroleum and other extractive industries formerly dominated by foreign companies.
[33] *Ibid.*
[34] *Ibid.*, pp. 17–18.

1920's.[35] Vladimir Kaigl, in an article published in the Soviet ideological journal *Voprosy filosofii* in January 1959, advanced counterarguments that might well have been drafted in response to those put forward by Horovitz:[36]

It is essential to assign given lines of production, by mutual agreement, to countries in possession of the most advanced technology, where they may yield a large effect in the course of a determinate period. An example of the application of the principle of ensuring the highest labor productivity, from the viewpoint of the entire socialist system, would be the mutually agreed specialization of, say, Rumania in the systematic development of chemical industries based on petroleum and gas, and of Bulgaria in the processing of non-ferrous metals all the way to the production of finished machinery products, as well as in labor-intensive types of agricultural production. Special circumstances of foreign trade very often predetermine the assignment of production programmes. Most of the difficulties of the individual socialist countries are concentrated on their passive balance of payments. In this connection it seems justified to try and solve these difficulties by means of measures affecting trade relations: thus, in order to secure a given level of import of raw materials and other products, the curtailment of machinery imports is resorted to. But the best way to eliminate a deficit in the balance of payments is to achieve a higher labor productivity. For this, however, one must produce and import more machines and equipment than hitherto, and, incidentally, machines of the highest technical level.[37]

Kaigl claims essentially that the interests of the socialist world as a whole require that specialization should correspond to differences in labor productivity. Machine building, for instance, should be concentrated in countries with the longest tradition in this sector. Moreover, from the viewpoint of the individual underdeveloped country the best way to catch up with the rest of the socialist world, and by the same token to solve its balance-of-payments problem, is to import

[35] Manoilescu wrote that the production of commodities should be determined not by how much a given commodity costs on the international market (compared to how much it would cost to produce at home) but by the productivity attainable per man in the production of these goods. As the attainable value of the output per man engaged in agriculture is smaller than the output per man in industry, agriculture suffers from an "intrinsic inferiority" as compared to industry; thus trade in agricultural commodities is "implicitly unequal" as opposed to trade in industrial commodities (as quoted and summarized in N. Spulber, *The Economics of Communist Eastern Europe* [New York and London: Technology Press and John Wiley, 1957], p. 277). Although Manoilescu's ideas are frequently reviled in Rumanian propaganda, I have it from good authority that Manoilescu's trade theories exerted influence on the thinking of some high officials responsible for external economic affairs in the 1960's.

[36] There is no reason to believe, of course, that Kaigl responded directly to Horovitz. Many "position papers" must have been presented at CMEA meetings and other conferences that never saw the light of day.

[37] V. Kaigl, "Zakonomernosti razvitiia ekonomicheskikh otnoshenii mezhdu stranami mirovoi sotsialisticheskoi sistemy," *Voprosy filosofii*, No. 3 (1959), pp. 37–39.

"effective" machines from experienced producers, such as Czechoslovakia, and thereby raise its labor productivity.

The tactical key to the passage, of course, is the reduction in machinery imports and its justification by a balance-of-payments problem, which fits Rumania perfectly.[38] Note also that the "example" given, suggesting that Rumania specialize in petroleum and gas chemistry, later became a very real issue dividing Rumania from the rest of the bloc.

A month after the appearance of Horovitz's article, discussions were held at a CMEA meeting in Moscow on the coordination of the long-term plans that were being elaborated in each country for the period 1960–1961 to 1965. The policies to be followed in the CMEA committees were laid down at a top-level meeting of Party representatives, which pressed for the "most effective utilization of the advantages of the socialist international division of labor." The representatives also urged the priority development of countries that were still industrially backward. This development, which should be "the object of a common effort of all socialist countries," was to be facilitated by aid "in such form as would also correspond to the interests of the developed countries."[39] The ninth session of CMEA (Bucharest, July 1958) and the tenth (Prague, December 1958) were expected to give concrete content to these resolutions. The deliberations of the tenth session were concerned with the perspective development of the metallurgical and chemical industries in each member state — which was to create a most delicate political problem in the next two years.

At this point it may be appropriate to introduce an ideological question that leaves considerable scope for speculation. This is the famous issue of the "more or less simultaneous transition to communism" and its relation to mutual aid in the bloc. This principle, first put forward by Ts. A. Stepanyan in 1958 in an authoritative article, stated that the uneven level of development of countries and peoples would gradually disappear "as the world socialist system expanded in the process of mutual aid and collaboration of all socialist countries. . . ."[40] Stepanyan did specify, however, that the European socialist countries, united in a single council for mutual economic aid, would be the first to enter communism as a group, while the Asian nations "having

---

[38] See p. 52.

[39] Machová, *op. cit.*, p. 163.

[40] Ts. A. Stepanyan, "Oktyabrskaia revolyutsiia i stanovlenie kommunisticheskoi formatsii," *Voprosy filosofii*, No. 10 (1958), pp. 34–35. The late Herbert Ritvo cites Stepanyan's article and relates it to the current strain in Sino-Soviet relations during the "great leap forward" campaign (Herbert Ritvo, ed., *The New Soviet Society* [New York: New Leader, 1962], pp. 232–233).

much in common in their economic and cultural development" would also simultaneously step into communism, but at a later date.[41] Khrushchev confirmed Stepanyan's thesis at the Twenty-first Party Congress of the CPSU in January 1959 but without differentiating between Asian and European countries.

The simultaneous-transition principle was probably linked to the resolutions on mutual economic help made at the Moscow meeting of CMEA in May 1958, which perhaps involved a tentative commitment by the better-off nations of the bloc to help the others. A hint to this effect can be found in a crucial article, also published in *Voprosy filosofii*, by I. P. Oleinik, a Soviet expert on Rumania and a staunch friend of the Rumanians. Oleinik pointed out that the leveling of historical differences in development, which forms the "material basis" for the more or less simultaneous transition to communism, has "not only a theoretical but a great practical interest, especially now that the USSR and the People's Democracies are elaborating their long-term plans of economic development and are implementing their coordination."[42] It is worth remarking that this statement was made in the crucial period between the Third Congress of the Rumanian Workers' Party[43] in June 1960 and the signing of the trade agreement between the Soviet Union and Rumania in November of that year when the pros and cons of Soviet aid must have been the subject of strenuous discussions in Moscow.[44]

Oleinik, incidentally, was the first to work out theoretical reasons why the less developed countries of the bloc have tended to grow faster than the others in the past, and would continue to do so until they caught up with their rivals — a notion that was later elaborated systematically in Rumanian writings. He also contested the idea, "which has appeared in our literature,"[45] that the primacy of output of the means of production applies to the socialist bloc as a whole but not to each of its individual members separately. (The argument he opposes could serve to rationalize the specialization in agricultural products of Bulgaria and Rumania.) Finally he stressed that "for the development of every socialist country the growth of a national

[41] *Ibid.*, p. 34.

[42] I. P. Oleinik, "Edinstvo i splochennost sotsialisticheskikh stran," *Voprosy filosofii*, No. 9 (1960), pp. 24, 27, and 28.

[43] In 1965, in connection with the renaming of the Party, this congress was referred to as the Eighth Congress of the Communist Party of Rumania.

[44] See p. 204.

[45] I found instances of this opinion in Czech and East German writings (see p. 193, note 26) but not in Soviet sources.

machine-building industry is of enormous importance." [46] In the light of Oleinik's background and interests, I construe these statements as expressions of support for the Rumanian stance on heavy industrialization with the aid of the more developed countries. As we shall see, however, Oleinik's views did not represent the official Soviet position, which, when it crystallized in late 1960 or early 1961, leaned in the other direction.

Curiously enough, the Rumanians, after the initial statement of their position in Horovitz's article of April 1958, held their peace for nearly two years — or at least published no controversial material of this type in the journals where we should expect to find it (*Lupta de clasă* and *Probleme economice*). The reason, I believe, is that their main consideration at the time was to obtain Soviet loans and assurances of deliveries of raw materials for their industrialization program for 1961–1965, and they did not want to jeopardize the delicate negotiations going on intermittently during this period by displaying their ill will on matters of specialization. [47]

The issue of credits came up in an interesting way at the November 1958 plenum of the Rumanian Workers' Party, where Gheorghiu-Dej announced that "in view of the optimal natural conditions obtaining in our country for intensifying the development of the chemical industry, I have considered it necessary to solicit from the Soviet Union the delivery on credit of a number of works for the chemical industry." He then added: "In the last few days I have received a letter from comrade Khrushchev notifying me that the Soviet government agrees to give us new help in the development of our chemical industry. Our delegation will go to Moscow in December to conclude the corresponding agreement." [48] The curious phrasing of this announcement suggests the following possible interpretation: If the Soviet Union and other members of CMEA think we have such "optimal" conditions for specializing in the processing of petroleum and gas products, they will have to grant us the credits to allow us to do so.

There is no record of any delegation having gone to Moscow in December to close the deal. A commercial agreement between Ruma-

[46] I. P. Oleinik, "Formy mezhdunarodnogo razdeleniia truda v lagere sotsializma," *Voprosy ekonomiki*, No. 5 (1961), pp. 67 and 68.

[47] This does not mean that the Rumanians backed down on any position taken by Horovitz but that their arguments were henceforth put in less controversial terms. The assertion that the priority development of heavy industry in each country was essential to the rapid development of the socialist camp as a whole was the most controversial theme reiterated in the next two years (see for instance the editorial in *Probleme economice*, No. 4 [1959], p. 8).

[48] *Scînteia* (December 2, 1958).

nia and the U.S.S.R. signed in February mentioned only routine exchanges of goods but no credits.[49] An article published in May in the Central Committee journal *Lupta de clasă* by the Minister of the Petroleum and Chemical Industry, who was in a good position to know about any negotiations going on, invoked fraternal aid as "a vital necessity" for Rumanian development and alluded to the "simultaneous transition principle" — the code phrase denoting an appeal for aid — but made no reference to any new Soviet concessions.[50] In August 1959, an article on Soviet aid finally revealed that an agreement had been concluded in the spring of that year "assuring us of the delivery from the U.S.S.R. of equipment for new chemical works, of which a part would be obtained on credit," under conditions similar to those received in December 1956.[51] According to a later Soviet source, "the Rumanian People's Republic received 61 million (new) rubles from the U.S.S.R. in 1956 [for the development of the Rumanian chemical industry], after which, in the course of fulfilling the agreement, the credit was raised to 83.5 million rubles"[52] (that is, by an extra 25 million dollars). An article published by two Rumanian economists in the Soviet journal *Voprosy ekonomiki* during the very month when the existence of the additional credit was initially divulged made no mention of this fact in their summary review of Soviet aid to Rumania.[53] It is hard to escape the impression that Gheorghiu-Dej did not get all that he had asked for.

But the Soviet Union was not the only source of credits that Rumania could tap. The morning after the close of the fateful plenum of November 26–28, and four days before the publication of Gheorghiu-Dej's speech on Soviet aid, *Scînteia* printed an interview granted to *The Washington Post* by Politburo member Chivu Stoica in which he reported that several reputable Western firms were "disposed to grant us credits" and that Rumania would accept these credits if they were

---

[49] *Scînteia* (February 3, 1959).

[50] M. Florescu, "Dezvoltarea relaţiilor economice dintre ţările sistemului mondial socialist," *Lupta de clasă*, No. 5 (1959), pp. 15 and 20. Florescu conceded that the negotiations at the tenth session of CMEA in December had been "difficult" but alleged that the proposals on specialization had finally been approved by all the participants (pp. 23 and 24).

[51] M. Mănescu and M. Nova, "Ajutorul frătesc al Uniunii Sovietice," *Probleme economice*, No. 8 (1959), p. 158.

[52] N. N. Dubimov, ed., *Sovremmennye mezhdunarodnye otnosheniia* (Moscow, 1964), p. 129.

[53] R. Moldovan and V. Rausser, "Uspekhi stroitelstva sotsializma v R.P.R.," *Voprosy ekonomiki*, No. 8 (1959), p. 69. A Soviet writer in an article published in October 1959 described in some detail the 270 million ruble credit granted to the R.P.R. in 1956 but also failed to mention any new loans (*Voprosy ekonomiki*, No. 10 [1959], p. 105).

in the country's interest. He then went on to reaffirm the Rumanian government's intent to expand the domestic metallurgical output as a basis for the metal-processing industry, which, along with the machine-building industry, represented "the principal condition of economic progress in our country." [54]

The November 1958 plenum marked a turning point in Rumania's foreign trade policy. It was probably on this occasion that the party leaders discussed and approved the major reorientation of Rumanian trade — away from the Soviet bloc, toward the West — that was described in the previous chapter. Already in the spring of 1959, Premier Ion Maurer made a discreet tour of Western Europe to explore the possibilities of expanding trade and of obtaining credits. Within a year or so, Rumania negotiated long-outstanding compensation claims with several Western countries including the United States and the United Kingdom. [55]

An interesting aspect of Rumania's search for credits in the West was that it coincided with the claim that Rumania's external accounts were at last balanced for the first time in several years. [56] In fact, as we have already seen, Rumania was able, from 1958 on, to embark on a much more rapid expansion of her industry. This expansion was facilitated by the increased availability of foreign exchange, with which a large increase in imports of machinery and equipment could be financed. The Rumanians were at last reaping the benefits of the Soviet concessions of 1954 and 1956; they could now dispose freely of their rich natural resources and use the proceeds to promote their industrialization plans rather than to compensate the Russians for ceded equipment or to reimburse past credits.

Although imports of machinery and equipment from Czechoslovakia and East Germany did increase after 1958, they rose much less than total imports in this category, owing to the shift in Rumanian purchases in favor of the West and, to a lesser extent, the Soviet Union. To make matters worse, Rumania insisted on exporting more machinery products to her CMEA partners, so that the absolute size of the deficit in machinery trade with these countries hardly went up at all. [57] This unwillingness on the part of Rumania to give the more industrialized CMEA nations their rightful share in her expanding market may account, from the beginning of 1960, for the increasingly specific and pointed Czech and East German recriminations against autarkic tendencies on

[54] *Scînteia* (November 29, 1958).
[55] *East Europe* (December 1960), p. 44.
[56] See Chapter 3, p. 172, note 53.
[57] Chapter 3, p. 171.

the part of "certain socialist countries," as for instance the following citation from an article in *Einheit*, the official organ of the Central Committee of the East German ruling Party.

> There are also subjective reasons for the tendency of international co-operation [among socialist countries] to lag behind the stage of development that has been achieved. It required a certain time to bring about a reconciliation between peoples which had been disrupted by the war unleashed by Hitler. In addition, a dogmatic conception of the theory of socialist industrialization tended to disregard the difference in conditions prevailing during the construction of socialism in the people's democracies compared to the conditions that prevailed during construction of socialism in the Soviet Union. In many countries, an attempt was made to build up all the branches of industries; the existence of a socialist world system was not sufficiently taken into consideration in practice.[58]

There are few pairs of countries in CMEA that were divided by World War II and could fit this description. Rumania and Czechoslovakia would of course qualify, as would Poland and East Germany.

The appearance of this piece nearly coincided with the publication in *Lupta de clasă* of a lengthy article, which, according to my informants in Bucharest, represented the first Party pronouncement on the intra-CMEA controversy. The article, simply entitled "Socialist Industrialization," was signed "C. Arnăutu," which may have been the pseudonym of a high Party official.[59] The author, besides reiterating the usual arguments for industrialization spearheaded by the expansion of heavy industry, struck a few controversial notes that linked his piece with earlier Czech and East German writings. He rejected what he termed the "absolutization" of the principle that only those branches of industry should be built up for which all the raw materials are available domestically. This approach disregards "the necessity of expanding the principal branches of heavy industry, in the first place of the machine-building industry."[60] He then alluded to "certain articles" according to which the priority expansion of heavy industry, in general, and of machine building, in particular, ought to be realized in the socialist world system as a whole but not in every individual socialist country (a view that was urged, as we have seen, by V. Kaigl). According to Arnăutu the interests of the socialist camp require that the principle operate in every socialist country.[61] After all

---

[58] Karl Morgenstern, "Zu einigen Fragen der sozialistischen internationalen Arbeitsteilung," *Einheit*, No. 4 (1960), pp. 621–628.

[59] C. Arnăutu, "Industrializarea socialistă," *Lupta de clasă*, No. 3 (1960), pp. 69–86.

[60] *Ibid.*, p. 75.

[61] *Ibid.*, pp. 84–85. Arnăutu pointed out in this connection that Czechoslovakia was attempting to even out disparities in development within her own borders. By

. . . not every type of industrial development can be construed as socialist industrialization. The development of a few extractive industries or of light industry alone — a so-called calico industrialization (*industrializare de stambă*) — does not really amount to industrialization. It cannot generate the technical progress necessary for the expansion of production in all branches of the economy.[62]

He then went on to criticize

. . . certain articles of propaganda, which present in a mechanical way the problem of the lack of professional or technical traditions and the shortage of qualified cadres in certain branches of industry, as if this problem could be a reason for abandoning the creation of a multilateral industry. . . . In social-ist countries that did not formerly have a developed industry but are now constructing such an industry, as for example, our own country, the problem presents itself in a different way. It is our task to create new traditions in the course of industrialization, to form the necessary cadres for the rapid development of a socialist industry. . . .[63]

The Issue of the Galaţi Steel Mill

While this debate was going on, a crucial policy issue was on the fire: the prospective development and expansion of Rumania's machine-building complex, including the iron and steel industry that was to serve as its input base. Already in December 1959 a Soviet report on the twelfth session of CMEA in Sofia hinted that little or no progress had been made in deciding on the countries that were to specialize in most standard types of machinery. In the list of the CMEA countries that were to expand their steel output significantly from 1961 to 1965, Rumania's name was glaringly omitted.[64] In March and April 1960, Alexander Bîrlădeanu was negotiating in Moscow with Kosygin and Soviet experts, presumably on Rumanian devel-opment plans, Soviet aid, and Soviet-Rumanian trade for the next five years. No official statements were made concerning these discus-sions. It is significant, in any case, that the directives for Rumania's

---

this he meant that if the law of priority development of heavy industry was to apply to individual regions, it must apply to each socialist country.

[62] *Ibid.*, p. 74.

[63] *Ibid.*, p. 79. The same month a review article appeared in *Probleme economice* advancing much the same arguments. The author of the review, M. Gheorghiu, attacked S. Vrțeli for implying in his book, *Industrializarea socialistă în R.P.R.*, that "a country without sufficient natural resources could not develop its own industry." (*Probleme economice*, No. 3 [1960], p. 130.) In April 1960, R. Moldovan, a vice-chairman of the Planning Commission, presented a paper at a conference in Prague where he followed the general lines traced out by Arnăutu. This paper was con-sidered important enough to be reprinted in *The World Marxist Review*, No. 8 (1960), pp. 73–74.

[64] *Vneshniaia torgovlia*, No. 2 (1960), p. 8.

Six-Year Plan, issued almost immediately upon the completion of these talks, contained maximum objectives for the country's industrialization, including a steel-output target of 3.3 million tons for 1965 and an increase of 120 percent in machine-building output over the six years.[65] These goals, one would assume, had to be approved at least tentatively by the Soviet government, since they implied large increases in iron ore imports and other materials from the Soviet Union.

At his keynote speech before the Third Party Congress[66] on June 20, 1960, Gheorghiu-Dej asserted that the Soviet Union would aid in the construction of a steel mill, a ten-year project that would eventually turn out 4 million tons of steel a year. This aid, he specified, included the delivery of a blooming-slabbing mill with an annual capacity of 3.3 million tons and a semicontinuous plate mill with a capacity of 1.5 million tons.[67]

I could find no other reference either in Rumanian or in Soviet literature to the alleged Soviet promise to deliver the equipment for the Galaţi mill.[68] Nikita Khrushchev himself made no reference whatever to it in his speech at the Congress, although he praised Gheorghiu-Dej as an outstanding figure in the international workers' movement and lauded Rumania's grandiose plans of industrialization.[69] These *politesses de circonstance* were a poor substitute for concrete promises.

On November 11, 1960, Rumania and the U.S.S.R. signed a commercial agreement for the next five years, which provided for Soviet technical aid in the construction of Galaţi but made no mention of the delivery of equipment, let alone of credits. It is not obvious what technical aid could contribute to the project if hardware was not to follow. In point of fact, various West European countries received important contracts for the delivery of equipment for the Galaţi mill in the next five years, but nothing concrete was heard about Soviet participation for several years.

---

[65] On the announcement of the other long-term plans, see United Nations, Economic Commission for Europe, *Economic Survey of Europe in 1959*, Chapter 3, p. 1; and *Economic Survey of Europe in 1960*, Chapter 2, pp. 25–26; Chapter 6, pp. 20 and 28.

[66] See note 70, p. 205.

[67] *Congresul al III-lea al Partidul Muncitoresc Romîn* (Third Congress of the Rumanian Workers' Party), June 20–25, 1960 (Bucharest, 1960), p. 27.

[68] For example, in September 1960, Dimitri Lazar, general secretary of the Ministry of Heavy Industry, described the main features of the Galaţi mill in essentially the same terms as Gheorghiu-Dej except for the omission of any mention of Soviet participation in supplying the equipment.

[69] *Ibid.*, pp. 194–196. J. F. Brown, in his well-documented article, "Rumania Steps Out of Line" (*Survey*, October 1963), suggested that Khrushchev's speech was evidence of support for Rumania's Six-Year Plan, and in particular for Galaţi. This seems very doubtful to me.

This sequence of events, reminiscent of the November 1958 episode, suggests again that Gheorghiu-Dej was making public what may have been a loose Soviet commitment in order to obtain concrete concessions that Khrushchev was reluctant to make. But Khrushchev ignored the Galaţi mill in his speech at the June Congress and then only vouchsafed the Rumanians a face-saving promise of technical aid the following November. Adding insult to injury, the Soviets proceeded to sign an agreement with Bulgaria on December 31st providing for a 650 million ruble credit to expand the Kremikovtsi steel works.[70]

At this juncture I should draw the reader's attention to another element in the deterioration in Soviet-Rumanian economic (and political) relations, that has never, to my knowledge, transpired in the press or in the periodical literature. The Soviet representatives in certain CMEA negotiations reportedly suggested that the Rumanians should make a greater effort to develop their cereals production in the next few years and, in particular, that they should undertake to export larger quantities of corn to the socialist market than they had envisaged in their draft of the Six-Year Plan. Khrushchev, who personally had a well-known interest in the cultivation of corn, is said to have pressed such a course on the Party leaders in Bucharest — too vigorously for the tastes of the latter, who had no desire for their country to resume its wartime role as purveyor of grain to Central Europe in exchange for Czech and German manufactures.

The Controversy Escalates

From December 1960, the public discussion of CMEA issues became more acrimonious.

The Rumanians opened a new round of the debate with a major article on "The importance of the economic aid of the USSR and of collaboration with socialist countries for the construction of social-

[70] Since these lines were written (they appeared in my article on the Rumanian dispute with Comecon in *Soviet Studies* of October 1964, p. 140), I learned in Bucharest that Khrushchev had indeed made either an oral or a written promise to Gheorghiu-Dej to deliver matériel for the Galaţi project; later on, however, he had been persuaded by the head of Gosplan of the U.S.S.R. that this would be an unwise course and he withdrew his support. Saltiel (*op. cit.*, pp. 110–115) argues that in February 1963 the Soviet leaders again altered their position and volunteered to provide slabbing and rolling equipment for Galaţi, some of which was actually delivered in 1964. The actual extent of these deliveries is not known. In any case, French, British, and German companies have been granted contracts for the construction of various parts of the mill, on some of which a good deal of work had already been completed by mid-1966. (One large blast furnace, built by a West German concern, was ready to go into operation by that date.)

ism in the R.P.R.," [71] which seemed to criticize the Soviet Union by implication for not making credits available for Rumanian industrialization.[72] The standard arguments concerning the disadvantages of narrow specialization, the necessity of taking into account dynamic factors in determining whether or not a given industry should be developed, and the benefits of industrial expansion on a broad front were again invoked.[73] In March 1961, for the first time since the onset of a controversy that had been conducted for at least three years in terms of carefully vague innuendoes, a more direct allusion to divergences among bloc economists crept into a review article by a Rumanian economist on an East German work on foreign trade.[74] The Rumanian, by way of lending his vigorous support to the East German author, attacked various views conflicting with the Rumanian Party's line on industrialization and foreign trade. He castigated "certain cadres" of East Germany's Ministry of External Trade who advocated buying mainly raw materials and foodstuffs from underdeveloped socialist countries and deplored the increasingly unfavorable structure of trade with developing countries intent on building up their machinery exports. The views of the East German economist Thiele also came in for sharp criticism. It was inadmissible, according to the Rumanian reviewer, that the division of labor should be based, as Thiele suggested, on the minimization of social labor costs. More generally, Thiele was accused of assigning an excessive role to the law of value in international trade instead of concentrating on the "law of proportional development." [75] The author of the review also argued that the priority development in each separate country of sector I (industries making producer goods) helped to consolidate the social foundations of the dictatorship of the proletariat by expanding the industrial labor force — a cogent argument for a country such as Rumania where

[71] F. Margineanu in *Probleme economice*, No. 12 (1960), pp. 12–34.

[72] The author cites Lenin (p. 20) to the effect that "the proletariat in advanced countries can and ought to help the retarded working masses and that the development of underdeveloped countries will emerge from the present stage when the victorious proletariat of the Soviet republic will extend a hand to these masses and bolster them." He then describes in detail the benefits of the November agreement, without mention of credits (pp. 25–26). Finally, he remarks that "as is well known, internal socialist accumulation constitutes the principal source of our efforts to develop the country, although Soviet credits create the possibility of obtaining a few supplementary means of production" (*unor mijloace suplimentare*, p. 28).

[73] *Op. cit.*, chiefly pp. 22–23.

[74] Review by L. Cretu of Gertrud Gräbig's *Internationale Arbeitsteilung und Aussenhandel im sozialistischen Weltsystem* (Berlin, 1960), in *Probleme economice*, No. 3 (1961), pp. 145–148. This source was cited and commented upon in William E. Griffith, *The Sino-Soviet Rift* (Cambridge, Mass.: The M.I.T. Press, 1964), p. 185, note 34.

[75] *Ibid.*, p. 147.

nearly two thirds of the economically active population were still engaged in agriculture.

The Central Committee meeting of the Rumanian Workers' Party of November–December 1961 was devoted to two topics, which both testify — although in very different respects — to the gradual emancipation of Rumania from Soviet tutelage: (1) a denunciation of the role played by the "*émigrés* from Moscow" (Pauker, Luca, *et al.*) between 1944 and 1952, who with the backing of the Soviets had suppressed the influence of native Communist groups;[76] and (2) a discussion of the Rumanian views on problems of trade and specialization, which hitherto had been advanced by individual authors without formal Party sanction. Gh. Gaston Marin, the chairman of the Rumanian Planning Commission, came close to an official Party statement of the Rumanian views on CMEA:

Our Party has always resolutely opposed and has always combated from a Marxist-Leninist standpoint those erroneous "theories" which, while defending the keeping of proportions between the branches of the national economy and the priority development of heavy industry on the scale of the whole socialist camp rather than within the framework of the individual socialist country, in fact deny the necessity of creating the technical and material base of socialism and present in a distorted manner the principles of specialization and cooperation within the framework of the socialist international division of labour.[77]

The Soviet position, mentioned earlier, seems to have swung in the direction of Czech and East German views in 1961. In February of that year a Soviet specialist on CMEA affairs pointed out that, even though the volume of foreign trade of all socialist countries had been growing, there remained wide disparities in the extent of participation in international trade of various socialist economies. "Many countries," he complained, "are far from exploiting the possibilities of the international division of labour for the development of their socialist production." [78] He refused to countenance the view that the operation of the law of value in international trade leads to antagonistic contradictions: "On the world socialist market, there is no mercenary spirit or speculation, no unequivalent exchange, characteristic of trade among

---

[76] See Chapter 2 in Stephen Fischer-Galati's volume, *The New Rumania: From People's Democracy to Socialist Republic* (Cambridge, Mass.: The M.I.T. Press, 1967); and Ghita Ionescu's, *Communism in Rumania 1944–1962* (London, New York, and Toronto: Oxford University Press, 1964), p. 334.

[77] *Scînteia* (December 12, 1961), cited by J. F. Brown, *op. cit.*, p. 23.

[78] I. Dudinskii, "Nekotoriye cherty razvitiia mirovogo sotsialisticheskogo rynka," *Voprosy ekonomiki*, No. 2 (1961), p. 42. It should be noted that Rumania's foreign trade per head is the lowest among the people's democracies.

capitalist countries." [79] After this implicit rejection of Rumanian views on the nonequivalence of exchange relations at world prices,[80] Dudinskii asserted the desirability of a transition to an international socialist price system, although he made no allusion to the necessity of shifting the terms of trade on the socialist market in favor of the underdeveloped countries.

In November 1961 the clearest expression of Soviet thinking on the correct criterion for determining international specialization came to light. The criterion put forward by the CMEA specialist Bogomolov turned out to be identical with the costs-minimization principle advocated by Kaigl as early as 1958, although it did leave room for the infant-industry argument by specifying that the analysis of comparative costs should be based on future- as well as on present-cost relations (a point insisted on by the Rumanians).[81] Despite this leftover from the typical compromises of the preceding two years, it was evident from the context that present profitability was meant to be the dominant consideration. This criterion, incidentally, must have met some opposition in Soviet circles, since, according to this same Soviet author,

> . . . a few of our economists follow a one-sided approach to the problem of the effectiveness or profitability of exchange. . . . They assert that putting the question in terms of the national-economic profitability of foreign trade introduces a certain mercenary element into the economic relations between socialist countries.[82]

These erroneous views he then refutes by invoking Mikoyan's authority.

It may seem surprising, in the light of these "integrationist" articles, which give the impression of a concerted attempt to define a Soviet position on matters of specialization in the bloc, that the Soviet economist I. P. Oleinik, a trusted friend of the Rumanians, kept on defending what he presumably took to be the interests of the underdeveloped countries in *Voprosy ekonomiki*,[83] *Mirovaia ekonomika i mezhdunarodnye otnosheniia*,[84] and finally right in Bucharest's own *Probleme economice*.[85] His, in any case, was the only exception I could find.

[79] *Ibid.*, p. 44.

[80] *Ibid.*, p. 131.

[81] O. Bogomolov, "Mezhdunarodnoe sotsialisticheskoe razdelenie truda na novom etape," *Voprosy ekonomiki*, No. 11 (1961), p. 97.

[82] *Ibid.*, p. 98.

[83] No. 5 (1961), p. 69.

[84] No. 8 (1961), pp. 8, 12, and *passim*.

[85] "Egalizarea nivelului dezvoltării economice a ţărilor socialiste," *Probleme economice*, No. 4 (1963), pp. 18–33. This article focused on the tendency of the underdeveloped countries to catch up with the more advanced economies, a favorite point of the Rumanians, but its position on the issue of specialization was either neutral or leaned toward the dominant Soviet position.

If I am right in supposing that the Soviet government adopted a less sympathetic position vis-à-vis the underdeveloped countries of the bloc around 1960, one may ask what causes could have prompted this policy shift. I am inclined to believe that the hesitancy of the Soviets in their trade-and-aid negotiations with the Rumanians in 1960 was due to domestic economic setbacks — compared at least with the sanguine expectations of rapid and uninterrupted growth that prevailed in 1958–1959. One of the problems that may have affected the Soviets' position directly was a deterioration in their balance-of-payments position with Western capitalist countries, which perhaps induced a switch of exports of equipment on credit from socialist countries to underdeveloped nations outside the bloc.[86] The crystallization of Soviet views in 1961 was probably the ideological manifestation of the tougher bargaining stance taken by the Ministry of Foreign Trade.[87]

Some key articles appeared in Czechoslovakia in 1961 and early 1962 that prepared the ground for the meeting of the Council for Mutual Economic Assistance of June 1962, at which the "Basic Principles of the International Division of Labor" were eventually agreed upon. An article in *Nová mysl* in May 1961 singled out as an obstacle to better coordination in the bloc the fact that "some underdeveloped countries" neglected their export commitments and thus jeopardized the fulfillment of their trading partners' plans.[88] At the time when the Third Five-Year Plan of Czechoslovakia (1961–1965) was already threatening to collapse, the failure to obtain raw materials that had been contracted for must have been critical indeed.[89] In April 1962 a theoretical article appeared that caused something of a sensation in Communist countries. This was Jiři Novozámský's paper on the equalization of development levels in the bloc. Novozámský called for a much greater degree of participation in the "socialist international division of labour" by the underdeveloped countries, whose structure of output had hardly been touched so far by the CMEA recommendations on specialization.[90] Greater specialization would both accelerate

[86] Cf. M. J. Garrison and M. H. Crawford, "Soviet Trade with the Free World in 1961," in *Dimensions of Soviet Power, op. cit.*, p. 454.

[87] The appeal to Mikoyan's authority just referred to may have been significant in this connection. The publication of the CPSU program (July 1961) with its very optimistic economic prospects seems to impugn my diagnosis of economic troubles. It must be kept in mind, however, that the program had been in preparation for some time and that, in any event, it need not necessarily reflect what the Party leaders may have assumed to be transient difficulties.

[88] *Nová mysl*, No. 5 (1961), pp. 609–610.

[89] For details, see J. M. Montias, "A Plan for All Seasons," *Survey*, No. 51 (April 1964).

[90] "Vyrovnávání ekonomické úrovně socialistických zemí," *Nová mysl*, No. 4 (1962), p. 433. See also Chapter 1, p. 16.

the growth of these less advanced countries and would make it possible for the more advanced countries to integrate their economies more fully into the world socialist system.[91] Novozámský touched on the delicate question of rates of accumulation, pointing out that the poorer countries of the bloc were enjoying levels of living that were relatively high for their per capita national incomes. To accelerate their development they could depend to some extent on loans from the more developed countries, but they would also have to raise the ratio of their investments to national income.[92] He went so far as to call for a greater degree of integration of the U.S.S.R. in the socialist world market for the sake of "expanded reproduction in the socialist world system and for maintaining proportional development in the framework of this system." [93] Although a greater volume of international lending among socialist countries was desirable to diminish gaps in the level of development, it would be wrong, in his opinion, to interpret the "transition to communism more or less simultaneously within one and the same historical epoch" [94] as a prediction of passage into that higher state "at the same hour." When the U.S.S.R. had completed building the Communist society, there would still be a few European countries that had not attained that stage, not to speak of the Asian states.[95]

The joint declaration on "The Basic Principles of the International Division of Labour," signed by all members of the Council for Mutual Economic Aid in June 1962, echoed many of the points made by Novozámský, although the underdeveloped countries apparently succeeded in watering down the more extreme demands on specialization sufficiently to accept the document. In the following summary I shall mark with a (C) the clauses echoing the Czech or East German position, with an (S) the clauses that seem to correspond to Soviet interests, and with an (R) the points that were probably introduced to placate Rumania or some other underdeveloped country in CMEA.

1. (C) "Comparative calculations of the economic effectiveness of investments in socialist countries, as well as of the economic effectiveness of foreign trade, serve in the coordination of national plans as an important, if not the only, criterion for determining rational ways to intensify the international division of labor." (R) In perfecting the international division of labor one should "take into account, along with calculations of economic effectiveness, the necessity of ensuring

[91] *Nová mysl*, No. 4 (1962), p. 425.
[92] *Ibid.*, p. 430.
[93] *Ibid.*, pp. 432–433.
[94] This was the formula adopted in the CPSU program (Ritvo, *op. cit.*, p. 232.)
[95] *Nová mysl*, No. 4 (1962), p. 436.

full employment, the preservation of equilibrium in the balance of payments, the role of a given good in raising labor productivity in the entire economy, the leveling of differences in economic development, and the consolidation of the country's defense capability." [96]

2. (C) "One of the most important methods of evaluating various alternative specialization plans is the calculation of the attendant reduction in current costs and in transportation costs as well as the reduction in investments, taking into consideration a time factor and a recoupment period." (R) "Considering that specialization measures are taken for a long period of time, one should have in mind the effect of technical progress on [these] value calculations and possible future changes in the indicators compared." [97]

Other important points included the following: (C) Underdeveloped countries should raise their rate of accumulation. (S) "Metallurgical plants with a complete cycle [from pig iron to rolled products] should be developed first of all in countries that are fully or in large measure supplied with domestic ores and technological fuels [coking coals] or at least with one of these raw materials." [98] (R) The machine-building industry should grow fastest in countries where it is least developed. (C) and (S) In the future, efforts to improve coordination should include means to secure fulfillment of contracts, with due regard to the volume, dates of delivery, quality, and technical level of the production to be delivered.

That this last point was a Soviet objective became apparent in August when Premier Khrushchev published his article in *Kommunist* calling for organizational measures to tighten up economic coordination in the bloc.[99] The establishment of a supranational organ with coordinating powers, which Khrushchev apparently had in mind, was

[96] "Základné princípy medzinárodnej socialistickej delby práce" (Basic principles of the international socialist division of labor), *Pravda* (Bratislava), June 17, 1962, p. 2. All the following quotations are from this same source.

[97] This seems to be a compromise within a compromise, inasmuch as the Rumanians never acknowledged that one could calculate explicitly the changes in comparative costs that would eventually place the underdeveloped country on an equal footing with its more mature competitor.

[98] This leaves out Albania, Hungary, and Rumania.

[99] Khrushchev's article echoed a number of Czech positions, including a strong emphasis on cost calculations and profitability as criteria for specialization. He recommended the creation of a common investment fund for member countries of CMEA but implied that only the states cooperating with the directives of CMEA on specialization would be allowed to draw aid from this fund. (N. S. Khrushchev, "Nasushchniie voprosy razvitie mirovoi sotsialisticheskoi sistemy," *Kommunist*, No. 12 [1962], p. 10.) Khrushchev's article is discussed in some detail by J. B. Thompson in "Rumania's Struggle with Comecon," *East Europe* (June 1964), pp. 7–9.

anathema to the Rumanian leaders, as they were later to make crystal-clear.[100]

Although the Principles of June 1962 were hailed in Moscow and Prague as a major achievement, they really left the opposing parties in the dispute more or less where they had stood before. It is not surprising that the controversy was soon resumed. Novozámský used Khrushchev's article as a springboard for demanding greater specialization and coordination, all the while assuring the underdeveloped countries that the progress of economic integration would in no way impair their political sovereignty.[101] He also leveled a general accusation to the effect that certain economies were producing and exporting machines that were technically below world standards and were more costly to produce than they should be according to their designed specifications — let alone than they would be if they were subject to a specialization agreement.[102]

In June 1962 Khrushchev visited Bucharest, perhaps to convince the Rumanian leaders that his plans for a reorganization of CMEA did not represent a threat to Rumania's economic sovereignty.[103] Khrushchev, in the speeches he made in Rumania, stressed the theme of cooperation in CMEA and expressed renewed sympathy for Rumania's industrialization plans but again failed to mention the Galaţi mill.[104]

In September, three months after Khrushchev's visit, Walter Ulbricht also called on the Rumanians. According to J. F. Brown, "it is probable that part of his mission was to get Rumania to modify its economic outlook." [105] Bruno Leuschner, who accompanied Ulbricht, spoke of "more decisive steps in perfecting the socialist division of labor . . . which would have to pervade even more the bilateral relations between

---

[100] See pp. 217–218.

[101] J. Novozámský, "Jednotné hospodařství socialistické soustavy," *Nová mysl,* No. 10 (1962), pp. 1165–1166.

[102] *Ibid.,* p. 1169.

[103] Brown, *op. cit.,* p. 23. Other accounts of the events of 1962–1963 are contained in the following articles: R. L. Braham, "Rumania: Onto the Separate Path," *Problems of Communism* (May–June 1964); J. B. Thompson, "Rumania's Struggle with Comecon," *East Europe* (June 1964); and George Gross, "Rumania: The Fruits of Autonomy," *Problems of Communism* (January–February 1966). An excellent treatment of the period 1962–1964 is contained in Fischer-Galati's *The New Rumania: From People's Democracy to Socialist Republic, op. cit.,* Chapter 4. His linkage of political and economic factors in the dispute forms the essential background of the description and analysis in the following pages.

[104] In his article of August 1962, Khrushchev gave the Galaţi issue a new twist when he alleged that blooming and slabbing mills had been made obsolete by the Soviet continuous-casting method. "As is known," he deplored, "this method has not been adopted by any of the socialist countries." (Khrushchev, *op. cit.,* p. 22.)

[105] Brown, *op. cit.,* p. 24.

socialist states." [106] The German visit was apparently not a success and resulted in a worsening of relations between Pankow and Bucharest.

In January 1963, J. Mervart, whose article had drawn a critical comment from Horovitz as early as 1958, resumed the campaign against autarkic tendencies in the bloc with a rather truculent article in *Nová mysl*. Mervart assailed the misguided policy adopted by "certain countries" of expanding steel production at a high cost, taking the volume of output as an index of economic progress rather than the efficiency of its manufacture (technology employed, amount of steel produced per unit of capacity, and so on). This efficiency, he wrote, "also depends on natural conditions, which are not favorable for the development of a domestic metallurgical base [in Hungary, Poland, and Rumania]. It will be more effective for these countries — with the possible exception of Poland — to import a larger proportion of their needs for metallurgical products from the Soviet Union, which has ideal natural conditions for and a high level of technology in the metallurgical industry." [107]

We now come to a turning point in Rumania's relations with CMEA, when, for the first time, the smoldering dispute came out in the open and attracted worldwide attention.

In mid-February 1963, the vice-premiers of member states met in Moscow to discuss "specialization in the world market." It may be speculated that the Soviets, with the backing of Czechoslovakia and East Germany, and perhaps of Poland, made a last-ditch effort on this occasion to reorganize CMEA into a supranational agency that would be capable of initiating and supervising the execution of specialization agreements. The split that resulted from this campaign was serious enough to prompt the Rumanian Communist leaders to call a meeting of their Party's Central Committee after the Rumanian delegation returned from Moscow. On this occasion, the Central Committee reaffirmed the instructions given to Alexander Bîrladeanu for the Moscow conclave and congratulated him for his representation of Rumania's stand at that meeting. The communiqué of the plenum read in part:

The plenary meeting reasserted its full agreement with the fundamental principles of the socialist international division of labor, adopted by the conference of the representatives of communist and workers' parties of the Comecon countries held in June 1962, in keeping with the main means of

[106] *Neues Deutschland* (September 18, 1962), cited by Brown, *op. cit.*, p. 25.
[107] J. Mervart, "Materialné-technická základna zemí RVHP," *Nová mysl*, No. 1 (1963), pp. 36–38.

successfully developing and deepening the socialist international division of labor and the coordination of national economic plans in the spirit of the principles proclaimed by the 1960 Moscow statement, of observance of national independence and sovereignty, of full equality of rights, comradely mutual aid and mutual benefit.[108]

Shortly thereafter, Gaston Marin granted an interview to *Corriere della Sera* in which he declared:

We are in the phase of bilateral discussion. Rumania has concluded agreements of this type with the Soviets, Bulgarians and Poles for the manufacture of certain types of machines. Comecon recognizes the right of every nation to develop and plan in keeping with its own national interests. Comecon is an organization of sovereign states.[109]

The stress on bilateralism was obviously out of tune with Moscow's efforts to promote multilateralism in the framework of CMEA.

In February 1963, on the eve of the Moscow meeting just discussed, Václav Kotyk, an eminent Czech expert on international relations, had alluded to political aspects of the divergences among CMEA members. Notwithstanding the title of his article, "The Unity of the Socialist Countries at the Present Stage," [110] Kotyk dealt, in effect, with the economic sources of disunity in the bloc.

One cannot exclude the possibility of certain difficulties and contradictions among [developed and less developed] countries; one cannot fail to see the significant differences in the economic level of the socialist countries and in the concrete historical circumstances of their development, which create the objective possibility of the occurrence of conflicting points of views. The experiences of individual socialist countries with the outside world are not the same. . . . Nevertheless, it is dangerous to magnify these national peculiarities.

He went on to accuse "certain socialist countries" of generalizing on the basis of "difficulties connected with their internal or their foreign situation" and of foisting their "incorrect or even correct conclusions" on other countries.[111] These remarks might apply to China or to Albania, but I suspect that they were directed chiefly at Rumania.

In March of the same fateful year, a Polish economist, siding with the underdeveloped countries of the bloc, rejected as "mistaken and lacking in objectivity" the Novozámský thesis about the need for relatively more intensive participation by the less developed countries in the socialist international division of labor. Invoking the example of

---

[108] *Scînteia* (March 8, 1963), cited by Brown, *op. cit.*, pp. 25–26.

[109] Cited by Brown, *op. cit.*, p. 26.

[110] V. Kotyk, "Jednota socialistiskýkh zemí v současné etapě," *Nová mysl*, No. 2 (1963), pp. 142–148.

[111] *Ibid.*, p. 148.

the coking industry, he observed that Rumania, Poland, and Hungary, "countries that are usually called less developed," used more advanced techniques and were achieving better results in economizing on scarce coking coals in the production of coke than were the other members of CMEA. It was up to Czechoslovakia to use a weaker mix of coking coals, possibly based on imported gas coals; this would allow her to export the better types of coking coals — to be mixed with ordinary coals in the countries that were short of high-grade coking coals. In this case, greater trading possibilities were being left unexploited by one of the most advanced economies.[112]

The regular CMEA meeting in May 1963 was no more successful than preceding encounters in ironing out disagreements within the group. Shortly thereafter, a high-level Soviet delegation led by Nikolai Podgorny came to Budapest with the aim, apparently, of bringing the Rumanians around to cooperation with CMEA. As on the Russians' former visit, both guests and hosts reiterated their previous points of views on specialization. Ceauşescu, the protégé and heir-designate of Gheorghiu-Dej, stressed the primacy of heavy industry, with the machine-building branch in the van of progress, while Podgorny evoked the gains in efficiency and labor productivity that could be achieved through greater specialization and coordination of production.[113]

The Rumanian leaders, far from being mollified by these representations, marked their continued disaffection with CMEA by failing to send a top representative to the conference of Party secretaries in Warsaw in June. This failure to participate, which exposed the seriousness of Rumania's dispute with CMEA, attracted wide attention in the West.

The Public Debate

By the time Gheorghiu-Dej had publicly displayed his ill will toward CMEA, political differences in the bloc were already aggravating the economic sources of discord. Most directly relevant here was the neutral or uncommitted stance adopted by Rumania on the Sino-Soviet dispute.[114] This in turn prompted the Chinese to court the Rumanians by espousing the latter's cause in matters of economic sovereignty. Several passages of the famous Chinese open letter of June 14, 1963, could be interpreted as a defense of the Rumanian positions, including, for example, the following paragraph:

[112] A. Pieńkowski, "Współpraca krajów RWPG a problem węgla koksującego," *Gospodarka planowa*, No. 3 (1963), pp. 4 and 5.

[113] Brown, *op. cit.*, p. 29.

[114] See Fischer-Galati, *op. cit.*, Chapter 4.

It is absolutely necessary for socialist countries to practice mutual economic assistance, cooperation and exchange. Such economic cooperation must be based on the principles of complete equality, mutual benefit and comradely mutual assistance. It would be great-power chauvinism to deny these basic principles and, in the name of "international division of labor" or "specialization," to impose one's own will on others, infringe on the independence and sovereignty of fraternal countries or harm the interests of their people.[115]

From about the middle of 1963, Rumanian propaganda, in contrast to its relative passivity in the late 1950's and early 1960's, began to take the initiative in stirring up the dispute.

The new journal *Viaţa economică* took up the cudgels in its very first issue. Its editor in chief, Costin Murgescu, leveled his fire against two authors, one a bourgeois economist and another an East German, linking both under the title "Pseudo-Theories Which Attempt To Deprive Industrialization of Its Contents." [116] The present writer of these lines was rather mildly reprimanded for his misguided criticism of certain aspects of Rumanian industrialization policy.[117] A lower circle in Inferno was reserved for the East German economist Gerhard Huber, who had had the temerity to argue that "passive industrialization" might be a proper goal for a socialist country under certain circumstances. According to his conception, certain developing countries should cease to give precedence to heavy industry and "pay more attention to agriculture and to the processing of agriculture products." [118] That the East Germans did not wish at this point to aggravate the controversy was shown, shortly after the appearance of Murgescu's critique, when Karl Morgenstern published an article in *Die Wirtschaft* [East Berlin] in which he also attacked Huber's notion of "passive industrialization" as "contrary to the fundamental principles of the socialist international division of labor." [119]

[115] "A Proposal Concerning the General Line of the International Communist Movement — The Open Letter of the Central Committee of the Communist Party of China in Reply to the Letter from the Central Committee of the Communist Party of the Soviet Union of March 30, 1963–June 14, 1963," *People's Daily* (June 17, 1963), quoted from William E. Griffith, *The Sino-Soviet Rift* (Cambridge, Mass.: The M.I.T. Press, 1964), p. 281.

[116] C. Murgescu, "Pseudoteorii care încearcă să golească de conţinut industrializarea," *Viaţa economică*, No. 1 (1963), p. 11.

[117] In my paper "Unbalanced Growth in Rumania," *American Economic Review*, Proceedings, May 1963.

[118] Murgescu, *op. cit.*

[119] Cited in *Viaţa economică*, No. 9 (1963), p. 11. Western commentators have, I believe, correctly interpreted Morgenstern's article as a conciliatory gesture; but the East German views are sufficiently variegated for such a difference of opinions to have emerged spontaneously. What leads me to accept the first hypothesis is that

The Rumanian counteroffensive against the integrationists in CMEA culminated in the publication of the "Statement on the Stand of the Rumanian Workers' Party Concerning the Problems of the World Communist and Working-Class Movement," issued by the Central Committee of Rumania's ruling Party in April 1964. This most official of pronouncements proclaimed to the world that Rumania would not brook interference in her policies, whether in the economic or in the political realm. The key passages bearing on Rumania's relations to CMEA are reproduced here.

Cooperation within CMEA is achieved on the basis of the principles of fully equal rights, of observance of national sovereignty and interests, of mutual advantage and comradely assistance.

As concerns the method of economic cooperation, the socialist countries that are members of CMEA have established that the main means of achieving the international socialist division of labor, the main form of cooperation among their national economies, is to coordinate plans on the basis of bilateral and multilateral agreements.

During the development of the relations of cooperation among the socialist countries that are members of CMEA, forms and measures have been projected, such as a joint plan and a single planning body for all member countries, interstate technical-productive branch unions, enterprises jointly owned by several countries, interstate economic complexes, etc.

Our party has very clearly expressed its point of view, declaring that, since the essence of the projected measures lies in shifting some functions of economic management from the competence of the respective state to that of superstate bodies or organisms, these measures are not in keeping with the principles that underlie the relations among the socialist countries.

The idea of a single planning body for all CMEA countries has the most serious economic and political implications. The planned management of the national economy is one of the fundamental, essential, and inalienable attributes of the sovereignty of the socialist state — the state plan being the chief means through which the socialist state achieves its political and socioeconomic objectives, establishes the directions and rates of development of the national economy, its fundamental proportions, the accumulations, the measures for raising the people's living standard and cultural level. The sovereignty of the socialist state requires that it effectively and fully avail itself of the means for the practical implementation of these attributions, holding in its hands all the levers of managing economic and social life. Transmitting such levers to the competence of superstate or extrastate bodies would turn sovereignty into a meaningless notion.

All these are also fully valid as concerns interstate technical-productive branch unions as well as enterprises commonly owned by two or several states. The state plan is one and indivisible; no parts or sections can be separated from it in order to be transferred outside the state. The management of

---

Morgenstern's views in the past had not been very different from Huber's (see Chapter 4, ftn. 58).

the national economy as a whole is not possible if the questions of managing some branches or enterprises are taken away from the competence of the party and government of the respective country and transferred to extrastate bodies.[120]

Returning the Chinese courtesy of the previous year, the Rumanian statement endorsed the participation of Communist states that were not at present members of CMEA — for example, China and the other Asiatic Communist states — in the affairs of the Council.[121]

One interesting consequence of the public airing of Rumanian views was that it justified the release of hitherto undivulged information on an earlier clash. The *World Marxist Review* and the Polish weekly *Polityka* disclosed the details of a controversial meeting of economists from the U.S.S.R. and Eastern Europe, at which the Polish economist and planner Jozef Pajestka had outlined a three-stage program for the gradual introduction of common planning among the CMEA countries. "The most reserved attitude" to his proposal had been shown by the Rumanian delegates. I. Rachmuth, a vice-director of the Institute for Economic Research in Bucharest, had defended Rumania's trade and development policy. "This policy," he argued, "strives to attain the highest technical level by buying the most modern licenses in the West (as does the German Democratic Republic)." He expressed fears lest Rumania tie up her trade too narrowly with stronger partners in CMEA at a time when she had not attained a level permitting her to deal with these partners on an equal basis. More generally, the Rumanians urged that it was inadmissible to "absolutize" the criteria of effectiveness in the field of specialization and cooperation, insisting that "in certain periods and with respect to certain fields, social-political considerations can sometimes predominate, which require that considerations of pure effectiveness be pushed aside temporarily." [122]

On June 5, 1964, Radio Bucharest voiced sharp objections to a Soviet broadcast in the Rumanian language calling for the "reinforcement of the Socialist community." [123] In answer to these critical comments on Rumania's economic policy, the Rumanian speaker had asked the following rhetorical question:

[120] "Statement on the Stand of the Rumanian Workers' Party Concerning the Problems of the International Communist and Working-Class Movement" (Bucharest: Meridiane Publishing House, 1964), quoted from William E. Griffith, *Sino-Soviet Relations*, 1964–1965 (Cambridge, Mass.: The M.I.T. Press, 1967), pp. 282–283.

[121] *Ibid.*, p. 284.

[122] *Polityka* (June 27, 1964), cited in *Polish Press Survey*, Research Department of Radio Free Europe (Munich, July 3, 1964), pp. 4–6.

[123] Cited in Saltiel, *op. cit.*, p. 38.

Is it not strange that those who are showing themselves to be against collaboration with other Socialist countries are approaching the capitalist states, asking them for technical aid, and are spending large amounts in foreign currency for this purpose? . . . To which Socialist countries [the Rumanian commentator asked] does this refer? Which of them are reproached for procuring equipment from capitalist countries and expending foreign currency for this purpose? Does the commentary perhaps refer to the USSR, which has developed and is developing its economic relations with the Western countries, with France, Britain, Italy, the United States, the German Federal Republic and other capitalist countries? Or does it refer to Poland, in whose foreign trade the relations with the capitalist countries have a share of approximately 40 percent? Or to Czechoslovakia which also has broad economic relations with the capitalist countries.[124]

It is significant that the Soviet broadcast focused its criticism on Rumanian purchases of machinery and equipment in the West, a line of attack that had never been taken so openly before (perhaps because it could too easily be construed as interference in the internal affairs of a sovereign state).

The debate reached its acme in June 1964 with the publication of a spirited Rumanian critique of various recent Soviet contributions to the geography of large economic regions. The critic's sharpest barbs were aimed at an article published the preceding February by a Soviet geographer named E. B. Valev, who had proposed the creation of an "interstate economic complex" in the lower Danubian region, which would have englobed a large part of Rumania as well as territories in Bulgaria and the U.S.S.R.[125] The author of the Rumanian broadside, C. Murgescu, editor of *Viaţa economică*, suggested by his citations, culled from a variety of papers written by Soviet economists and geographers between 1962 and 1964, that the idea of regional complexes spreading across national boundaries had not sprung spontaneously but had been sanctioned by Soviet authorities.[126] The econ-

---

[124] *Summary of World Broadcasts*, Part II, *Eastern Europe*, BBC Monitoring Service, No. 1573 (June 8, 1964).

[125] E. B. Valev, "Problems of the Economic Development of the Danube Districts of Rumania, Bulgaria, and the U.S.S.R.," *Vestnik Moscovskogo Universiteta*, No. 2 (March–April 1964). This article appeared in Rumanian translation along with the critique, "Concepts Contrary to the Basic Principles Guiding Economic Relations Between Socialist Countries," in *Viaţa economică*, No. 24 (1964). Both were reprinted in *Probleme ale relaţiilor economice dintre ţările socialiste*, Biblioteca "Viaţa economică," No. 2 (1964), pp. 47–59.

[126] According to Murgescu, the more recent proposals, "being very concrete in their essence — ignoring the notions of sovereignty, state frontiers and national economy — exhibit a general non-individualized character" (p. 14). A Rumanian official confirmed to me in 1965 that it was the general belief in Bucharest that the notion of multistate complexes could not have been put forward in public if it had not first been approved at a high level in the Soviet Union.

omist G. Sorokin in *Voprosy ekonomiki* had advanced the opinion as early as 1962 that "the creation of interstate complexes represents a new, superior and stable type of the international socialist division of labor." He specified in this connection that specialists from the Soviet Union and from other socialist countries had already proceeded to the elaboration of a few concrete projects of this type.[127] G. Karhin had argued in *Ekonomicheskaia gazeta* in 1963 that the development of socialist nations had been hampered by the existence of national boundaries, which cut across natural economic regions.[128] In early 1964, the geographer P. M. Alampiev advocated the development of interstate complexes as a step toward the formation of a grand economic ensemble governed by a unique plan. He discerned a contradiction between the future transformation of a socialist world economy ruled by a single plan and the development of regional complexes "within the boundaries of sovereign states . . . which have their own balance of national income, their own balance of payments and their own independent planning." [129] Similar pleas for interstate complexes were presented by other Soviet geographers at the Twentieth International Geographical Congress in London. The gist of these proposals, according to Murgescu, consisted in "detaching from a national economic whole certain territories in order to subject them to the deeper influence of the international division of labor. Their ultimate import is that they are *attempting to theorize about a process of dismemberment of the national economies and of the national territories of certain socialist states.*" [130]

In his article Murgescu also categorically rejected the proposal made by the geographers Maergois and Probst, and supported by Alampiev, of transferring manpower from labor-surplus to labor-deficit countries. "The notion of international migration," Murgescu asserts, "is incompatible with socialism. . . . The idea of planning the dislocation of labor from its own milieu . . . could only denigrate socialism, compromise it in the eyes of the peoples struggling toward its construction." [131]

The article by E. B. Valev was the logical continuation of these earlier more or less theoretical efforts. Valev urged the creation of a Lower-Danubian Complex, which, according to Murgescu's calcula-

---

[127] C. Murgescu, "Concepţii potrivnice principiilor de bază ale relaţiilor economice dintre ţările socialiste," in *Probleme ale relaţiilor* . . . , *op. cit.*, p. 7, reprinted from *Viaţa economică* (June 12, 1964).

[128] *Ibid.*

[129] *Ibid.*, p. 8. The reference to each country's independent "balance of national income" alludes to the autonomous planning of investments in each country, which inhibits the free flow of capital among Communist countries.

[130] *Ibid.* (Italics in the original.)

[131] *Ibid.*, p. 13.

tions, would incorporate 86 percent of all Rumania's oil and gas production, 54 percent of her machine-building output, 51 percent of her chemical industry, 58.5 percent of her wheat, and 60 percent of her corn harvests.[132] His calculations, based on the map published by Valev, indicate that out of 150,000 square kilometers of territory assigned to the complex in the Valev proposal, Rumania would contribute 100,000 square kilometers, Bulgaria 38,000, and the U.S.S.R. 12,000. Three fourths of its population would be Rumanian (9 million out of a total of 12 million).[133]

While the core of Murgescu's opposition to the Valev proposal lay in his belief that the Lower-Danubian Complex would encroach on Rumanian national sovereignty, he also had some specific objections to its cavalier treatment of problems bearing on the output of consumption of steel and electric power, which were of vital importance for Rumania's industrialization. Valev wrote that "a precise specialization" is being planned in Comecon among the metallurgical complexes of Galați, Hunedoara, and Reşiţa (all in Rumania), of Sofia (Kremikovtsi) and of the Dnieper Region "with respect to the types of rolled products produced on a large scale."

It is true [Murgescu retorts] that when metallurgical problems were discussed in CMEA, the problems of specializing the production and the assortment of certain individual mills (combinates) were discussed for the following countries: Bulgaria (Kremikovtsi), Czechoslovakia (Košice), German Democratic Republic (Eastern *kombinat*), Poland (the mill near Kraków), Hungary (the mill on the Danube) and the USSR (for unspecified mills — nothing was said about a mill situated on the Dnieper). This was the framework in which specialization was studied, not among the three Danubian regions belonging to three states. As far as the Galați mill is concerned, Rumania indicated that *her economic requirements compel her not to modify either the specialization of production envisaged for the mill, nor its assortment, nor the dates at which its component parts will be put into operation.* Our country agreed to *coordinate* the output of rolled production projected for the Galați mill, in the framework of the usual process of coordinating plans and on the basis of bilateral consultations.[134]

In other words, the Rumanians had expressed their willingness to mesh their productive output with that of their partners in CMEA after the structure of production had been decided for the mill on the basis of domestic requirements. They did not wish to *adapt* this structure to foreign demands. (It is not surprising in view of these adverse comments on specialization in the metallurgical industry that Rumania did not join the CMEA association of steel producers known as *Intermetall*,

---

[132] *Ibid.*, p. 15.
[133] *Ibid.*, p. 16.
[134] *Ibid.*, p. 22. (Italics in the original.)

which is said to wield extensive powers in determining the structure of output and the marketing of metallurgical products in Poland, Czechoslovakia, East Germany, and Hungary.)

What will happen, Murgescu then asks, to consumers of metal located outside the limits of the complex? "The author is generous enough not to let them perish of metal hunger." Valev provides for "reinforced links" between the metallurgical and machine-building industries of the "old regions of Rumania, Bulgaria and the U.S.S.R. and the Lower-Danubian Complex." With a touch of sarcasm Murgescu suggests that these reinforced links might call for the establishment of "diplomatic relations" between the parts of Rumania within the complex and the parts outside it.[135]

Murgescu was particularly exercised by the notion that the electric power generated in the lower Dnieper region of the U.S.S.R. would be conveyed across Rumanian territory for the use of Bulgaria, without benefit to the Rumanian regions in the complex, which would remain dependent on the present network. He also objected to Valev's proposals concerning the allocation of petroleum, Rumania's most abundant source of power, which would have the effect, in his opinion, of depriving Rumanian regions outside the complex of all petroleum produced within its limits.

All these scientific proposals of specialists are narrowly bound up with *practical* aspects of certain problems. . . . Even though, for instance, Rumania's consumption of electric power and fuels per capita is at present, and is projected to be in the future, considerably lower than that of all other members of CMEA, proposals have been put forward repeatedly for covering the deficits of certain countries at least in part by Rumania (even though our country already exports electric power to Czechoslovakia and Bulgaria and methane gas to Hungary). In February 1964 specialists of *Energosetiproekt*[136] (Moscow), unsolicited by us, drew up a study . . . titled "Rumanian Power," in which it was affirmed that these resources (the authors have in mind Rumanian liquid fuels, gas and water power) could cover partially the deficit in electric power of Hungary and Bulgaria.[137]

Murgescu finds it impossible to reconcile such transfers of energy from a country with a low consumption per capita to economies with a higher consumption with the "objective tendency" of equalizing the levels of development of socialist countries.

The Rumanian editor's analysis of Valev's paper and of earlier Soviet contributions to the topic was presumably calculated to arouse

[135] *Ibid.*, p. 23.
[136] An organization charged with the elaboration of hydraulic projects in the U.S.S.R.
[137] *Viața economică* (June 12, 1964).

indignation rather than to initiate a serious discussion. But the cumulative weight of his arguments should be enough to convince any detached observer that the Soviet geographers had indeed meddled in Rumanian internal affairs, at a time when the Rumanians had already shown that they would not tolerate such interference. With or without official approval, the Russians had trespassed the bounds of propriety hitherto observed in relations within CMEA. The publication of Murgescu's article must have driven home to the highest Soviet authorities that Valev *et al.* had gone too far. O. Bogomolov, one of the chief Soviet specialists in CMEA affairs, was given space in *Izvestia* to refute and castigate Valev. "Professor Valev's approach," Bogomolov wrote, "was fundamentally wrong and not in line with Soviet communist policy designed to strengthen economic ties with fraternal countries on the basis of the principles of equal rights and sovereignty." [138]

After this climactic episode, the debate calmed down, although no reconciliation of views has taken place. The Rumanians have not ceased their carping about integrationist writings from other nations of the camp, but the tone of their critiques has not risen again to the pitch of the diatribe against Valev. The most significant contribution to the debate in the last year or two was made by Professor Ion Rachmuth, who went to the extreme of rejecting the theory of specialization according to comparative advantage, even in cases where the consequence of its adoption would be greater output and consumption for all countries involved, as long as this pattern of specialization happened to widen the disparity in development levels between trading partners at different stages of development.[139] Fairness and equivalence, in other words, take precedence over efficiency. This is as protectionist an argument as one can find in the extensive literature on this subject.

Most recently an institutional problem has supervened that may widen the breach between the more and the less industrialized members of CMEA. The more developed nations may be about to embark on a Yugoslav-type decentralization in which domestic enterprises would participate directly in foreign trade, at least for certain types of import and export transactions. The least developed members of CMEA, Bulgaria and Rumania, have no intention of pushing decentralization that far. Rumania, for one, has taken only the most hesitant steps to curb the overriding power of the Planning Commission with respect to industrial ministries. This divergence of attitudes toward institutional reform erupted at the Moscow Conference of CMEA experts on

[138] Cited in *The New York Times*, July 3, 1964.
[139] I. Rachmuth, "Unele aspecte ale acţiunii legii valorii pe plan internaţional," *Probleme economice*, No. 9 (1964), pp. 9–11.

International Specialization and Cooperation in February 1966. One of the topics that aroused "a lively discussion," according to a Czech reporter, was the problem of determining between what institutions or other agents specialization agreements should be concluded.

The experts from countries where a new system of management and national economic planning is under preparation (Czechoslovakia, the German Democratic Republic, Hungary and the USSR) recommended, or assumed, that the contracting partners in specialization agreements would be productive enterprises, associations and general administrations, together with foreign trade enterprises. The experts who came out most decidedly against this conception were those from Bulgaria and Rumania, according to whom an enterprise cannot fully represent statewide interests and cannot make sure that the engagements it has undertaken will be respected by other organizational units or the whole territory of the state.[140]

The perennial problem of a proper price basis for trade between CMEA members was again thrown up in the discussion. Some of the less developed members of CMEA voiced their unhappiness about the January 1966 revision of CMEA prices, which, by changing the reference point for intra-CMEA prices from world market prices of 1957–1958 to world market prices of 1960–1964, had allowed the deterioration of the terms of trade for primary products in the West to impinge on the CMEA market. The Bulgarians, true to form, pressed for a price system detached from the world market, which "practically would have the effect of raising the prices of agricultural products and raw materials and of reducing the prices of machinery." The Soviet representatives suggested that prices of specialized machinery should be lowered to offset speculative and monopolistic tendencies in pricing these goods on the world market. They were also of the opinion that the prices of agricultural products and raw materials in CMEA were not sufficiently attractive for the producers of these goods. The Czechs, predictably, came out for continued use of world prices in CMEA trade: "We are not of the opinion that the prices of specialized machinery produced in socialist states should be made to deviate in one or another direction from the level of world prices." [141] According to the same Czech report, the delegates from East Germany, Hungary, Poland, and Yugoslavia "expressed themselves in a similar vein." If this exhausts the list of countries supporting the Czechoslovak position, we may infer that the Soviet Union, Bulgaria, and Rumania must have been lined up on the opposite side of the argument, and hence, presumably, that they all supported an autonomous principle of price formation. This array suggests

[140] M. Polívka, "Mezinárodní specializace na nový základ," *Hospodářské noviny*, No. 10 (1966), p. 10.
[141] *Ibid.*

that the Soviet Union still does not identify its interests on all issues with those of the more developed countries. This is quite understandable in view of the fact that its structure of trade resembles that of the less developed countries more than it does that of the specialized exporters of manufactures such as Czechoslovakia and East Germany. The U.S.S.R., as well as Bulgaria and Rumania, would clearly stand to gain from a revision of the relative prices of raw materials and manufactured goods.[142]

Facts and Arguments in the Dispute

What generalizations, finally, can we draw from this fastidious chronicle of disagreements within the socialist common market? The most meaningful, it seems to me, turn on the relation between the "material base" and the "superstructure" of the controversy, that is, between conflicts of interests among members and the divergent theories and principles they have generated.

We almost always found a strict correspondence between the interests of the parties to the dispute as they conceived of them and the theoretical arguments they advanced. I detected no exception to this rule in Rumanian or in Czech writings. In the Soviet case, the issue is wrapped up in a skein of partially contradictory interests arising from a multiplicity of economic and political goals. On the one hand, the Soviet Union is primarily concerned about the unity of the bloc that it leads; it must therefore play a neutral or conciliatory role in disputes among the people's democracies, especially since Communist China has challenged this leadership and threatened to exploit divisions in CMEA to augment its own influence in Eastern Europe. On the other, the Soviets carry the heavy burden of meeting Eastern Europe's deficit in raw materials and foodstuffs. At a time when their resources were strained to achieve excessively ambitious targets in the early 1960's, it is understandable that they hesitated to underwrite the Galaţi mill project, which, they must have calculated, would tie up scarce capital if the equipment was delivered on credit and would force them to increase their deliveries of iron ore at a high cost in mining and transportation. (In the end, they compromised by supplying the ore but holding back on the equipment.) On the issue of a "unique plan" for CMEA, which would coordinate and allocate resources *ex ante* rather

---

[142] For an unequivocal statement of the Soviet Union's stance on raw-material prices, see O. Bogomolov's important article, "Aktual'nye problemy ekonomicheskogo sotrudnichestva sotsialisticheskikh stran," *Mirovaia ekonomika i mezhdunarodnye otnosheniia*, No. 5 (1966), p. 22.

than mesh *ex post* the decisions taken by the planning authorities of member states, the Soviet leaders faced a quandary. Such a plan would have the advantage of promoting the development of the Soviet bloc as a whole, since it would deepen interstate cooperation and specialization; but any Soviet move to support an organization of CMEA with executive powers was sure to antagonize the Rumanians, who were bent upon following their own devices.

It is not surprising, in view of this diversity of aims, that it took some time for the Soviet position to crystallize. Until Khrushchev took a clear stand in favor of a "Comecon with teeth" in 1962, Soviet writings were distinguished either by their refusal to commit themselves on the divisive issues or, when substantive opinions were expressed, by their mutual disagreement. In retrospect, Khrushchev's decision to slight the cause of intrabloc harmony, apparently in order to salvage Soviet economic interests, does not seem to have been a wise one. The alienation of Rumania must be more costly in terms of Soviet prestige and leadership in the socialist camp than the price Moscow would have had to pay to finance Galați or to compensate Czechoslovakia for the loss of her Rumanian market. (This price should of course be measured in terms of the domestic economic objectives that might have been forgone if more economic aid had been extended to the people's democracies.)

In East Germany, there were also divergences of views between Ministry of Foreign Trade officials concerned with economic advantage and ideologically motivated economists with a sense of "proletarian internationalism." My impression also is that the G.D.R. pressed less hard than Czechoslovakia for the organizational tightening up of the Council for Mutual Economic Assistance. Here we should consider two points. First, East Germany, having achieved her status as a major supplier of manufactures in Eastern Europe only after 1953, suffered no loss of markets in the wake of the New Course, as did Czechoslovakia; she was therefore less afflicted by Rumanian autarkic policies. Second, her tenuous situation as a state unrecognized by a majority of the world's nations might have made her more willing to sacrifice direct economic interests for the sake of the power, cohesion, and prestige of the Soviet bloc. This speculation may help to explain the diversity of views that coexisted in a country where, on many other issues, a singleness of viewpoint was enforced.

We saw that Czechoslovak writings, except for minor differences in emphasis,[143] followed a consistent line, quite in keeping with Czechoslo-

---

[143] Of all Czech writers, D. Machová seems to have gone furthest toward meeting the points raised by the less developed countries, although, in the last analysis, she sided with the positions taken by Kaigl, Tauchman, Mervart, and Novozámský.

vakia's commercial interests. They attempted to induce their less developed partners to boost their rate of accumulation without expanding their capital goods industries at a faster rate than their consumer goods industries. The only way this could be done was for them to import more machinery and equipment, presumably from the industrially mature economies of the camp. They were also encouraged to raise their rate of accumulation so that they would not have to dun the more advanced countries for credits with which to buy this equipment. The Czechs opposed the "excessive efforts" of the less developed countries to raise the proportion of manufactures in their exports — to achieve a closer balance in trade by commodity groups — because this tended to reduce the amounts of foodstuffs and raw materials they could obtain from these suppliers. They pressed for a tighter organization of CMEA, which they calculated would lead to greater specialization among its member states. The *ex ante* coordination of plans under the aegis of an organization endowed with greater executive powers — another point on the Czechoslovak agenda for reform — was meant to preserve her markets for manufactures and simultaneously to ensure a regular supply of the foodstuffs and raw materials she wished to buy in return for these manufactures from the less developed countries. The Czechs also looked to their own interests in their theoretical writings on prices. Even though they had been satisfied to reap the gains of the "price stop" during the Korean War, they later argued for the use of world prices in socialist trade so that they would not have to export manufactures and import food and raw materials at more disadvantageous relative prices than those prevailing on capitalist markets.

The reader will recall that the Rumanians refrained from engaging in a controversy with the integrationists in CMEA until at least 1958. This silence was not necessarily damaging to their position. They chiefly desired the freedom to conduct their economic affairs as they saw fit. They had nothing to gain by irritating the dispute. Unlike the Czechs who needed the cooperation of the less developed countries to accomplish their ends and had to resort to suasion and propaganda to sway their partners, it was sufficient for the Rumanians to exercise their economic sovereignty to preserve their interests. The Rumanian government, for example, canceled short-term agreements to buy equipment from and sell foodstuffs and raw materials to Czechoslovakia in 1953 and 1954 when it embarked on its New Course.[144]

See in particular her article "K otázce působení hodnotových vztahů při vytváření proporcionality hospodářství mezi zeměmí socialistackého tábora," *Nová mysl*, No. 11 (1958), pp. 36–51.

[144] Interview material. For a fairly candid discussion of this problem, see D. Machová, *ČSSR v socialistické mezinárodní dělbě práce* (Prague, 1962), pp. 134–135.

Prague had something to complain about after 1953, but not Bucharest.

One may argue, alternatively, that the Rumanians held their peace because, until at least 1958, they were politically very weak and could hardly afford to incur Moscow's displeasure by sowing discord within CMEA. At this point it is too early to choose between economic and political explanations for Rumania's forbearance.

When the Rumanian Communists chose to respond to the more or less overt attacks against the protectionist policies of the less developed countries, they did so because they felt that their plans for a broad, multisided, industrialization were threatened, first by moves to put teeth into the organization of CMEA that might have forced Rumania into a pattern of specialization contrary to these plans, and second, by Soviet schemes to hold back radical expansion of Rumania's metallurgical and machine-building complex, which was at the very core of her strategy of development. Even after Rumanian propaganda entered the debate, it did so for some time with diffidence, responding only to issues that might have practical consequences. The Rumanians did not object in principle to specialization within branches of industry, as long as they were allowed to develop every major branch of industry that might be needed to build up a "complex, balanced economy." (That in practice they did not subscribe to specialization agreements that could have forced them to give up lines of production they were already engaged in or which they envisioned for the foreseeable future was another matter.) It is worth pointing out that Rumanian publications on problems of economic integration never criticized developed socialist countries in the way Czechoslovakia or East Germany assailed the policies of underdeveloped countries in the bloc. Rumania had no quarrel with the policies pursued by Czechoslovakia or East Germany. After all, these countries were in a weak bargaining position, striving to market manufactures that were in relatively abundant supply within the bloc in exchange for the scarce raw materials and foodstuffs Rumania had to sell. The Rumanians were apprehensive that their developed partners would exert political power or influence on the Soviet Union to turn the tables on them. As it turned out, the industrially advanced members of CMEA did try to swing the Soviet Union to their side and were even joined, at least for a time, by Poland, which was not considered to belong among the developed countries in the bloc.

The close correspondence between the real problems faced by individual countries and the theories developed by their economists to justify their position does not mean that all these problems found their echo in the press or in economic literature. To my knowledge, none of the participants in the controversy grappled with the delicate issue of the technological deficiencies in machine and equipment exports from the more developed CMEA countries, which undoubtedly influenced Rumania to shift some of her purchases to the West. High Rumanian officials who were interviewed on this subject were frank about the shortcomings of Czechoslovak exports. The steel of the boilers that Czechoslovakia supplied for chemical and power installations was not so resistant to corrosion as specifications required. Due to technical problems, there were substantial delays in the construction of the power plants that the Czechs were building in Rumania with their own equipment. Only once, in the radio broadcast from a Soviet source already cited, did any party to the controversy criticize directly Rumania's heavy purchases of equipment from the West. No one complained that she was depriving the bloc of much-needed corn, petroleum, lumber, and other primary materials to pay for these imports. Yet the most casual conversation with CMEA experts in other countries of the bloc will reveal that these were matters of grave concern to them.[145] The controversy never reached a point where these matters were discussed publicly in complete frankness, perhaps because it was obvious to everyone that squabbling on the subject of trade with the West was injurious to the unity of the bloc vis-à-vis the "imperialist camp" and that, in any case, almost every country of CMEA had something to reproach itself for in this regard (as the Rumanians were prompt to point out in their retort to the broadcast just alluded to).

Finally, a word of speculation may be in order about the effects on Rumania's trade of her dispute with CMEA, and with the Soviet Union in particular. We saw in the preceding chapter that the Rumanians shifted a significant part of their imports of machinery and equipment and of their exports of raw materials and foodstuffs from CMEA to Western Europe between 1958 and 1962. In 1963 and 1964, the new trade relations established in the previous four years were stabilized. In 1965, however, trade returns show that Rumania's dependence on CMEA was reduced both with respect to machinery and to raw-material imports. There is some indication that Bucharest has been turning from the Soviet Union toward alternative sources of supply for iron ores and other materials required for Rumania's industrialization.

[145] A hint on the subject was dropped in Czechoslovakia's journal of international affairs in 1964: "In the future, it will be necessary to overcome exaggerated nationalistic tendencies . . . whose roots lie in differences in economic development but also in the partial successes which may be achieved — even though temporarily — by individual countries in orienting [their trade] toward other regions of the world" (J. Krylová, "Socialistické industrializace," *Mezinárodní politika* [July 1964], p. 294). The Bucharest economist who pointed this article out to me claimed that it was meant as a direct challenge to Rumanian policies.

India, Brazil, and the United Arab Republic are being called upon to provide a significant portion of Rumania's iron ore requirements (which total nearly 3 million tons a year). This diminished reliance on the Soviet Union can only strengthen Rumania's hand in CMEA negotiations: the threat to curb the delivery of raw materials in exchange for manufactures is one of the last economic trumps that Moscow has left to keep the Rumanians from going astray. If this threat can be parried and if Western markets can be found for the products of Rumania's new industries, the Rumanians will be safe to pursue their independent economic policy.

CHAPTER FIVE

A SUMMING UP

In recent years the Communist rulers of Rumania have identified themselves increasingly with the aspirations of the progressive intellectuals of the *ancien régime* who advocated industrialization under state guidance.[1] These men, for the most part, were inspired by economic nationalism and were either indifferent or hostile to socialist ideas. For them industrialization under the aegis of the state was a *sine qua non* of national power.

Economists and statesmen such as M. Kogălniceanu and A. D. Xenopol in the nineteenth century and Stefan Zeletin, Mitiţa Constantinescu, and I. N. Angelescu in the twentieth are now praised for their progressive views, even though they represented the class interests of the bourgeoisie, because "under numerous circumstances and at various times, the interests of the industrial bourgeoisie coincided with national interests." [2]

One is struck by the essential continuity of views between the early proponents of industrialization who urged high import tariffs on manufactures to protect Rumania's nascent industries — those, for example, who fought against the tariff convention with the Austro-Hungarian Empire in the 1880's — and the present-day opponents of integration in the framework of CMEA. A clear parallel can also be drawn between old and new views on the type of industrialization that would best suit the interests of the Rumanian state: those men are said to deserve the gratitude of the Rumanian people who fought the takeover of Rumania's resources by foreigners and opposed the excessive concentration of industrial investments — also chiefly by foreigners — in export industries that did not benefit the nation at large. At the present time the more or less overt criticism of the old Soviet-Rumanian joint com-

---

[1] Cf. Nicolae Ceauşescu, "Partidul Comunist Român — Continuator al luptei revoluţionare şi democratice a poporului român, a tradiţiilor mişcarii muncitoreşti şi socialiste din România," *Agerpres Supplement* (Bucharest, 1966), p. 14.

[2] I. Veverca, "Mihail Kogălniceanu despre dezvoltarea economică a României," *Probleme economice*, No. 7 (1966), p. 98. See also *Probleme economice*, No. 12 (1966), p. 47.

panies, which exploited Rumania's resources mainly with an eye to the external market, falls in with this nationalist tradition.

The Communists pride themselves on their ability to fulfill the aspirations of their ideological predecessors, which, as they see it, remained largely sterile under the old social order on account of the obstacles put in the way of their realization by selfish private interests.

The industrialization strategy of the Communist regime is most clearly expressed in the investment programs of the Five-Year Plans.[3] Judging by the composition of these programs, particularly by the consistently high proportion of total investments allotted to heavy industry, we may affirm that the same broad goals have been pursued throughout the postwar period. We may detect a greater emphasis in recent years on industrial diversification, to create what the Rumanians call a "complex, many-sided and equilibrated economy"; but it may be argued that this autarkic trend is appropriate to a later stage in the country's development in the framework of the same over-all strategy, since the economy is now less pressed to build up a small number of export industries to finance large purchases of equipment in addition to meeting raw-material requirements (as it was in the early 1950's). The wider range of manufactures available for export also makes it easier to practice diversification.

The investment program also gives expression to the systematic policy of building plants on the basis of the latest world technology, no matter how capital-intensive it happens to be. This policy conflicts with the aim of providing as many peasants as possible with job opportunities in the cities, an aim that apparently fits on a lower rung of the planners' priority scale. As we have seen, the concentration of investments in industries that were capital-intensive to start with and that were slated to become even more capital-intensive as a result of these technologically advanced investments has led to a growing divergence between the modern, capital-intensive plants of heavy industry and traditional, labor-intensive manufactures in light industry. Nevertheless, it would be premature at the present state of our knowledge to criticize the Rumanians for their technological fetishism. We have no way to judge, looking in from the outside, whether new plants in high-priority sectors, especially when they are built from imported components or based on foreign know-how, come in packages whose factor proportions are more or less fixed by the existing technology or whether real alternatives exist of utilizing unskilled labor from low-priority sec-

---

[3] Note that the output program is not as faithful an expression of planners' aims, since the low-priority sectors — light industry and agriculture — are usually assigned targets that can only be fulfilled under ideal conditions, while the targets for heavy industry are much more likely to be fulfilled.

tors to economize on capital outlays in the "progressive" sectors. It is possible that the excess labor tied down in light industry or in agriculture (due to the lack of capital in these sectors) is poorly suited to work in heavy industry: female textile workers and sheep herders may have a very low opportunity cost in terms of the capital that they could replace in the metallurgical or machine-building industries.

Collectivization of the farm sector under state tutelage was another option taken by the ruling party that was both an end in itself and a means to other ends. From 1958 to 1962 collectivization helped to raise the share of produce marketed outside the state sector. It would seem also that it facilitated the imposition of direct controls over production, particularly to promote the expansion of technical crops, instead of allowing the output decisions of farms to be guided by the price system.

If we can make the simplifying assumption that the planners' goals and priorities were more or less the same throughout the postwar period, what can we say about the tactics that were employed to realize these objectives? Did similar problems evoke the same responses when they recurred, or were the planners eclectic in their improvisations? I think that a stable pattern of responses to changing circumstances can be made out.

The long-term plans, which were always framed with an optimistic outlook, demanded a strenuous investment effort each year if they were to be fulfilled even in their broad outline. How high a level the planners set for state investments depended on three basic factors:

1. The political climate of the moment. (In 1953–1954 and in 1956–1957, for instance, an unsettled and menacing political situation dictated retrenchments in the investment program for the benefit of consumers.)

2. The state of the balance of payments. (In 1955, in spite of more favorable political circumstances, investments remained sluggish, because there was insufficient foreign exchange left, after meeting external obligations and the minimum raw-material purchases needed to keep industry operating at or near capacity levels, to import a large volume of machinery and equipment. Domestic machinery production, which was still specialized in a small number of lines, could not satisfy the demand that would have been generated by a larger level of investments. In addition, the shortage of foreign exchange made it necessary to export lumber and cement that would otherwise have been consumed by the construction industry.)

3. The prospects for the forthcoming harvest and, more specifically, for state procurements of foodstuffs. The state fund for agricultural products is the main source of consumer goods that can be used to

absorb the wages and salaries paid out by the investment sectors, including construction enterprises and the machine-building industry. A poor harvest and a depleted state fund, coupled with a high level of investments, tend to disturb the macroeconomic balance of the economy. A symptom of this disequilibrium is likely to be an excess of currency in circulation and rising prices on the peasant market. It also poses a balance-of-payments problem, which cuts down on the opportunities of using imports to absorb the additional purchasing power released by investments. (Between 1958 and 1960 the extraction of larger surpluses from the peasantry and from state farms helped to clear the way for the upswing in investments during those years, although other favorable circumstances, such as the government's renewed confidence in maintaining a secure political hold over the population after the events that upset Eastern Europe in the fall of 1956 and the alleviation of Rumania's external obligations, also contributed significantly to this recovery.)

These were the factors directly determining the level of investments; others exerted an *indirect* influence through the balance of payments. The stagnation of petroleum output and the conservation of timber, for instance, both had a depressing effect on investments by depriving the economy of foreign exchange earnings that could have been used to buy investment goods or that would have made it possible to reduce food exports, which in turn would have allowed more domestic resources to be channeled into capital accumulation.

When I claim that planners "responded" to a variety of circumstances, I imply, of course, that they had a choice, that their decisions were not just a mechanical adjustment to changing constraints. The balance-of-payments crisis brought on by the liquidation of Soviet-Rumanian companies and by the repayment of old debts need not have inhibited investments, if the authorities had resolved to force a decline in individual consumption. In order to ram through this policy in the face of potential popular unrest, more resources would have had to be devoted to "ideological persuasion" and to the "repression of hostile elements." Stalin in the past, and Chinese and Albanian Communist leaders more recently, have demonstrated that a pliant population can, within certain limits, be coerced into sacrificing consumption. But such a Draconian policy has been eschewed by the Rumanian Party, at least in recent years. Nevertheless, it must be recognized that once they had made the major political decision to maintain minimum living standards and, if at all possible, to improve them from year to year, the planners were fairly restricted in the range of their responses.

In pursuing its investment strategy, Rumania, like the other industrializing members of CMEA, had a signal advantage over most underdeveloped countries in the rest of the world: it could translate any surpluses of primary goods it could spare from domestic consumption into imports of capital goods at constant terms of trade (determined, after a varying lag, by world price relations). Since "world prices" in use on the CMEA market tended to understate the relative scarcity of raw materials and foodstuffs relative to manufactures, primary commodities tended to be in short supply in CMEA. Hence the Rumanians faced a perfectly elastic demand for their corn, meat, timber, and petroleum exports. It so happened also that these exportables could be marketed in Western Europe at constant prices, at least for the quantities Rumania could supply. In contrast with such nations as India and Pakistan, which are said to face an inelastic demand for their staple exports and may on occasion suffer from the inability to convert their potential saving into capital formation (except by lavishing labor on projects that could more efficiently be carried out with imported machinery), Rumania had considerable freedom in choosing whether to import capital goods or to use domestic capacities to produce them. This leeway must have raised the marginal efficiency of investment, compared to what it would have been without this extra degree of freedom.

The next question I should like to speculate on is whether Rumania's conflict with Comecon was an "objective" concomitant of the strategy and tactics adopted by its leadership or whether it was the product of "subjective" elements of discord on both sides.

Some light may be shed on this question by comparing Rumania's policies with the policies of its fellow members of CMEA.

In Tables 5.1 and 5.2 I have tried to analyze the machinery trade of five CMEA members between 1958 and 1965 to bring to light changes that have occurred in the regional orientation of their exchanges in this group.

These tables reveal a remarkable pattern in the geographic distribution of machinery exchanges by individual CMEA members. To start with, we observe a manifest tendency for trade in machinery products among CMEA members to be more closely balanced in 1964–1965 than in 1958. Rumania and Bulgaria, the least developed countries, imported four to five times as much machinery from their fellow members of CMEA in 1958 as they exported; in 1965 these two countries imported only 50 to 60 percent more from CMEA members than they exported. On the other hand, Hungary and Czechoslovakia, which exported to CMEA nearly twice as much machinery as they imported in 1958, cut

TABLE 5.1. The Relation of Machinery Imports to Machinery Exports of Rumania, Poland, Hungary, Bulgaria, and Czechoslovakia with CMEA and the Rest of the World in 1958, 1960, 1962, 1964, and 1965 (*Imports as Percentage of Exports with Each Region*)

	1958		1960		1962		1964		1965	
	CMEA	Rest of the World	CMEA	Rest of the World	CMEA	Rest of the World	CMEA	Rest of the World	CMEA	Rest of the World
Rumania	400	51	206	124	195	826	217	403	153	486
Poland	126	98	108	113	115	199	88	98	98	114
Hungary	52	27	86	45	85	93	86	165	84	96
Bulgaria	492	120[a]	360	250[a]	335[b]	93[b]	175	302	157	393
Czechoslovakia	51	18	58	27	55	40	61	40	63	55

[a] Since both machinery imports from, and exports to, the "rest of the world" were very small in 1958 and 1960, relatively slight errors in estimating trade with CMEA may lead to significant errors in the balance of machinery trade with the rest of the world.

[b] 1961.

Sources and methods: Rumania: Tables 3.15 and 3.16 of Chapter 3. Poland: 1958: L. Ciamaga, *Od współpracy do integracji* (1965), p. 170; 1960: *Handel zagraniczny*, No. 7 (1961), p. 295; 1962: *Rocznik polityczny i gospodarczy 1963* (Warsaw, 1963), pp. 315–316. (It was assumed that imports of machinery from socialist countries not members of CMEA made up the same fraction of total machinery imports — 0.6 percent — as in 1960); 1964: the value of exports of machinery to CMEA was first estimated from the percentage of total exports to CMEA in *Czechoslovak Foreign Trade*, No. 10 (1965), p. 5; imports of machinery from CMEA were then calculated from the ratio of imports to exports in trade in this group with CMEA given in *Mirovaia ekonomika i mezhdunarodnye otnosheniia*, No. 5 (1966), p. 22. Hungary: 1958: Ciamaga, *op. cit.*, p. 171; the surplus in machinery trade with CMEA in that year is given in G. M. Sorokin, ed., *Stroitel'stvo kommunizma v SSSR* (Moscow, 1962), p. 110; this surplus was subtracted from machinery exports to CMEA (based on a percentage in *Czechoslovak Foreign Trade*, No. 10 [1965], p. 5) to obtain the value of imports; 1964: *Statisztikai évkönyv 1964* (Budapest, 1965), p. 226, and J. Kovács and L. Vékony, *A szocialista országok gazdasági együttműködése* (Budapest, 1965), pp. 27–28; 1962: trade in machinery and equipment with all socialist countries is given in *Magyar statisztikai évkönyv 1962* (Budapest, 1963), p. 254; machinery imports from and exports to non-CMEA socialist countries were estimated on the assumption that they bore the same relation to total imports and exports in trade with this group of countries as in 1964. Bulgaria: 1958: Ciamaga, *op. cit.*, p. 171; 1960: *Vŭnshna tŭrgovia*, No. 6 (1961), p. 6; 1961: imports were computed from exports and imports in 1955 (Ciamaga, *op. cit.*), an index of imports plus exports from 1955 to 1961 in V. Wacker and B. Malý, eds., *Mezinárodní socialistická dělba práce* (Prague, 1964), p. 246, and the absolute value of exports in 1961 based on percentages in *Ikonomichesko i sotsialno razvitie na NRB* (Sofia, 1964), p. 272. Czechoslovakia: 1958: Ciamaga, *op. cit.;* 1960 and 1964: *Czechoslovak Foreign Trade*, No. 10 (1965), p. 5. All countries 1965: Based on percentages of total imports from and exports to CMEA in *Plánované hospodářství*, No. 12 (1966), p. 63, and *Hospodářské noviny*, No. 29 (1966), p. 3

TABLE 5.2. Imports of Machinery and Equipment of Rumania, Poland, Hungary, Bulgaria, and Czechoslovakia from CMEA and from the Rest of the World in 1958, 1960, 1962, 1964, and 1965 (*Percentage Breakdown, Total Imports of Machinery = 100*)

	1958		1960		1962		1964		1965	
	CMEA	Rest of the World	CMEA	Rest of the World	CMEA	Rest of the World	CMEA	Rest of the World	CMEA	Rest of the World
Rumania	89.1	10.9	74.5	25.5	61.2	38.8	70.4	29.6	62.3	37.7
Poland	66.5	33.5	73.3	26.7	76.4	23.6	81.8	18.2	81.5	18.5
Hungary	77.4	22.6	81.3	18.7	83.1	16.9	80.2	19.8	83.0	17.0
Bulgaria	94.6	5.4	93.8	6.2	95.0[a]	5.0[a]	84.9	15.1	81.5	18.5
Czechoslovakia	82.9	17.1	85.5	14.5	83.1	16.9	84.9	15.1	81.1	19.9

[a] 1961.

Sources and methods: Rumania: Table 3.15. Other countries: same sources and methods as in Table 5.1.

back their surpluses to some 20 and 60 percent of their exports in this category, respectively (Table 5.1).

This relative curtailment in the import and export balances of CMEA members in their reciprocal trade in machinery did *not* occur in their exchanges with the "rest of the world." Here all five East European states suffered a "deterioration" in their balances in this group — imports rising at the relative expense of exports. Bulgaria and Rumania ended up importing four to five times as much from the "rest of the world" — that is, from Western Europe — as they exported to these other countries — chiefly to the underdeveloped nations and to the Communist states of Asia. It is evident that the policy of "bilateral balancing by commodity groups," whereby the less industrialized members of the Soviet bloc sought to cover as large a proportion as possible of their purchases of machinery from each trading partner by exporting machinery in return, applied only to the CMEA area. Exports of machinery by the industrializing countries of CMEA to France, Germany, Italy, and the United Kingdom, their chief suppliers in this commodity group outside CMEA, remained negligible.

Turning now to the second table, we find that Rumania and Bulgaria more than tripled the proportion of their machinery imports originating outside the CMEA area between 1958 and 1965. Between 1962 and 1965 Rumania was purchasing some 30–40 percent of its machinery imports from the West — a significantly higher proportion than any of the other four countries. Bulgaria and Rumania, it should be noted, acquired a much smaller proportion of their machinery imports outside the CMEA area in the initial year than did the remaining countries. Poland and Hungary, which bought an above-average proportion of their machinery in the West in 1958, had reduced that proportion down to or below the five-country average by 1965. The distribution of Czechoslovakia's machinery imports between the two areas fluctuated without a clear tendency during the entire seven-year period.

Trade statistics released by the Organization for Economic Cooperation and Development for 1965 disclose the value of machinery and equipment exports by European members of O.E.C.D., the United States, Japan, and Yugoslavia to the various East European states. The absolute value of these exports to individual CMEA members is shown in the following tabulation, along with their value computed per capita of the importing country's population.

	O.E.C.D. and Other Western Exports of Machinery and Equipment to Individual CMEA Members (millions of U.S. dollars)	Per Capita (U.S. dollars)
U.S.S.R.	451	2.0
Rumania	146	7.7
Poland	117	3.7
Hungary	73	7.3
Bulgaria	69	8.5
Czechoslovakia	129	9.2
East Germany	82	4.8

Source: O.E.C.D., *Statistical Bulletins,* Series C, *Commodity Trade: Exports,* January–December 1965 (Paris, 1966), pp. 90–94.

As these figures stand, Czechoslovakia had the largest per capita imports of machinery and equipment from the West. However, if we wished to "normalize" these data by adjusting them for differences in national income as well as population, we should find Bulgaria and Rumania leading the list, with 1.8 dollars of machinery imports from the West per 100 dollars of per capita national income, compared to 1.4 dollars for Hungary, 1.1 dollars for Czechoslovakia, 74 cents for Poland, 57 cents for East Germany, and 32 cents for the U.S.S.R.[4]

As we saw in the last two chapters, surpluses in raw materials and foodstuffs — so-called "hard goods" — are used by the less developed countries of CMEA to pay for their deficits in machinery; *mutatis mutandis* the more developed countries pay for their deficits in hard goods

[4] These adjustments are based on the per capita national income estimates cited in Chapter 4, p. 190, note 13.

with surpluses in their machinery trade (as well as with surpluses in manufactured consumer goods). Other sources of foreign exchange that can be used to buy manufactures include the net proceeds of the tourist trade and of other invisible earnings and capital imports. The combined impact of these additional resources finds its expression in the negative balance of merchandise trade. In Table 5.3 I have attempted to divide the surpluses and deficits in raw materials and foodstuffs and the total balance of merchandise trade between CMEA and the rest of the world with the aim of illuminating the trends in machinery exchanges discussed in the foregoing pages.

Some theoretical speculations may be helpful to interpret the data set forth in Table 5.3.

Suppose a member of CMEA wished to acquire from Western suppliers as large a share as possible of its total imports of manufactured goods. If we take as given this country's total imports from and exports to all regions in each commodity group, then it might choose to pursue the following options: it might (1) export as large a share as possible of its own manufactures to the West; (2) reduce the surplus (or increase the deficit) in its hard goods exchanges with CMEA; (3) shift its imports of raw materials and foodstuffs from CMEA to the West; (4) reduce the import balance (or increase the surplus) in trade in manufactures with CMEA. As the calculations in the footnote indicate,[5] the degree of free-

---

[5] Consider the following distribution of Rumanian exchanges between CMEA and other countries in 1965 (in millions of U.S. dollars).

	CMEA	Other Countries	Total
Exports of manufactures	+269	+57	+326
Exports of raw materials and foodstuffs	+430	+346	+776
Imports of manufactures	−300	−192	−492
Imports of raw materials and foodstuffs	−318	−268	−586
Total	+81	−57	+24

Suppose Rumania could export no more than $57 million of manufactured goods outside the CMEA area and that it was obliged to export a 35 percent greater value of raw materials and foodstuffs to CMEA than it imported from CMEA. Then an increase from $268 million to $300 million in imports of raw materials and foodstuffs from "other countries" would have the following consequences:

	CMEA	Other Countries	Total
Exports of manufactures	+269	+57	+326
Exports of raw materials and foodstuffs	+386	+390	+776
Imports of manufactures	−288	−204	−492
Imports of raw materials and foodstuffs	−286	−300	−586
Total	+81	−57	+24

Thanks to the reorientation of the country's imports of raw materials and foodstuffs, imports of manufactures from the West would rise from $192 to $204 million in the second. Simultaneously the import balance in trade in manufactures with CMEA would have to fall (from $31 million to $19 million).

TABLE 5.3. SURPLUSES (+) AND DEFICITS (−) IN HARD GOODS (RAW MATERIALS, SEMIFABRICATES, AND FOODSTUFFS) AND IN TOTAL TRADE WITH CMEA AND THE REST OF THE WORLD IN 1958, 1960, 1962, 1964, AND 1965 (Millions of U.S. Dollars)

	1958		1960		1962		1964		1965	
	CMEA	Rest of the World	CMEA	Rest of the World	CMEA	Rest of the World	CMEA	Rest of the World	CMEA	Rest of the World
Rumania										
Hard goods	+50	+14	+102	+50	+53	+81	+31	+59	+112	+78
Imports minus exports	+38	−25	−32	−37	+65	+58	+110	+58	−81	+57
Total	+88	−11	+70	+13	+118	+139	+141	+117	+31	+135
Poland										
Hard goods	−63	−17	−149	−40	−138	−37	−105	−84	−179	−51
Imports minus exports	+142	+25	+143	+27	+196	+44	−34	+10	+124	−12
Total	+79	+8	−6	−13	+58	+7	−139	−74	−55	−63
Hungary										
Hard goods	−129	−50	−177	−93	−208	−82	−222	−137	−249	−69
Imports minus exports	+11	−42	+87	+15	+25	+24	+40	+103	+32	−18
Total	−118	−92	−90	−78	−183	−58	−182	−34	−217	−87
Bulgaria										
Hard goods	+65	+6	+91	−12	+141[a]	−6[a]	+63	−3	+114	+14
Imports minus exports	−3	−3	+46	+15	+10	−7	+33	+49	−56	+55
Total	+62	+3	+137	+3	+151	−13	+96	+46	+58	+69
Czechoslovakia										
Hard goods	−257	−214	−390	−305	−445	−253	−502	−232	−555	−236
Imports minus exports	−66	−97	−66	−47	−112	−11	−81	−66	−6	−10
Total	−323	−311	−456	−352	−557	−264	−589	−298	−561	−246

[a] 1961.

Note: In order to estimate the net availability of foreign exchange that each country had at its disposal to finance imports of manufactures, deficits in total merchandise trade were *added* to surpluses in hard goods. Thus in the table trade deficits are preceded by a plus sign and surpluses by a minus sign.

Sources and methods: Except where noted, imports and exports of raw materials, semifabricates, and foodstuffs were calculated as residuals after subtracting the estimates of machinery imports and exports used in Tables 5.1 and 5.2 and estimates of trade in consumer goods from total exchanges with CMEA countries (as given in the official statistical yearbooks, unless specified). For 1965, imports of raw materials and foodstuffs can be computed for all countries from the percentages of total imports from CMEA in *Hospodářské noviny,* No. 29 (1966), F. 3. To arrive at exports of raw materials and foodstuffs, one needs, in addition to machinery exports, to estimate exports of consumer goods. This was done by assuming that CMEA accounted for the same percentage of exports in this group as in 1964, for which year information was available in the case of Czechoslovakia, Poland, and Hungary. For Bulgaria, it was assumed that this share was the same as in 1963 (see below).

Rumania: Tables 3.18 and 3.19 and sources indicated in these tables. Poland: the breakdown of imports from and exports to all socialist countries in 1960, 1962, and 1964 is given, respectively, in *Rocznik polityczny i gospodarczy 1962, 1963, and 1965* (Warsaw, 1962, 1963, and 1965), pp. 314 and 317, pp. 315 and 318, and pp. 332 and 334; exports of consumer goods to socialist countries in *Handel zagraniczny*, No. 56 (1966). p. 261; imports and exports of raw materials in trade with CMEA in 1958 in J. Novozámský, *Vyrovnávání ekonomické úrovně zemí RVHP* (Prague, 1964), p. 109, and in 1960 and 1962 in B. Malý, *Rozvoj komplexu národního hospodářství ČSSR* (candidate dissertation, Prague, 1965), p. 173; exports of raw materials to CMEA in 1964 were estimated from percentages in *Czechoslovak Foreign Trade*, No. 10 (1966), p. 7. Rough adjustments were made to reduce trade in consumer goods and in imports of foodstuffs with "all socialist countries" to trade with CMEA members only. The error involved in so doing is believed to be small, since machinery and raw materials represent the bulk of trade with socialist countries that are not members of CMEA, whose trade, as a whole, came to less than 10 percent of imports or exports in all years covered. Hungary: 1958, 1960, 1962, and 1964: trade in raw materials with CMEA was estimated from data in Malý, *op. cit.*, Novozámský, *op. cit.*, and *Czechoslovak Foreign Trade*, already cited. Breakdowns of trade by commodity groups between socialist and nonsocialist countries are given for 1962 and 1964 in *Statisztikai évkönyv 1962 and 1964*, pp. 254 and 226, respectively. Surpluses and deficits with CMEA in 1960 are broken down by commodity groups in G. M. Sorokin, ed., *Stroitel'stvo kommunizma v SSSR* (Moscow, 1962), p. 110. Exports of foodstuffs to socialist countries in 1958 and 1960 are from I. Vajda, *Szocialista külkereskedelem* (Budapest, 1963), p. 254; exports in all four groups to socialist countries in 1962 and 1964 can be computed from percentages in S. Czeitler, *Ipari termékeink a világ piacon* (Budapest, 1965), p. 30. As in the case of Poland, trade with CMEA in certain commodity groups had to be estimated from data relating to trade with all socialist countries. A breakdown of imports from and exports to

Communist China for 1960, in J. Karácsony, *Külkereskedelmünk helyzete és feladatai* (Budapest, 1963), p. 72, helped to make this adjustment. Bulgaria: trade by commodity groups with all countries in 1958 and 1960 is from *Vŭnshna tŭrgovia na Narodna Republika Bŭlgaria: Statisticheski sbornik* (Sofia, 1963); in 1964 and 1965 from *Zahraniční obchod*, No. 9 (1966), pp. 8–9. Trade in raw materials in 1958 may be reconstructed from percentages in the works already cited by Novozámský and Malý. The surplus in trade in foodstuffs was estimated from the average surplus for 1958 to 1960 in J. Lipták, *Mezinárodní dělba práce v zemědělství zemí RVHP* (Prague, 1965), pp. 159–160, from which the surplus for 1960 was subtracted (Sorokin, *op. cit.*). The resulting average for 1958–1959 was divided up between the two years in the same proportion as the surplus in foodstuffs with all countries in 1958 and 1959. Surpluses and deficits for 1960 are all from Sorokin, *op. cit.* For 1964, exports of raw materials were derived from percentages in *Czechoslovak Foreign Trade*, No. 10 (1965), p. 7. Exports of foodstuffs to CMEA in 1964 were assumed to bear the same relation to total exports of foodstuffs as in 1963. These in turn were estimated from a breakdown of Bulgarian exports by commodity groups and by area of destination in *Ikonomichesko i sotsialno razvitie na NRB* (Bŭlgarska akademiya na naukite, Sofia, 1964), p. 272. Imports of consumer goods in 1964 were assumed to be divided between CMEA and other countries in the same proportion as in 1965 (for which year they were calculated as an exact residual after subtracting known imports of machinery, raw materials, and foodstuffs, as already explained). 1961: exports to CMEA by commodity groups were estimated from *Ikonomichesko i sotsialno razvitie*, already cited. Planned and contracted imports of consumer goods from CMEA for 1961 are given in *Vŭnshna tŭrgovia*, No. 6 (1961), p. 6. It was assumed that actual imports in this group were equal to plan. Imports of raw materials and foodstuffs were obtained by subtracting imports of machinery and consumer goods from total imports from CMEA. Czechoslovakia: for 1958, same sources and methods as for Poland, Hungary, and Bulgaria; for 1960 and 1964, complete breakdowns by commodity groups between CMEA and the rest of the world are given in *Czechoslovak Foreign Trade*, No. 10 (1965), p. 5; for 1962, comparable statistics are to be found in Malý, *op. cit.*, p. 160. Total imports and exports by area and by commodity groups for 1960, 1962, 1964, and 1965 are from *Facts on Czechoslovak Foreign Trade 1966* (Prague, 1966), pp. 76, 78, 110, and 112.

dom such a country would have in varying the combination of these policies is quite restricted. In the last analysis the two crucial variables determining the ability of one of the less developed members of CMEA to shift its purchases of manufactures toward the West would be the willingness of its partners in the socialist common market (1) to purchase a larger proportion of manufactures in return for their exports of these goods to the country in question and (2) to tolerate a reduction in their deficit in trade in raw materials and foodstuffs vis-à-vis that country.[6]

It is hardly necessary to add that an increased deficit or a reduced surplus with the rest of the world would augment a country's capacity to import manufactured goods outside CMEA. It is slightly less evident that if the increased deficit occurred with the CMEA area, it could not be used to import more manufactured goods from the West unless CMEA partners agreed to expand their exports of raw materials and foodstuffs without requiring any compensating increment in these commodity groups.

Looking now at the data in Table 5.3, we find that Rumania and Bulgaria were the only CMEA members among those listed to accumulate surpluses in raw materials and foodstuffs with either the CMEA area or the rest of the world. In 1958 and 1962 Poland ran deficits in "hard goods" with the rest of the world but earned sufficient amounts of foreign exchange from credits and possibly from invisible items in its balance of payments to cover the deficit in these commodity groups, leaving enough besides to finance a deficit in trade in manufactures outside CMEA. Poland in other years, and Hungary and Czechoslovakia in all periods examined, ran deficits in hard goods and surpluses in manufactures.

Between 1958–1960 and 1964–1965 Rumania approximately doubled its exports of hard goods to the rest of the world ("the West") without curtailing its average surplus with CMEA in these groups. In 1965 Bulgaria was able at last to generate a surplus in hard goods of $14 million with the West, while simultaneously increasing its surplus in these groups with CMEA. In the period 1958 to 1965 Bulgaria and Rumania both reduced the share of CMEA in their imports of hard goods and curtailed their relative deficit in manufactures with this area.

[6] In note 5 it may be noted that if exports of raw materials and foodstuffs to CMEA were reduced from $430 in the first table to $400 (the regional distribution of imports of these goods remaining the same), imports of manufactures from other countries would rise from $192 to $222 million. Note also that a developed country attempting to shift its imports of raw materials and foodstuffs away from CMEA sources of supply would have to increase its surplus in trade in manufactures with CMEA and increase its deficit in trade in raw materials and foodstuffs with that area.

From their deficits in total trade with the "rest of the world," in Table 5.3, we may infer that the credits and earnings on tourism and other invisible items of trade received by Rumania and Bulgaria made an important contribution to the foreign-exchange resources needed to finance their deficits in manufactures. For Bulgaria, in point of fact, these earnings were the principal means of financing its deficit in manufactures in 1964 and 1965, whereas for Rumania the surplus of imports over exports covered a little less than half the total deficits in manufactures in these two years.

Czechoslovakia and Hungary incurred much larger deficits in raw materials and foodstuffs with respect to the world as a whole in the 1960's than in 1958. If it had not been for the willingness of the Soviet Union to take over the bulk of this deficit — by increasing its surplus in hard goods correspondingly — they would have had to curtail their purchases of manufactures in the West. As it was, they had to curb their credits and other nonmerchandise expenditures in the West to maintain an approximately constant share in their purchases of manufactures outside CMEA.

To recapitulate, we conclude from the analysis of our sample of CMEA members that countries running a deficit in raw materials and foodstuffs with CMEA, such as Poland, Hungary, and Czechoslovakia, were forced to trade closely with those among their Comecon partners that were still willing to take machinery and consumer goods in exchange for raw materials and foodstuffs. The pressure on each country to reduce to a minimum its deficit in raw materials and foodstuffs with CMEA compelled the more developed countries, which suffered from an over-all deficit in these two groups, to shunt most of their supplies of these goods to the CMEA market. The exportable surpluses of raw materials and foodstuffs that they had left after meeting their import requirements from CMEA were not sufficient to purchase from the West any substantial proportion of their total imports of machinery or consumer goods. Bulgaria and Rumania, the least developed members of CMEA with the exception of Mongolia, were in a position, by contrast, to buy large amounts of machinery from the West because (1) they disposed of sufficient supplies of raw materials and foodstuffs to generate a surplus in these groups with CMEA and still have enough left over to pay for their imports of "soft" goods outside the Communist trade area, and (2) they received credits from the West (after 1960) to reinforce their earnings of foreign exchange in Western markets.

The question may be raised as to why the more developed countries did not cut back their imports of machinery and consumer goods *from* CMEA. The answer is that they were forced to buy large amounts of these "soft" goods from the newly industrialized members of the bloc if they wished to sell them more of these goods than they bought from them. Bulgaria, for example, would not buy nearly as much machinery from Czechoslovakia and Hungary if these two partners did not agree to buy machinery from her in return as part payment for these purchases. Only after meeting these "tied-sales" conditions were the more industrialized partners permitted to buy "hard" goods to fulfill their more urgent needs.

In the past ten years politics have determined how each country's potential share in trade with the West has been utilized. In 1958 Rumania and Bulgaria were both capable of buying a substantial share of their machinery requirements in Western Europe because they already disposed of surpluses in hard goods with CMEA that they could shunt to the West, but political conditions were not yet ripe for them to do so. At that time, Poland, which received substantial credits from the West in 1958, had the means and enough political autonomy to buy a fairly large proportion of her machinery imports from outside CMEA. In 1959–1960 the Rumanians chose to draw on their political power to shift trade toward the West. Bulgaria followed suit around 1963 when political circumstances became favorable.[7] When Poland's deficit in raw-materials trade with CMEA deepened and she began to accumulate a surplus in over-all trade with the West instead of a deficit, she lost some of her old margin in hard currency and was forced to reorient her purchases of manufactures toward CMEA sources.[8]

The Soviet Union, which runs a large surplus in hard goods with the rest of CMEA and buys an above-average proportion of her machinery imports in the West, and East Germany, whose trade pattern is exactly the opposite, would, I believe, both conform to this same pattern, although I cannot document this as precisely as for the other five countries.

A consequence of the logic of the trade relations I have described is that as Rumania and Bulgaria continue to industrialize they may *in the long run* tighten up, rather than loosen further, their trade links with

[7] If these conjectures are correct, they would also explain why Communist China had no trouble shifting her trade radically from CMEA toward Western markets after 1961. China did not need CMEA as an outlet for her manufactures. There was nothing therefore to deter her from switching the direction of her trade. On the other hand, it would be extremely difficult for Czechoslovakia or East Germany to carry out a switch of this kind if political conditions came about that would make such a move attractive to the governments of these two countries.

[8] This economic explanation for the evolution of Poland's machinery trade does not rule out, of course, the possibility that political factors might have prompted a tightening of Poland's ties with CMEA.

CMEA.[9] This is so for two interrelated reasons: first, as their raw-material requirements and as their consumption of domestically produced food keep on rising, they will become increasingly dependent on the Soviet Union, *qua* supplier of these goods; second, they will soon be generating a trade surplus in consumer goods and machinery, for the disposal of which they will have to look to their fellow members of CMEA, and again especially to the Soviet Union, the sole remaining country willing to barter materials for manufactures. This retrogression can only be forestalled if the Balkan countries of CMEA can secure outlets for their manufactures in the West. Credits, of course, would help to tie the trade of these countries to the West, but in the long run these loans will have to be repaid, at least in part, in the form of manufactures, if they are not to impose an intolerable burden on the balance of payments of the recipients. It is too early to say whether the present *détente* between Eastern and Western Europe will proceed far enough in the next few years to allow this new pattern of trade to emerge.[10]

If we now turn to the broader aspects of Rumania's future development, it may be appropriate to add some final remarks on the subject of "intensive" versus "extensive" industrialization, which we began discussing at the end of Chapter 1. The question that poses itself is whether an expansion based on the creation of productive facilities essentially similar to those already in existence in the more advanced nations can go on for a long period without running into some of the difficulties that have recently beset the more industrially mature nations of CMEA. Now it is true that Rumania's industry and her other modern sectors have a long way to go before they exhaust the reservoir of labor power still waiting to be drained in her collectivized agriculture. It is still a relatively simple matter for the Rumanian planners to draw off the additional manpower they need in other sectors by substituting modest amounts of capital for the prospective migrants from the countryside. The cost of doing so is limited to the provision of standard equipment for farms, including trucks, mechanical sowers,

[9] In the short run, of course, they may still wish to exploit more fully their *potential* trade with the West. It is evident that Bulgaria at least has not yet exhausted these possibilities.

[10] The 1966 agreement between Rumania and France, which is said to provide for Rumanian exports of manufactured goods on a substantial scale, may herald a new attitude on the part of West European countries. But it may also be a *sui generis* consequence of the special cultural and political ties binding together these two Latin countries. The establishment of diplomatic relations with the Bonn government and the April 1967 trade agreement with Israel may also open up new opportunities for Rumanian exports of manufactures, in part at least as a result of joint-investment ventures and of licensing arrangements.

pickers, automatic balers, and harvesters, and the construction of modest housing facilities, hospitals, and schools to accommodate the new entrants into the urban labor force. The age structure of the Rumanian farm population is much more favorable than it is in the developed socialist countries. It is still possible to invest resources in the agricultural sector with a relatively high pay-off, especially if the institutional framework of agriculture can be reshaped so as to provide the collective farmers with incentives that seem to be lacking at the present time.

The more immediate problem that Rumania will face in her transition to a mature industrial economy lies in the industrial sphere. Her first phase of industrialization encompassed mainly the reproduction of technologies mastered before, during, or shortly after World War II in the Soviet Union, East Germany, and Czechoslovakia. In the second phase, from 1958 to 1965, Rumania drew on the most recent technologies of these same nations together with some of the more up-to-date achievements of Western Europe. Except in the manufacture of oil-drilling equipment, where Rumanian engineers were responsible for a number of innovations, Rumania's scientific contribution was small, consisting mainly in the adaptation of foreign processes to local conditions. One may wonder how competitive Rumania's industrial products will be on the world market — especially in the West — if they remain the outcome of processes mastered a few years beforehand in the scientifically more advanced countries. This relative backwardness can be overcome only if strong inducements are provided within the enterprise to develop new processes or to introduce technical improvements wherever they may originate. Rumania will soon resemble Hungary and Czechoslovakia, industrial countries with a very narrow resource base, which have had considerable difficulty shifting from an "extensive" to an "intensive" type of growth chiefly because of the inflexibility of the centralized economic systems they have been saddled with for so many years. It is hard to escape the impression that Rumania also will eventually have to abandon the system that has successfully carried the economy through the first stages of industrialization and devise some sort of market mechanism to guide enterprise managers toward the more sophisticated decisions necessary in an industrially complex economy.

These arguments are exceedingly verbal. But unfortunately the quantitative evidence that would allow us to assess the *Konkurrenzfähigkeit* of Rumanian industry is almost entirely lacking. We know that manufacturing costs have been falling, and we guess that the costs of production of certain primary materials, including petroleum, have been rising. Thus we surmise that Rumania's comparative disadvantage in manufacturing is probably significantly less today than it once was. But we do not have at our disposal any information on the effects of diversification on the costs of producing industrial goods for a limited market. Neither do we know anything about the value added in terms of foreign currency from manufacturing products for export that have a large foreign-exchange content, such as steel and many types of heavy machinery. We know a good deal more about recent *trends* in the Rumanian economy than about its strengths and weaknesses at the present time.

Even if we knew all there is to know about the relative costs of industrial and agricultural products, their evolution in the past and their probable tendency in the future, we should still be incapable of giving an objective appraisal of the policy of industrial protectionism practiced by the Rumanians. For there are at the root of this policy certain subjective judgments about the value of industrialization per se and about the temporary sacrifices that are worth bearing for its sake, which we cannot criticize objectively. If these value judgments were limited to the volume of industrial output, then we might side with Rumania's critics who claim that Rumanian industry could grow faster if more efficient machines were imported from advanced countries. But in point of fact the Rumanians want no part of a "calico industrialization." They are willing to pay a high price — or to require from the Rumanian population a heavy sacrifice in terms of consumption forgone — to develop a "complex, multisided industry," which they consider the hallmark of true development. In the last analysis, only the Communist rulers of Rumania can decide whether these hardships are necessary and how much longer they should be borne.

INDICES OF RUMANIAN
INDUSTRIAL PRODUCTION *

This appendix describes the technical aspects of our industrial production index for Rumania. We believe ours is one of the first attempts at such an independent recalculation. It was made possible by the recent publication in a statistical handbook that gave more detailed industrial data than had been previously available. The official Rumanian industrial production index claims a very rapid growth during the postwar period. One purpose of our recalculation is to check the general validity of this claim; another is to provide a measure of output that can be compared with indices prepared in Western countries for estimating the growth both of capitalist and of Communist economies.

The official index is based on the gross value of output. It is calculated by the enterprise method; that is, the gross value of total industrial output equals the summation of the gross outputs of individual enterprises of socialist industry, of craftsmen outside cooperatives, and of small-scale private industry. The gross value of output in 1938, 1948, and 1950–1955 was expressed in terms of 1948 wholesale factory prices; output in the years 1955–1963 was expressed in terms of 1955 wholesale factory prices. The index for earlier years is linked to the index for 1955–1963 via 1955, for which output in both sets of prices has been calculated by the Central Direction of Statistics.[1] In essence, the official Rumanian index is based on the same methodology as the gross-output indices in other CMEA countries.

The chief objectives raised by Western scholars against gross-output indices of the type represented by the Rumanian official index are these: (a) quantities are weighted essentially by gross value rather than by value added, so that products fabricated in several stages tend to be overrepresented; (b) changes in the degree of vertical integration of the industry, for which adequate adjustment is likely to be difficult

* This appendix was written in collaboration with Pong S. Lee.
[1] *Anuarul statistic al R.P.R. 1965*, p. 132; *Dezvoltarea industriei R.P.R.: Culegere de date statistice* (Bucharest, 1965), pp. 3–5.

248

if not impossible, bias the indices; (c) the failure to take into account production by small-scale producers and craftsmen in earlier years imparts an upward bias to the index, inasmuch as this small-scale output is relatively more important at an early stage of industrialization; and (d) the method of valuing new products at base-year prices, when the level of current prices diverges significantly from that prevailing in the base year, is generally defective.

While our sample index has many weaknesses of its own, we have tried to make these explicit, and the reader can evaluate for himself the reliability of our measure. The methodology underlying our index is essentially the one developed by students of Soviet and East European growth.[2] Our measure is a quantity index of sample products aggregated by value-added weights for industries (based on 1958) and by 1948–1950 wholesale prices for commodity groups. The first part of this appendix discusses the product coverage of our index, the second part considers the weighting system, and the last part evaluates our indices and compares them with official measures.

Product Coverage

The number of products with positive outputs in the years listed that were used to represent the growth of Rumanian industry is shown in Table A.1 for various branches of industry. The product coverage varies from branch to branch. Relatively homogeneous branches such as coal, petroleum, and electric power seem to be adequately represented. Despite the large number of products listed, the coverage is undoubtedly much less comprehensive in branches that have a very heterogeneous final output-mix, such as machine building and metalworking, chemicals and food. We should point out, in defense of our product coverage that many of the series counted as single products are themselves aggregates of a number of more homogeneous categories. For example, freight cars (goods and tank wagons) consist of six individual series, while industrial steam boilers include three series. Thus the coverage is considerably better than the simple enumeration of products would indicate.

Two special problems related to product coverage should be men-

[2] Maurice Ernst, "Overstatement of Industrial Growth in Poland," *Quarterly Journal of Economics* (November 1965), pp. 623–641; Alexander Gerschenkron, *A Dollar Index of Soviet Machinery Output, 1927–1928 to 1937,* Rand Report R-197, Santa Monica, Calif., 1951; N. M. Kaplan and R. H. Moorsteen, "An Index of Soviet Industrial Output," *The American Economic Review* (June 1960), pp. 295–318; D. R. Hodgman, *Soviet Industrial Production, 1928–1951* (Cambridge, Mass.: Harvard University Press, 1954).

TABLE A.1. PRODUCT COVERAGE OF LEE-MONTIAS INDEX,
1938, 1948, 1953, 1958, AND 1963

Industrial Branch	Number of Products				
	1938	1948	1953	1958	1963
Electric power	1	1	1	1	1
Fuel	15	15	15	15	15
Ferrous metallurgy	4	4	4	4	4
Machine building and metalworking	28	32	48	62	60
Chemicals	22	27	31	35	35
Building materials	10	10	10	12	13
Lumber and woodworking	11	11	13	13	13
Cellulose and paper	3	3	3	4	4
Glass and ceramics	5	5	5	5	5
Textiles	8	8	8	8	8
Leather and hides	1	1	1	1	1
Food	22	22	22	22	22
Soap and cosmetics	1	1	1	1	1
Total number of products	131	140	162	183	182

tioned specifically: (*a*) our treatment of outputs produced but not recorded in the early years; and (*b*) the treatment of new products, that is, of items that were not produced in the early years of the period under consideration. The inclusion of the first category in the sample without adjustment for quantities produced in earlier years will obviously cause an upward bias in the index. On the other hand, leaving such products out of the sample is unacceptable because, insofar as these products tend to grow more rapidly than average, their omission will give rise to a downward bias. The machine-building and metalworking industry and the chemical industry are the two branches where the likelihood of error due to the inclusion of new or hitherto unrecorded products was particularly high. We decided to extrapolate the growth of output of products that were produced in earlier years but not recorded on the basis of their growth rates in later years as recorded in the official statistics. As for new products, we opted to add the value of their current output to the sample without adjustment for earlier years.[3]

Sufficient information on quantity outputs was not available for three branches: nonferrous metallurgy, printing, and clothing. We had to rely on the official gross-value indices for these branches. Any bias that may result should be relatively minor since the relative shares of the three branches are small (less than 7 percent of the total in 1958).

[3] This procedure is only acceptable, of course, if the new products are not over-represented in the sample of products entering the index.

We also used the official index of machine-building output for the period 1938–1948, due to the exceptionally poor coverage of our sample for these years.

The Weighting System

The weights used in our calculations are given in Columns 5 and 6 in Table A.4. The weights used in aggregating subgroups into branches, and branches into all industry, are "imputed" rather than "earned," by which we mean that the weights express the relative importance of the entire subgroup or branch and not just of the sample of products for which we have quantity data.

The weighting proceeded in three stages: (*a*) physical outputs within subgroups of commodities were weighted by 1948–1950 wholesale prices or by prices related thereto; (*b*) employment data were used in aggregating subgroups into branches, except in two instances where the structure of the value of gross output, as estimated in the official statistics, was used as the source of weights instead of employment; (*c*) our estimates of value added for industrial branches (defined as wages and salaries plus amortization allowances) served to aggregate the branches into total industrial production.

AGGREGATION INTO SUBGROUPS. We had access to 1948–1950 wholesale prices for 105 of these products.[4] Prices of the remaining 80 products were estimated as follows: We selected a pair of products in the sample, for one of which we had a 1948–1950 Rumanian price and for the other not. We then took the ratio of the Soviet prices of these two products and calculated the Rumanian price of the second product on the assumption that relative prices for this particular pair of products were the same in the two countries. In our aggregation of commodities into subgroups we eliminated those semifabricates within each subgroup that were predominantly consumed as inputs into other products of the same subgroup (for example, pig iron and crude steel used in the making of rolled steel products). The total number of products included in the base year was 183. Our value-added weights and employment data were derived from data referring to 1958. The index for subgroups takes the form:

$$C_j = \frac{\sum_{i=1}^{s} Q_i^n P_i}{\sum_{i=1}^{s} Q_i^b P_i} \tag{1}$$

[4] Comișionea de Stat al Planificării, *Catalogul prețurilor constante* (Bucharest, 1950); and Ministerul Industriei Grele, *Catalogul prețurilor comparabile* (Bucharest, 1957).

where C_j is the output index for the jth subgroup, P_i is the wholesale price of 1948–1950 of the ith commodity in the subgroup, Q_i^b is its physical output in 1958, and Q_i^n is its physical output in the nth year (i runs from 1 to s, the total number of commodities in subgroup j).

AGGREGATION INTO BRANCHES. In aggregating various subgroups into branches of industry, we used employment data, since wage rates and amortization charges for individual subgroups were not available. The data on distribution of employment into subgroups refers to 1959 rather than 1958 (for which no breakdown into subgroups was available); these data cover all branches except lumber and woodworking.[5] For lumber and woodworking, we arbitrarily assigned 60 percent to forestry and 40 percent to the woodworking subgroup. Employment data for the machine-building and metalworking industry were available for four subgroups, including "machine building," as such, which alone represented 58.6 percent of total employment in the industry in 1959. To obtain a finer breakdown of this last subgroup, we divided it into 8 commodity aggregates on the basis of the structure of gross output in 1958 as officially evaluated.

Our aggregation of subgroups into industrial branches was made according to one or the other of the alternative formulae:

$$I_k = \sum_{j=1}^{J} C_j \frac{E_j}{\sum\limits_{j=1}^{J} E_j} \quad \text{or} \quad I_k = \sum_{j=1}^{J} C_j \frac{G_j}{\sum\limits_{j=1}^{J} G_j} \tag{2}$$

where I_k is the index of output of branch k, C_j is from Formula 1, $(E_j)/(\sum E_j)$ is the jth subgroup's relative weight on the basis of 1958 employment, and $(G_j)/(\sum G_j)$ is the jth subgroup's relative weight on the basis of 1958 official gross value ($j = 1$ to J, the total number of subgroups in branch k).

The number of employees in 1958 for various branches and subgroups is shown in Column 2 in Table A.4.

AGGREGATION INTO TOTAL INDUSTRIAL PRODUCTION. Wages and salaries for various branches of industry were computed by multiplying the average annual wage per employee in 1958 by the average number of persons employed in the branch in 1958.[6] Wages and

---

[5] *Anuarul statistic al R.P.R. 1965*, Table 98, pp. 186–187; and *Dezvoltarea industriei R.P.R.: Culegere de date statistice* (Bucharest, 1964), Chapter 3.

[6] The ratio of the average monthly wages in the metallurgical, machine-building, chemical, light, and food-processing industries to the monthly wage in coal mining in April–June 1958 is given in *Probleme economice*, No. 11 (1958), p. 44. Wage relatives for missing industries were interpolated in these ratios by analogy (e.g.,

salaries and amortization allowances as percentages of total costs in each branch of republican industry are available for 1963.[7] We estimated the structure of industrial costs in 1959 from these 1963 data on the basis of relative changes in employment and fixed capital between 1959 and 1963. Our estimated ratios of amortization allowances to wages and salaries for various branches in 1959 are shown in Column 4 of Table A.4. Amortization charges for individual branches were derived by applying the ratio of amortization to wages and salaries for 1959 to the wages and salaries that we estimated for 1958.

The formula for the aggregation of branches into total industrial production is

$$P = \sum_{k=1}^{K} I_k \frac{VA_k}{\sum_{k=1}^{K} VA_k} \tag{3}$$

where P is the index of output for all industry, I_k is from Formula 2, and VA_k is the value added in the kth branch of industry ($k = 1$ to K, the total number of branches in all industry).

Official and Independently Calculated Indices

Our indices of Rumanian industrial output are shown in Table A.2. In Table A.3, our indices for branches and total industry are compared with the official indices for each five-year period and for the entire twenty-five years between 1938 and 1963.

For industry as a whole, our index shows a lower growth rate than does the official index.[8] For the whole time span of twenty-five years, the official index shows an increase in industrial output over one fourth larger than our index. The greatest divergence between the two measures occurs between 1948 and 1953; the gap is reduced in the 1953–1958 period; finally, the two indices show virtually identical growth during the last five-year period, 1958–1963.

Part of the divergence between the official indices and our own can be explained by differences in coverage. For example, our index of

petroleum with coal mining, cellulose and paper with light industry). The average monthly wage for all industry was estimated at 700 lei from a figure for 1962 deflated by an index of industrial wages and salaries in *Anuarul statistic al R.P.R. 1965*, p. 128. (Note that since the weights are proportional to the *relative* wage bills, errors in absolute magnitude of the monthly wage cannot bias the calculations.)

[7] *Dezvoltarea industriei R.P.R.: Culegere de date statistice*, p. 154; *Anuarul statistic al R.P.R. 1965*, pp. 104, 186–189. Since the percentage distribution of fixed capital by branches was not available for 1958, our estimation refers to 1959.

[8] For official indices see Table 1.5; *Anuarul statistic al R.P.R. 1965*, pp. 148–149; and *Dezvoltarea industriei R.P.R.: Culegere de date statistice* (Bucharest, 1965), pp. 124–125.

TABLE A.2. Lee-Montias Indices of Rumanian Industrial Output, 1948, 1950, 1953, 1955, 1958, 1960, and 1963 (*Percentages, 1938 = 100*)

Industrial Branch	1948	1950	1953	1955	1958	1960	1963
Electric power	132.8	187.0	301.9	384.1	547.3	677.0	1,033.9
Fuel	77.8	99.2	156.4	175.8	198.5	213.0	244.9
Ferrous metallurgy	106.6	173.5	206.0	192.2	293.4	589.9	876.4
Machine building and metalworking	87.0	116.6	224.6	267.5	535.9	796.9	1,062.6
Chemical	117.2	200.4	328.9	403.6	633.1	965.1	2,060.4
Building materials	119.4	179.6	312.9	390.5	483.5	605.1	824.7
Lumber and woodworking	83.8	135.3	182.7	179.3	205.1	246.3	374.0
Cellulose and paper	118.2	158.2	194.9	246.3	273.3	323.5	486.1
Glass and ceramics	141.4	171.2	271.2	326.5	413.2	466.7	704.7
Textiles	86.4	171.5	216.7	262.6	249.4	315.7	393.1
Leather and hides	127.7	326.4	330.1	383.6	475.5	726.9	848.4
Food	82.0	116.2	165.5	199.2	236.1	271.6	433.6
Soap and cosmetics	88.8	188.9	332.8	311.1	355.0	411.1	421.6
Nonferrous metallurgy	n.a.	n.a.	n.a.	n.a.	n.a.	n.a.	n.a.
Clothing	n.a.	n.a.	n.a.	n.a.	n.a.	n.a.	n.a.
Printing and bookbinding	n.a.	n.a.	n.a.	n.a.	n.a.	n.a.	n.a.
Total industry[a]	89.8	140.6	206.6	233.1	305.8	407.0	575.1

[a] Nonferrous metallurgy, clothing, and printing are included in the over-all index on the basis of the official indices for these branches.

output in the power industry is identical with the official index of electric-power output measured in kilowatt hours. The official gross-value index based on the enterprise method differs from the index of power output for all our subperiods, but particularly in the years 1948 to 1953. For the entire twenty-five-year period, the official gross-value index shows an increase about 64 percent greater than the increase in power output. The official gross-value index may include repairs and other ancillary activities that would not be counted as industrial output in the West. The divergence between the two indices for such a homogeneous product as electric power clearly confirms the need for the calculation of an independent index.

The same significant divergence between the two indices can be observed for machine building and metalworking, chemicals, building materials, glass and ceramics, and food processing in the 1948–1953 period.

For machine building and metalworking, our estimate of the growth rate between 1938 and 1948 is based on the official index. The significant divergence between the official index and ours for this branch

TABLE A.3. COMPARISON OF OFFICIAL WITH LEE-MONTIAS INDICES

Industrial Branch	1948 (1938 = 1)		1953 (1948 = 1)		1958 (1953 = 1)		1963 (1958 = 1)		1963 (1938 = 1)	
	(1)	(2)	(1)	(2)	(1)	(2)	(1)	(2)	(1)	(2)
Electric power	1.56	1.33	2.88	2.27	1.88	1.81	2.01	1.89	17.00	10.34
Fuel	.76	.78	2.09	2.01	1.41	1.27	1.57	1.23	3.51	2.45
Ferrous metallurgy	1.21	1.07	1.69	1.93	1.96	1.42	2.51	2.99	10.00	8.76
Machine building and metalworking	.87	.87	4.52	2.58	1.91	2.44	2.26	1.98	17.00	10.63
Chemical	1.01	1.17	3.72	2.81	2.09	1.92	2.92	3.25	23.00	20.60
Building materials	1.17	1.19	4.98	2.62	1.70	1.55	1.82	1.71	18.00	8.25
Lumber and wood-working	.99	.84	2.17	2.18	1.48	1.12	1.65	1.82	5.26	3.74
Cellulose and paper	1.20	1.18	1.73	1.65	1.38	1.40	2.29	1.78	6.58	4.86
Glass and ceramics	1.33	1.41	2.87	1.92	1.81	1.52	1.73	1.71	12.00	7.05
Textiles	.91	.86	2.70	2.51	1.38	1.15	1.63	1.58	5.53	3.93
Leather and hides	1.02	1.28	2.13	2.58	1.62	1.44	1.58	1.78	5.55	8.48
Food	.62	.82	2.40	2.02	1.47	1.43	1.46	1.84	3.19	4.34
Soap and cosmetics	.84	.89	2.65	3.75	1.55	1.07	1.28	1.19	4.40	4.22
Total industry	.85	.90	2.91	2.31	1.59	1.48	1.89	1.88	7.41	5.75

Columns (1): Official index.
Columns (2): Lee-Montias index.

for the 1948–1953 period may have been caused by the expansion of armaments manufactures, although there is no statistical evidence to support this conjecture. If we consider the material inputs consumed by this industry — particularly the supply of rolled steel from domestic and foreign sources — we are even more inclined to question the 4.5-fold increase in the official index in machine building and metal-working (compared to our estimate of a 2.5-fold increase).

Despite their divergences, the two indices both agree in their general trends: it is clear that a great industrial spurt took place in the 1948–1953 period, which was followed by a marked deceleration in the years 1953–1958; this slowdown was then overcome, and rapid growth was resumed in the 1958–1963 period.[9] All branches of industry exhibited their highest rates of growth in the 1948–1953 period, with the exception of ferrous metallurgy and cellulose and paper, which grew fastest in the 1958–1963 period. Only two branches — leather and hides and food processing — showed faster rates of growth in our index than the official growth rates over the entire twenty-five-year span. The reliability of our index of output of the leather and hides

[9] See Chapter 1.

TABLE A.4. DERIVATION OF WEIGHTS FOR LEE-MONTIAS OUTPUT INDEX

Products and Physical Units [a]	1948–1950 Price per Unit (millions of lei) [d]	Number of Employees (thousands) [m]	Average Wage per Year [n]	Ratio of Amortization to Wages and Salaries [o]	Value-Added Weight (total industry = 100) Branch	Subgroup
I. *Electric Power (million kwh)*	8.00	14.1	12,000	27.0:13.8	3.10	
II. *Coal (thousand tons)*		48.5	13,680	13.9:42.0	5.48	
Pit coal	2.14					
Lignite	1.24					
Brown coal	1.83					
III. *Petroleum and Methane Gas Extraction*		37.4	12,000	19.4:7.4	10.09	
1. *Crude petroleum and casing head gas*		23.2				6.26
Crude petroleum (thousand tons)	2.00					
Casing head gas (million m³)	0.21	12.3				
2. *Processing of petroleum products (thousand tons)*						3.32
Gasoline	5.35					
Kerosene	2.60					
Gas oil	2.54					
Mineral oil	16.00					
Petroleum bitumen	4.00					
Paraffin	2.00					
Liquid gas	3.95					
Refinery gas	4.00					
Fuel oil	1.10					
3. *Methane gas extraction (million m³)*	0.71	1.9				.51
IV. *Ferrous Metallurgy (including mining)*		48.6	11,888	5.5:8.9	5.79	
1. *Ferrous metallurgy (thousand tons)*		42.3				5.04
Solid finished rolled metals	30.00					
Steel tubes	48.40					
2. *Mining (thousand tons)*		6.3				.75
Iron ores	1.3					
Blast furnace cokes	8.5					

V. *Machine Building and Metalworking*							
1. *Electrical engineering*		255.5	11,140	4.4:20.3	21.48	26.8	6.02
Electric motors (thousand kw)	15.00						
Electric generators (thousand kva)	30.00						
Electric transformer (thousand kva)	1.2						
Electric insulating conductor and cables (thousand km)	5.17e						
Radios (thousand units)	11.00						
Refrigerators (thousand units)	39.60g,h						
Washing machines (thousand units)	33.00g,h						
2. *Metal construction and products*		31.5					1.23
Ball bearings (million units)	2,192.00e						
Forgings and pressing (thousand units)	299.40e,g						
3. *Machine building*b		197.2					.24
Power-generating equipment							
industrial steam boilers (thousand units)	3,500.00						
steam turbines (thousand units)	1,000.00						
internal-combustion motors (hp)	.02b						
Metalworking and equipment							.64
lathes (thousand units)	495.50e,g						
planers (thousand units)	5,414.00e,g						
milling machines (thousand units)	544.00e,g						
grinding machines (thousand units)	475.00e,g						
technical equipment for metalworking (thousand tons)	74.00e						
Hoisting equipment							.28
winding engines (thousand units)	352.2e,g						
mining winches (thousand units)	125.40e,g						
electric traveling cranes (unit)	10.00f						
automobile cranes (thousand units)	1,000.00e						
pioneer-type cranes (thousand units)	906.75f						

TABLE A.4. (continued).

Products and Physical Units[a]	1948–1950 Prices per Unit (millions of lei)[d]	Number of Employees (thousands)[m]	Average Wage per Year[n]	Ratio of Amortization to Wages and Salaries[o]	Value-Added Weight (total industry = 100) Branch	Subgroup
Machinery for extractive and construction industry					2.65	
complete drilling rigs (thousand units)	2,019.20[e]					
roller bits (thousand units)	566.10[e]					
mud pumps (thousand units)	1,088.00[e]					
excavators (unit)	2.70[e]					
bulldozers (thousand units)	206.20[i]					
compressor cylinders (thousand units)	558.70[e]					
Agricultural machinery (thousand units)					4.53	
scrapers	2,307.00[i]					
tractor-drawn ploughs	245.00					
mechanical disk harrows	262.10[i]					
tractor-drawn drills	60.00					
tractor-drawn cultivators	200.00					
tractor-drawn grain combine harvesters	2,000.00					
corn combine harvesters	1,246.90[i]					
threshing machines	760.00[f]					
silo fodder-harvesting combines	410.00[i]					
tractors	1,200.00					
Transportation equipment (thousand units)					3.04	
standard-gauge diesel locomotives (120 hp)	2,445.70[f]					
diesel electric locomotives (2,100 hp)	50,000.00[f]					
steam locomotives	10,000.00					
tramway rail cars	3,700.00[f]					
passenger coaches	9,000.00					

goods and tank wagons		1,600.00
automobiles		750.00[j]
trucks		1,500.00
Equipment for chemical industry (thousand tons)	.34	
technical equipment for chemical industry		150.00[e]
technical equipment for petroleum refining		151.00[e]
Others	2.52	
technical equipment for building and refractory materials (thousand units)		25.67[e]
technical equipment for forestry and woodworking (thousand units)		34.33[e]
technical equipment for reed, cellulose, and paper industry (thousand units)		34.10[e]
technical equipment for light industry (thousand units)		25.37[e]
technical equipment for food industry (thousand units)		19.65[e]
centrifugal pumps (thousand units)		308.76[f]
compressors (thousand m³ per minute)		143.80[f]
cameras (thousand units)		7.00[g,h]
roentgen apparatus (thousand units)		591.72[i]
electric meters (thousand units)		55.00[j]
pig iron heating radiators (thousand tons)		54.81[e]
pig iron pressure pipes (thousand tons)		54.81[e]
gas cookers (thousand units)		13.00
liquid gas cylinders (thousand units)		5.30
sewing machines (thousand units)		22.60
bicycles (thousand units)		11.00

TABLE A.4. (continued).

Products and Physical Units[a]	1948-1950 Prices per Unit (millions of lei)[d]	Number of Employees (thousands)[m]	Average Wage per Year[n]	Ratio of Amortization to Wages and Salaries[o]	Value-Added Weight (total industry = 100)	
					Branch	Subgroup
VI. Chemicals		43.9	11,000	8.4:12.9	4.94	
1. Basic chemicals (thousand tons)		15.9				1.79
Soda ash	7.00					
Caustic soda	20.00					
Hydrochloric acid	11.84					
Sulfuric acid	15.00					
Acetic acid	187.40					
Compressed ammonia	64.20[e]					
Carbide	37.00					
Carbon black (inactive)	31.00					
Active carbon black	60.00					
Methanol	67.00[e]					
Butanol	—[l]					
Acetone	180.00[g]					
Phenol	—[l]					
Naphthalene	59.00[e]					
Benzine	59.00[e]					
Toluene	82.00					
Xylene	78.00[e]					
2. Chemical Fertilizers (thousand tons)		1.9				.21
Phosphatic fertilizers	26.00					
Nitrogenous fertilizers	43.00					
3. Chemical Fiber and Yarn (thousand tons)		3.4				.39
Synthetic fiber and yarn	412.00					
Artificial fiber and yarn	432.00					
Plastic and synthetic resins	124.00					

4. *Medical and Pharmaceutical*						
Antibiotics (ton)	10.00	6.0				.67
Sulfamides	—					
Vitamins	—					
Chemical and pharmaceutical synthetic products	—					
Pesticides	—					
5. *Rubber, Plastic, and Asbestos Products*						
Tires (cars, planes, tractors) (thousand units)	9.00	9.4				1.06
Rubber footwear (thousand pairs)	.80					
Synthetic rubber	—					
Rubber technical goods	—					
6. *Others (thousand tons)*						
Varnishes	223.00	7.3				.82
Organic dyestuffs	1,300.00					
Tanning substances	195.00					
Bone and leather glues	211.00[e]					
Detergents	75.00					
VII. *Building Materials*						
1. Cement (thousand tons)	2.05	74.9	9,600	8.6:22.0	6.20	1.58
2. *Reinforced-Concrete Prefabs (thousand m³)*	—	19.1				.77
3. Refractory Materials (thousand tons)		9.3				.62
Fireproof bricks	4.59[k]	7.5				
Silicic refractory bricks	3.59[k]					
4. *Others*						
Lime (thousand tons)	2.40	39.0				3.23
Plaster (thousand tons)	2.90[j]					
Masonry materials (million units)	3.10					
Roofing materials (million units)	5.00					
Tarred cardboard (million m²)	24.50					
Cement pipes (ton)	—					
Marble block (m³)	—					
Reed sheet (thousand m²)	—					

TABLE A.4. (continued).

Products and Physical Units[a]	1948–1950 Prices per Unit (millions of lei)[d]	Number of Employees (thousands)[m]	Average Wage per Year[n]	Ratio of Amortization to Wages and Salaries[o]	Value-Added Weight (total industry = 100) Branch	Subgroup
VIII. Lumber and Woodworking[c]		212.8	9,320	3.7:31.5	13.75	
1. Forestry Operations						8.32
Pitprops (thousand m³)	2.00[e]					
Pulpwood (thousand m³)	3.00[e]					
Firewood (thousand m³ of piled timber)	.92[e]					
Coniferous trees (thousand m³)	2.17					
Beech (thousand m³)	3.00					
Oak (thousand m³)	4.70					
2. Woodworking						5.43
Veneer (thousand m²)	.10					
Plywood (thousand m³)	4.20					
Lumber-core plywood (thousand m³)	5.00					
Fiber building board (thousand tons)	2.00[e]					
Pressed slabs (thousand tons)	0.80[j]					
Furniture (million lei)						
Matches (billion boxes)	35.35[j]					
IX. Cellulose and Paper		10.5		9.5:17	.99	
1. Cellulose and Paper		8.7	9,800			.82
Paper (thousand tons)	26.00					
Cardboard and millboard (thousand tons)	20.42[h]					
Paper bags (thousand units)	11.68[e]					
2. Reed (ton)	—[l]	1.8				.17
X. Glass and Ceramics		14.6	9,320	7.3:37.1	1.01	
1. Glass		11.7				.81
Window glass (million m²)	46.00					
Glassware (thousand tons)	70.00					

2. Chinaware and Faïence (thousand tons)		2.9				.20
Household faïence	10.00[j]					
Faïence sanitary goods	10.00[e]					
Household chinaware	70.00[j]					
XI. *Textiles*			9,320	3.3:12.6	9.20	
1. Flax, Hemp, and Jute Fabrics (million m²)	250.00	*126.1*				.56
2. Cotton and Cotton-Type Fabrics (million m²)	160.00	7.3				4.13
3. Woolen Fabrics (million m²)	700.00	53.7				1.96
4. Silk Fabrics (million m²)	200.00	25.4				.71
5. Knitwear (million units)		9.2				1.71
Cotton knitwear	120.00	2.2				
Woolen knitwear	400.00					
Silk knitwear	200.00					
6. Other		22.2				.17
Stockings and socks (million pairs)	140.00					
XII. *Leather and Hides*			9,320	2.4:15.8	3.20	
Leather footwear (million pairs)	2,000.00	*50.2*				
XIII. *Food*			8,904	1.8:6.0	8.15	
1. Meat (thousand tons)	150.00	*113.4*				1.38
Meat preparations	216.00	19.1				
2. Dairy		11.8				.85
Milk (million hl)	1,400.00					
Cheese (thousand tons)	200.00					
Butter (thousand tons)	340.00					
3. Vegetable Oils and Fats (thousand tons)	70.00	3.9				.28
4. Sugar (thousand tons)	48.00	14.9				1.07
Confectionery	140.00					
5. Canning (thousand tons)		9.9				.71
Canned meat	154.00					
Canned vegetables	64.00					
Canned fruits	64.00					

TABLE A.4. (continued).

Products and Physical Units[a]	1948–1950 Prices per Unit (millions of lei)[d]	Number of Employees (thousands)[m]	Average Wage per Year[n]	Ratio of Amortization to Wages and Salaries[o]	Value-Added Weight (total industry = 100) Branch	Value-Added Weight (total industry = 100) Subgroup
6. *Alcoholic Beverages*		18.0				1.29
Rectified alcohol (million decaliters)	800.00					
Starch glucose (thousand tons)	90.00					
Rectified alcoholic beverages (million decaliters)	800.00					
Beer (thousand hl)	1.50					
7. *Others (thousand tons)*		35.8				2.57
Whole bread	7.89[h]					
White and fancy bread	14.94[h]					
Flour pastes	10.27[j]					
Biscuits	25.00[j]					
Hulled rice	10.50					
Salt	12.00[j]					
Tobacco products	500.00					
XIV. *Soap and Cosmetics*		1.8	8,904	1.5:5.8	.12	
Soap (thousand tons)	150.00					
XV. *Nonferrous Metallurgy*		26.6	11,140	4.8:17.3	2.37	
XVI. *Clothing*		47.5	9,320	.3:10.5	2.82	
XVII. *Printing*		17.2	9,800	4.8:36.8	1.19	

[a] Roman numerals denote branches. Arabic numerals denote subgroups.

[b] The machine-building subgroup was further divided into eight subgroups according to 1958 official gross-value weights (*Dezvoltarea industriei socialiste în R.P.R.*, p. 202).

[c] No employment breakdown is available. As an approximation of value added, 60 percent and 40 percent of the 1958 official gross value were assigned to the forestry and woodworking subgroups, respectively (*Dezvoltarea industriei R.P.R.: Culegere de date statistice* [Bucharest, 1964], p. 202).

[d] 1948–1950 wholesale prices, unadjusted for the monetary reform of 1952. Prices are expressed per aggregate unit (in parentheses). *Source,* except in the cases noted: Comişionea de Stat al Planificării, *Catalogul preţurilor constante* (Bucharest, 1950); and Ministerul Industrei Grele, *Catalog preţurilor comparabile* (Bucharest, 1957).

[e] N. M. Kaplan and W. L. White, *A Comparison of 1950 Wholesale Prices in Soviet and American Industry,* Research Memorandum, RM-1443 (Santa Monica, Calif.: Rand Corporation 1955).

[f] R. Moorsteen, *Prices and Production of Machinery in the Soviet Union, 1928–1958* (Cambridge, Mass.: Harvard University Press), 1962.

[g] Supplement to R. V. Greenslade and P. Wallace, "Industrial Production in the U.S.S.R.," in *Dimensions of Soviet Economic Power* (Washington, D. C.: Joint Economic Committee, 1962), pp. 115–136.

[h] L. Turgeon, "Levels of Living, Wages and Prices in the Soviet and United States Economies," in *Comparisons of U.S. and Soviet Economies* (Washington, D. C.: Joint Economic Committee, 1960), pp. 319–340.

[i] A. S. Becker, *Prices of Producers' Durables in the United States and the U.S.S.R. in 1955,* Research Memorandum RM-3432 (Santa Monica, Calif.: Rand Corporation, 1959).

[j] Estimated from relative market prices in the West.

[k] L. Turgeon and A. Bergson, *Prices of Basic Industrial Goods in the U.S.S.R., 1950 to 1956, A Preliminary Report,* ASTIA Document AD 144262 (Santa Monica, Calif.: Rand Corporation, 1957).

[l] Products for which no prices could be obtained. Their values were estimated by comparing the official and our gross-value distributions for a subgroup that includes these products.

[m] The total number of employees in the entire branch is in italics. The data are from *Anuarul statistic al R.P.R. 1965,* pp. 186–187. The employment breakdown into subgroups is based on *Dezvoltarea industriei: Culegere de date statistice,* Part II (Bucharest, 1965).

[n] The ratio of the average monthly wage in the metallurgical, machine-building, chemical, light, and food-processing industries to the monthly wage in coal mining in April–June 1958 is given in *Probleme economice,* No. 11 (1958), p. 44. Wage relatives for missing industries were interpolated in these ratios by analogy (e.g., petroleum with coal mining, cellulose and paper with light industry). The average monthly wage for all industry was estimated at 700 lei from a figure for 1962, deflated by an index of industrial wages and salaries in *Anuarul statistic 1965,* p. 128. (Note that since the weights are proportional to the *relative* wage bills, errors in the absolute magnitude of the monthly wage cannot bias the calculations.)

[o] The numerator of the ratio is the percentage of amortization allowances to total cost, while the denominator is the percentage of wages and salaries to total cost in each branch. The ratios were extrapolated for 1959 from the 1963 official ratio on the basis of relative changes in fixed capital and employment between 1959 and 1963 (*Ibid.,* pp. 116–117, 174; *Anuarul statistic al R.P.R. 1965,* pp. 104, 186–187).

industry is limited because our sample covers only one product, namely, leather footwear.[10] With regard to the food-processing industry, a sharp rise in the output of dairy products caused our index to increase about 26 percent more than the increase in the official gross-value index for the period 1958–1963; this resulted in a higher growth rate for the entire period than the official index. The recorded increase in the output of milk products reflects in part the recording of production hitherto carried out on the farm or by small private units. If the official rates of growth of the leather and the food industry were used instead of the aggregated series in our index for 1958 to 1963, this would reduce the index relative for 1963 on a 1958 base from 188 to 183 and the annual rate of growth from 13.4 to 12.8 percent.

The derivation of the weights used in our index is shown in Table A.4.

[10] Soles and leather for uppers were excluded from the sample because they are inputs to footwear.

NATIONAL INCOME

Published Statistics

The only data pertaining to Rumania's aggregate social accounts that have been regularly published in the statistical yearbooks are the following: (1) indices of national income (produced) and of gross social product,[1] together with indices of the gross value of output and of value added in the six principal productive sectors, all in "comparable prices";[2] (2) the ratio of national income to gross social product and of value added to the gross value of output for each productive sector, calculated in current prices; (3) the percentage breakdown of national income and of gross social product by productive sectors, also in current prices.[3] All these published statistics are reproduced in Tables B.1, B.2, B.3, and B.4.

The concept of national income in Rumania differs from that used in the Western economies mainly in two respects: it excludes "nonproductive services" (administration, passenger transportation, hospital services, and so on), and it includes turnover taxes, which are levied chiefly on consumer goods.

Two sets of national income accounts are constructed: national income "produced" and national income "distributed" or "utilized." The difference between the two equals the surplus on the balance of payments in current account (the surplus must be subtracted from, or the deficit added to, national income produced to obtain national income distributed).[4] National income distributed is the sum of "consumption" plus "accumulation." Consumption is broken down into its

---

[1] Gross social product equals national income plus materials consumed by producing enterprises plus depreciation on the economy's total fixed assets.

[2] Essentially, comparable prices are current prices of 1948 for 1950 to 1955 and current prices of 1955 for all years from 1955 on. The indices of "physical volume" expressed in comparable prices of 1950 and 1955 are linked to each other via the index relatives for 1955, which both these indexes have in common.

[3] A percentage breakdown by sectors in "comparable prices" was discontinued after 1959.

[4] On the foreign trade surplus, see pp. 278–279.

principal components in Table B.5, based on recently released data.

Other elements of the consumption fund include the material expenditures of social and cultural institutions and the rents (*uzură*) on both private and state housing.[5]

Since data on retail sales in socialist trade are available, the absolute value of the (material) consumption fund may be estimated by dividing the value of these sales by their percentage share in total consump-

TABLE B.1. Indices of Gross Social Product for the Entire Economy
and by Productive Sectors, 1938, 1948, 1950–1965
(*Calculated in "Comparable Prices," 1938 = 100*)

	Gross Social Product	Industry	Con- struction	Agri- culture and Forestry	Transpor- tation and Communi- cations	Mer- chandise Trade	Other Branches
1948	66	82	87	62	58	42	56
1950	99	146	227	73	79	59	68
1951	124	181	336	94	91	76	71
1952	135	214	440	87	112	75	63
1953	156	241	549	103	132	79	72
1954	159	257	475	101	140	86	77
1955	184	294	567	119	157	101	82
1956	185	314	688	95	172	95	76
1957	205	350	661	119	178	96	79
1958	213	390	713	102	177	97	78
1959	235	431	778	123	177	91	82
1960	261	495	924	126	201	91	92
1961	290	556	1,100	136	232	106	93
1962	308	626	1,200	124	253	106	96
1963	335	698	1,300	128	290	128	76
1964	373	789	1,400	137	319	146	84
1965	406	n.a.	n.a.	n.a.	n.a.	n.a.	n.a.

Source: Anuarul statistic al R.P.R. 1965, p. 101; Statistical Pocket Book of the Socia Republic of Romania 1966, p. 39 (hereafter referred to as Statistical Pocket Book 1966)

tion, with the following results: for 1950, 34.8 billion lei; for 1955, 64.1 billion lei; for 1959, 78.2 billion lei; for 1962, 100.6 billion lei; and for 1963, 102.3 billion lei. These numbers served as the basis for the consumption index in current prices in Table 1.20.

The accumulation fund in official statistics is defined as the sum of investments in fixed capital, major ("capital") repairs, increases in working capital, reserves, and the value of cattle herds, minus depre-

[5] S. Dinculescu, V. Dumitrescu, and F. Buzan, "Probleme metodologice privind indicatorii utilizării finale a venitului național," *Revista de statistică*, No. 2 (1963), pp. 75–76.

ciation on all fixed assets.[6] The available data on trends in consumption and accumulation are also shown in Table 1.20.

Prices

To arrive at national income in constant prices, the Central Direction of Statistics deflates each of the sectoral components of national income produced by an index of the sector's prices. This must also be

TABLE B.2. INDICES OF NATIONAL INCOME AND OF VALUE ADDED BY
PRODUCTIVE SECTORS, 1938, 1948, 1950–1965
(Calculated in "Comparable Prices," 1938 = 100)

	National Income	Industry	Con- struction	Agri- culture and Forestry	Transpor- tation and Communi- cations	Mer- chandise Trade	Other Branches
1948	67	94	78	59	60	49	64
1950	99	164	238	70	81	65	75
1951	130	212	323	95	99	87	87
1952	136	248	404	82	130	79	75
1953	157	282	504	98	154	85	87
1954	156	299	375	88	164	91	89
1955	192	358	518	119	189	103	94
1956	177	368	619	74	207	90	90
1957	206	415	657	110	221	91	89
1958	213	471	714	88	218	90	82
1959	241	522	837	117	223	81	89
1960	267	611	1,128	117	265	84	102
1961	294	696	1,105	122	310	96	98
1962	307	793	1,163	108	337	93	102
1963	336	885	1,205	112	400	115	97
1964	375	1,018	1,306	117	438	135	99
1965	409	1,149	1,348	119	475	146	95

Source: Anuarul statistic al R.P.R. 1965, p. 102; Statistical Pocket Book 1966, p. 43.

done to calculate consumption and accumulation at "comparable prices." The construction of these price indices presents special problems, which were acknowledged by a team of Rumanian statisticians in an interesting methodological paper contributed to a statistical conference in 1961.[7] In industry, for example, the basic material for the

[6] *Ibid.*, p. 72.
[7] I. Răvar, C. Ciobarsu, P. Scarlat, *et al.*, "Cu privire la metodologia de calcul al produsului social, cheltuielilor materiale şi al venitului naţional," in *Studii de statistică: Lucrările consfătuirii ştiinţifice de statistică* (November 27–29, 1961), pp. 294–327.

calculation of the gross product of industry is the gross value of output, which differs from the former by the inclusion of certain semifabricates and of turnover taxes that are excluded from the latter. It is particularly difficult to estimate what the value of turnover taxes would have been at "constant prices" for the current volume of output when tax rates fluctuated over time. The authors give various procedures for arriving

TABLE B.3. Ratio of National Income to Gross Social Product and of Value Added to the Gross Value of Output for Each Productive Sector, 1938, 1950–1965 (*Current Prices*)

	National Income	Industry	Con- struction	Agri- culture and Forestry	Transpor- tation and Communi- cations	Mer- chandise Trade	Other Branches
1938	48.9	38.6	40.0	62.2	50.0	65.0	30.6
1950	51.2	48.4	41.9	55.7	52.5	76.0	37.0
1951	53.0	48.8	37.7	60.8	51.6	80.1	37.4
1952	50.4	48.3	36.0	56.6	50.8	72.5	38.6
1953	51.4	48.6	35.9	58.9	51.3	75.5	36.7
1954	48.8	44.2	30.3	58.6	48.6	73.3	33.2
1955	50.8	45.0	36.2	62.5	48.7	69.6	34.6
1956	46.6	42.4	37.2	55.4	50.4	64.2	35.0
1957	50.2	43.6	40.9	64.7	52.0	58.3	30.7
1958	47.3	40.4	41.4	62.3	50.7	63.5	29.0
1959	49.0	40.4	44.9	65.3	51.4	64.8	31.8
1960	48.5	40.8	45.1	65.2	51.9	68.6	33.1
1961	48.3	41.8	43.0	63.6	52.1	67.5	29.1
1962	47.1	41.8	41.6	61.6	51.7	66.2	30.2
1963	44.4	37.1	37.6	61.2	53.6	68.5	34.2
1964	43.5	37.2	36.6	58.3	53.7	67.4	31.1
1965	43.3	36.8	36.3	59.0	52.8	66.8	30.2

Source: Anuarul statistic al R.P.R. 1965, p. 100; Statistical Pocket Book 1966, p. 42.

at the value of turnover taxes in constant prices but do not claim that the problem has been solved in a satisfactory manner. As we shall see, price movements were fairly large during certain years, and errors in deflation may easily cause the difference between growth and retro-gression for national income as a whole in these years.

We can readily compute the price indices corresponding to the deflators used by the Central Direction of Statistics for each of the six sectors of national income produced *in percentage relation to the price index for national income as a whole*. We do this by making use of the following formula in any year t:

TABLE B.4. PERCENTAGE BREAKDOWN OF GROSS SOCIAL PRODUCT AND
OF NATIONAL INCOME BY PRODUCTIVE SECTORS, 1938,
1950–1965 (*Current Prices*)

	Industry	Construction	Agriculture and Forestry	Transportation and Communications	Merchandise Trade	Other Branches
			Gross Social Product			
1938	39.0	5.4	30.2	6.4	11.2	7.8
1950	46.6	7.4	25.8	4.2	7.9	8.1
1951	44.9	8.1	28.0	3.6	7.9	7.5
1952	49.5	9.8	23.2	4.1	7.6	5.8
1953	44.7	9.6	29.6	3.9	6.0	6.2
1954	43.9	8.0	30.6	4.0	6.6	6.9
1955	44.9	7.9	30.5	3.9	6.7	6.1
1956	47.2	9.6	27.0	4.2	6.0	6.0
1957	46.0	8.2	31.2	3.9	4.6	6.1
1958	50.0	8.7	26.4	3.8	5.4	5.7
1959	49.6	8.8	28.3	3.5	4.8	5.0
1960	52.4	9.7	24.6	3.5	4.6	5.2
1961	52.0	9.7	25.1	3.4	4.6	5.2
1962	55.0	10.0	22.5	3.5	4.4	4.6
1963	56.2	9.9	21.6	3.5	5.1	3.7
1964	56.3	9.7	22.0	3.4	4.7	3.9
1965	57.0	9.4	22.0	3.3	4.7	3.6
			National Income			
1938	30.8	4.4	38.5	6.5	14.9	4.9
1950	44.0	6.0	28.0	4.3	11.8	5.9
1951	41.4	5.7	32.2	3.5	11.9	5.3
1952	47.5	7.0	26.0	4.1	10.9	4.5
1953	42.2	6.8	33.9	3.9	8.8	4.4
1954	39.7	5.0	36.7	4.0	9.9	4.7
1955	39.8	5.6	37.6	3.7	9.2	4.1
1956	43.0	7.6	32.1	4.6	8.2	4.5
1957	39.9	6.7	40.2	4.1	5.4	3.7
1958	42.7	7.7	34.8	4.1	7.2	3.5
1959	40.9	8.0	37.8	3.7	6.4	3.2
1960	44.1	9.0	33.1	3.8	6.5	3.5
1961	45.0	8.7	33.0	3.7	6.5	3.1
1962	48.8	8.8	29.4	3.9	6.2	2.9
1963	46.9	9.3	29.8	4.2	7.9	2.9
1964	48.1	8.2	29.5	4.2	7.3	2.7
1965	48.5	7.8	30.0	4.0	7.2	2.5

Source: Anuarul statistic al R.P.R. 1965, p. 99; Statistical Pocket Book 1966, p. 41.

$$\frac{\text{Net output of sector } x \text{ in current prices in year } t.}{\text{Percentage change in prices of sector } x \text{ from base year to year } t} \times \frac{\text{percentage change in national-income prices from base year to year } t}{\text{national income in current prices in year } t} = \begin{array}{l}\text{share of sector } x \\ \text{in national income in} \\ \text{year } t \text{ at base-year prices.}\end{array}$$

Now the ratio of the net output of sector x in current prices to "national income in current prices" in the formula is known for the years 1950 to 1965 and so is the right-hand side ratio, which expresses the same share, but in constant prices, for the years 1950 to 1959. It

TABLE B.5. Percentage Breakdown of the "Consumption Fund" in 1950, 1955, 1959, 1962, and 1963 (*Current Prices*)

	1950	1955	1959	1962	1963[a]
Purchases in socialist retail trade	35.3	43.3	46.2	52.7	56
Purchases on the peasant market	9.3	10.0	9.4	6.5	6
Nonproductive consumption of agricultural producers from their own production	26.8	27.1	25.4	23.1	22
Other elements of the consumption fund	28.6	19.6	19.0	17.7	16
Total consumption fund	100.0	100.0	100.0	100.0	100

[a] The breakdown for this year was estimated from a diagram and is subject to a small error.

Source: S. Ţaigar, *Veniturile populaţiei şi nivelul de trai in R.P.R.* (Bucharest, 1964), p. 86; *Dezvoltarea complexă şi echilibrată a economiei naţionale* (Bucharest, 1965), p. 37.

is easy to see that the percentage ratio of the price index for the sector to the price index for national income as a whole is equal to the ratio of the sector's share in national income in current prices to the sector's share in constant prices for any year. An alternative, slightly more complicated, method can be used to calculate these same indices of relative prices in the absence of sector shares in constant prices, for which we have data only until 1959. It can be verified that the ratio of the price index of any sector to the price index of national income in a given year also equals the ratio of the sector's share in national income in the given and in the base year, divided by the ratio of the index of the value of the sector's net output in the given year to the index of national income for that year, both expressed in constant prices. The price relatives for 1959 in Table B.6 show that the alternative methods yield very close results (A corresponds to the first method discussed, B to the second).

TABLE B.6. Percentage Ratio of the Deflator for Individual Sectors to the Deflator for National Income, 1950–1960

	Industry	Construction	Agriculture and Forestry	Transportation and Communications	Merchandise Trade	Other Branches
1950	100.0	100.0	100.0	100.0	100.0	100.0
1951	95.2	92.1	111.1	87.5	98.3	101.9
1952	97.5	93.3	107.9	82.0	104.8	104.7
1953	88.1	84.0	136.1	76.5	90.7	102.3
1954	77.5	82.0	163.8	72.7	95.2	106.8
1955	79.7	82.6	152.4	71.2	95.8	107.9
1956	77.7	86.3	192.5	74.4	90.3	113.1
1957	74.2	83.4	189.3	72.0	67.6	109.1
1958	72.3	90.8	212.2	75.9	96.0	116.7
1959						
A	70.5	92.1	194.8	75.5	106.7	110.3
B	70.6	91.7	195.6	75.4	105.9	111.2
1960	72.2	90.5	188.7	72.2	115.4	117.8
1961	71.2	92.2	199.7	66.1	110.4	120.4
1962	70.5	92.2	210.0	67.0	113.1	112.3
1963	66.6	92.4	223.6	66.8	109.8	128.8
1964	66.4	93.7	237.9	67.9	113.1	131.6
1965	64.7	93.3	257.4	64.8	111.9	137.2

Sources and methods: The data in the table for 1950 to 1955 and for 1959A were obtained as the ratio of each sector's share in national income in current prices to its share in national income in constant prices, both of which are to be found in *Anuarul statistic al R.P.R. 1960*, pp. 104–105; for 1956–1958, 1959B, and 1960–1965, the data were obtained as the ratio of the sector's share in national income in current prices in the given and in the base year, divided by the ratio of the index of the value of the sector's net output in the given year to the index of national income for that year, both expressed in constant prices.

The relatives derived by the two methods, which were compared for all sectors for 1956 to 1959, showed disparities of less than one percent, well within the normal range of rounding errors. Somewhere in the data for the years 1956 and 1957, although the two methods are in close agreement, some mistake must have crept into the original material, since it is obviously inconceivable that every one of the sector's relatives should have declined, or, looking at the matter inversely, that the price index for national income should have grown more, or dropped less, than the index for every individual sector.

In general, the relatives of Table B.6 make sense. As we should expect, prices of agricultural and forestry products rose throughout most of the period compared to the prices of industrial products;

moreover, the divergence between the two price indices widened in 1953–1954 and in 1956, years in which marked increases in agricultural prices are known to have occurred.

We can calculate the absolute changes in prices in each sector in 1958 by making use of the fact that industrial net output went up by 127.5 percent in current prices from 1950 to 1958 and by 187.2 percent in comparable prices.[8] These two relatives imply that by 1958 prices of industrial products had fallen to 79.2 percent of their 1950 level. But we also know from Table B.6 that the ratio of this price relative to the price relative for national income as a whole came to 72.3 percent. The price relative for national income, therefore, must have been 109.5 percent of 1950. Using this result and the ratios of Table B.6 for other sectors, we find that agricultural prices in 1958 stood at 232 percent of 1950, that construction prices were nearly on the same level as in 1950, that prices in the transportation sector were at 83 percent of their 1950 level, prices in merchandise trade at 105 percent, and prices in "other branches" at 128 percent of this base year.

We also have an independent way of calculating the implicit deflators used for 1957 to 1963. The key to these estimates is supplied by the following index relatives of gross social product in current prices on a 1957 base: 102.3 in 1958, 109.8 in 1959, 122.2 in 1960, 141.5 in 1961, 150.2 in 1962, and 169.7 in 1963.[9] With the aid of the percentage ratios in Table B.3, we may reconstruct the official deflator for national income.[10] The index of prices for any sector may then be derived from the index of prices for national income as a whole, making use of the price relatives in Table B.6. All the indexes so constructed for the years 1957 to 1963 may be linked to 1950 on the basis of the price indices for 1958 (on a 1950 base) that we derived from the increase in the net output of industry in current and in constant prices. This leaves us with the years 1951 to 1956 for which we have no strictly precise basis from which to estimate the absolute levels of the deflators. It is known, however, that construction prices stayed more or less constant from 1950 to 1954 and dropped by 7 percent in 1955.[11] Moreover, if we compare the value of investments in structures and assemblies, which

---

[8] *Probleme economice*, No. 3 (1960), p. 10.

[9] I. Răvar in *Dezvoltarea complexă și echilibrată a economiei naționale* (Bucharest, 1965), p. 21.

[10] As may easily be verified, an index of national income in current prices on a 1957 base may be constructed by multiplying for each year the relative for the index of gross social product in current prices by the ratio of national income to gross social product in the given year to the same ratio in the base year. The index of prices may then be calculated by dividing the resulting index of national income in current prices by the index of national income in fixed prices given in Table B.1.

[11] *Revista de statistică*, No. 5 (1958), p. 25.

should come close to the value of construction works, in 1959 and in 1955 prices, we find an average difference of 4.7 percent,[12] which is roughly consistent with the figure given for 1955 and with the index relative for 1959 that we found independently of these estimates. No large error should arise from the assumption that construction prices varied in the described manner. Once the prices of this one sector were fixed, of course, all others were easily determined via the relatives of Table B.6 (see Table B.7).

TABLE B.7. Reconstructed Official Price Deflators, 1950–1955, 1957–1963 (*1950* = *100*)

	National Income	Industry	Con- struction	Agri- culture and Forestry	Transpor- tation and Communi- cations	Mer- chandise Trade	Other Branches
1950	100.0	100.0	100.0	100.0	100.0	100.0	100.0
1951	108.5	103.3	100.0	120.5	94.9	106.7	110.6
1952	107.1	104.4	100.0	115.6	87.8	112.2	112.1
1953	119.0	104.8	100.0	162.0	91.0	107.9	121.7
1954	122.0	94.6	100.0	199.8	88.7	116.1	130.3
1955	112.6	89.7	93.0	171.6	80.2	107.9	121.5
1957	117.4	87.1	98.0	222.2	84.5	79.4	128.6
1958	109.5	79.2	99.5	232.4	83.1	105.1	127.8
1959	107.6	76.0	98.7	210.4	81.1	113.9	119.7
1960	107.1	77.3	101.5	202.1	77.3	123.6	126.2
1961	112.2	79.9	103.4	224.2	74.2	124.4	135.0
1962	111.2	78.5	102.5	233.5	74.5	125.9	124.7
1963	108.0	72.0	99.8	241.4	72.1	139.6	139.6

Sources and methods: Tables B.2, B.4, and B.6, and methods described in the text.

I cannot find a satisfactory explanation for the absolute decline in industrial prices from 1957 to 1958 at a time when prices of producer goods, net of turnover taxes, were stable; and no reductions in retail prices of industrial goods took place during the year that could auto- matically have reduced turnover taxes on industrial consumer goods.[13] It is interesting that the value of turnover taxes collected in the budget went down by 7 percent from 1957 to 1958 (even though retail sales were about the same in the two years), while enterprise profits rose by

[12] Computed as the average ratio of investments in structures and assemblies for 1955 to 1959, in 1959 and in 1955 prices (*Anuarul statistic al R.P.R. 1959*, p. 207; and *Anuarul statistic al R.P.R. 1965*, p. 340).

[13] The official retail price index for industrial consumer goods showed virtually no change from 1957 to 1958 (see Table 1.23 of Chapter 1).

35 percent.[14] This suggests that the cut in turnover taxes was not passed on to consumers in the form of lower prices. If this reasoning is correct, the drop in industrial prices was arbitrarily determined and had an artificial effect in reducing the national-income deflator for the year. (Since, in principle, the current value of national income must also have been reduced artificially by this price change, the manipulation should not have biased the change in national income in comparable prices.)

The implicit deflator calculated by Michael Kaser from a comparison of national income in current prices with the official index of national income in constant prices diverges significantly from the results that I obtained for the period 1955–1960:

IMPLICIT PRICE INDICES FOR RUMANIA'S NATIONAL INCOME

	Kaser[a]	Montias
1955	100	100
1960	112	95
1961	109	100
1962	n.a.	99
1963	113	96

[a] "An Estimate of the National Accounts of Rumania Following Both Eastern and Western Definitions," *Soviet Studies* (July 1966), p. 87.

If Kaser's index were correct, then it follows from the price relatives for 1955 and 1960 in Table B.6 that construction prices in 1960 should have been 22.7 percent above 1955 levels.[15] In my opinion an increase of this magnitude is unlikely to have occurred.[16]

Estimates of National Income

Table B.8 sets forth my calculations of official estimates of national income distributed in current and in constant prices. The link between national income in current and in constant prices for 1950 is supplied by the official deflator, as reconstructed in Table B.7 from data referring to national income produced. It was taken that the price indices for the alternative concepts of national income could not differ sig-

[14] *Anuarul statistic al R.P.R. 1965*, p. 447.

[15] $90.5/82.6 \times 112 = 122.7$.

[16] Nominal wages in the construction industry rose by 51.4 percent from 1955 to 1960, and labor productivity by 34 percent (*Anuarul statistic al R.P.R. 1965*, pp. 128, 368). Hence labor costs must have risen by approximately 13 percent. Material costs were approximately constant, since no major changes occurred in the prices of building materials during this period. An increase in total net costs in excess of 10 percent therefore seems improbable.

nificantly enough to affect the calculations in Table B.8. The increase
in national income in constant prices from 1959 to 1963 as calculated
in Table B.8 amounts to 42.5 percent, as compared to 41 percent according to the index cited in Table 1.20. A difference of this magnitude
could easily be due to rounding errors.

TABLE B.8. A Reconstruction of Official Estimates of National
Income Distributed in Selected Years, 1950 to 1963
(*Billions of post-1952 Lei*)

	Current Prices			Constant (1950) Prices
	National Income Distributed	Consumption	Accumulation	National Income Distributed
1950	39.1	34.8	4.3	39
1955	77	64	13	68
1957	92.6	78.5	14.1	79
1959	93.4	78.2	15.2	87
1962	126.1	100.6	25.5	113
1963	133.9	102.3	31.6	124

Note: Due to rounding errors, the sum of accumulation and consumption may
differ slightly from national income in certain years.

Sources and methods: Current prices: consumption estimates are taken from
Table B.5, except for 1957, which is based on a percentage relation to 1962 in
Dezvoltarea complexă și echilibrată a economiei naționale (Bucharest, 1965), p. 36. The
ratio of accumulation to national income in 1963, which was inferred to be in
current prices, was taken from *Pravda* (Bratislava, January 6, 1966) (see Table
1.21). National income was then derived by elementary algebra. Accumulation
in other years was computed by deflating the estimate for 1963 by the index of
accumulation in current prices reproduced in Table 1.20. Constant prices: National
income in constant prices: Values in current prices divided by the national-income
deflator of Table B.7.

In Table B.9 I make use of the estimates of Table B.8 to calculate
the ratio of investments in fixed capital to national income from 1955
to 1963.

In the following pages the conjectural method of calculating national income produced from national income distributed involves
utilization of budget data on the income from foreign trade, which,
according to a Rumanian specialist interviewed in 1962, were said to
represent the total net profit on both imports and exports. The statistics available cover 1951, when the net income of foreign trade
equaled 2.8 billion lei, 1956, when it equaled 4.8 billion lei, and the
plan for 1959, when it was set at 6.6 billion lei.[17] If my understanding

[17] *Economia României între anii 1944–1959* (Bucharest, 1959), p. 539.

TABLE B.9. Investments in Fixed Capital and Their
Ratio to National Income, 1955, 1959–1963

	Investments in 1959 Prices (1955 = 100)	Ratio of Investments to National Income Distributed[a]
1955	100.0	18.2
1959	136.7	19.8
1960	174.8	23.5
1961	220.7	n.a.
1962	260.6	27.4
1963	275.2	28.0

[a] Ratio of state and cooperative investments in fixed capital at 1959 prices to national income deflated by an implicit price index based on 1959 (derived from Table B.7).
Sources: Table B.8 and Anuarul statistic al R.P.R. 1965, p. 337.

of these budgetary receipts is correct, then the deficit on merchandise trade, that is, the true deficit on current account, exclusive of invisibles, can be derived from these data as follows.[18]

Receipts from foreign trade = $M^D - M^F + X^F - X^D$, where M^D and X^D are imports and exports in domestic prices and M^F and X^F are imports and exports in foreign-exchange lei. Since we know M^F and X^F for all three years, we can easily compute the deficit on merchandise trade in domestic prices. Thus:

$$M^D - X^D = R + (M^F - X^F),$$

where R equals the net budgetary receipts from foreign trade.

[18] The assumption made here is that income from foreign trade does not enter national income produced directly. According to a United Nations survey of national income methodology in Eastern Europe, the Soviet Union and several other members of CMEA (but not East Germany) include in national income *produced* the net gain on foreign trade at the level at which actual imports would be balanced by exports. Only the difference between the import surplus at domestic prices and this surplus contributes to the gap between national income produced and distributed. It is my impression from the methodological discussions in Rumanian statistical literature that this technique was not adopted in Rumania, but this is by no means certain. If this method *was* in use in Rumania, I should not be able to reconstruct national income produced from national income consumed and from the net budget differences referred to in the text (see United Nations, Economic Commission for Europe, *Economic Bulletin for Europe*, Vol. 11, No. 3 [1959], p. 58). The error in estimating national income produced from data on national income distributed if the methodology followed by the Central Statistical Office were that allegedly employed in the Soviet Union rather than that described in the text would be of the order of 2 to 3 percent for the most recent years. This difference should then be *added* to the estimates of national income produced in Table B.10 to arrive at a correct evaluation.

Our results are tabulated in billions of lei:

	R	$M^F - X^F$	$M^D - X^D$
1951	2.8	0.056	2.86
1956	4.8	−0.3	4.5
1959 (plan)	6.6	−0.13	6.47

Let us suppose that the plan for 1959 was fulfilled and that there was neither surplus nor deficit in the balance of invisibles. Then national income produced should have been 86.9 billion lei in 1959 (the difference between 93.4 billion lei distributed and the deficit of 6.5 billion lei). We can then use the index of national income produced in comparable prices in Table B.1 to compute the value of national income in 1959 prices and then convert the results into current prices with the price deflators of Table B.7. The results are shown in Table B.10.[19]

TABLE B.10. ESTIMATES OF NATIONAL INCOME PRODUCED AND DISTRIBUTED FROM 1950 TO 1963 (*Billions of Lei*)

	National Income Produced		National Income Distributed	Apparent Deficit on Current Account
	(at 1959 prices)	(at current prices)	(at current prices)	(in domestic prices)
1950	35.9	33.4	39.1	5.7
1951	47.0	47.3	50.2	2.9
1952	49.2	49.0	n.a.	n.a.
1953	56.7	62.6	n.a.	n.a.
1954	56.4	63.4	n.a.	n.a.
1955	68.9	72.1	77.0	4.9
1956	63.9	n.a.	n.a.	4.5
1957	74.3	81.1	92.6	11.5
1958	76.8	78.2	n.a.	n.a.
1959	86.9	86.9	93.4	6.5
1960	96.2	95.9	n.a.	n.a.
1961	105.9	110.5	n.a.	n.a.
1962	110.6	114.2	126.1	11.9
1963	121.3	122.3	133.9	11.6

Sources: Tables B.1, B.7, and B.8, and budgetary receipts cited in the text.

[19] The United Nations estimate in 1950 prices was equal to 30.3 billion post-1952 lei (*Economic Survey for Europe in 1955*, p. 246). Note also that Kaser's estimates in *Soviet Studies*, which were derived from value added in industry and from the share of the latter in national income produced, come within about 5 percent of my own estimates for 1962 and 1963. Kaser's estimates of national income produced in current prices (in billions of lei) are as follows: in 1955, 69.1; in 1960, 108.3; in 1961, 115.6; and in 1963, 138.6 (*op. cit.*, p. 87).

THE RELATION OF IMPORTS TO CONSUMPTION AND OF EXPORTS TO PRODUCTION FOR STAPLE PRODUCTS IN RUMANIAN TRADE

We begin our analysis by examining the import dependence of the textile industry, which before World War II imported a larger proportion of its materials consumption than any other industry. In 1936, 79.9 percent of its materials consumption was imported, compared to 40.9 percent for the electrotechnical industry, 30.3 percent for metallurgy, 26.1 percent for ceramics, 10.8 percent for construction materials, 8.5 percent for food processing, and 2.5 percent for lumber.[1] No such aggregative measure of import dependence being available for the postwar years, we must look at import-to-consumption ratios for the principal materials processed by the textile industry.

Natural fibers form the basis of Rumania's textile industry.[2] The principal fibers, in order of importance, are cotton, silk, wool, hemp, and flax. All cotton fiber is at present imported, whereas domestic production accounts for the bulk of consumption of wool, hemp, and flax. Some raw silk is produced in Rumania, but it is believed that most of the raw materials for the silk-weaving industry are procured abroad.[3] The available data on the import dependence of the textile industry are assembled in Table C.1. They show a quite successful drive for self-sufficiency in wool and flax, in contrast to the abandonment of the efforts made until the mid-1950's to build up domestic sources of cotton fiber.

[1] *Enciclopedia Romăniei* (Bucharest, 1938–1939), Vol. III, p. 817.

[2] In 1958, 73.3 percent of yarn consumption consisted of natural fibers while the rest was of chemical origin. By 1965, the proportion of chemical fibers was slated to rise to 31.2 percent (*Mezinárodní socialistická dělba práce*, V. Wacker and B. Malý, eds. [Prague, 1964], p. 270).

[3] In 1963 the silk industry procured 1,295 tons of silk cocoons and produced 26.6 million square meters of silk fabrics, not including artificial silk (*Industria Rominiei 1944–1964* [Bucharest, 1964], p. 704, and *Dezvoltarea industriei R.P.R.: Culegere de date statistice* [Bucharest, 1964], p. 357). No other information on the raw-material consumption of the industry is available to the author.

TABLE C.1. IMPORTS AND APPARENT CONSUMPTION OF COTTON, WOOL, AND FLAX IN SELECTED YEARS, 1950 TO 1963
(*Thousands of Tons*)

	1950	1955	1958	1960	1962	1963
Cotton: Imports	29	39	46	51	61	65
Procurements from domestic production	6	14	4	—	—	—
Apparent consumption	35	53	50	51	61	67
Import-to-consumption ratio	83.7	73.3	92	100	100	100
Wool: Imports of All Woolen Fibers[a]	13.3	7.6	6.2	4.8	0.7	0.7
Imports of wool only	n.a.	n.a.	2.8	2.4	0.3	0.3
Procurements from domestic production	7.4	9.8	13.8	14.5	19.1	19.6
Apparent consumption	20.7	17.4	20.0	19.3	19.8	20.3
Import-to-consumption ratio	64.2	43.6	30.1	24.9	3.2	3.4
Flax: Imports	n.a.	5	n.a.	5	—	—
Procurements from domestic production	13	31	n.a.	36	61	52
Apparent consumption	n.a.	36	n.a.	41	61	n.a.
Import-to-consumption ratio	n.a.	14.2	12.6[b]	12.0	—	—

[a] Including rags.
[b] 1959.

Note: "Imports of All Woolen Fibers" are estimated from import-to-consumption ratios, while "imports of wool" are taken from official statistics of imports.

Sources: Cotton: Imports of raw cotton from the U.S.S.R. for 1950 and 1955 are given in I. P. Oleinik, *Dezvoltarea industriei Romîniei în anii Regimului Democrat-Popular* (Bucharest, 1960), p. 157; the share of imports from the U.S.S.R. in total cotton imports (*Probleme economice*, No. 10 [1957], pp. 122–123) was used to calculate total imports from these data. Imports of cotton since 1958 are from *Anuarul statistic al R.P.R. 1964*, p. 442. Wool and flax: *Dezvoltarea complexă și echilibrată a economiei naționale* (Bucharest, 1965), pp. 73 and 115; *Probleme ale creării și dezvoltării bazei tehnice-materiale a socialismului în R.P.R.* (Bucharest, 1963), p. 189; *Dezvoltarea industriei socialiste în R.P.R.* (Bucharest, 1959), pp. 394–395; *Dezvoltarea agriculturii R.P.R.* (Bucharest, 1961), pp. 368–369.

Before concluding this short discussion of the import dependence of the Rumanian light industry, I may mention that 45 percent of the raw hides consumed in Rumania in 1949 were imported, but only 22 percent in 1963.[4]

From the fairly abundant data published about the iron and steel industry, we can estimate the relation of output and consumption to trade for key metallurgical products for the years 1950 to 1965. This has been done in Table C.2.

The import ratios for coking coals, coke, and iron ores are generally quite high, perhaps high enough to justify the proposition, often

[4] *Dezvoltarea complexă și echilibrată a economiei naționale* (Bucharest, 1965), p. 117.

TABLE C.2. Trade Dependence of the Metallurgical Industry:
Output, Consumption, and Trade in Raw Materials
and Rolled Steel Products (*Thousands of Tons*)

	1950	1956	1958	1960	1962	1964	1965
Coking Coals							
Output	65	413	730	994	1,130	1,193	1,220
Imports	n.a.	n.a.	152	416	750	718	706
Consumption	n.a.	n.a.	882	1,410	1,880	1,911	1,926
Import-to-consumption							
ratio (percent)	n.a.	n.a.	17.2	29.5	39.9	37.6	36.7
Metallurgical Coke							
Output	72	256	563	820	1,119	1,146	1,135
Imports	n.a.	n.a.	616	656	719	946	930
Consumption	n.a.	n.a.	1,179	1,476	1,838	2,092	2,065
Import-to-consumption							
ratio (percent)	80.2[a]	64.2[a]	52.2	44.4	39.1	45.2	45.0
Iron Ores							
Output	392	694	743	1,460	1,738	1,932	2,479
Imports	600	513	753	917	1,920	2,305	2,623
Consumption	992	1,207	1,496	2,377	3,658	4,237	5,102
Import-to-consumption							
ratio (percent)	60.5	42.5	50.3	38.6	52.5	54.4	51.4

	1950	1955	1958	1960	1962	1964	1965
Rolled Steels and Pipes							
Output	450	565	777	1,592	2,121	2,608	2,933
Import	n.a.	264	655	933	1,088	1,356	1,199
Export	n.a.	8	49	470	561	508	577
Consumption	n.a.	822	1,383	2,055	2,468	3,456	3,555
Import-to-consumption							
ratio	36.2	32.1	47.4	45.4	44.1	39.2	33.7
Export-to-output ratio	n.a.	1.4	6.3	29.5	26.4	19.5	19.7

[a] All cokes.

Sources and methods: Output statistics for all selected years and trade statistics for
the years 1958 to 1964 for all the items listed are given in *Anuarul statistic al R.P.R.
1961*, p. 317, and in *Anuarul statistic al Republicii Socialiste România 1966* (Bucharest,
1966), pp. 172, 474, and 476. Import-to-consumption ratios for coke in 1950 and
1956 and for rolled steels (including pipes) in 1950 and 1955 are from *Probleme
economice*, No. 12 (1957), pp. 21–22. For iron ores, 1950 imports are from A. Bodnar,
Gospodarka europejskich krajów socjalystycznych (Warsaw, 1962), p. 156; 1956 imports
of ores are based on data in I. P. Oleinik, *Razvitie promyshlennosti Rumynii . . .*
(Moscow, 1959), p. 159. Rolled steel exports in 1955 are derived from an export-
to-output ratio in V. Wacker and B. Malý, eds., *Mezinárodní socialistická dělba práce*
(Prague, 1964), p. 202.

covertly alluded to in CMEA publications, that Rumania does not have a proper "raw-material basis" for a steel industry.[5] In any case, large quantities of semifabricated steel were also imported.[6]

The efforts made by the Rumanian planners to lessen their dependence on imports of coke and iron ores were successful only up to about 1961; thereafter the pace of industrial expansion outran capacity increases in the domestic production of these materials.

Despite great strides in the production of metal-consuming industries, the import-to-consumption ratio for rolled steels steadily declined from 1958 to 1965; the export-to-output ratio, however, after rising to a peak of 29.5 percent dropped to less than 20 percent in 1964 and 1965, thus releasing supplies for domestic consumption.

The goal of self-sufficiency also embraced nonferrous metals, at least for products that had some sort of raw-material basis in the country, as was the case for lead and zinc and, to a more limited extent, for copper. In 1957 the output of the first two just matched consumption, while 50 percent of copper consumption was satisfied from domestic production in that year. The Five-Year Plan ending in 1965 called for export surpluses equal to 6 percent of consumption for lead and 17 percent for zinc; two thirds of copper consumption was now to be made up domestically. The plan for 1965 also envisaged that aluminum production would be sufficient to cover all domestic requirements, even though no primary aluminum at all had been turned out in 1957. On the other hand, Rumania is totally deficient in deposits of nickel ores. All requirements for metallic nickel were met from imports in 1957, and no change was expected in this situation by 1965.[7]

The chemical industry also moved toward greater self-sufficiency over the years of postwar industrialization, while simultaneously increasing its dependence on foreign outlets for a part of its production. In 1950, exports came to less than one third of imports; by 1965 exports came to within 4 percent of imports. It was estimated that 8.7 percent of the total output of chemicals was exported in 1959; in the plan for 1965, this proportion was slated to increase to 20 percent,

[5] See Chapter 4, p. 213. Whether steel production in the quantities produced at present is rational can, of course, be determined only by way of complex economic calculations going far beyond simple comparisons of imports and outputs.

[6] In connection with the average import ratios in the table, it may be noted that 40 percent of the steel products delivered to the Rumanian machine-building industry around 1960 were imported. (*Ekonomicheskoe sotrudnichestvo i vzaimopomoshch' sotsialisticheskikh stran*, A. D. Stupov, ed., *op. cit.*, p. 254.)

[7] B. Malý, *Rozvoj komplexu národního hospodařství ČSSR v mezinárodní socialistické dělbě práce* (candidate dissertation, Prague, 1965), p. 181; and J. Novozámský, *Otázky vyrovnávání ekonomické úrovně* . . . (candidate dissertation, Prague, 1962), p. 143.

and did in fact about reach this share by the target date.[8] The three main staples of the industry's export program have been carbon black, soda ash, and caustic soda. The average export-to-output ratios for these three products from 1960 to 1963 were roughly 65, 57, and 55 percent, respectively.[9] The bulk of exports consists in semifabricates and the bulk of imports in finished products — a normal state of affairs for a country developing a new industry of this type.[10]

The petroleum industry remains, as before World War II, an essential source of foreign exchange, although the share of oil products in total exports has suffered a sharp setback in recent years — from 36 percent in 1955 to 16 percent in 1964 — most of the drop having taken place since 1960.[11] (It was argued in Chapter 3 that the ratio of exports to output for the industry as a whole must have dropped after 1960.)[12] For the period up to 1955, we have estimates by the Soviet economist I. P. Oleinik — according to whom 73 percent of the output of petroleum products was exported in 1938, 60.7 percent in 1951, 63.4 percent in 1953, and 58.0 percent in 1955.[13] According to another source, which covers only gasoline, kerosene, and gas oil, 69 percent of the combined output of these three products was exported in 1955; the Second Five-Year Plan foresaw a decline in the ratio to 50 percent by 1960.[14] From the statistics for individual products in Table C.3, it would appear as if the aggregate share for "white products" had indeed fallen substantially since the late 1950's, but this trend has been partly offset by the substitution in the export program of fuel oil and lubricating oils for the declining lighter fractions. This tendency reflects the progress made in boosting the proportion of crude products undergoing catalytic cracking and vacuum distillation in the 1960's.[15]

In the 1950's an extraordinarily large proportion of Rumania's cement output was sold abroad. The export-to-output ratio for this basic building product was as high as 53.4 percent in 1950; it then fell steadily, due chiefly to enormous increases in output, descending to a low mark of 27.3 percent in 1964. The quantities involved were quite

[8] I. Burştein in *Dezvoltarea complexă şi echilibrată a economiei naţionale* (Bucharest, 1965), p. 291; *Probleme economice*, No. 4 (1966), p. 118.

[9] Cf. *Rumania in the International Trade 1944–1964*, p. 84.

[10] Import surpluses on finished items, such as pharmaceutical products and organic dyes, have remained quite large (see *Anuarul statistic al R.P.R. 1965*, pp. 440–443).

[11] *Anuarul statistic al R.P.R. 1965*, p. 438.

[12] Chapter 3, p. 150.

[13] I. P. Oleinik, *op. cit.*, p. 222.

[14] I. D. Kariagin, *Neftianaia promyshlennost' Rumynii* (Moscow, 1958), p. 323.

[15] See Appendix D on the petroleum industry, pp. 302–303.

TABLE C.3. OUTPUT, CONSUMPTION, AND EXPORT RATIOS FOR PETROLEUM
PRODUCTS (*Thousands of Tons and Percentages*)

	1950	1955	1958	1960	1962	1964	1965
Gasolines							
Output	1,502	2,635	2,821	2,792	2,400	2,512	2,458
Export	1,146	2,362	2,258	2,466	1,871	1,655	1,444
Consumption	390	273	563	326	529	857	1,014
Export-to-output ratio	76.3	89.6	80.0	88.3	78.0	65.9	58.7
Kerosene							
Output	736	1,362	1,529	1,289	1,234	990	965
Export	250	675	667	676	602	338	280
Consumption	427	687	862	613	632	652	685
Export-to-output ratio	34.0	49.6	43.6	52.4	48.8	34.1	40.9
Gas Oil							
Output	731	1,626	1,807	2,376	2,910	3,386	3,600
Export	336	834	1,480	1,286	1,648	1,900	1,979
Consumption	578	692	327	1,090	1,262	1,486	1,621
Export-to-output ratio	46.0	51.3	81.9	54.1	56.6	56.1	55.0
Fuel Oil							
Output	1,681	4,037	3,930	3,824	3,952	3,839	3,773
Export	n.a.	n.a.	552	1,229	1,468	1,894	1,639
Consumption	n.a.	n.a.	3,378	2,595	2,484	1,945	2,134
Export-to-output ratio	n.a.	n.a.	14.0	32.1	32.1	49.3	43.4
Lube Oils							
Output	125	162	212	311	346	448	483
Export	n.a.	n.a.	94	211	205	303	294
Consumption	n.a.	n.a.	118	100	141	145	189
Export-to-output ratio	n.a.	n.a.	44.3	67.8	59.2	67.6	60.9

Sources and methods: Output statistics in all years listed and export data for 1960,
1962, and 1964 are from *Anuarul statistic al R.P.R. 1961*, p. 317, and from *Anuarul
statistic al Republicii Socialiste România 1966* (Bucharest, 1966), pp. 172, 474, and
476. Exports in 1958 are from *Rumania in the International Trade 1944–1964*, p. 88.
Exports and consumption of white products (gasoline, kerosene, and gas oil) were
derived from data in I. D. Kariagin, *Neftianaia promyshlennost' Rumynii* (Moscow,
1958), pp. 329–333. According to this source 69 percent of the output of the
light fractions was exported in 1955. It appears probable that this share was
obtained by summing the tonnages of output and exports of the three light products. The separate consumption of each of the three products in 1955 was computed from a percentage breakdown of this total (on p. 323). Index numbers
relating consumption of the three products in 1955 and in 1950 (p. 318) yielded
the consumption data for 1950. All export statistics for 1950 and 1955 were obtained by subtraction, on the likely assumption that imports were negligible.

large for a less developed country, rising from 549,000 tons in 1950 to some 1.0 to 1.2 million tons between 1957 and 1962,[16] during which period Rumania is said to have accounted for around 10 percent of world cement exports.[17]

Timber is too heterogeneous a group to permit such simple and unambiguous calculations. Exports consist of relatively unprocessed products such as pulpwood, semifabricates such as plywood, and highly finished products such as furniture. The proportions in output and in exports among these groups has been changing. In 1950, for instance, 60.2 percent of the value of the total exports of lumber and lumber products consisted of pine lumber and 0.7 percent of furniture; in 1962 the former made up only 27.8 percent of these total exports and the latter 15.4 percent.[18] Thanks to the government's policy of processing an increasing proportion of timber output, the value of products obtained from a cubic meter of timber rose by 64 percent from 1959 to 1963. Finished and semifinished products made up 14 percent of timber exports in 1950 and 40 percent in 1962.[19] Export-to-output ratios, as well as their trends through time, have tended to differ appreciably according to the type of lumber and to the degree of processing to which it was subjected. For pulpwood, the ratio went up from 8.4 percent in 1958 to 40.2 percent in 1963; for sawn softwood it fluctuated between 30 and 35 percent between 1958 and 1963, then jumped suddenly to 53 percent in 1964, with 1.4 million cubic meters exported. (This recent increase may have resulted from an extraordinary measure to meet a deterioration in the balance of payments.) For plywood, the ratio rose steadily from 21.7 percent in 1958 to 43 percent in 1964. With regard to furniture, all data we have consist in statistics of exports in *valută* lei and of output in domestic (constant) prices. The quotient of these two (not fully comparable) aggregates increased from 5 percent in 1959 to 8 percent in 1964.[20] These quotients undoubtedly understate the true ratios in terms of comparable values because the *valută* leu represents somewhat more than one domestic leu, but the upward trend is still significant.

The average ratio for all lumber products could not have differed

[16] Cement exports in 1950, 1952, 1954, and 1957 were computed from an index of exports with a link to 1958, the first year for which exports are given in the *Anuarul statistic al R.P.R. 1964*. The index was published in *Economia Rominiei între anii 1944–1959, op. cit.*, p. 577.

[17] *Rumania in the International Trade, op. cit.*, p. 93.

[18] *Valorificarea superioară a resurselor naturale* (Bucharest, 1965), p. 170.

[19] *Ibid.*, pp. 90–91.

[20] All these export and output data are to be found in the *Anuarul statistic al R.P.R. 1964* and *1965*, pp. 172 and 461, except for pulpwood output, in *Dezvoltarea industriei, R.P.R.: Culegere de date statistice* (Bucharest, 1964), pp. 308–309.

very much from 30 percent in 1950 and 35 percent in 1962, judging from the ratios for the important products listed.[21]

Foodstuffs contributed nearly 50 percent of total exports in 1948; the absolute level of the exports in this group oscillated around a constant mean for about a decade, while the total value of exports was increasing. They thus lost their dominant position in the export program. Rapidly expanding procurements of farm products made it possible to step up exports to double the 1958 level by 1960 and to triple it by 1964. By this latter date, foodstuffs contributed a greater share of total exports than did petroleum products (22–23 percent).

There is clear evidence of declining export-to-output ratios in the agricultural sector in the mid-1950's, followed by a sharp rise in the 1960's. This conclusion follows from a comparison of trends in agricultural net and gross output with trends in the export of foodstuffs. While agricultural exports, valued in foreign currency prices, fluctuated around a stable mean between 1948 and 1958, the gross output of agriculture rose by 67 percent.[22] By 1964, however, exports were running at three times their 1948 level, while both net and gross output were only about 2.2 times as large as they were in this base year. If exports were deflated by an index of the prices at which Rumania sells her foodstuffs abroad, this would probably reduce the disparity between the two trends but would not eliminate it altogether.

We have only fragments of information about the composition of agricultural exports in the 1950's. In spite of exceedingly low consumption levels at the time, Rumania found it possible to export some 240,000 tons of grain in 1950.[23] This may have accounted for a third of commercial exports of foodstuffs in that year, or about 5 percent of the total output of all grains. Meat, oil seeds, eggs, vegetables, and fruits must have made up most of the rest. The burden of food exports on the economy was even heavier if we consider that food delivered to the Soviet Union on reparations account was not included in these statistics.

In 1955 the surplus of grain exports over imports exceeded 200,000

[21] The output of sawn timber, which made up the bulk of exports in the early 1950's, went up by 8 percent from 1950 to 1954, then went down again to the level of 1950 in 1957. According to published indexes of exports of lumber products based on 1950, exports stood at 133 in 1952, at 157 in 1954, at 151 in 1957, and at 144 in 1958 (*Economia Romîniei între anii 1944–1959*, *op. cit.*, p. 577). See also *Valorificarea superioară* . . . , *op. cit.*, p. 170.

[22] *Anuarul statistic al R.P.R. 1965*, pp. 101 and 328.

[23] Juliús Lipták, "Podminky mezinárodní socialistické dělby práce v zemědělství," in *Výzkumne práce* (Výzkumný ústav narodohospodářského plánování), No. 52 (December 1963), p. 52. On exports plus additions to reserves in 1952 and 1953, see Chapter 1, p. 31.

tons, despite wheat imports of 302,000 tons.[24] Corn exports must then
have topped 500,000 tons; this was slightly less than 10 percent of
estimated production and not far from 20 percent of total marketed
output, including sales on the free market.[25] Meat exports to the Soviet
Union alone were 8,500 tons in 1955 and 22,900 tons in 1956,[26] or 5
percent of state meat procurements.[27] For the years from 1958 on we
have export statistics for individual products. Meat exports increased
from 4,400 tons in 1958 to 33,000 tons in 1960. We may estimate from
the fact that meat exports averaged 29,000 tons from 1958 to 1960 that
they must have risen to about 45,000 tons in 1961 and 1962.[28] This
was 16 percent of industrial meat output and 31 percent of total retail
sales of meat and meat products. If the meat sold abroad had been
consumed domestically it would have added about 8–10 percent to
domestic consumption in 1961–1962.[29]

Exports of cereals, consisting for the most part of corn, averaged
470,000 tons from 1958 to 1960 and 1,230,000 tons from 1961 to 1964.
This was 5 and 12 percent, respectively, of average cereals production
in these two periods. Corn alone represented 80 percent of cereals
exports from 1958 to 1962.[30] The ratio of corn exports to the corn harvest rose from 10 percent, for the period 1958 to 1960, to 22 percent
for 1961 to 1964. Exports of corn amounted to 60 percent of total corn
procurements from 1958 to 1962 and to about 50 percent in 1963
and 1964.[31]

Imports and exports of sugar went through a number of gyrations
after 1958. After reaching a peak in 1962 with 310,800 tons, exports
declined to 34,500 tons in 1965. If we take an average for 1960–1965,
we find that net sugar exports — exports minus imports — came to

[24] *Ibid.*, p. 52.

[25] *Probleme agricole*, No. 1 (1957), p. 13.

[26] *Vneshniaia torgovlia SSSR za 1956 god* (Moscow, 1958), p. 86.

[27] *Ibid.*, Table 2.16, and *Dezvoltarea agriculturii 1965*, p. 587.

[28] Export statistics for 1958, 1959, and 1960 are to be found in *Rumanian Foreign Trade* (Chamber of Commerce of the R.P.R.), No. 2 (1960), p. 10, and No. 1 (1961), p. 12. The average for the five-year period is from J. Lipták, *Mezinárodní dělba práce v zemědělství zemí RVHP* (Prague, 1965), p. 178.

[29] See Table 2.16. Meat consumption per head in 1958 was equal to 23.4 kilograms, less than 50 percent of Poland's and 55 percent of Hungary's at the time (Table 1.15). It is doubtful whether per capita consumption has risen more than 20 percent from 1958 to 1961–1962.

[30] Exports of corn averaged 658,000 tons from 1958 to 1962 (Lipták, *Mezinárodní dělba práce . . .*, p. 178).

[31] *Anuarul statistic al Republicii Socialista România 1966*, pp. 181, 475, and 477, and Chapter 2. My estimates of the ratio of exports to procurements for 1963 and 1964 assume that corn made up the same proportion of cereals exports in those two years as in 1958 to 1962.

97,000 tons a year, or over a quarter of average output in these years.[32] For a country with an average consumption per head of less than 15 kilograms in the early 1960's — the lowest in CMEA apart from Albania and Mongolia — these exports represented an appreciable sacrifice. The large volume of sugar and meat exports exposes the readiness of the Rumanian government to postpone increases in living standards for the sake of buying the foreign machines and materials necessary to keep pressing ahead with its industrialization drive.

[32] *Anuarul statistic al R.P.R. 1965,* pp. 175, 441, and 443.

THE PETROLEUM INDUSTRY AND ITS ROLE IN RUMANIA'S ENERGY BALANCE

The Extraction of Crude Oil

Although my brief survey of the Rumanian economy does not pretend to be comprehensive, the omission of the petroleum industry as a separate subject of analysis would leave too wide a gap in the coverage of the present study. Those readers who are familiar with Rumania's petroleum industry before the war will wish to know how it developed in the postwar years and, more specifically, the reasons why it failed to keep up with the progress accomplished in other sectors of the economy.

A few preliminary statistics on the extraction of crude oil will provide the framework for the subsequent discussion. Total output of crude oil reached a prewar peak in 1936 with 8.7 million tons. It dropped to 4.5 million tons in 1945, and to less than 3 million tons in 1946; it then fluctuated around that low point until mid-1947, recovered the prewar peak in 1953, and continued to make fairly rapid headway until 1955. From that year on, production progressed very slowly; it increased by less than 15 percent over the entire decade 1955 to 1965, reaching 12.6 million tons at the latter date.

This slow and apparently "organic" evolution may give the erroneous impression that the extraction of crude is going on much under the same conditions and in the same fields as before the war. Yet, already in 1959, 80 percent of crude oil output came from deposits discovered after 1948.[1] Since then the share of new deposits in total output has risen to at least 85 percent.[2] Most of these new deposits are in "new regions" — the Bacău district (Moldavia), Piteşti in the Argeş district (western Muntenia), Craiova in Oltenia, and the Bu-

---

[1] I. Desmireanu in *Probleme ale creării şi dezvoltării bazei tehnice-materiale a socialismului în R.P.R.* (Bucharest, 1963), p. 174.

[2] *Valorificarea superioară a resurselor naturale* (Bucharest, 1965), p. 14.

charest region, only the first of which produced any significant amount of oil before World War II. The Prahova fields in the Ploieşti district, which accounted for some four fifths of output in 1930–1931 and a little less than 50 percent in 1936, were producing some 4.5 million tons in 1955–1956, about as much as at their maximum prewar level in the early 1930's. Their output has probably receded since that time.[3] Table D.1 provides information on the output of the four principal producing regions.

The regional breakdown of crude petroleum output in 1963, which I estimated by roundabout methods, was so extraordinary, and in comparison with 1960 gave rise to such unexpected trends, that at first I did not trust the results of my calculations. Yet I believe there is enough evidence to support the general trends that these data reveal, namely the decline since 1960 in the output of all regions hitherto producing significant amounts of crude oil and the simultaneous emergence of the Bucharest region as an important and dynamic producer.[4]

A major geological discovery of petroleum deposits in the Bucharest region must have occurred in the late 1950's. This is confirmed by the fact that the region became an important focus of investments in petroleum in the 1960's, absorbing 12.2 percent of all investments in this branch of industry (including refining) from 1960 to 1964.[5] Yet the Rumanian censors, as far as I have been able to ascertain, have sought to conceal this discovery from the public. The Rumanian press

[3] Cf. the graphs on p. 100 of *Dezvoltarea economiei R.P.R. pe drumul socialismului 1948–1957* (Bucharest, 1958), and the statistics in Table D.1.

[4] The breakdown of each region's gross industrial output by branch, although it aggregates all fuels into one group, provides corroborating evidence of the Bucharest region's importance as a petroleum producer. In 1963, 3.5 percent of all fuels were produced in the Bucharest region, where they made up 15.6 percent of the region's industrial output (*Dezvoltarea industriei R.P.R.: Culegere de date statistice*, p. 140). Since no coal or lignite was produced in the region and only a relatively small percentage of the country's methane output (6.3 percent in 1961), it is clear that nearly all this value of output refers to petroleum extraction. After subtracting an estimate of the value of methane produced in the region, based on the assumption that 10 percent of total methane output was contributed by Bucharest in 1963, I deduced that petroleum extraction in the region accounted for 0.287 percent of the total industrial output of Rumania. Since petroleum extraction represented 2.0 percent of total industrial output in that year, the share of the Bucharest region in this sector must have been about 14 percent. This would correspond to 1.74 million tons. The output of the other regions and residual errors would cause the difference between this figure and the estimate for "other regions" in Table D.1. One may also interpolate output data for 1962 for Argeş and Oltenia on the assumption that yearly rates of increases (for Argeş) and of decline (for Oltenia) were constant from 1960 to 1963. This yields an output for "other regions" equal to 1.2 million tons for 1962.

[5] *Anuarul statistic al R.P.R. 1965*, p. 364.

TABLE D.1. Production of Crude Oil by Regions, 1936, 1946, 1950–1965 (*Thousands of Tons*)

	Ploieşti	Argeş	Oltenia	Bacău	Bucharest and Other Regions	Total
1936	8,606	—	—	—	—	8,703
1946	4,050	—	—	200	—	4,257
1950	4,814	—	—	233	—	5,047
1952	5,537	942	n.a.	n.a.	—	8,002
1953	n.a.	662	n.a.	2,020	—	9,058
1955	5,332	1,722	1,404	2,096	—	10,555
1956	4,477[a]	1,959	2,293	2,184	—	10,920
1957	n.a.	2,101	2,800	n.a.	n.a.	11,180
1959	3,841	2,650	2,810	2,089	48	11,438
1960	3,909	2,740	2,430	2,109	311[b]	11,500
1962	3,511	n.a.	n.a.	1,614	n.a.	11,864
1963	3,000	3,650	2,135	1,500	2,000	12,230
1964	n.a.	3,533	n.a.	n.a.	n.a.	12,395
1965	n.a.	3,268	1,483	n.a.	n.a.	12,571

[a] Of which about 3.8 million tons came from the Prahova fields alone.

[b] Of which 260,000 tons came from the Bucharest region alone.

Sources: For 1950, 1955, 1959, and 1960, *Anuarul statistic al R.P.R. 1961*, p. 147; other data are based on percentages from the following sources: for 1936, 1946, 1953, 1956, and 1957: *Dezvoltarea economiei R.P.R. pe drumul socialismului 1948–1951* (Bucharest, 1958), pp. 89, 90, and 100. Percentages of total crude output in *Republica Populară Romînă: geografie a patriei* (Bucharest, 1964), yielded the outputs for Ploieşti and Bacău for 1962. The 1965 estimates for Oltenia and Argeş are similarly based on the percentages of those regions in total output as given in *Viaţa economică*, No. 28 (July 15, 1966), pp. 8–9. For the production of Argeş in 1952, 1953, and 1957, see the index of output in *Petrol şi gas*, No. 8 (1959), p. 344; the production of Argeş in 1964 is based on its share in total output in 1964, *Congresul al IX-lea al Partidului Comunist Român* (Bucharest, 1965), p. 530. The breakdown by regions for 1963 was obtained as follows: for Argeş and Oltenia: from the proportion of gross output of the petroleum industry (which consisted in extraction only) to the total gross output of the respective regions in 1959 and 1963 and from the index of the gross output of the regions one may compute the approximate percentage changes in petroleum extraction in the two regions between the two dates; the absolute volume of production can then be obtained by applying these indices to the official data on extraction for 1959 (the shares of petroleum in gross output are from *Studii de economie socialistă* [Bucharest, 1961], pp. 190–192, for 1959, and *Industria Romîniei 1944–1964* [Bucharest, 1964], pp. 155–157, for 1963). For the Bacău and Ploieşti regions, which possess refining facilities, a similar procedure was used to construct index relatives for 1963 on 1960 (for Bacău) and for 1963 on 1959 (for Ploieşti) (based on the share of the output of the petroleum industry in gross output in *Revista de statistică*, No. 11 [1961], and *Viaţa economică*, No. 3 [July 24, 1964], p. 8). From the known share of petroleum extraction in Ploieşti out of the country's total in 1959, from the average prices of refined products in Ploieşti refineries compared to the over-all average (*Industria Romîniei 1944–1964*, p. 303), and from gross-output data for petroleum extraction and refining combined it was possible to estimate that 82 percent of

and scholarly publications have ignored the existence of the deposits.[6] I cannot offer any convincing reasons why this blackout should have been imposed.

The development of new fields in the early 1950's was achieved by dint of massive investments in geological surveys and exploratory drilling. In 1951, one fifth of all state and cooperative investment outlays was spent on the petroleum industry, which absorbed three fourths of all expenditures on geological prospecting. Outlays on well drilling alone accounted for 8.1 percent of the country's total investments by state and cooperative organs.[7] The extent of these drilling operations before and after World War II is shown in the data in Table D.2, while the concentration of exploratory drilling in the new regions in the early 1950's is illustrated in Table D.3.

These data are indicative of a major shift in emphasis after 1951. One may conjecture that the yield in terms of new reserves discovered per meter drilled must have been higher in the new than in the old regions, so that it seemed more advantageous to concentrate exploratory efforts in Piteşti, Oltenia, and Bacău than in the old regions. (The availability of new types of deep-drilling equipment produced by the Soviet Union and by the joint Soviet-Rumanian company in Rumania must have facilitated the shift in emphasis to the new deposits, which, at least in the Bacău region, lay at greater depths than did the old.)

The volume of oil reserves in Rumania has not, to my knowledge, been disclosed in any Rumanian source since World War II. Since yearly output, as we shall see, comes to a significant fraction of total "industrial reserves," and since new deposits are from time to time

[6] The only reference to the discovery I have been able to find is a bare mention of "the successes obtained by the young petroleum industry of the region" in a speech by a delegate from the Bucharest region at the Ninth Congress of the Party (*Congresul al IX-lea, op. cit.*, p. 355). A detailed description of industrial activity and an economic map of the Bucharest region published in *Viaţa economică* in 1964 (No. 49 [December 4, 1964], pp. 8 and 9) omitted all mention of the discovery of oil or, for that matter, of the existence of a fuel industry.

[7] *Anuarul statistic al R.P.R. 1965*, pp. 339 and 336; *Valorificarea superioară a resurselor naturale, op. cit.*, p. 13. See also Table D.2.

petroleum output was refined in the Ploieşti region; the rest, or 18 percent, was refined in the Bacău region in the base year. As for the 6 percent increment in crude output from 1959 to 1963, which we know to have been processed, it was assumed that the same percentage distribution of crude between the Ploieşti and Bacău refineries prevailed as in 1959. Average price data for 1963 from the same source were then used to break down the value of petroleum output in the two regions between extraction and refining. Once this was done, an index of extraction for both regions was readily computed. The output of "other regions," presumably chiefly represented by the Bucharest region, was derived as a residual.

TABLE D.2. WELL-DRILLING OPERATIONS 1936, 1942–1963
(*Thousands of Meters Drilled*)

	Total	Exploration	Prospecting[a]	Exploitation and Injection
1936	329.0	35.2	—	293.8
1942	344.0	47.0	—	297.0
1948	308.5	101.0	—	207.5
1949	517.9	163.3	—	354.6
1950	657.3	206.1	—	447.5
1951	825.3	425.2	—	394.1
1952	879.0	384.1	—	426.8
1953	936.6	418.7	—	517.9
1954	812.2	377.0	—	435.2
1955	870.0	473.7	—	396.3
1956	897.4	540.0	—	357.4
1957	876.6	471.6	—	405.0
1958	671.0	336.1	42.4	292.5
1959	851.6	411.4	128.9	311.3
1960	944.5	449.6	210.3	284.6
1961	965.9	419.4	164.5	382.0
1962	1,145.6	421.7	209.1	514.8
1963	1,248.5	431.6	217.9	599.0

[a] Including structural drilling.

Sources: Industria Romîniei 1944–1964 (Bucharest, 1964), p. 284; *Dezvoltarea economiei R.P.R. pe drumul socialismului 1948–1957* (Bucharest, 1958), p. 85.

TABLE D.3. EXPLORATORY DRILLING BY REGIONS, 1950–1955 AND 1958
(*Thousands of Meters*)

	Moldavia (Bacău)	Oltenia	Western Muntenia (Pitești)	Other New Regions	Old Regions[a]
1950	19.1	—	46.2	32.2	108.6
1951	49.7	31.6	123.1	14.6	206.2
1952	45.7	58.3	131.0	13.3	135.8
1953	53.8	41.7	201.2	57.9	64.1
1954	63.7	52.3	122.7	78.2	60.0
1955	90.0	54.0	152.0	131.0	47.0
1958			269.9		66.2

[a] Chiefly Ploiești.

Sources: I. P. Oleinik, *Dezvoltarea industriei Romîniei în anii Regimului Democrat-Popular* (Bucharest, 1960), p. 215; *Economia Romîniei între anii 1944–1959* (Bucharest, 1959), p. 137.

discovered, the volume of reserves is subject to variation, usually up-
wards but sometimes also downwards, when current output exceeds
new discoveries.[8]

A crucial variable in the management of mineral resources is the
ratio of yearly extraction to total industrial reserves or its inverse,
which states the number of years that reserves would last if no more
were henceforth discovered and if present rates of consumption were
continued. What we have to go on to estimate total reserves are percentage changes in this ratio,[9] an index relative of percentage changes
in the volume of reserves between 1948 and 1961, and an estimate of
the actual state of reserves prior to the nationalization of the industry
in 1948.[10] From these we may reconstruct the approximate volume of
industrial reserves from 1950 to 1961 and the plan for 1965 (Table D.4).

The ratio of output to reserves rose from 1958 to 1961, fell when
large new deposits were opened up in the "new regions" in 1952–1953,
and then stayed fairly constant up to 1956.[11] Industrial reserves were
expanded to an unknown but presumably significant extent around
1957 by the inclusion of the potential increase in the yield that could
be extracted by the injection of gas and water under pressure and by
other modern methods.[12] Thus the improvement in the ratio from

[8] "Industrial reserves," the category of reserves most widely used in Rumania
and to which all percentage increases refer, comprise deposits that are known
firmly enough to serve as the basis for investment decisions (in refinery capacity,
conducts, and so on). At the very least such a deposit must have been "demonstrated" by two successful bores (for details, see N. Grigoraş, "Criterii de classificare
a rezervelor de petrol şi gaz," in *Petrol şi gaz*, No. 12 (1958), pp. 532–533).

[9] This ratio was said to have declined by 16 percent from 1956 to 1959 and was
slated to be 24 percent smaller in 1965 than in 1956 (*Probleme ale creării şi dezvoltării
bazei tehnice-materiale a socialismului în R.P.R.* [Bucharest, 1963], p. 181). Since we
know oil output in 1956 and 1959 and the plan for 1965, it is easy to translate these
changes in the ratio into index relatives of the volume of reserves itself.

[10] See sources to Table D.4. Other estimates from non-Rumanian sources seem
to be either inaccurate or based on some other definition than the one on which
the data in Table D.4 are based. I. P. Oleinik, for instance, cites a figure of 150
million tons referring to a year shortly after World War II (*Dezvoltarea industriei . . . ,
op. cit.*, p. 193). This presumably includes possible as well as proved reserves. An
estimate for the late 1950's or for 1960 of 80 million tons cited in *Hospodářské noviny*,
No. 34 (1962), p. 8, appears seriously on the low side. The data in Table D.4 are
consistent with an estimate of reserves — 130 million tons — published in 1961,
which would presumably refer to the late 1950's, in *Mezinárodní socialistická dělba
práce* (V. Wacker and B. Malý, eds. [Prague, 1964], p. 17). See also note 13.

[11] Note that the Rumanian consumption ratio was high by world standards even
at its lowest point, if we consider that the average ratio for all petroleum producers
was said to be 6.2 percent in 1936 and 2.55 percent in 1958. (*Petrol şi gaz*, No. 8
[1960], p. 332.)

[12] Reserves in the Ploieşti region are said to have risen by 38 million tons from
1955 to 1960, in part owing to an increase in the estimated potential of output
from secondary recovery. (*Congresul al III-lea al Partidului Muncitoresc Romîn* [Bucha-
rest, 1960], p. 268.)

TABLE D.4. VOLUME OF INDUSTRIAL RESERVES AND RATIO OF OUTPUT TO
RESERVES SELECTED YEARS, 1940–1961, 1965 PLAN
(*Millions of Tons*)

	Industrial Reserves[a]	Output of Crude Oil	Ratio of Output to Reserves (percent)
1940	86	5.7	6.6
1948	54	4.1	7.6
1950	49	5.1	10.2
1951	48	6.2	12.9
1955	100	10.6	10.6
1956	102	10.9	10.2
1958	124	11.3	9.1
1959	130	11.4	8.8
1960	124	11.5	9.3
1961	160	11.6	7.3
1965 (Plan)	156	12.2	7.8

[a] On January 1 of given year.

Sources and methods: 1940 and 1948: I. D. Kariagin, *Neftianaia promyshlennost'
Rumynii* (Moscow, 1958), pp. 188, 191. The 1961 estimate is based on the approxi-
mate increase in reserves from January 1948 in *The Oil Industry in Rumania*
(Bucharest, 1963), p. 21. Estimates for other years were derived from the index
relatives in *Probleme ale creării și dezvoltării bazei tehnice-materiale a socialismului în
R.P.R.* (Bucharest, 1963), pp. 174, 176, and 181; *Dezvoltarea industriei socialiste în
R.P.R., 1959*, p. 111, and *Petrol și gaz*, No. 7 (1960), p. 269.

1950 to 1955, in spite of a great increase in the yearly extraction of
crude oil, appears more substantial than the diminution in the ratio
of subsequent years. The former resulted from the discovery of new
deposits, the latter, in part at least, from a change in the mensuration
of previously known deposits. The exploration of deposits in the "new
regions" (Bacău, Oltenia, and Argeș) was not opening up any very
promising new prospects in the late 1950's. On the contrary, there is
at least tentative evidence suggesting that reserves in the new regions
were being depleted even more quickly than in the old. This may be
surmised not only from the stagnation or decline in output in the three
regions (Table D.1) but also from the fact that the consumption-to-
reserves ratio in the Ploiești region around 1960, which was said to
equal 4.2 percent, was less than half as large as the average estimated
(in Table D.4) for the country as a whole.[13] Finally, the sudden increase

[13] *Congresul al III-lea al Partidului Muncitoresc Romîn, op. cit.*, p. 268. Incidentally,
this percentage implies that reserves in the Ploiești region were equal to about 93
million tons (cf. Table D.1). If, as mentioned, reserves in this region increased by
38 million tons between 1955 and 1960, then they amounted to 55 million tons in
1955. But the industrial reserves of Ploiești came to 55 percent of the entire industrial

in reserves in 1961 is probably related to the discovery, already mentioned, of new deposits in the Bucharest region.

In view of the stagnation or recession of output in most regions, it is not surprising to discover that the Rumanian fields are not gushing oil as exuberantly as they once did. The amount of crude oil extracted per productive well, which amounted to 4,520 tons per year in 1936, had fallen to less than 2,000 tons in 1950; this yield recovered partly in the 1950's as a result of the discovery of new deposits reaching a peak close to 3,000 tons in 1955, only to drop again in the late 1950's

TABLE D.5. SHARES OF DIFFERENT PROCESSES USED IN PETROLEUM EXTRACTION, 1950, 1955, 1958, 1961, AND 1963 (*Percentages*)

	1950	1955	1958	1961	1963
Captured eruption	30.8	52.0	42.9	30.7	28.6
Pumping	44.5	37.9	n.a.	54.7	60.7
Gas-lift	23.2	9.8	13.3	14.1	10.4
Other methods	1.5	0.3	n.a.	0.5	0.3
All methods	100.0	100.0	100.0	100.0	100.0

Sources: I. P. Oleinik, *Dezvoltarea industriei Romîniei în anii Regimului Democrat-Popular* (Bucharest, 1960), p. 216; *Economia Romîniei între anii 1944–1959* (Bucharest, 1959), p. 145; *Industria Romîniei 1944–1964* (Bucharest, 1964), p. 291; *The Oil Industry in Rumania* (Bucharest, 1963), p. 40.

and early 1960's as exhaustion set in. In 1961 and in 1963 production per well amounted to about 2,300 tons, or less than 7 tons per day.[14] It is also significant that only 8 percent of crude oil output in 1958 was from newly bored wells, compared to 22.8 percent in 1951 and 11.8 percent in 1955.[15]

Another sign of gradual exhaustion is the drop in the proportion of crude oil obtained by natural eruption from "gushers" (Table D.5).

Needless to say, oil extracted by pumping and by the injection of

reserves of the country at that date (Kariagin, *op. cit.*, p. 197). Hence total reserves were 100 million tons in 1955, thus confirming the estimate arrived at independently in Table D.4.

[14] The total number of active wells at various dates are given in the following sources: for 1936, I. Oleinik, *op. cit.*, p. 215; for 1950 and 1956, in *Dezvoltarea economiei R.P.R. pe drumul socialismului 1948–1957, op. cit.*, p. 90, and the graph p. 100b; for 1955, in *Petrol și gaz*, No. 8 (1959), p. 324; for 1961, from *The Oil Industry in Rumania* (Bucharest, 1963), p. 43. The 1963 estimate is based on a percentage relative to 1950 in *Industria Romîniei 1944–1964, op. cit.*, p. 291.

[15] *Petrol și gaz*, No. 4 (1959), p. 134.

water and gas is much more expensive than oil captured from natural eruption.[16]

Many wells that had been retired from production prior to 1955 were "reactivated" in subsequent years, in connection with the injection of gas and water into deposits that had been more or less exhausted by traditional methods. The number of these reactivated wells increased by nearly two thirds from 1955 to 1958, and by another 77 percent from 1958 to 1961.[17]

The more intensive exploitation of existing deposits is reflected in the much greater proportion of the estimated capacity of these deposits that is being extracted now than in the past. This proportion is said to have risen from about 15 percent before World War II to an average of 45 percent in 1960 or 1961.[18]

I suspect that a policy decision was taken in 1957 or 1958 to scale down the exploration of new deposits and to concentrate on the more thorough exploitation of known fields. This is borne out in part by the drastic curtailment of exploratory drilling in 1957 and 1958 and in part by the extraordinary reduction in the number of sterile drilling operations conducted in the Ploieşti and in the Piteşti regions between 1955 and 1959.[19] It is also suggestive that the average cost of drilling per meter went down from 1,950 lei in 1958 to 1,250 lei in 1959.[20] Since such a steep decline could not have been the result of a major technical breakthrough, I surmise that it must have been due at least in part to the scaling down of activities in the more inaccessible regions where drilling was most expensive, among others the mountainous, deep-lying deposits of Moldavia.

On the occasion of the 1960 Congress of the Communist Party, explicit reference was made to the need for "stabilizing" petroleum reserves and for reducing the excessive costs of new discoveries. Efforts, henceforth, were to be centered on increasing production from old deposits.[21] By 1965, 77 percent of extraction was to be achieved by

[16] Cf. *Congresul al III-lea al Partidului Muncitoresc Romîn, op. cit.*, p. 269, and the statement in *Economia Romîniei între anii 1944–1959, op. cit.*, p. 146, to the effect that oil extracted by the injection of gases costs 120 percent more than by natural eruption.

[17] *Probleme ale creării . . . , op. cit.*, pp. 178–179.

[18] *Probleme economice*, No. 8 (1961), p. 54.

[19] The proportion of sterile wells in the total of wells drilled in the Ploieşti fields fell from 46 percent in 1955 to 31 percent in 1959; in the Piteşti region, sterile drilling fell from about 50 percent in 1955 to only 13 percent in 1959 (*Congresul al III-lea, op. cit.*, pp. 268, 530).

[20] *Ibid.*, p. 230.

[21] M. Florescu, Minister of the Petroleum and Chemical Industries, in *Petrol şi gaz*, No. 8 (1960), pp. 331-332 and 338. One Soviet expert, writing about 1957, was of the opinion that the Rumanians, far from lavishing excessive funds on the

means of water injection, which would make it possible to produce 2.3 million tons per year more than by traditional methods.

Although the excesses of the mid-1950's have been curbed, exploratory drilling at great depth is still taking place on a large scale. It is said that the depth of wells drilled is over 50 percent greater than before World War II (over twice as great for geological exploration alone).[22]

Little is known about the prospects for the years 1965 to 1970 except for the 1970 target itself — 13.1 to 13.3 million tons — which comes to about 5 percent more than in 1965.[23] This increase will be accomplished, it would seem, chiefly by the more intensive exploitation of old deposits by water injection and other modern methods. This may indicate that the substantial contribution to reserves made by the discoveries in the Bucharest region in the first half of the 1960's is not expected to be duplicated in the second half.

To conclude this melancholy chronicle of the stagnation of oil production in Rumania, it is pertinent to mention that Bucharest has recently contracted to import crude oil from Iran before 1970.[24]

The Processing of Oil Products

On the eve of World War II, fifty-nine petroleum refineries were in operation in Rumania with a total capacity of nine million tons for primary processing and two million tons for cracking.[25] This capacity was only utilized to the extent of about two thirds, crude oil output fluctuating at levels appreciably below the capacity levels of the refineries. The yield of gasoline, measured in proportion to the total input of petroleum processed, was only 24.3 percent, compared to 37.5 percent in the United States.[26]

For several years after World War II, petroleum output was so low

---

development of crude oil resources, were not making sufficient efforts to expand industrial reserves. Already by 1955 "the proportionality was upset between the extraction of oil and the prospection for new reserves. This led to a significant decline in the tempo of expanded reproduction in the oil industry. A task that should not be put off is the establishment of correct, rational proportions which would fulfill the requirements of the law of planned (proportional) development of the oil industry." From the context and the passages that follow, it is clear that the author has in mind the expansion of reserves to suit the actual rate of extraction rather than the contraction of output to conserve existing reserves (I. D. Kariagin, *Neftianaia promyshlennost' Rumynii* [Moscow, 1958], p. 228).

[22] *Lupta de clasă*, No. 5 (1965), p. 17.
[23] *Congresul al IX-lea, op. cit.*, p. 757.
[24] *Scînteia*, November 4, 1966.
[25] Oleinik, *op. cit.*, p. 218.
[26] *Ibid.*, p. 219.

that refining capacity was more than sufficient to cope with volume requirements, although the quality of products left much to be desired. The average octane number of the gasoline produced, for example, was only 56.2 in 1950, which was quite low by international standards.[27]

The policy of *Sovrompetrol*, which ran the industry from 1950 to 1955, was to invest chiefly in extraction and to keep outlays on refineries to a minimum.

Investment outlays on processing facilities (Table D.6) came to less

TABLE D.6. INVESTMENTS IN THE PETROLEUM AND GAS INDUSTRY, 1951–1963 (*Millions of Lei*)

	Total Petroleum and Gas Industry	Petroleum Extraction	Gas Extraction	Refining	Total as Percent of Investments in All Industry
1951	1,714	1,581	79	54	36.8
1952	1,874	1,666	94	114	30.8
1953	2,425	2,063	89	273	29.2
1954	1,912	1,632	47	233	25.7
1955	2,056	1,685	63	308	24.8
1956	2,277	1,813	27	437	25.6
1957	2,293	1,844	87	362	28.3
1958	2,186	1,658	212	316	25.9
1959	2,070	1,591	231	248	22.0
1960	2,642	1,678	433	531	22.0
1961	3,034	2,071	515	448	21.1
1962	3,220	2,427	524	269	18.6
1963	3,530	2,528	644	358	18.1

Source: Industria Romîniei 1944–1964 (Bucharest, 1964), p. 282.

than 10 percent of all investment in the oil petroleum industry from 1951 to 1955. The sums allotted to the processing branch of the industry went to replace war-damaged, worn-out, or obsolete equipment in primary refining. Little or nothing was done to improve the low quality of refined products, whose yield, expressed as the value of products obtained per ton of crude oil, deteriorated. An index of this ratio declined steadily from 1951 to 1954, when it reached a low point of 94 percent of the 1950 level; it only recovered and surpassed this base level in 1958.[28] The proximate reason was that no expansion of secondary processing — thermal or catalytic cracking of fuel oil and other residues — was carried out in this period, so that the limited

[27] *Economia Romîniei între anii 1944–1959, op. cit.*, p. 141.
[28] *Probleme economice*, No. 11 (1963), p. 21.

facilities inherited from prewar days accommodated a smaller proportion of the expanding supply of crude oil than it did in 1950.[29] In view of the policy of specialization in the Soviet bloc, the stress on quantity rather than on quality may not have been a bad thing, since processing facilities were available in most of the countries importing Rumanian oil. From a mercantilistic viewpoint, however, it meant that Rumania had to forgo the extra foreign exchange that could have been earned from further refining of its products without depleting its limited oil deposits.[30]

Starting with 1955, substantial headway was made in the secondary refining of petroleum products. In 1956 and 1957 new thermal cracking capacities, together amounting to 1.1 million tons, began functioning in Darmaneşti and Ploieşti. From that time on the new policy of "valorification" of Rumania's resources held sway, and vigorous efforts were deployed to improve the yield and quality of petroleum products.

A number of indicators testify to this progress. The average octane number of all gasoline produced in Rumania, which stood at 59.5 in 1955 (close to the prewar level), rose to 61.4 in 1959 and 71.2 in 1963.[31] The value of products obtained per ton of crude oil refined increased from 95.4 percent of the 1950 level in 1955 to 106.9 in 1959, 123.0 in 1961, and 146.7 in 1963.[32] The yield of higher fractions of diesel oil increased at the expense of fuel oil and other low-value products, as illustrated by the data in Table D.7.

Thanks mainly to the progress made in imparting greater value in the course of processing to the petroleum extracted, the gross output of the refining branch of the industry rose by 66 percent from 1958 to 1962, while the volume of crude oil refined increased by only 8.5 percent during the same period.[33]

While the capacity for the primary distillation of crude oil kept up with the slowly increasing volume of oil extracted in the late 1950's and early 1960's, the gradual curtailment of output in certain areas must have created a regional imbalance between the supply of crude oil and refining capacities. Prior to 1960, the capacity of the refining

[29] *Ibid.*, p. 21.

[30] Prior to 1956, for example, Czechoslovakia imported fuel oil from Rumania for further processing. After that date, owing to the Rumanian decision to cease exporting unprocessed products, the Czechs began to import raw products from the Soviet Union in order to utilize their own refining capacities (D. Machová, *ČSSR v socialistické mezinárodní dělbě práce* [Prague, 1962], p. 203).

[31] *Industria Romîniei 1944–1964, op. cit.*, p. 306.

[32] *Dezvoltarea industriei R.P.R.: Culegere de date statistice* (Bucharest, 1964), p. 206.

[33] *Probleme economice*, No. 11 (1963), p. 23; and *Anuarul statistic al R.P.R. 1965*, p. 152.

TABLE D.7. PERCENTAGE BREAKDOWN OF THE OUTPUT OF REFINERY
PRODUCTS, 1955, 1959, AND 1964

	1955	1959	1964
Gasoline	25.4	24.1	20.2
Aromatic products (benzene, toluene, xylene)	—	—	0.6
Kerosene and white spirit	13.2	11.4	8.3
Diesel oil	15.7	20.4	28.3
Lubricating oils	1.5	2.5	3.5
Fuel oil	37.4	33.3	30.0
Others	6.8	8.3	9.1
Total	100.0	100.0	100.0

Source: *Industria Romîniei 1944–1964* (Bucharest, 1964), p. 307.

facilities in the Bacău region was approximately equal to the output of the region. The petroleum mined in all other parts of the country, including the Pitești and Oltenia regions, was refined around Ploiești. When production began to decline in Bacău, while it suddenly surged in the new fields of the Bucharest region, there must have developed a local surplus of refining capacity in the former and a deficit in the latter. I surmise that crude oil had to be transported from the south to the refineries at Onești and Darmanești in the Bacău region, a solution which, though costly, at least made it possible to process all available oil.[34]

In most recent years efforts have been concentrated on the expansion of catalytic cracking reforming and on the expansion of facilities yielding high-grade oils. A measure of the growing importance of these technically advanced processes is given in Table D.8.

According to the plan data for 1970, the value of petroleum products obtained per ton of crude refined is slated to rise by another 11.2 percent from the level attained in 1965, which was already 37 percent higher than in 1960.[35] The major investments projected for this five-year period consist of a catalytic cracking plant with a capacity of 1,100,000 tons and installations for catalytic reforming with a capacity of 500,000 tons.[36] The modest scale of this program by the standards

[34] The assumption that crude oil was imported for processing in the Bacău region in order to meet the total demand for refining capacity underlies the construction of the estimates for 1963 in Table D.1.

[35] A. Boaba, "Industria petrolului în cincinal," *Viața economică*, No. 3 (January 21, 1960), p. 5.

[36] *Ibid.*

TABLE D.8. PERCENTAGE RATIO OF THE OUTPUTS OF SECONDARY
PROCESSING RELATIVE TO THE OUTPUT OF PRIMARY
DISTILLATION

	1938	1959	1963	1966
Atmospheric distillation	100.0	100.0	100.0	100.0
Vacuum distillation	3.1	10.4	15.5	27.6
Thermal cracking	22.4	28.8	26.7	25.8
Catalytic cracking	—	—	3.7	3.8
Catalytic reforming	—	—	8.6	13.2
Coking	—	0.57	1.95	6.0
Oils	1.2	3.73	3.98	3.9
Absorption and fractioning of gases	—	—	4.5	19.7
Others	1.07	1.97	7.0	

Sources: Industria Romîniei 1944–1964 (Bucharest, 1964), p. 304; and Valorificarea
superioară a resurselor naturale (Bucharest, 1965), p. 28; Viața economică, No. 26
(July 1, 1966), p. 5.

set in the last decade probably reflects the pessimistic outlook of the
planners regarding the future of oil output and the fact that the
valorification campaign launched in the mid-1950's has by now accomplished the aims that had originally been set for it.

Gas and Solid Fuels

Petroleum today, while it still holds pride of place as the principal
fuel exported and as a major foreign-exchange earner, has lost its first
rank both in production and consumption in terms of calorific content.
It has been displaced by natural gases — methane and casing-head
gases from oil wells — which are cheaper to produce and less costly in
investment outlays.[37] Reserves of methane alone were estimated at
575 billion cubic meters in the early 1960's, or forty-five times the
production reached in 1965.[38] The outlook for natural gas is still
bright, while the prospects for petroleum are tarnished by impending
exhaustion.

As a consequence of rapid industrialization, the demand for fuels of

[37] On the basis of recent cost estimates for investment projects, a Rumanian
economist calculated that petroleum was 2.2 to 2.6 times as costly in investment
outlays as methane (in lei per ton of conventional fuel produced per year) and that
the production costs of petroleum were 90 percent greater than those of methane.
A comparison with lignite also shows up to the advantage of methane, both in
investment outlays and production costs (I. Desmireanu in Probleme ale creării și
dezvoltării, op. cit., p. 182).

[38] Mezinárodní socialistická dělba práce, op. cit., p. 169; and Statistical Pocket Book 1966,
p. 91.

all sorts has grown by leaps and bounds over the years.[39] Although production (as can be seen in Table D.9) has also expanded at great speed, the exportable surplus has dwindled.

TABLE D.9. PRODUCTION AND CONSUMPTION OF PRIMARY ENERGY IN TERMS OF CONVENTIONAL FUEL (*Thousands of Tons of Conventional Calorific Content*)

	Production	*Consumption*
1938	16,388	9,101
1948	12,416	n.a.
1950	15,100	11,500
1953	24,695	17,600
1955	27,977	20,600
1957	30,387	23,100
1959	33,534	25,350
1961	36,612	29,845
1963	42,021	33,900

Source: Dezvoltarea industriei R.P.R. 1944–1964 (Bucharest, 1964), p. 249, except for consumption in 1938, which is based on the proportion of net exports to output cited in *Dezvoltarea industriei socialiste în R.P.R.* (Bucharest, 1959), p. 24.

In 1938 exports of fuels amounted to 44 percent of total production; by 1963 the export-to-output ratio had fallen to 19 percent.

TABLE D.10. PERCENTAGE BREAKDOWN OF PRIMARY-ENERGY PRODUCTION BY TYPES OF FUELS

	1938	*1950*	*1955*	*1959*	*1963*
Superior coals	9.3	12.1	8.0	8.3 ⎫	
Inferior coals	1.4	2.8	3.3	3.8 ⎭	12.7
Petroleum	57.7	47.8	54.0	48.7	41.6
Natural gas	16.4	26.4	26.9	34.0	41.0
Wood for fuel	14.1	9.5	6.4	4.1	3.1
Hydraulic energy	1.1	1.4	1.4	1.1	1.6
Total	100.0	100.0	100.0	100.0	100.0

Source: Industria Rominiei 1944–1964 (Bucharest, 1964), p. 250.

Table D.10 breaks down the production statistics of the preceding table by types of fuels.

[39] From 1955 to 1961 consumption of primary energy rose at a rate of 6.4 percent per year in Rumania, as against 5.6 percent in Czechoslovakia, 5 percent in Hungary, 4.9 percent in Poland and Sweden, and 3.5 percent in France (*Industria Rominiei 1944–1964, op. cit.*, p. 249).

Considering that the output of methane went up by 27 percent from 1963 to 1965, while that of petroleum rose by a mere 3 percent, it is apparent from Table D.10 that the share of natural gas in total energy produced must now surpass the share of petroleum.

Statistics of fuel consumption exclude all sources of energy destined for "specific uses" such as gasoline for motors, kerosene for lighting, and coal for coking. A breakdown of consumption of materials used directly as fuels or to produce electricity is available for a few benchmark years (see Table D.11).

TABLE D.11. The Percentage Composition of Fuels Consumed in Terms of Primary Energy, 1938, 1950, 1955, 1958, 1961, 1965, and 1970

	1938	1950	1955	1958	1961	1965	1970 (plan)
Solid fuels	55.7	35.2	24.4	25.1	26.4	24.3	28.0
Coal	26.4	17.6	14.3	16.6	n.a.	n.a.	n.a.
Wood	29.3	17.6	10.1	8.5	n.a.	n.a.	n.a.
Liquid and gaseous fuels	44.3	64.8	75.6	74.9	73.6	75.7	72.0
Petroleum[a]	26.7	25.8	34.6	29.9	n.a.	n.a.	n.a.
Natural gases	17.6	39.0	41.0	45.0	n.a.	n.a.	n.a.

[a] Diesel and fuel oil.

Sources: For 1938, 1950, 1955, and 1958: Dezvoltarea industriei socialiste în R.P.R. (Bucharest, 1959), p. 27; for 1961: Mezinárodní socialistická dělba práce, V. Wacker and B. Malý, eds. (Prague, 1964), p. 163; for 1965 and for 1970 (plan): Hospodářské noviny, No. 1 (1966), p. 10.

As we might expect, the share of wood for fuel in total consumption has been declining, while the share of natural gases has been steadily rising from 1938 on. The relative importance of solid fuels in the Rumanian energy balance is still quite small, compared to Czechoslovakia where they represent 91.9 percent of fuel consumption, Poland (94.5 percent), and East Germany (96.6 percent); even in the oil-rich U.S.S.R., solid fuels made up 60.2 percent of consumption in 1961.[40] For lack of detailed statistics after 1958, we cannot demonstrate that methane continued to displace petroleum in the consumption of fuels in subsequent years, although an analysis of the fuels consumed in the electricity sector alone suggests that this substitution must have gone on throughout the Six-Year Plan. Fuel oil and diesel oil, which accounted for 28.2 percent of the fuel consumed by the power industry

[40] Mezinárodní dělba práce . . . , op. cit., pp. 162–163.

in 1958, dropped to 6.3 percent in 1964, while the share of natural gases went up from 44.4 to 75.0 percent between the two years.[41]

The fuels policy of the Rumanian government is guided by the following principles. Fuels must be assigned first to "specific uses" — methane and petroleum to the chemical industry for the production of rubber and petroleum derivatives, gasoline and diesel oil for internal combustion engines, coal for coking and metallurgical uses. After their specific uses have been met, inferior coals and methane are given over to the production of heat energy. Fuel oil and diesel oil, insofar as possible, should be allotted for heating purposes only in installations adapted to consume no other type of fuel: every effort should be made to economize on liquid fuels so as to leave as much as possible for export.[42]

Methane and benzine from primary distillation are the basic raw materials of the petrochemical industry. The former is a primary ingredient in the manufacture of nitrogen fertilizers and artificial rubber. Petroleum is transformed into valuable intermediate chemicals such as glycerin and acetone and into final products, including plastics, dyes, insecticides, solvents, lacquers, synthetic fibers, and explosives.

The Rumanian government's strategy has been to develop the petrochemical industry along chains of "forward linkages," starting with the primary refinery products and ending up with highly valuable products of complex syntheses. Thus the Craiova chemical and gas complex was set up to produce nitrogen fertilizers from methane. In the production process, acetylene was generated as an inexpensive by-product, which formed the basis for the creation of a plant for the production of acetic acid, butanol, and octanol. These materials will eventually be processed into plastics in factories set up for this purpose. Similarly the Petrochemical Combine at Brazi began with the manufacture of primary petrochemicals and is now about to undertake the synthesis of polyesters for the manufacture of synthetic fibers.[43] Early in the course of the Third Five-Year Plan (1966–1970), Rumania's petrochemical industry will have a processing capacity, measured in the carbon content of the basic petrochemicals, of 450,000 tons per year, or 24 kilograms per inhabitant, which will place it in the forefront of European producers.[44]

[41] *Anuarul statistic al R.P.R. 1965*, p. 184.

[42] See, for example, I. D. Stăncescu, "Rolul termificării în folosirea raţională a combustibililor în R.P.R.," *Revista de statistică*, No. 8 (1960), pp. 10–11.

[43] *Valorificarea superioară* . . , *op. cit.*, pp. 56–57.

[44] *Ibid.*, p. 57.

SELECTED BIBLIOGRAPHY

Books on the Rumanian Economy

I. COLLECTIVE WORKS

    A. Publications of the Institute of Economic Research of the Rumanian Academy of Sciences (Institutul de cercetări economice, Academia R.P.R.)

Dezvoltarea economică a Rominiei 1944–1964 (The economic development of Rumania 1944–1964). Bucharest: Editura Academiei R.P.R., 1964.

Dezvoltarea economiei R.P.R. pe drumul socialismului 1948–1957 (The development of the economy of the Rumanian People's Republic on the path to socialism 1948–1957). Bucharest: Editura Academia R.P.R., 1958.

Economia Rominiei între anii 1944–1959 (The economy of Rumania between the years 1944–1959). Bucharest: Editura Academiei R.P.R., 1964.

Probleme ale creării și dezvoltării bazei tehnice-materiale a socialsmului în R.P.R. (Problems concerning the creation and development of the technical-material basis of socialism in the Rumanian People's Republic). Bucharest: Editura Academii R.P.R., 1963.

Probleme ale dezvoltării și consolidării agriculturii socialiste (Problems of the development and consolidation of socialist agriculture). Bucharest: Editura Academii R.P.R., 1960.

Studii de economie socialistă (Studies in the socialist economy). Bucharest: Editura Academii R.P.R., 1961.

    B. Other Collective Works

Agricultura Rominiei 1944–1964 (The agriculture of Rumania 1944–1964). Bucharest: Editura Agro-silvică, 1964.

Dezvoltarea agriculturii în R.P.R. (The development of agriculture in the Rumanian People's Republic) (Ministerul Agriculturii în R.P.R.). Bucharest: Editura Agro-silvică de Stat, 1958.

Dezvoltarea complexă și echilibrată a economiei naționale (The complex and equilibrated development of the national economy). Bucharest: Editura Politică, 1965.

Geografia economică a R.P.R. (The economic geography of the Rumanian People's Republic) (M. Hașeganu, ed.) Bucharest: Editura Științifică, 1957.

Nova geografia a patriei: Republica Populară Romîna (A new geography of the fatherland: The Rumanian People's Republic). Bucharest: Editura Științifică, 1964.

Romania (S. Fischer-Galati, ed.). New York: Frederick A. Praeger, 1957.

Valorificarea superioară a resulselor naturale (The superior valorization of natural resources). Bucharest: Editura Politică, 1965.

II. MONOGRAPHS ON RUMANIA

Ionescu, Ghita, *Communism in Rumania*. London, New York, Toronto: Oxford University Press, 1964.

Kariagin, I. D., *Neftianaia promyshlennost' Rumynii i ekonomicheskie problemy eë razvitie v usloviakh narodno-demokraticheskogo stroia* (The oil industry of Rumania and the economic problems of its development under the conditions of the People's Democratic Regime). Moscow: Gosudarstvennoe nauchno-tekhnicheskoe Izdatel' stvo Neftianoi i Gorno-toplivoi Literatury, 1958.

Karra, V. A., *Stroitel'stvo sotsialisticheskoi ekonomiki v Rumynskoi Narodnoi Respubliki* (The construction of the socialist economy in the Rumanian People's Republic). Moscow: Akademiia Nauk, 1953.

Levente, Mihai, E. Barat, and M. Bulgaru, *Analiza statistico-economică a agriculturii* (The statistical-economic analysis of agriculture). Bucharest: Editura Ştiinţifică, 1961.

Madgearu, Virgil, *Rumania's New Economic Policy*. London: P. S. King and Sons, 1930.

Oleinik, I. P., *Dezvoltarea industriei Romîniei în anii Regimului Democrat-Popular* (The development of Rumania's industry in the years of the Democratic-Popular Regime) (Translation from the Russian). Bucharest: Editura Politică, 1960.

Roberts, Henri L., *Rumania: Political Problems of an Agrarian State*. New Haven, Conn.: Yale University Press, 1951.

Saltiel, J. P., *L'Attitude de la Roumanie vis-à-vis d'une planification supranationale*. Paris: Cahiers de l'ISEA (G-22, No. 168), 1965.

Spulber, Nicholas, *The Economics of Communist Eastern Europe*. New York: Published jointly by The Technology Press of M.I.T. and John Wiley & Sons, 1957.

Strat, Aurelian, *Des possibilités de développement industriel de la Roumanie*. Paris: Presses Universitaires, 1931.

Ţaigar, Simon, *Veniturile populaţiei şi nivelul de trai în R.P.R.* (The population's incomes and levels of living in the Rumanian People's Republic). Bucharest: Editura Politică, 1964.

III. BOOKS ON EASTERN EUROPE CONTAINING IMPORTANT INFORMATION ABOUT THE RUMANIAN ECONOMY

Bodnar, Artur, *Gospodarka europejskich krajów socjalistycznych* (The economy of European socialist countries). Warsaw: Książka i Wiedza, 1962.

Ciamaga, Lucjan, *Od współpracy do integracji:* (From cooperation to integration). Warsaw: Książka i Wiedza, 1965.

Hertz, F., *The Economic Problems of the Danubian States*. London: V. Gollantz, Ltd., 1947.

Kaser, Michael, *Comecon: Integration Problems of the Planned Economies*. London: Oxford University Press, 1965.

Konečný, Čestmir, *Socialistický mezinárodní úvěr* (Socialist international credit). Prague: Nakladelství Ceskoslovenské Akademie Věd, 1964.

Lipták, Juliús, *Mezinárodní dělba práce v zemědelství zemí RVHP* (The international socialist division of labor in agriculture of the countries of CMEA). Prague: Nakladelství Politické Literatury, 1965.

Machová, Dušana, *ČSSR v mezinárodní socialistické dělbě práce* (Czechoslovakia in the international socialist division of labor). Prague: Nakladelství Politické Literatury, 1962.

Novozámský, Jiři, *Vyrovnávání ekonomické úrovně zemí RVHP* (The leveling of the economic levels of the CMEA countries). Prague: Nakladelství Politické Literatury, 1964.

Pryor, Frederic L., *The Communist Foreign Trade System.* Cambridge, Mass.: The M.I.T. Press, 1963.

Vajda, Imre, *Nemzetközi kereskedelem.* Budapest: Közgazdasági és Jogi Könyvkiado, 1959.

Wacker, V., and B. Malý, eds., *Mezinárodní socialistická dělba práce* (The international socialist division of labor). Prague: Nakladelství Politické Literatury, 1964.

Zaleski, Eugène, *Les courants commerciaux de l'Europe Danubienne.* Paris: Librairie Générale de Droit et de Jurisprudence, 1952.

Periodicals

Bulletin of the Chamber of Commerce of the R.P.R.
Documents, Articles, and Information on Romania (Bucharest: Agerpres)
Lupta de clasă
Probleme agricole
Probleme economice
Revista de statistică
Revue Roumaine des Sciences Sociales (Série de Sciences Economiques)
Viața economică
Economic Bulletin for Europe (United Nations)

Statistical Publications

Issued by the Central Direction of Statistics (Direcția Centrală de Statistică):

Anuarul statistic al R.P.R., 1958, 1960, 1961, 1964, 1965 (Statistical annual of the Rumanian People's Republic). Bucharest, 1958, 1960, 1961, 1964, 1965.

Anuarul statistic al Republicii Socialiste Românîa 1966 (Statistical annual of the Rumanian Socialist Republic). Bucharest, 1966.

Dezvoltarea agriculturii R.P.R. (The development of agriculture in the Rumanian People's Republic). Bucharest, 1961.

Dezvoltarea agriculturii R.P.R.: Culegere de date statistice (The development of agriculture in the Rumanian People's Republic: Collection of statistics). Bucharest, 1964.

Recensămintul populaţiei din 21 februarie 1956: Rezultate generale (The population census of February 21, 1956: General results). Bucharest, 1959.

Statistical Pocket Book of the Socialist Republic of Romania 1966. Bucharest, 1966.

Studii de statistică: Lucrările consfătuiri ştiinţifice de statistică (27–29 noiembrile 1961) (Studies in statistics: Proceedings of the Scientific Conference on Statistics, November 27–29, 1961). Bucharest: Editura Ştiinţifică, 1962.

Studii de statistică: Lucrările celei de-a-doua consfătuiri ştiinţifice de statistică (29 noiembrile–1 decembri, 1962) (Studies in statistics: Proceedings of the Second Scientific Conference on Statistics, November 29–December 1, 1962). Bucharest: Editura Ştiinţifică, 1963.

Anuarul statistic al Oraşului Bucureşti 1959, 1963, Direcţia Orăşenească de Statistică Bucureşti (Statistical annual of the City of Bucharest). Bucharest, 1959, 1963.

INDEX

* Page numbers followed by a lowercase "n" refer to footnotes, those followed by a capital "T" refer to tables.